T0028550

LAST STANDS

ALSO BY MICHAEL WALSH

Nonfiction

Carnegie Hall: The First One Hundred Years (with Richard Schickel)
Who's Afraid of Classical Music?
Andrew Lloyd Webber: His Life and Works
Who's Afraid of Opera?
So When Does the Fat Lady Sing?
Rules for Radical Conservatives (as David Kahane)
The People v. the Democratic Party
The Devil's Pleasure Palace
The Fiery Angel

Fiction

Exchange Alley
As Time Goes By
And All the Saints

The Devlin Series

Hostile Intent
Early Warning
Shock Warning

LAST STANDS

WHY MEN FIGHT WHEN ALL IS LOST

MICHAEL WALSH

ST. MARTIN'S
PRESS

NEW YORK

First published in the United States by St. Martin's Press,
an imprint of St. Martin's Publishing Group

Printed in the United States of America. For information, address
St. Martin's Publishing Group, 120 Broadway, New York, NY 10271.

www.stmartins.com

Designed by Steven Seighman

Library of Congress Cataloging-in-Publication Data

Names: Walsh, Michael, 1949– author.
Title: Last stands : why men fight when all is lost / Michael Walsh.
Other titles: Why men fight when all is lost
Description: First edition. | New York : St. Martin's Press, 2020. | Includes index.
Identifiers: LCCN 2020028406 | ISBN 9781250217080 (hardcover) |
ISBN 9781250217097 (ebook)
Subjects: LCSH: Battles—History. | Military history—Miscellanea. | Courage. |
Honor.
Classification: LCC D25.5 .W34 2020 | DDC 355.4/8—dc23
LC record available at https://lccn.loc.gov/2020028406

10 9 8 7 6 5 4 3 2

*For Alexandra Elisabeth, Clare Veronica, Ada Clare,
and Sorcha Kathryn, to help you understand how you got here*

They landed on a wild but narrow scene,
Where few but Nature's footsteps yet had been;
Prepared their arms, and with that gloomy eye,
Stern and sustained, of man's extremity,
When Hope is gone, nor Glory's self remains
To cheer resistance against death or chains,—
They stood, the three, as the three hundred stood
Who dyed Thermopylæ with holy blood.
But, ah! how different! 'tis the cause makes all,
Degrades or hallows courage in its fall.

—BYRON, "THE ISLAND, OR, CHRISTIAN AND HIS COMRADES" (1823)

Oliver said: "Companion, sir, I believe
We may have a battle with the Saracens on our hands."
Roland replies: "May God grant it to us! . . .
Now let each see to it that he employ great blows,
So that no taunting song be sung about us!"

—*LA CHANSON DE ROLAND* (C. 1040–1115), TRANSLATED BY GERARD J. BRAULT

There is one hope for the defeated
That he cannot hope in victory.
Is it not better to die as a man,
Than to live in shame before the eyes of all?

—MIKLÓS ZRÍNYI, *THE SIEGE OF SZIGET* (1651) TRANSLATED BY LÁSZLÓ KŐRÖSSY

The human heart . . . is then the starting point in all matters pertaining to war.

—COL. ARDANT DU PICQ, *BATTLE STUDIES* (1880)

CONTENTS

PROLOGUE

THE PROFESSIONAL IS PERSONAL

SINCE A WRITER MAY NOW ONLY WRITE ABOUT WHO HE OR SHE personally is or what he or she has experienced in an "authentic" way, and since the political, *mutatis mutandis*, is now personal, please permit me some personal history.

My parents were married in September 1948, when they were both 22 years old; I was born 13 months later, on the U.S. Marine Corps base in Camp Lejeune, North Carolina, the first of five siblings. John J. Walsh and Ann Patricia Finnegan were high school sweethearts in Malden and Medford, Massachusetts, back in the days when it was not at all uncommon for young American men and women to meet and fall in love at an early age, pledge their troth, and head into life and family while still in their teens and early twenties. In fact, this was normal.

Less than two years later, while we were living in Berkeley, California, and awaiting transfer to the American territory of Guam, my father, a newly promoted first lieutenant, was suddenly directed instead to Japan in order to stage for a landing in Korea, where war had broken out on June 25, 1950, between the Communist north and the U.N.-backed south of the peninsula, which had been divided along the 38th parallel after World War II. In a lightning strike, the Soviet-backed north had invaded the south along a wide front, pushing the troops of the Republic of Korea into what became known as the Pusan Perimeter along the southeast coast. It looked for all the world that they would soon be overrun and shoved into the sea.

At the time, there were few if any American forces in Korea. What was left of a rump American military presence in Asia was in Japan, where much of its materiel had been sold to the Japanese, including amphibious landing vehicles (LSTs); they had welded the drop-fronts shut in order to use them as commercial barges. Assigned to a weapons company in the Second Battalion, Fifth Marines (aka the "2/5")—the most decorated company in Marine Corps history—my father went ashore at Pusan in the midst of chaos. "Who's in command here?' he asked the first Marine he saw. "You are, sir," came the reply. In one-hundred-degree heat and with artillery incoming, he jumped into a shell crater on the Obong-ni Ridge and found himself sharing the space with a dead North Korean. Welcome to war in Korea.

My father, already a man at the age of 24, immediately took command and has never relinquished it—as no real man ever does, at least not willingly, and except by death. So this book is a testament not only to him but to the concept of manliness itself.

The Marines and other allied forces established control over the Pusan Perimeter. Meanwhile, back in Washington, President Truman and his military commander, Douglas MacArthur, decided that the objective was not simply to push the North Koreans out of the south but to liberate the north from Communist influence. Just five years after Soviet troops demolished Berlin, it was the first hot battle of what became the Cold War—a war that would last for 39 years, ending only when the Berlin Wall fell[1] and, two years later, the Soviet Union itself dissolved.

Like many surprise attacks, the landing at Inchon on September 15, 1950, could have gone badly. Coming ashore in the concrete harbor, the Marines had to use wooden ladders to climb over the welded-shut fronts of the LSTs, where they immediately faced withering

1. An event that, as it happens, I witnessed in person, and I have a piece of the Wall that I knocked out myself with a borrowed sledgehammer in my study to prove it. I brought it back to America in my carry-on. "*Wer hat ein Stück Berliner Mauer?*" asked the woman scanning the bags at Tegel airport. "*Ich,*" I replied, and everyone in line cheered.

fire from the entrenched North Korean troops. The casualty rate for Marine infantry officers in such a situation runs between 60 and 75 percent killed or wounded, owing to the Marine tradition of officers hitting the beach first: you're either a casualty and replaced or you're the leader.

My father's best friend, 1st Lt. Baldomero "Baldy" Lopez, the son of a Spanish immigrant, was captured in a memorable photograph clambering up a seawall from the LST next to my father's; the night before, Baldy had said, "John, I'm going to die tomorrow." He was shot in the arm and the chest as he was hurling a grenade. He smothered the pineapple with his body and was killed instantly, and was later awarded the Medal of Honor. A reporter who witnessed the event later wrote, "He died with the courage that makes men great."

And that was just the beginning of my father's baptism by fire, which went on to include the battle for Seoul—for the Marines, the most harrowing and (to use the current term) "traumatic" battle of the war, and which he refuses to talk about to this day, even at age 94. Every civilian, even the *mama-sans*, was a potential enemy combatant, and many was the Marine who died when a peasant woman deployed an AK-47 from beneath her skirts and shot him in the back. The Marines quickly learned to trust no one, and to take no prisoners. Today, this might be called a "war crime." Back then, it was called survival.

Still to come was the last stand at the Chosin Reservoir, in which Dad's unit, the 2/5, wrote itself into Marine Corps legend. My mother only learned of his safe return to Allied lines in the depths of the 1950–51 winter, when she saw an AP photograph of him in the local newspaper. He was standing up, in full winter gear, his rifle at the ready at present arms, leaning against an abutment, sound asleep.

In other words, I grew up with heroism, although I didn't know it at the time; after all, I was only 15 months old. And yet, Operation Chromite—for so the landing was termed—and its emotional consequences have been with me throughout my life. How does a son, the firstborn, live up to such a father? What does it mean to be a man measured against an example like his? Years later, when I dedicated my novel *And All the Saints*—a first-person "autobiography" of the twentieth-century Irish-American gangster Owen Vincent Madden—to him, his father, and my Irish-born great-grandfather, I wrote in the inscription: "To my father, who's still teaching me how to be a man."

He read it, looked up at me, and said, "You've always known how to be a man." That was how he told me what he thought of that book. What he thinks of this one, I hope he will let me know.

INTRODUCTION

TO DIE FOR

"The state of peace among men living side by side is not the natural state; the natural state is one of war," wrote Immanuel Kant in *Perpetual Peace: A Philosophical Sketch* (1795). "This does not always mean open hostilities, but at least an unceasing threat of war." Indeed, war is the natural state of man, and the history of the world is written in blood. In *Leviathan* (1651), the philosopher Thomas Hobbes evoked the biblical Ishmael when he spoke of the "war of every man against every man," and a glance at Genesis 16:12 provides the archetype: "And he will be a wild man; his hand *will be* against every man, and every man's hand against him; and he shall dwell in the presence of all his brethren."

To observe that war is crucial to civilizational advancement is also to observe the following: that human beings have a larger purpose than simply living out their threescore and ten. That men are born to father children and defend them and their women against other men who would kill them or otherwise take advantage of them.[1] That men understand that their enemy—on both the individual and sexual level—is other men, rarely women. That men are not in competition with women but with other men. That the measure of a real man is not how much money he makes (although that is one metric, to use current jargon) but what he has done in his life: how far he has sailed, how well he has loved, how he has raised his children, and how much, or little, they love him. What he has contributed to the historical record, what he has left

1. One of the most celebrated wars in history, that of the Greeks versus the Trojans recounted in Homer's *Iliad*, was fought over a woman.

in the way of posterity, and for posterity; his mark, whether it be empire or a simple X.

In other words, war is not only in our blood, it is our familial birthright and burden. Wish it away though we might, it is the inevitable result of the frictions among human beings and their political extensions, kingdoms, nations, and nation-states. No matter how we may pretend it doesn't exist, erase the memory of our martial past, attempt to eradicate it, or deny its existence altogether, war—or its existential threat—is always with us, and will be until the day mankind vanishes.

It is fashionable today to regard war as the exception and peace the rule, but a simple glance at an unexpurgated and unbowdlerized history of the world—ancient or modern—quickly shows the essential nature of bellicosity and its importance to the survival of and, ofttimes, the advancement of the human species. War, or the specter thereof, is the principal means of scientific advancement, of territorial expansion, and of the defense of those personal, social, and political elements a society holds dear.

Every age, it seems, yearns for peace but—heeding the old Roman maxim, *Si vis pacem, para bellum*—prepares for war. This is no less true today than it was in the time of Vegetius in his famous tract, *De re militari* from the fourth or mid-fifth century A.D. The history of the West, from the end of the Roman Empire to the present day, attests to the truth of the observation. Just when we think that the great geopolitical issues of the day have been settled by force of arms, along comes Clio, the Muse of History, to remind us otherwise:

> England has now been blest with thirty-seven years of peace. At no other period of her history can a similarly long cessation from a state of warfare be found. It is true that our troops have had battles to fight during this interval for the protection and extension of our Indian possessions and our colonies; but these have been with distant and unimportant enemies. . . . There has, indeed, throughout this long period, been no great war, like those with which the previous history of modern Europe abounds. . . . It would be far too much to augur from this, that no similar wars

> will again convulse the world; but the value of the period of peace which Europe has gained, is incalculable; even if we look on it as only a truce, and expect again to see the nations of the earth recur to what some philosophers have termed man's natural state of warfare.
>
> —Edward Shepherd Creasy, *The Fifteen Decisive Battles of the World: From Marathon to Waterloo* (1851)

Thus the view from mid-nineteenth century England, with the corpse of the Little Corporal safely entombed, breathing well-deserved lungfuls of fresh air devoid of gunpowder and the stench of rotting flesh and emptied entrails after the tumult of the Napoleonic Wars. And yet the preambulatory conflict of the Franco-Prussian War was only two decades in the future, and the unimaginable horrors of the First World War were already stirring in the souls of the artists, writers, and composers who could sense the slouching advent of the murderous beast but were powerless to stop it. As it turned out, the Treaty of Paris in 1815 was simply a *caesura*, the briefest pause in the historical record, before the harvest of death continued anew. Nothing, it seems, can stop the Kantian categorical imperative.

Because war's price is too terrible to contemplate rationally, diplomacy has emerged over the centuries as a preferable alternative to physical conflict, and yet when diplomacy fails, war nonetheless breaks out. (The reverse is almost never true—except when the side that is about to lose begs for terms, almost always refused.) And then, men whose fallen fathers are still freshly in their graves, their widows still in weeds, their children barely out of knee pants, once more present arms and take to the battlefields, confident that their sons will willingly follow them into the smoke and haze and dust of death.

Why? Few are overtly in favor of war, and yet it has been a part of the human condition as long as there have been men to fight it. Indeed, some men thrive on it, and some require it in order to realize their passions and destinies. In American history alone, Washington was elevated by it; Grant was relieved from alcoholism and obscurity by it; Patton was transfigured by it and, when it ended, disappeared along with it. Some of history's greatest figures saw it as an opportunity, but more often others regarded it as a sacred duty, a moral obligation. The proper use and management of armed might is one of the themes of Machiavelli's *The Prince*: "Where there are good arms there must be good laws . . . whoever has good arms will always have good friends."[2]

How retrograde, how antique to our modern ears this all sounds. And yet it is quintessentially male, the inherited patrimony of one of the two sexes, and the most fundamental defense mechanism against the loss of home and hearth and, most important, progeny. For war is at root a masculine engagement, undertaken on behalf of females and children—in large measure to win and protect the former and to ensure the survival of the latter—a truth not lately much told or acknowledged. Children, once the future of a society, are now seen, in the right-thinking quarters of the postindustrial and sumptuously feminized West, as a burden both economic and social; women are regarded by some as fully capable of holding their own in any contests with men, whether mental, emotional, or physical, without any distinction or allowances; and as for men, well, the sooner they disappear into the dustbin of history, the better. After all, as the antiwar slogans of the 1960s put it, "War is unhealthy for children and other living things." And who, historically, has fought—started, won, lost, or finished—wars?

We tend these days to think of war—when we think of it at all, so remote has it become—in near-bloodless terms, a luxury we ought no longer to afford. It has become an embarrassing relic of our past, something at once uncivilized and unnecessary. Although the United States has been engaged in a near-continuous series of wars, large and small, since the First World War, and has been embroiled in European and

2. "Above all, any prince or republic that wants to prevail must have armed forces that are its own in every possible way," writes the Italian-born Angelo Codevilla in the introduction to his translation and annotation of *The Prince*. "Soldiers and citizens must be one and the same. The prince, or the republic's leading men, must command the troops personally and must do whatever it takes to keep the troops happy and devoted. The foundation of political power is the willingness of an army to fight and win. Nothing substitutes for that." Certainly not, the modern reader might observe, "soft power," which neither frightens nor convinces anybody.

international affairs for even longer, war—with the notable exceptions of the Revolution, the War of 1812, and the Civil War of 1861–65—has largely avoided these shores. And that last war was the bloodiest in our national history, a cataclysm so powerful that its social and political effects are still being felt today.

It is, however, a war we honor. It was a war to save the Union and free the slaves, a war that pitted brother against brother, father against son, fought in essence in the short distance between Washington, D.C., and Richmond, Virginia, a war that cost more than 600,000 lives in a country numbering at the time only 31 million souls. It was a war—"a great civil war," in Lincoln's famous formulation in his Gettysburg Address—worth fighting and winning. "We Are Coming, Father Abraham, Three Hundred Thousand More," went the poem by James S. Gibbons, set to music by America's first great composer-songwriter, Stephen Foster, in 1862. Men and boys from Maine and Michigan shouldered arms to kill men and boys from Virginia and Alabama because the cause was worth it—no matter what the price.

This is, by any standard, the very definition of heroism. (The word derives from the Latin for "illustrious man" and, even earlier, from the Greek for "demigod," with the added nuance of "defender" or "protector.") War has always been elemental, involving spears and swords, clubs and arrows, cannonballs and canisters, all instruments of death. In the great battles of the past, armies clashed with the express purpose of slaughtering each other until one had had enough and surrendered, fled, or simply gave up to be butchered in the field like cattle. Hunger and thirst both took their toll, as did diseases against which there was no effective treatment or cure. When their ships were rammed, the oarsmen died and the men above decks were tossed into the sea to drown. Once hostilities were offered and accepted, as in Greek and Roman times—generally after a day or two of maneuvering around the battlefield for maximum tactical and operational advantage—the conflict was waged to its conclusion, which was more often than not decided on a single day in one location.

The pitiless brutality of it is literally beyond modern imagination. Heads and limbs were hacked off, eyes put out, soldiers beaten to death. The French national epic poem, *La Chanson de Roland,* depicts men being split from skull to breastbone by the stroke of a sword, while at Hastings, the Danish axes wielded by the Saxon housecarls were said to cleave both rider and horse in twain at a single blow. Despite the massed formations of the Greek phalanxes and the Roman legions, at root the clash of armies was a clash of individuals, a prolonged series of simultaneous hand-to-hand combats, encounters from which only one man at a time could emerge victorious. The modern notion of a humanitarian, "proportional" war (surely an oxymoron) was utterly foreign to them. A soldier's job, as Patton put it so bluntly and yet so eloquently in a speech to his Third Army during World War II, was to kill or die: "No bastard ever won a war by dying for his country. He won it by making the other poor dumb bastard die for his country."

The classical scholar and military historian Victor Davis Hanson notes:

> As observers as diverse as Aldous Huxley and John Keegan have pointed out, to write of conflict is not to describe merely the superior rifles of imperial troops or the matchless edge of the Roman gladius, but ultimately the collision of a machine-gun bullet with the brow of an adolescent, or the carving and ripping of artery and organ in the belly of an anonymous Gaul. To speak of war in any other fashion brings with it a sort of immorality: the idea that when hit, soldiers simply go to sleep, rather than are shredded, that generals order impersonal battalions and companies of automatons into the heat of battle, rather than screaming nineteen-year-olds into clouds of gas and sheets of lead bullets, or that a putrid corpse has little to do with larger approaches to science and culture.[3]

There is no sanitizing it. War is, in fact, to use the voguish term, "toxic," in the sense that killing and inflicting of severe physical pain is precisely its point. No one in his right mind would willingly engage in it were it not for a host of other factors, some of them genetic and sexual, some spiritual, some psychological; some vain, and some base,

---

3. Victor Davis Hanson, *Carnage and Culture* (Knopf Doubleday Publishing Group), Kindle Edition.

and some entirely unknown, even to the warriors themselves. And yet, from the dawn of recorded history, men have felt the need, the obligation, and the duty to take up arms against an enemy and fight for what they believe in, whether the defense of territory or in conquest, rapine, and plunder. Noble or base, it does not seem to matter.

At the same time, it is essentially masculine; there are no reliable accounts of nations of women warring against other women with spear, pike, hatchet, sword, bayonet, carbine, machine gun, or nuclear weapon. When war breaks out, as it inevitably does, fastidiousness goes out the window, and—in particular, when the fight is defensive and dire—men, not women, are called to arms. That they go, fearful but generally unflinching, is a continual wonder, but it is also a "celebration" of masculinity—which, in its essence, is simply another word for duty, honor, and country. In the view of the demon god Thanatos, women are born to give birth, to provide the next generation of cannon fodder; in the view of the priapic god Eros, women are born to provide the next generation of heroes.

None of this is diminishment. Rather, it is complementary. The sexes are different. A country whose women lose their virtue and whose men lose their nerve—the Soviet Union is the most recent example of this historical truth[4]—soon vanishes into history. When every man is a petitioner, a lackey, or a slave, and every woman a whore, that country is finished. A land of "strong" (i.e., in defiance of previous social norms with no immediate consequences, or even opposition) women and weak men is a dead country. As the cultural historian Camille Paglia inflammatorily wrote in the first chapter of her magisterial treatise *Sexual Personae* (1990),

> Nature's cycles are woman's cycles. Biologic femaleness is a sequence of circular returns, beginning and ending at the same point. Woman's centrality gives her a stability of identity. She does not have to become but only to be. Her centrality is a great

---

4. In my own personal experience in the Soviet Union between April 1986 and the summer of 1991, nearly every young woman was a trollop and every man corruptible, as if the Cold War had already been lost.

> obstacle to man, whose quest for identity she blocks. He must transform himself into an independent being, that is, a being free of her. If he does not, he will simply fall back into her. . . . The western idea of history as a propulsive movement into the future, a progressive or Providential design climaxing in the revelation of a Second Coming, is a male formulation. No woman, I submit, could have coined such an idea . . . if civilization had been left in female hands, we would all still be living in grass huts.

Of course women can be physically heroic,[5] and many have been, although generally in the absence of available men. But most women are not, by nature, martial; they gestate, conserve, and protect life. For every Boadicea from Celtic Britain or Volscian Camilla in the *Aeneid*, there are millions of their male counterparts, some sung, most unsung. In the teeth of battle, those men did not talk, palaver, or powwow. They fought, died, and lie buried, often piecemeal or in fragments, in cemeteries or forgotten battlefields, long since plowed under. And yet they live on in the hearts and minds and the DNA of their descendants of both sexes. To paraphrase what Lincoln said of Grant: they fight.

In his account of the Battle of Mutina (present-day Modena) in Cisalpine Gaul in 43 B.C. between troops loyal to the Roman senate, assisted by Octavian (the future emperor Augustus), and those of Mark Antony, the Greek historian Appian of Alexandria notes the stone bravery of the Roman forces confronting one another:

> Being veterans they raised no battle-cry, since they could not expect to terrify each other, nor in the engagement did they utter a sound, either as victors or vanquished. As there could be neither flanking nor charging amid marshes and ditches, they met together in close order, and since neither could dislodge the other they locked together with their swords as in a wrestling match. No blow missed its mark. There were wounds and slaughter but no cries, only groans; and when one fell he was instantly borne away

5. Consider, for example, the Soviet female flyers and sharpshooters on the Eastern Front in World War II.

> and another took his place. They needed neither admonition nor encouragement, since experience made each one his own general. When they were overcome by fatigue they drew apart from each other for a brief space to take breath, as in gymnastic games, and then rushed again to the encounter. Amazement took possession of the new levies who had come up, as they beheld such deeds done with such precision and in such silence.

Antony, perhaps the most charismatic and tragic of the great men who fought Rome's civil wars, was besieging forces commanded by Decimus Brutus, one of Julius Caesar's assassins, to whose aid Octavian had come.[6] (Antony eventually broke off the battle after heavy casualties on both sides; he and the future emperor, to be called Augustus, would shortly thereafter form an alliance against the plotters, crushing them at Philippi the following year.)

It was Roman versus Roman as the legions squared off against each other, knowing there would be quarter neither asked nor given: the courage this took is practically unimaginable today, as is the indifference to suffering. Death was, ultimately, a matter of duty and accepted by soldiers as their lot, should it come. The coward who fled was not viewed as prudent but as criminal, unmanly, and was generally executed when caught, as an example to others.[7]

Despite the steady advance of martial technology, things did not materially change for centuries. Even as late as World War I, single combat between soldiers had not entirely disappeared, especially when bayonets were fixed and encounters in no-man's land sometimes ended with each man having run the other through, fatally. In the nuclear age, warring nations now have the capacity to annihilate the other side at the push of a button, but a postapocalyptic world will take humanity right back to where we started: hand-to-hand combat, to the death.

This is a brutal notion, and one that our fastidious times do not want to entertain. Surely, the argument goes, there must be a better way to

6. It seems that politics has made for strange bedfellows throughout human history.

7. The Romans took a particularly dim view of pusillanimity.

resolve human disputes. Diplomacy—talking—is said to be war by other means, but in reality war is diplomacy by other means, and far more dispositive. When has a major conflict been settled by high-level talks and a "peace process"? True, the Peace of Westphalia in 1648 concluded the Thirty Years' War between Catholic and Protestant European states and ratified the Dutch emancipation from Habsburg Spain. But that only came about because the losing side was exhausted and enervated by the bloodshed and simply couldn't fight any longer.[8] Westphalia also set off a prolonged balancing act among the Great Powers and the royal families that headed them until it all collapsed in the mud and blood of Ypres, Passchendaele, and the Somme.

To put it in modern terms, war has long been a binary choice: win or lose, live or die, conquer or give way. It is neither pretty nor politically correct. And yet, it is human—all too human, in Nietzsche's formulation. It is, in fact and in essence, masculine; no matter how "modern" man gets, he will never entirely abandon his biological and genetic roots and impulses. Historically, men organize themselves around status and power, both of which are often won at the point of a spear, while women from time immemorial have assumed the status of the men in their lives, by whatever means achieved, generally sexually. Men are Romans, women are Sabines. This is true of every culture, and in every time and place. That we find it regressive and deplorable today says more about our ahistoricism than the supposed prejudice of our ancestors.

Latter-day sensibility, and a loss of faith in traditional Western religions, has decreed that there is, literally, not a fate worse than death. We have, in our wisdom, transformed our short span of existence into a kind of living Purgatory, where life itself is misery and palliative surcease can only be found via drugs, sex, or therapy. That there might exist a teleologically aspirational end state is unthinkable; past and future have vanished, to be replaced by an eternally torturous present that can only be endured, and not transformed. Death becomes no one; if there

---

8. One of the bloodiest wars in history, largely fought in what is now Germany, the Thirty Years' War resulted in the deaths of an estimated eight million people. Atrocities against civilians—especially by the Croatian cavalry fighting on the side of the Catholic League—shocked all Europe by their brutality.

is nothing worth living for, except for the sake of living, then what is worth dying for?

Still, no matter how feminized he may become—in attitude, emotions, and, latterly, even in vocal timbre and physique—a man can never entirely reject his essentially masculine way of seeing the world: as one in which the strong survive and the weak perish, whether he is a gladiator, a Wall Street arbitrageur, or even a capon-voiced NPR commentator. No one should "take care" of a man once he hits puberty and grows into what we once called manhood. He is, or should be, responsible for himself and those who look to him for physical protection and leadership. The defense of women and children is not a paternalistic plot, sketched in some prehistoric Lascaux cave, but a noble and essential prerequisite of all civilizations grounded in physical reality, and not something lightly to be forsaken. Fighting battles in faraway lands for cultural protection and expansion is not necessarily predatory imperialism or malevolent colonialism but a hedge against future disaster.

For masculinity is, *in extremis*, lethal. Males fight. They fight for both the present and for the future. The enemy who's killing them now, in the moment of combat, may well—will—fall to one of their sons. The revenge drama is one of the theater's mainstays for a reason. It is elemental. It forms much of human history. It is also progress, for without survival there can be none. Men fight for power, for love, for sex, for money, for wealth and possessions. The basest crime statistics prove it. So do the lists of geniuses in every form of intellectual, scientific, and artistic endeavor.

To be a male—in any century, apparently, but the twenty-first—is to be born if not raised, Spartan-like, with an understanding that the world is not your friend but your adversary or your enemy. The cuddly, anthropomorphic animals of fables and cartoons men know to be capable of ripping their throats out at any moment. The belligerent drunk at the bar challenging them to fight they know cannot be reasoned with, and when he charges, their only choices are fight or flight. There are many factors to consider in making those choices, but in the end they come down to self-preservation, by any means necessary. The only culture that doesn't defend itself is one bent on suicide.

Historically, nations have recognized this powerful biological fact and have sought to channel it by inducting their young men into the armed forces, whether those of the ancient Greeks or contemporary China. The priapic thrust of young manhood must needs be given an outlet: fucking or fighting are generally the choices, as China is now discovering—and confronting, with the abandonment of its actuarially ill-conceived "one child" policy—even as it fields the world's largest army.[9] And, in the end, what are armies for but to direct the physical and sexual energies of young men, for whom combat and procreation are the most primordial instincts of manhood, into war?

Instead, we are witnessing an attempt at profound cultural and historical change—the transformation of men into women and women into men, at will, and on a mere say-so—that is as audacious as it is insane.[10] The profoundly ahistorical, anticultural, and unscientific assertion that something as elemental as biology can be altered on a personal whim is something unique in human history; autonomy without God—indeed the replacement of nature, Nature's God,[11] or God himself by mere humans who have abandoned their sense of the transcendental and substituted instead a perverse desire to abjure the evidence of their own genitals in the pursuit of a counterfactual.

This is not to say there aren't exceptions to all norms, even the biologically Mendelian. Nature has her sports: two-headed snakes, Cyclopean calves, albinos, hermaphrodites. But to say that something as elemental as sex is arbitrarily "assigned" (by whom?) is absurd, a cultural-Marxist[12] attempt to play God. "Stereotypes" are stereotypes

---

9. Historically, China is a nonhegemonic power regarding the West. It has been defeated many times by its neighbors—Japan conquered it twice in the 1930s—and yet, like Russia, China relies on its sheer intractable size to preserve its fundamental national character.

10. At the Battle of Salamis, watching his fleet being destroyed, Xerxes was thrilled by the performance of his Greek ally, Queen Artemisia of Halicarnassus, exclaiming: "My men have turned into women, my women into men!" But such women were, and are today, extremely rare.

11. As Jefferson phrased it in the American Declaration of Independence.

12. Many on the modern left deny that such a thing exists. For an analysis of cultural Marxism, and how to combat its pernicious influence, please see my books:

(fixed images) for a reason: they are largely true and therefore broadly useful. Stereotypes are not conspiracies but rather the evolved shorthand of decades, centuries, millennia, of folkish and cultural data, which can only seem "offensive" in retrospect and out of cultural context. But the exception cannot be the rule.

Iconoclasm is a luxury in which only stable societies can indulge; once it becomes institutionalized, it turns into a battering ram wielded by a resentful minority against the larger, historically based, cultural entity toward which its animus is directed. To put it in Hegelian Marxist terms: the antithesis has superseded the thesis, thus negating the need for a synthesis. This is the goal of all "progressivism."

Nature, however, has greater powers of resistance than mere humans. The straw-man argument of desirable stasis is an imaginary social goal, attributed to conservatives in today's intellectually bifurcated *agora*, and is held by precisely nobody, on either left or right, with the possible exception of those advocates of "sustainability," the zero-sum theory of humanity enforced by the coercive power of government.

In life, however, nothing is static, and nowhere is that more evident than in war. No major battle ends the way it began; wars cease only when one side is conquered or cannot continue. "Negotiated settlements" are essentially truces by both sides and rarely survive even a few years, which is to say, until one side feels emboldened to take up the cudgels once more. War is the great leveler, the great decider. When civilizations collapse, as all must and do, they do not simply dissolve from enervation (although that is always a factor; today we might call it guilt), but by conquest: just ask Romulus Augustulus, the last Western Roman emperor.[13] When Caesar attempted to emasculate the Roman senate by having himself named dictator[14] for life, the senators fought

---

The Devil's Pleasure Palace (2015) and its sequel, *The Fiery Angel* (2018), both from Encounter Books.

13. In 476, the Pannonian-born barbarian, Odoacer, deposed the fifteen-year-old boy, whose reign lasted less than a year.

14. "Dictator" was a constitutional provision in Roman government, conferring absolute power in a military emergency for a maximum term of six months upon the *magister populi*, who commanded the army; his deputy, who commanded

back with poiniards and *pugiones*, but once the Julio-Claudian line of emperors had run its course, ending with Nero,[15] the senate was of little consequence. By the fifth century, Rome was begging to be put out of its misery, and the barbarian tribes who had settled in Italy under Roman aegis were only too happy to oblige. Nature abhors a vacuum.

And so, in the end, when they knew that all was lost, when they knew they not only would not survive but also that they would never see their families, wives, children again, they set their jaws, fixed their bayonets, emptied their revolvers, used their rifles as clubs, shot their mounts for breastworks, and piled their dead high. They broke their spears in the bodies of their enemies, used their swords for stabbing instead of slashing, and, when all else was exhausted, employed their teeth and fingernails as weapons, until they could fight no longer.

As you will read in these pages, the Romans did it at Cannae, and again at the Teutoburg Forest; so did Custer's men at the Little Bighorn. The Christian Hungarians and Croatians at Szigetvár embraced a final, suicidal charge as preferable to surrender or supine slaughter at the hands of the Muslim Turks, but cleverly planned to take as many invaders with them as they could, even after death. The Jews held off the Romans at Masada and the Germans in Warsaw until they could fight no longer. Men died also at Thermopylae, at Roncevaux, at Hastings, and before the door of St. Peter's in Rome. They perished at the Alamo and at Camarón in Mexico, in the Tennessee mud at Shiloh and at the godforsaken Little Bighorn in Montana. The fought to the end at Khartoum, as well as Rorke's Drift, Stalingrad, and the Chosin Reservoir, because death was always preferable to dishonor, for without his honor, and his fidelity to his training, his country and, most important, his comrades, a man was nothing. Even when, against all the odds, a few of

---

the cavalry, was called the master of the horse, or *magister equitum*. Caesar took advantage of this provision to effectively overthrow the Republic.

15. "What an artist dies in me!" the most dissolute and cowardly of the first five emperors exclaimed as his freed slave killed him in 68 A.D.

them survived or even won through to victory, they still were prepared to make the ultimate sacrifice.

Which brings us to one of the paradoxes of Western civilization: a culture based on the primacy of the individual serves the common good better via the mechanism of willing self-sacrifice than the regimented, collectivist societies of the East. Western soldiers do not have to be prodded into battle by political commissars. They do not have to be conscripted on a vast and permanent scale. They need not be propagandized to come to the defense of the homeland. The individual, while extolled politically, is dispensable militarily—for the good of all the other individuals.

Indeed, death in battle was glorious—that was the word the ancients used, repeatedly—the end state to which masculine humanity aspired. For some things were worth dying for. To the individual soldier, the goal was not survival of the individual, although that was always preferable to the alternative. Men in war generally fought as long and as ferally as they could as the end approached; as the Spartan maxim had it, you emerged from battle either with your shield or on it. But when the end appeared, whether in the form of Persian arrows, Turkish cannons, captured Winchesters in the hands of American Indians, or Chinese AK-47s, these heroes never flinched. They fought to the last man, to the limits of masculine human endurance, and beyond. They suffered willingly the sword thrusts, stab cuts, arrow wounds, gunshots, legs and limbs blown asunder by artillery, the battlefield butchery, scalping, and even decapitation—things that no men other than criminals would ever inflict upon women but do willingly inflict upon one another in their service.

We now arrive at the central question: Why do men fight? What or whom is worth dying for? Property is disposable and fungible—more important, it can be reacquired through conquest, prosperity, or sharp dealing. The answer, as we shall see in these pages, is surprisingly simple: they fight for themselves, for their brothers-in-arms, and therefore for their women and children and for their country, which is the expression of the family. Without women, there are no children, and without children, there is no future. And without a country—a *patria*, which means "fatherland"—there is nothing but the tribe, the family, the self.

And so men sacrifice themselves, finding in that sacrifice not only glory (as risible and even "offensive" as that word seems in our louche yet murderous age) but in defense of all the structures of society from the individual (expendable) to the family (replaceable, although less so now than formerly), to the town, city, polis, province or state, and finally nation. *E pluribus unum.*

Almost no one dies for an abstract idea. No one dies for democracy, or fascism, or communism, or National Socialism, or "Europe." He dies instead for America, or Italy, or Russia, or Germany—for the nation-states that emerged from the ruins of the Roman Empire, or in the case of the Islamic *ummah*, for a seventh-century Arabian Peninsula faith that combines the pertinent elements of both Judaism and Christianity (long preexistent in the region). While it is true that the Crusades were a European reaction against the occupation of the Holy Land by the Islamic Arabs and their religiously colonized subjects, including the Turks and, soon enough, the religiously and militarily hapless Persians, the Christian reaction to the Muslim conquest was essentially transnational: a kind of prefigured NATO in the service of the Cross of Christ. Soldiers, of whatever stripe, are trained not simply to win—although that is the optimal outcome—but to die, that their fellows might win.

Therefore, what is heroism? What are its moral components? Is it altruism, love, self-sacrifice? What are its amoral components—fear of cowardice, lust for glory, pride? Why was it once celebrated, and now often dismissed as anachronistic at best, foolish and vainglorious at its worst? Is it something unique to the Greco-Roman, Judeo-Christian West, or is it found universally—and, if so, how does it differ from culture to culture? Can it be separated from religious faith, or at least some sort of ethical code? Is it innately human, implanted by the divine, or both?

In an age of victimhood and identity politics, heroism is increasingly regarded as an antiquated relic of the "patriarchy" as if, historically at least, there had ever been an alternative. Is it "racist" to sacrifice yourself for your own kind rather than submit to the sword of the alien enemy seeking to supplant you? By regarding all cultures as equal, or even superior, to one's own, has not treason therefore become the highest form of patriotism? The cultural-Marxist import of "Critical Theory" would have us ask these questions, not to illuminate the moral issues, which have long since been decided, but to sow doubt about our most basic social concepts: a pacifist, post-Christian, feminized West seemingly can no longer take its own side in a quarrel.[16] Accommodation, inclusivity, tolerance, and, above all, shame have become the new watchwords. In a politically correct culture, only a fool would sacrifice himself for something as fashionably objectionable as the traditional nuclear family or as base as personal honor.

As the British epistolarians Trenchard and Gordon wrote in "Cato" Letter No. 15 (1721), "In those wretched countries where a man cannot call his tongue his own, he can scarce call any thing else his own. Whoever would overthrow the liberty of the nation, must begin by subduing the freedom of speech; a thing terrible to publick traitors."[17] But here we are. Even heroism has now, it seems, become politically incorrect.

We cannot afford it to become so.

This is not simply a matter of semantics, or of changing mores. Heroism—in *The Devil's Pleasure Palace* and *The Fiery Angel,* I referred to its cultural transcription as the Heroic Narrative—is the core of our self-understanding. If the importance of the individual is central to the social and political meaning of the West, if we are not to be cogs in a wheel or clerks in a gigantic post office, then our fates as free and autonomous men and women are what must most concern us—far more than the static and sometimes destructive collectivism that seeks to supplant our agency. Western art and culture is the story of heroes, not groups. What may seem today to be antiquated concepts of honor, virtue, glory, and the chivalric protection of women and children we forsake at our existential peril. The great stories of our patrimony are the stories of heroes, generally martial, not diplomats or committees.

What features do these stories have in common? The first is the embrace (often, at first, reluctant) of a great cause, one that allows, or propels, the individual into the service of his people. Concomitant with this commitment is the hero's acceptance that he may have to give his

16. The poet Robert Frost's famous definition of a "liberal."

17. A quotation often erroneously attributed to Benjamin Franklin.

life in this endeavor, that there are some things, big things, worth dying for so that others might live, or live freely. Self-sacrifice is, after all, the ultimate sacrifice.

Thus we have what might at first appear to be a paradox: that it is often by acting in one's self-interest—"selfishly"—that the hero effects the collective good via self-abnegation. If he fails, his tribe, people, or nation may fall with him, but even in death he can still succeed, and often does, which is why we still honor his memory.

We don't have to look very far for the roots of this cultural tradition. It's the heart of the Jesus story[18] and the Christian religion, which forms the basis of the Western civilization that emerged from the ruins of the Western Roman Empire between 476 A.D. and the coming of the Holy Roman Empire under Charlemagne in 800 A.D. This period is often, wrongly and derisively, referred to as the "Dark Ages," but there was nothing benighted about the emerging nations and nation-states that originated during these 324 years. In the Christian New Testament, for example (John 15:12), Jesus commands his disciples to love one another as he has loved them. Further: "Greater love hath no man than this, that a man lay down his life for his friends" (John 15:13). Even with the coming of Christianity, the slain warrior is guaranteed a place in Valhalla.

Indeed, all organized religions include some sort of sacrifice as part of their founding mythos or revelation; at the core of every faith, whether pagan or monotheistic, lies an impulse to propitiation, gratitude, and favor-seeking. In the Jewish Bible, Abraham is prepared to slay his son, Isaac, and burn his body upon a makeshift altar because that's what his God, Yahweh, had ordered him to do as a test of his spiritual fidelity and obedience.[19]

Abraham's reward was not only the life of his son but a promise from Heaven that his progeny would multiply like grains of sand on the shore, "and thy seed shall possess the gate of his enemies, And in thy seed shall all the nations of the earth be blessed; because thou hast obeyed my voice" (Genesis 22:17–18). This parable has many

---

18. The hidden religious origins of many of the battles treated in this book will surprise those modern readers who think largely in secular terms.

19. See Extract 1 at the end of this book.

meanings, but one less-remarked upon is the temporal power bequeathed by God to Abraham as a reward for his resolution. From the beginning of recorded history, then, sacrifice has been intertwined with military victory. The willingness to surrender something so essentially dear, a human life, whether our own or someone very close to us, in order to achieve a larger (although not necessarily higher) goal is part of our nature. It's not only spiritual, it's also transactional and transcendental.

Self-sacrifice should not be confused with, or mistaken for, altruism. Far too often, the purpose of, call it Pharisaic, altruism is to make the benefactor feel good about himself at the expense of the recipient, for gratitude can quickly turn to shame and resentment, while the flipside of generosity is contempt. Further, altruism is optional. One can choose whether to give or perform a service gratis. The men who fought and died in history's greatest battles generally had no choice; whether conscripts and cannon fodder or consuls and generals, their path to the ultimate tests of courage and fortitude was foreordained upon the opening of hostilities and the engagement in battle. We must, however, ask: Can there be heroism in the service of a bad cause, or at least a cause that seems to us, in retrospect, suspect? The soldiers who fought and died in the conflicts under discussion here, or who just barely survived them, did not have the luxury to think about such matters, as they furiously battled to save themselves, their families, their property, and their way of life.[20] The onrushing horror of what was shortly to confront them—not simply death but, in many cases, death preceded and accompanied by agonizing torture—focused their minds: if they could not stay alive, then they were going to take as many of the enemy with them as they could before succumbing. Last-stand heroism, it seems, can be a form of pre-posthumous revenge.

Indeed, the reasons for heroism are varied, and in the course of this book we will examine many of them, both in a traditional light and

---

20. Western notions of private property, especially land, animate much of military history. As we shall see in Chapter XII, the communist Soviet Union temporarily forsook atheism for nationalism during the Second World War.

through a contemporary lens. But at the heart of the matter lies the heart itself. And despite all the advances of rationalist science, that most precious of human organs remains the most complex and mysterious. At its most basic, war, like love, is a matter of the heart, which is why, as the old saying goes, all's fair in both.

That is why this book is not a traditional military history. War is not simply about the act, or facts, of war itself. It is not simply about the *how* or the *when* or even the *why* but rather about the cultural circumstances that precipitated it and the men who fought it. The battles under discussion are not included simply because the "good guys" won, or lost. More important to our consideration is the battle's "afterlife,"[21] its perpetuation in the larger culture, however retold, recast, or even fictionalized, and in whatever form. That we remember engagements that occurred more than two millennia ago says something about them, and about us. In a strong, self-confident culture, the past guides the present into the future; countries that come to—or have been forced by conquest to—hate or eradicate their own histories quickly disappear from maps and hearts. In revolutionary societies from the Mohammedan conquests to the French, Russian, and Chinese revolutions, the winners sought to erase the past and begin the world anew. But this is, as history shows, impossible.

From a look at our martial history from the ancient Greeks to the present day, it might appear that—*pace* father Abraham—the earthly god of man is neither Yahweh nor Jesus Christ but Baal, the bloodthirsty, horned god of the Phoenicians and the Carthaginians, Rome's mortal enemies. Baal is closely identified with the Carthaginian practice of child sacrifice (shades of Abraham, but of far different moral import). When Rome became Christian in the early fourth century under Constantine, it was not the passive Jewish Jesus whose ethos triumphed during the late Empire but the Canaanite Lord Baal. For, at that point,

---

21. A term employed by the late British polymath Jonathan Miller in his book *Subsequent Performances* (Faber and Faber, 1986): "The amplitude of Shakespeare's imagination admits so many possible interpretations that his work has enjoyed an extraordinary afterlife unforeseeable by the author at the time of writing."

incessant warfare was Rome's lot, both in the West and, for a thousand years more, in the East as well.

The Crusades during the first half of the second millennium—Christian retaking of what had been first Roman territory and then the literal birthplace of Christianity in the Holy Land, the Levant, Anatolia, and Greece—were the high-water mark of the Church Militant. The Ottoman Muslim conquest in 1453 of Constantinople—the Second Rome and the seat of the shrinking Eastern Empire—marked its end as a force for regional domination; the Cross and the broadsword had been exchanged for the Crescent and the scimitar. Perhaps, as Gibbon argues in *The Decline and Fall of the Roman Empire*, it was Christianity that hollowed out the Roman martial tradition, along with waning Roman fertility, the increasing reliance upon foreign mercenaries, and the extension of citizenship to the German barbarians, many of them veterans of the legions. Today, as the Christianized West enters its fully secular, post-Christian phase, it may eventually have to revert to its pre-Christian pagan, visceral roots as it battles the religiously animated bloodlust of Islam.

And then the bloodshed will be terrible.

Do not mistake paganism's potency. Adolf Hitler's National Socialist movement, with its roots deep in the barbarian German resistance to Rome (i.e., the West), flourished in the soil of the Third Reich's militant anti-Christianity; the Nazis, many of them nominally Christian by birth or baptism, saw nothing admirable in passivity. They no more showed tolerance, mercy, or forbearance to their enemies than the Romans did to their foes—or, for that matter, than Arminius and his men did to the Roman legions under Varus in the Teutoburg Forest during the reign of Augustus.[22]

In the decisive battles of both antiquity and the modern era the slaughter was extensive, but the outcome was definitive. The Greeks repelled the Persian Empire at Marathon, Salamis, and Plataea, and Alexander crushed it at Gaugamela. It was in Greece that the Roman Civil War was decided, where the fate of the Roman Republic was

---

22. See Chapter II.

settled when Caesar defeated Pompey, where Octavian and Mark Antony destroyed Cassius and Brutus, and where Augustus finished Antony and Cleopatra. Charles Martel halted the northward expansion of the Umayyad Muslims under Abdul Rahman at Tours. At Hastings, the Normans superseded the Anglo-Saxons; at Waterloo, Wellington ended Napoleon's brilliant military career and neutralized France as a Great Power, while at Stalingrad, the pride of the Wehrmacht died in the snows east of the Urals, on the fringe of the vast Soviet interior.

But what of the battles in which the losing side won in the end? The most spectacular of these has come down to us as the very definition of heroism, the willingness to fight when everything either was, or seemed at the time, lost. The original Last Stand at Thermopylae, in 480 B.C., set the template for all that followed: a small band of Spartans and other Greeks holding back the mighty army of the Persian king, Xerxes, until on the third day the Persians found a way over and around the Greeks through the mountains and wiped them out, but at a terrible cost in manpower and, more important, pride.

Thermopylae also created a high bar for all subsequent last stands in that it has had a 2,500-year afterlife, not only militarily but also politically, historically, and artistically. The names of almost all the men who fought at the Hot Gates under the Spartan king, Leonidas, are lost to history, although their poetic valedictory by Simonides of Ceos still echoes down the ages: "Go tell the Spartans, stranger passing by, that here obedient to their laws we lie." For men trained from youth to prize martial valor above all else, a life well ended was a life well lived, no matter his age or station; king and commoner died alike, and for the same reason.

Sometimes last stands turn out to apply to both sides. At the Battle of Shiloh, Grant and Sherman were caught unawares by the Confederate Army of Mississippi bearing down on their position at Pittsburg Landing on the western bank of the Tennessee River. In the teeth of tremendous casualties, however, the Union forces held fast until reinforcements arrived, and the day was saved—and the Confederacy lost, in retrospect, its best chance to take both Union generals off the chessboard in a single move—and lost its own best general as well. Custer's last stand at the

Little Bighorn against the forces of Crazy Horse and Sitting Bull in the early summer of 1876 has been the subject of innumerable paintings, posters, books, and movies, with each successive generation choosing to see one of the most remarkable Americans who ever lived through the prism of their own contemporary politics and prejudices. The Indians may have destroyed Custer, but that victory was also their last, and it led directly to the slaughter at Wounded Knee that concluded the Indian Wars of the late nineteenth century.

The events set off by Thermopylae and all the last stands that came after have echoed down the ages, the cultural values expressed therein preserved, literally, in story and song. They include the development and preservation of Greek art, poetry, drama, philosophy, and culture, including the very notion of political self-determination itself. Western civilization was germinated in the bloody ground of Thermopylae, a martial Pallas Athena springing from the bruised brow of Zeus. As the Ground Zero of Western notions of selfless heroism, Thermopylae has come to symbolize both the power and the glory of a last stand, in which the tactical defeat resulted in a larger strategic victory, fueled by the conflicting emotions of courage, bravery, revenge, anger, fear, and pride. And yet the story never grows old.

Similarly, in most of the other battles treated herein, their cultural resonance outweighs even the violence, the dash, and the grit and sand in their souls in their tragic encounters with fate: Roland at Roncevaux (778 A.D.) was immortalized not only in *La Chanson de Roland,* the French national epic written more than two hundred years after the battle itself, but also in Ariosto's hugely influential sixteenth-century Italian-language poem, *Orlando Furioso*; Handel alone wrote three operas based on the Ariosto poem.

The Song of Roland finds a poetic echo in the struggle between a small Hungarian-Croatian defensive force and the Turkish host of Suleiman the Magnificent at the Siege of Szigetvár in 1566: the epic poem *The Siege of Sziget*, written by the great-grandson of the commander, Miklós Zrínyi, whose final sally-forth against hopeless odds is still celebrated in Central Europe to this day—as is its surprising, posthumous conclusion, which stopped the Turkish advance into Europe for more than a century. For Szigetvár turned out to be Suleiman's last stand too.

Every American is familiar with the story of the Alamo and the annihilation of the defenders at the hands of Santa Anna—a battle that led to "Texian" independence and, shortly thereafter, statehood; it also created the legends of Davy Crockett and Jim Bowie, and provided Walt Disney with rich source material for both a motion picture and a television series. Another last stand, that of the roughly 60 members of the French Foreign Legion against three thousand Mexicans fighting to cement their independence from France at Camarón in 1863, is unknown to most Americans. Yet it is acknowledged and celebrated in both France and Mexico as the beginning of the legend of the *Légion étrangère* as well as a crucial step in ridding Mexico of the Emperor Maximilian and expelling the last of the European powers from North America.

No book about last stands would be complete without a look at two epic British battles in Africa: the engagement at Rorke's Drift in Natal in 1879, in which a small detachment of 150 British soldiers held off a three-to-four-thousand-strong force of Zulu warriors in a fight that matched British discipline, tactics, and firepower against the double-envelopment strategy (notably used by Hannibal at Cannae thousands of years earlier) of the Zulu chieftain, Prince Dabulamanzi kaMpande. Eleven Victoria Crosses, Britain's highest military honor, were awarded to the survivors; the British and colonial forces lost only 17 killed and 15 wounded. It has been memorialized on film in *Zulu* (1964), with a young Michael Caine as Lt. Gonville Bromhead.

Six years after Rorke's Drift came Gen. George "Chinese" Gordon's tenacious defense of Khartoum, located at the junction of the White and Blue Niles in the Sudan. Gordon was defeated by Muslims under one Muhammad Ahmad, a charismatic figure who had proclaimed himself the Mahdi, the Expected One, comparable in Muslim eschatology to the Jewish *Moshiach* and the Christian Second Coming of Christ. Gordon—the subject of one of the four profiles comprising the acidic *Eminent Victorians* (1918) by the Bloomsbury Group writer Lytton Strachey—was killed when the "dervishes" overran the city, but the British took their revenge at the Battle of Omdurman in 1898, calming the *jihad* for nearly a century. Gordon's story is told, only partly fictionalized, in the 1966 movie starring Charlton Heston as Gordon and Sir Laurence Olivier, in resplendent blackface, as the Mahdi.

Although there are plenty of last stands in Chinese, Japanese, Indian, African, and South American history, for this volume I have chosen battles that primarily involved Westerners. There are notable last stands in the histories of many other cultures, including the Battle of Saragarhi (1897) between a small force of 21 Sikhs fighting in the service of the British Indian Empire and more than a thousand rebellious Afghan Pashtuns—but those I must leave to other historians. This is not a matter of simple jingoism but a reflection of my own personal interest and experience growing up in a military family that has served the United States practically since its arrival from Ireland in the late nineteenth century.

I have also omitted the Battles of Manzikert (1071) and Hattin (1187), two crucial Western defeats that led to the crippling of the Byzantine Empire and the end of the Crusader Kingdom of Jerusalem, in favor of another pivotal confrontation between Islam and the West: Szigetvár. Both Hattin and Manzikert were military disasters that resulted from headstrong and incompetent leadership on the part of the losing side, while Szigetvár exemplifies themes basic to this book. For my primary intent here is to reflect upon how our Western notions of heroism—duty, honor, country, in the face of overwhelming odds—evolved and why they still matter to the survival of our civilization.

In these pages, I have sought to tell the stories with as much reliance on primary sources as possible, even given their notorious overestimation of the number of troops that fought at the time, and of the ensuing casualties. Modern historians have properly brought these conflicts into accurate focus, but it was Herodotus, Livy, Tacitus, Suetonius, up through the contemporary news reports by the journalists of the nineteenth and twentieth centuries, that created the framework of the stories and have given them their historical resonance.

For ancient history is not simply ancient history, whether cultural or military. The strategies and tactics used by the Greeks and Romans remained in use for thousands of years and are still with us in modified forms today. In his 1941 treatise *How Wars Are Fought*, the British military historian J. E. A. Whitman, a former captain in the Royal Artillery, writes this about the development of tactics:

> It would at first sight seem that the practice of major battles must change almost yearly, and that a text-book published in, say, 1920 must have been hopelessly out of date by 1939. . . . Yet the essence of major tactics has not changed so greatly as some writers would have us believe. The methods of its application have altered—that is all. It may startle some to know that in the general tactical principles now adopted by Britain and Germany, and practiced by them for many generations, those of Britain can be traced back in an almost direct line to the tactics of the Romans, while those of Germany show an equally close genealogical descent from the tactics of Alexander the Great.

The difference between the two ancient patrimonies is largely in the use of cavalry, of which Alexander was a master and which the Romans often treated as a kind of protective afterthought along their flanks. Alexander destroyed the Achaemenid Persian Empire at Gaugamela (also known as the Battle of Arbela) in 331 B.C. with his innovative use of his cavalry, his unorthodox angling of his mobile central phalanx, and his audacious willingness to hang his left flank out to dry under his best general, Parmenion, until he had routed the Persian left flank and driven Darius II from the field. Similarly, the Romans learned the hard way at Cannae in 216 B.C. just how valuable cavalry could be when Hannibal used his horsemen to surround and envelop the legions, resulting in their near-total destruction at the hands of the Carthaginian. On the other hand, the Roman armies, led by the Republic's two consuls, crushed Hannibal's brother, Hasdrubal, at the Battle of the Metaurus just five years later, using their superior numbers (which had been useless at Cannae) to overwhelm the Carthaginian left flank and thus turn the tide, killing Hasdrubal in the process. In the end, it comes down to the genius of the general, the discipline of the troops, the state of their armaments, and their willingness to endure danger and privation until victory is achieved.

In considering the selected battles, I have endeavored not only to relate the kinetic action as clearly as possible—the "fog of war" is both a help and a hindrance to heroism, which often evinces itself in improvisation and innovation born of desperation—but also the larger cultural resonance of why these battles were fought, what the participants on both sides hoped to gain by fighting them, what the outcomes were, and why they were important to the military and cultural history of the West. The proximate *casus belli* in each case was different, but in every instance the wars were fought over territory, religion, economic and political systems, and the desire to impose or defend a way of life the men of the time felt was worth dying for.

So quickly has our society changed—so quickly has the West lost the cultural confidence that marked it for 2,500 years—that the very fact of these confrontations has become "politically incorrect."[23] In crude, reductionist terms, some try to portray the inevitable, generally antithetical, conflicts of civilizations and cultures as a kind of proto-"racism" (an inflammatory word of twentieth-century coinage unknown to the ancients or even, until about the 1970s, to the moderns), and "xenophobia"—never mind that humanity has, from its most primitive origins, been tribal and learned to be wary, if not downright fearful, of strangers and outsiders. Indeed, my own Irish surname, Walsh (*Breathnach* in Irish) derives from the Anglo-Norman word for "foreigner" or "stranger,"[24] which was applied by the invaders to the native inhabitants of the British Isles, such as the Welsh. Strongbow's invasion of Ireland in 1170, barely a century after the Conqueror defeated Harold at Hastings in 1066, was launched from Wales—"the land of foreigners" to the Anglo-Normans but *Cymru* to the Welsh, which means, essentially, "our country." Tribalism is built into our very languages and nomenclatures, and no discussion of Western history is possible without referring to it.

Etymology may not be destiny, but it is history. And while the history of the future is as yet unwritten, and unknowable, the history of the past is, often literally, engraved in stone, carried around in our DNA, and boldly proclaimed by our very names. In a time that prizes "authenticity" and "identity," it is passing strange that this most fundamental aspect of identity is dismissed as "jingoism" while transient sexuality is regarded as fixed and immutable—until fashion or personal whim

23. A concept originating with Trotsky that is itself a hallmark of cultural Marxism.

24. In Wagner's opera *Die Walküre,* the second in *The Ring of the Nibelung* saga, Wotan is called *Wälse,* and his children *the Wälsungs,* reflecting the word's Nordic roots.

dictates otherwise. History may not describe an "arc," but it most certainly does blaze a trail, like that of a comet (Greek: "long-haired"), leaving only the void of the future to be yet filled in.

The Pax Americana that has obtained since Korea has averted subsequent global conflicts, although it has been marked by dozens of smaller wars, including the clashes in Vietnam, Afghanistan, Iraq, and elsewhere in the Middle East.

But a will to win has not characterized any American war effort since Roosevelt's speech to Congress after Pearl Harbor in late 1941:

> As commander in chief of the Army and Navy, I have directed that all measures be taken for our defense. But always will our whole nation remember the character of the onslaught against us. No matter how long it may take us to overcome this premeditated invasion, the American people in their righteous might will win through to absolute victory. I believe that I interpret the will of the Congress and of the people when I assert that we will not only defend ourselves to the uttermost, but will make it very certain that this form of treachery shall never again endanger us. Hostilities exist. There is no blinking at the fact that our people, our territory, and our interests are in grave danger. With confidence in our armed forces, with the unbounding determination of our people, we will gain the inevitable triumph—so help us God.

Since then, micromanaging has largely been the order of the day, with conflicts fought to inconclusive standstills. Lyndon Johnson fiddled with bombing targets while American cities burned; George H. W. Bush invaded Iraq, then abruptly walked away from the lightning victory, leaving a noisome sewer behind that has festered for decades. After the attacks of September 11, 2001, George W. Bush re-intervened in Iraq, despite the fact that Saddam Hussein had little, if anything, to do with the destruction of the World Trade Center. Barack Obama deposed the Libyan strongman Muammar Gaddafi for no strategic reason and created yet another failed Arab state.

Hovering over much of the period was the Cold War, fought in secret in the back alleys of Berlin and by proxies around the world. Still, the sudden collapse of the Soviet Union following the fall of the Berlin Wall in 1989 unleashed long-dormant forces, an event largely unremarked at the time but clearly evident today. The Soviet invasion of Afghanistan in late 1979 and the covert pushback by the United States led directly to the rise of Islamic radicalism, aided by the flood of weapons into the Hindu Kush war zone, and blowing back on the United States in the form of the September 11, 2001, attacks on Washington and New York. The religious wars of the sixteenth century, as violent as they were, thus can be seen as an interlude in the far longer struggle between Islam and the West, which has been ongoing since the seventh century and shows no signs of abating; this particular "arc of history" is remarkably static and unbending.

In sum, the essence of the human condition is the struggle for physical survival. It is, ultimately, a losing struggle. The Greek Byzantines at the Hellespont outlasted Rome by a millennium, but in the end—their territory shrunken and their ability to field an army gone—Constantinople was overrun and the empire disappeared. Once-fearsome Prussia, which dominated European military affairs from the sixteenth century, vanished into the mists of history at the end of World War II. The Zulu Kingdom is no more, although it has been in part replicated in modern southern Africa.

Thus, heroism is not solely about culture, history, ethnicity, and religion. Rather it is, at root, about masculinity. *Pace* the legendary Amazons, and aside from a handful of female-dominated societies in places like Africa, China, and the subcontinent, there has never even been a successful or effective matriarchy, and certainly not one of any geopolitical significance. In the main—there are always exceptions such as Golda Meir and Margaret Thatcher—women (and feminized men) make poor political leaders in times of existential strife; their natural inclination to feminine virtues such as tolerance, as well as their innate sympathy for the stranger or the outsider, leads them to seek to understand their opponents rather than defeat them unconditionally and with all necessary force.

Whether we like it or not, masculinity and its attendant bellicosity is, in fact, the glue that preserves and holds civilizations together. A primal force, it is deadly to both friend and enemy. It is amoral: in a last stand, there is no turning of the other cheek to receive the slap. Instead, one gets the thrust to the heart. As much as it pains the modern West to admit it, war appears to be the natural state of mankind, and peace the aberration, exactly as Kant argued.

"Soft countries," remarked the ancient Persian king Cyrus, "breed soft men." War brings death and misery in its wake—"Hell," in William T. Sherman's famous aphorism—but it also brings great technological advances, as swords are turned into better plowshares, and rockets designed to rain down death upon London become transports to the moon and the stars. It serves as a kind of North Star of valor and courage on the parts of both men and, increasingly, women—who, it seems, will be called upon in greater numbers to fight for civilization in the future. The time when civilians could opt out of global conflicts is long past, and so it remains true that the best way to preserve the peace is to prepare for war—and hope it never comes.

But come again it will. We must know its nature and its history in order to cope with it when it does. And mostly, we must understand the nature of the beast who fights it—and why.

CHAPTER I

"GO TELL THE SPARTANS"

THE BATTLE OF THERMOPYLAE (480 B.C.)

IT IS THE *FONS ET ORIGO* OF THE HISTORY OF WESTERN MILITARY SUPERIORITY, fortitude, self-sacrifice, and heroism, a fight against impossible odds that was won in the losing of it. Had not the three hundred Spartans—and several thousand other Greeks—held the Hot Gates of Thermopylae for a numerologically portentous three days, the West might never have developed as a contentious but politically and spiritually potent counterweight to Eastern despotism, conformity, and submission.

For more than two thousand years, historians ancient and modern have located the origins of Western civilization at this narrow pass, threaded between the mountains and the sea, which an invading Persian army needed to traverse in order to annihilate Eve's most rebellious of progeny and reduce them to mere spokes in the wheels of a million soul-crushing chariots. For three days, a small army of Greeks, led by the Spartans, blocked the way not only into Greece but the nascent West itself: the land that would give birth just a decade later to Socrates, and then to Plato and Aristotle. Even as the crows feasted on the carrion of Greek and Persian bodies, Thermopylae defined once and for all what it meant to be Greek, Western, human.

What a contrast they offered, these two armies. In the clash between the massed might of the Achaemenid Persian Empire and the quarrelsome, contentious Greeks of the young city-states, we have the most dramatic expression of the differences between Oriental collectivism and Occidental orneriness. An army of conscripts versus a small force of free men. Between men who were poked and prodded and speared by the slave-drivers of the Aryan king lest they think of turning back from the fight, and men for whom it was second nature to take their part in the phalanx and move to the front. Just ten years earlier, the Athenians and the Plataeans had doubly enveloped the Persian army under Darius and crushed it at Marathon. Owing to the sacred festival of Carneia, the Spartans had not participated in that battle; now, ten years later, it was their turn to win the glory.

On the morning of the battle, the Persians sent a scout toward the Greek encampment at the narrow pass of Thermopylae to ascertain its state of readiness for the attack that was on its way. Writing around 440 B.C., Herodotus—the Father of History—tells us:

> The Persian rider approached the camp and took a thorough survey of all he could see—which was not, however, the whole Greek army; for the men on the further side of the wall which, after its reconstruction, was now guarded, were out of sight. He did, none the less, carefully observe the troops who were stationed on the outside of the wall. At that moment these happened to be Spartans, and some of them were stripped for exercise, while others were combing their hair. The Persian spy watched them in astonishment, nevertheless he made sure of their numbers, and of everything else he needed to know, as accurately he could, and then rode quietly off. No one attempted to catch him, or took the least notice of him.
>
> —*The Histories*, translation by Aubrey de Selincourt

In a dazzling display of logistical expertise, Xerxes, the commander of a mighty army that had crossed the Hellespont (the Dardanelles, south of present-day Gallipoli) and moved north and west through Thessaly before heading south to launch his conquest of Greece—and thereby succeed in 480 B.C. where his father, Darius, had failed ten years earlier at the Battle of Marathon—could not believe the report: how could men facing certain death at the hands of his Mede archers and his ten thousand Immortals, just a fraction of his total strength of half a million or so men,[1] be so calm and relaxed?

A Greek defector—Demaratus, a former king of Sparta—had the answer:

> Once before, when we began our march against Greece, you heard me speak of these men. I told you then how I saw this enterprise would turn out, and you laughed at me. I strive for nothing, my lord, more earnestly than to observe the truth in your presence, so hear me once more. These men have come to fight us for possession of the pass, and for that struggle they are preparing. It is the custom of the Spartans to pay careful attention to their hair when they are about to risk their lives. But I assure you that if you can defeat these men and the rest of the Spartans who are still at home, there is no other people in the world who will dare to stand firm or lift a hand against you. You have now to deal with the finest kingdom in Greece, and with the bravest men.[2]

And so the Spartans[3] at Thermopylae calmly went about their ablutions in the teeth of the Persian horde, flexing their limbs and combing out their long hair. The three hundred Spartans, who spearheaded a total force of some seven thousand Greek soldiers, may have thought they were defending a fragmented and contentious Greek people, with whom they were—and would be again—often at odds on the battlefield. In reality, they were defending the young civilization of the West from

---

1. Estimates vary widely, from 120,000 to 2.6 million. At one point in *The Histories*, Herodotus confidently puts the number of Persians at Thermopylae at an utterly fantastic 5,283,220 men, not counting eunuchs, female cooks, and concubines.

2. Aside from military training, Spartan girls were educated in much the same way as the boys, including competing naked in athletic competitions—something that surprised and appalled other Greeks—and learning songs and poetry.

3. Upon first encountering Spartan envoys at Sardis in the sixth century B.C., the first great king of Persia, Cyrus, was said to have asked some other Greeks present, "Who are the Spartans?"

what we once called "oriental despotism,"[4] a term for the top-down tyranny of the East in contradistinction to the early Greek self-governing city-states. They were citizens, husbands, sons, and fathers united in a common purpose against a polyglot, largely mercenary or slave force being driven by a hereditary megalomaniac with no worlds left to conquer in the East, but great ambitions in the West.

Though their ideas of what constituted freedom 2,500 years ago may not be precisely ours, the foe they battled is recognizably the same today. Like his spiritual and even ethnic progeny, Xerxes demanded submission, obeisance, and the surrender of the Greeks' weapons. Their answer, like their sacrifice, has echoed down the ages: Μολων λαβε!—"Come and take them!"

As Wellington said of Waterloo,[5] it was "the nearest-run thing you ever saw in your life." So also was Thermopylae and its aftermath. Had Xerxes succeeded in his conquest of Greece, how different the history of the European West would have been and, given the history of Persia since, how much poorer the world would be.

Unlike Waterloo, which was inevitable the moment Napoleon returned from Elba, Thermopylae was something of a miracle. The proximate outcome, the annihilation of the Spartans and the temporary Persian occupation of much of Greece, including an evacuated Athens (which was burned), matters little. The Persians were defeated later that same year at sea at Salamis and beaten on land by a coalition of Greek city-states at Plataea in 479, ending the Achaemenid Persian threat.

A century and a half later, the Hellenistic armies of Alexander the Great swept east across Mesopotamia and routed the Persian forces of Darius III, demonstrating the superiority of Western arms and, more important, tactics against the god-kings and nomads of the East—a

---

4. "For example, the encounters between the Greeks and Persians, which followed Marathon, seem to me not to have been phenomena of primary impulse. Greek superiority had been already asserted, Asiatic ambition had already been checked, before Salamis and Plataea confirmed the superiority of European free states over Oriental despotism." Creasy, *Fifteen Decisive Battles.*

5. And, as we shall see, was also true of the Battle of Hastings.

superiority that would last with some notable exceptions[6] for nearly eight hundred years, until the arrival of the Huns in Europe in 441.[7] After extracting tribute from the Eastern Empire, the Huns under Attila sets their sights on Roman Gaul, but were finally stopped in the Western Empire's last gasp at the Battle of Châlons in 451.

But that was all far in the future when the Greek city-states first got word of the impending Persian invasion in the fifth century B.C. Many of the Greeks at that time were of the opinion that to submit to the Persians would not be such a bad thing, and many of them did. But they were lesser players: the real power lay with the Spartans on land and the Athenians at sea. Athens held the balance of power in the debate. As Herodotus notes,

> If the Athenians, through fear of the approaching danger, had abandoned their country, or if they had stayed there and submitted to Xerxes, there would have been no attempt to resist the Persians by sea; and in the absence of a Greek fleet, it is easy to see what would have been the course of events on land. . . . Thus the Spartans would have been left alone—to perform great deeds and to die nobly. Or, on the other hand, it is possible that before things came to the ultimate test, the sight of the rest of Greece submitting to Persia might have driven them to make terms with Xerxes. In either case, the Persian conquest of Greece would have been assured . . .

Ah, but Pythia,[8] the female voice of the Oracle, speaking for Apollo, seemed at first to counsel against resistance. When the Athenians went to Delphi, the prediction they heard was dire: "Why sit you, doomed ones? Fly to the world's end!" she advised. One of the

---

6. Principally, the Roman-Persian wars fought against the Parthians and the Sassanids between 54 B.C. and 628 A.D. Shortly before his assassination in 44 B.C., Caesar had announced a new campaign against the Parthians.

7. Alexander's teacher, Aristotle, advised him to be a leader to the Greeks but a master to the barbarians.

8. For twelve centuries a series of "Pythias" spoke on behalf of the god.

Athenians decided to ask for a second opinion from the prophetess, this time sweetening their request with olive branches in hand. The results were somewhat more reassuring: "Divine Salamis, you will bring death to women's sons, when the corn is scattered, or the harvest gathered in." Even so, there was a dispute about her meaning until Themistocles (the architect of the Athenian fleet, who would become their commander at Salamis) confidently explained that it foretold victory.

As some of the fractious Greek city-states began to see the wisdom in cooperation rather than abject capitulation, three spies were sent into Asia to gather information on the Persian army, even then preparing for the invasion. They succeeded, but before they could make their escape they were caught and tortured by the Persians. They were about to be executed when Xerxes countermanded the death sentences and brought the men into his presence. Rather than killing them, the overconfident Xerxes instructed his guards to take them to observe his army and navy, to marvel at how mighty they were, and then to return home to tell the Greeks what they had seen.

By seeking to intimidate the Greeks in this way, Xerxes hoped to avoid the necessity of bloodshed. Similarly, he was not above appeals to brotherhood, as when (or so the story goes) he reminded the Argive Greeks of their possible kinship:

> Xerxes sent a man to Argos before his army started on its march. "Men of Argos," this person is supposed to have said upon his arrival, "King Xerxes has a message for you. We Persians believe that we are descended from Perses, whose father was Danae's son Perseus, and whose mother was Andromeda the daughter of Cepheus. Thus we are of the same blood as yourselves, and it would not be right for us to make war upon the people from whom we have sprung, any more than it would be right for you to help others by opposing us. Rather you should hold aloof from the coming struggle and take no part in it. If things turn out as I hope they will, there is no people I shall hold in greater esteem than you."

Other accounts hold that the Argives bristled at the Spartans' demand for complete control of the land operations. In any case, the Argives sat this one out.[9]

Things got worse for the Greeks. An embassy was sent to Gelon, the ruler at Syracuse of the most powerful Greek colony, Sicily, who refused to offer help. The Greeks on the island of Corcyra (Corfu) at first agreed to contribute to the fleet, then welshed, on their belief that the Greeks stood no chance against the Persians and that therefore they would receive more merciful treatment from Xerxes if they were innocent of aiding Athens and Sparta. The Cretans bailed. The Thessalians petitioned other Greeks for help, but once the Persians arrived, they switched sides.

In the end, the Greek defenders decided on a two-pronged plan: to hold the narrow pass, sandwiched between a mountain and the sea, at Thermopylae, while blockading the narrow straits toward Thermopylae at Artemisium[10]—a twin-bottleneck strategy that the Greeks hoped would negate the Persians' superior numbers, hamper their ability to maneuver at close quarters, and give the Hellenes a fighting chance, even as they made plans to fall back to the more easily defended Peloponnese, where Sparta was located, a southern peninsula connected to the Greek mainland by the Isthmus of Corinth.

And so, in August or September of 480 B.C., they lined up, the Persians pressing down from the north, the Greeks manning the pass of Thermopylae, where they had rebuilt a low wall (at the narrow part of the pass, the "middle gate," originally constructed by the Phocians against Thessaly) that had fallen into disrepair. As a defensive wall,

---

9. Herodotus admits he does not know the truth behind the Argives' decision, then goes on to say, "If all mankind agreed to meet, and everyone brought his own sufferings along with him for the purpose of exchanging them for somebody else's, there is not a man who, after taking a good look at his neighbor's suffering, would not be only too happy to return home with his own. . . . My business is to record what people say, but I am by no means bound to believe it—and that may be taken to apply to this book as a whole."

10. After the defeat at the Hot Gates, and an inconclusive naval battle with the Persians that inflicted heavy casualties on both sides, the Greek fleet abandoned Artemisium and regrouped at Salamis.

it wasn't much, but it did provide a certain amount of concealment, and gave the Greeks something to defend, as well as a fallback position should they be pushed back by the physical pressure of the attackers.[11]

Although each of the Greek contingents had its own leader, the acknowledged commander overall was Leonidas, one of the kings of Sparta (there were generally two[12]) and a descendent of Hercules—symbolically as well as militarily appropriate, since the Hot Gates featured an altar to the mythical hero. According to legend, Hercules had jumped into a nearby river in order to wash off the Hydra's poison as he completed the second of his ten labors, thus turning the waters forever hot. The Spartan force was small—the Spartans were once again celebrating their festival of Carneia, dedicated to the god Apollo—and intended largely to bolster the courage of the other Greeks until, the holiday over, the main Spartan army could take the field. To complicate matters, the Olympics were also underway, which accounted for the paucity of the forces supplied by other Greek states.

As it had happened, the Delphic oracle had had some words for the Spartans as well:

Hear your fate, O dwellers in Sparta of the wide spaces;
Either your famed, great town must be sacked by Perseus' sons,
Or, if that be not, the whole land of Lacedaemon
Shall mourn the death of a king of the house of Heracles,
For not the strength of lions or of bulls shall hold him,
Strength against strength; for he has the power of Zeus,
And will not be checked until one of these two he has consumed.[13]

---

11. Similar in function to the "mealie bag" wall the defenders at Rorke's Drift improvised in their battle with the Zulus in 1879, as we shall see.

12. As there were Roman consuls, following the expulsion of the Tarquins in 509 B.C. Even after the advent of the emperors, two consuls, elected annually, continued to be the norm.

13. A shorter version reads: "The strength of bulls or lions cannot stop the foe. No, he will not leave off, I say, until he tears the city or the king limb from limb." The meaning is the same: either Sparta must be destroyed, or its king must die.

Upon seeing the size of the Persian host, the Greeks debated abandoning Thermopylae, falling back, and calling for reinforcements. But, according to Herodotus, Leonidas cast the deciding vote to stay and fight it out. He was not a young man, past 50 and possibly approaching 60, and he must have known the chances of him and his men surviving the encounter were slim; with that in mind, he had personally selected the men of the three hundred as those with sons at home, so that if they were killed, their bloodlines would continue. It is said that, upon leaving Sparta, he advised his wife, Gorgo, that in the event of his death, she should "marry a good man, and have children."[14]

The Greeks were armed, as they always were, with long spears (for thrusting at close quarters, not for throwing), short swords, and shields. They had no archers, since they believed that killing an enemy from a distance was cowardly and that a proper warrior battled face-to-face. Organized into their customary phalanx—a bristling hedgehog, 64 men across and 18 men deep—they were ready for both offensive and defensive maneuvers. The phalanx, which was later enhanced by Alexander with the addition of cavalry in order to protect its vulnerable flanks and rear, could either press forward, like a giant threshing machine, or turtle down, shields in place, as it was bombarded by enemy missiles, until the frontal attack came. The initial clash of forces resembled nothing so much as a rugby scrum, albeit an especially lethal one.

Battles—sometimes whole wars—in classical antiquity were generally one-day affairs. A great deal of planning and maneuvering went into choosing the perfect spot (generally an open plain) at the right season (summer or early fall) and the right weather conditions (dry, but not too hot). More akin to a siege than a pitched set piece, Thermopylae lasted a full three. It even started late: Xerxes paused four days in position at the northern end of the pass, waiting for the small Greek force to give way in the face of the manifestly overwhelming odds. Finally, the Persian potentate gave the signal for the attack to begin, which it did, with a shower of arrows from his Medean archers and then an assault.

---

14. Which indicates she was still of child-bearing age. From antiquity, older, successful men often selected younger women to be the mothers of their children, a kind of Darwinian imperative.

The Greeks resisted charge after charge, staying in tight formation, their oak-and-bronze shields protecting them first from the arrows and later from the swords of the attackers. Generally superior in training, weaponry, armor, and motivation to the Persian army, even the non-Spartan Greeks were more than a match for the Medes and the Cissians (from what is today western Iran, along the Persian Gulf), hewing them down almost at will. Herodotus drily notes that Xerxes had in his army "many men, but few soldiers." Even when the Persian elite troops, the Immortals, entered the fray, they too were repelled, for at close quarters and robbed of their superior numbers across such a narrow front, they could not compete with the Greeks either.

What preserved the Greeks on the first two days of Thermopylae was not only their tactics, bravery, and fighting spirit but the security of their position. It was inevitable that they would eventually be worn down by constant fighting, but as long as the Persians could neither outflank them nor get to their rear, they could hold out for a long time, at least until reinforcements could arrive from the south. To keep their men fresh, the Greeks rotated their separate commands, each taking a turn on the front line: all except the Phocians, whose region included Delphi, who were assigned to guard the rear—and, crucially, the path up and over the mountains to the west that could debouch an enemy behind the Greek lines.

The legend is that the Greeks were unaware of this path, and it was thanks to the treachery of the traitor Ephialtes of Trachis[15] that the Persians learned of it and, on the night between the second and third day of battle, sent troops along it in order to take the Greeks by surprise. The truth is that Leonidas and the Greeks did know about it, which is why there was a Phocian garrison stationed along its course to prevent just such an attack. Ironically, the path had been forged by the local Malians, who discovered

15. Herodotus also notes that two other men, Onetes and Corydallus, have also been suspected of providing the information to Xerxes, but the historian rejects the charge and pins the blame on Ephialtes: "It was Ephialtes, and no one else, who showed the Persians the way, and I put his name on record as the guilty one." The Spartans later put a bounty on the traitor's head, and in due course he was killed in Thessaly c. 470 B.C. by one Athenades, although apparently for an unrelated reason; the bounty, however, was paid.

it after the Phocians had walled off the pass—the same wall the Greeks had had to rebuild as they prepared their defenses against the Persians.

In retrospect, it was a fatal miscalculation by Leonidas and the Greeks, but what choice did they have? To have devoted more troops protecting against a rear-guard attack that might never come would have made no sense. The Spartans and the other Greeks were tough, but they were still mortal; they were falling in battle as well, at perhaps a tenth of the rate of the Persians, but falling nonetheless.

A Persian force under Hydarnes moved at dusk, following Ephialtes along the narrow path through the night and arriving at the summit around dawn. They were as surprised to see the Phocians as the Phocians were to see them, and a brief battle ensued; at first Hydarnes thought these men might be Spartans, but Ephialtes assured him they were not. The skirmish ended with a Phocian retreat back up the mountain, preparing a defensive position. But Hydarnes contemptuously ignored them and instead headed down the hill and toward the principal enemy, the Spartans under Leonidas.

It soon enough became clear to Leonidas that their position was hopeless. For the Spartans, of course, retreat was not an option, but Leonidas did not hold the other Greeks to Spartan standards and offered them a chance to retreat while there was still time. Accordingly, the bulk of the surviving Greek forces departed for home, and to raise the alarm among the other city-states about the approaching Persian horde. Staying with the three hundred Spartans were the Thespians and Thebans—although how willingly the Thebans remained is a matter of some dispute. Even though Leonidas understood the battle was lost, and that he and the Spartans would go to their death in a headlong charge beyond the Phocian wall and well into the contested pass, he still needed a small rear guard interposed between Hydarnes and the retreating Greeks, who would otherwise be overtaken and slaughtered before they could put enough distance between themselves and the Persians.

At breakfast on the third day, Leonidas is supposed to have said (most likely apocryphally, although Plutarch[16] paraphrases it), "Eat well, for tonight

16. In the *Apophthegmata Laconica.*

we dine in Hades"—an apt Spartanism, especially since the entrance to Hades was said to be right there at the Hot Gates. With the outcome decided, all that was left was the glory. Writes Herodotus: "The Greeks, who knew that the enemy were on their way round the mountain track and that death was inevitable, put forth all their strength and fought with fury and desperation. By this time most of their spears were broken, and they were killing Persians with their swords." As Seneca famously observed, "He who falls obstinate in his courage, if he has fallen, he fights on his knees."

As the Persians closed in, the Thebans surrendered on their feet, but the rest of the Greeks gathered round Leonidas on a small hillock, where they died to the last man, finally perforated by the Medean arrows that announced the beginning of the battle 72 hours before. (Two of Xerxes's brothers died on the field as well.) The enraged Persian king demanded Leonidas's body be brought to him, but the Greeks held the Persians off four times, defending their dead king until they too died.[17] Leonidas's head was severed, and exhibited.

Years later, the Greeks erected a monument to the men who died at Thermopylae, and to the Spartans in particular, with inscriptions by the poet Simonides of Ceos. The first reads:

Four thousand here from Pelops's land
Against three million once did stand.

While the words (in the translation by de Selincourt) honoring the Spartans proclaim:

Go tell the Spartans, you who read;
We took their orders, and here lie dead.

Of a foundational epic, you can't ask for much more. At the dawn of Western history, it has it all: individualism versus the supranational state; men fighting for hearth and home and family against slaves

17. Echoing the struggle for the body of Patroclus in *The Iliad*. As we shall see, the Saxon Huscarls performed a similar service for their king, Harold, at Hastings.

prodded by spears to enhance the transient glory of an earthly king. The Greeks, whether they thought about it or not, also were preserving and enhancing their advances in philosophy, drama, poetry, and the theater, in addition to their military and militaristic contributions to Western civilization. By contrast, the Achaemenid Persians left nothing of lasting value beyond some technological achievements and bureaucratic procedures involving the administration of such a large, if fragile, empire. What artistic contributions they might have made would be swept away by the Arab conquest and the imposition of Islam on the formerly Zoroastrian nation in the middle seventh century.

Which, even as early as 480 B.C., brings us to one of the salient differences between East and West, and which forms the central question of this book: What is worth fighting and dying for? The prodded mercenaries, given the choice of death at the point of a spear or death by the lash, fought for basic survival, but as the clashes between West and East showed throughout the ancient world, the calcified East was no match for a rising and vigorous West. Alexander and his Hellenistic army launched history's first *blitzkrieg* across Egypt and central Asia with nary a reversal, deposing dynasties as he went. It wasn't until the rise of the Islamic Crescent that the "oriental" world found a motivation—conquest in the name of a higher cause other than king or emperor—that would sweep its armies to victory from Egypt to Indonesia in half a millennium. To stop Islam and roll it back, it took a vigorous Christianized West, inheriting the mantle of both halves of the Roman Empire, and fighting also in the name of its faith.

The long odds the Greeks faced at Thermopylae are something of a leitmotif running down the ages. No matter how the story ends, there is something inherently romantic about the hopelessness of the conflict. And more: that the losing side so often went on to win the larger war illustrates the Greek philosopher Aristotle's prescription in the *Poetics* that reversals of fortune are the very stuff of drama. Greek dramatists took current events and spun them into theatrical gold. Aeschylus—a veteran of the stunning Greek victory over Darius at

Marathon in 490 B.C.—based his play *The Persians* (472 B.C.) on the Battle of Salamis.[18]

And yet, perhaps strangely, the battle's afterlife has existed largely via history and not popular culture. We have no extant, contemporaneous play about Thermopylae, although Byron, Houseman, Eliot, Plath, Dickinson all alluded to it in verse. With the exception of *The 300 Spartans* (1962) and, more recently, director Zack Snyder's *300*, the 2006 live-action adaptation of Frank Miller's graphic novel, the events at the Hot Gates have been more often referred to than illustrated or dramatized. The 1978 Vietnam War film *Go Tell the Spartans* employed the resonance of Simonides's epitaph to hint at the futility of the American war effort in Indochina, but otherwise had nothing to do with the story.

Perhaps it's because Thermopylae needs no gloss to keep echoing down the ages. Western history began at the Hot Gates, and for centuries those gates have guarded the front lines of what Samuel Huntington has memorably called "the clash of civilizations," in this case the border between Orthodox Christian Greece and Muslim Turkey; the line between the now-defunct empires of the eastern Romans and the Ottomans. Which way is Heaven, and which way Hell?

Ask any young male about the appeal of Thermopylae and you will get an answer that would not have surprised any Western boy: the chance to fight and perhaps die in battle for a cause at once larger than yourself is irresistible. For, in the end, and at the end, what were the Greeks really fighting for? Just five decades after the Persian Wars ended, Athens and Sparta went at each other in the vicious Peloponnesian War, from which neither side benefitted. Periclean Athens, the apogee of ancient Greek civilization, attacked the prosperous Corinthian Greek island of Sicily in 415 B.C., with disastrous results from which it never recovered.

---

18. *The Persians* was the second part of a trilogy whose bookends are lost to us, except by name. The first play was called *Phineus*; the second, *Promethus Pyrkaeus*, or Prometheus, the Fire-Kindler.

In 1851, the British military historian Sir Edward Creasy listed the fight for Syracuse as one of the fifteen decisive battles of the world, a calamity that ended Greek aspirations to cultural dominance of the Mediterranean and opened the way for Rome to turn the Middle Sea into a Roman lake. The plucky little city-state of Athens that had saved the West at Salamis had become a bully, an oppressor, and a regional hegemon with a thirst for expansion:

> At Marathon . . . we beheld Athens struggling for self-preservation against the invading armies of the East. At Syracuse she appears as the ambitious and oppressive invader of others. In her, as in other republics of old and of modern times, the same energy that had inspired the most heroic efforts in defence of the national independence, soon learned to employ itself in daring and unscrupulous schemes of self-aggrandizement at the expense of neighbouring nations. In the interval between the Persian and Peloponnesian wars she had rapidly grown into a conquering and dominant state, the chief of a thousand tributary cities, and the mistress of the largest and best-manned navy that the Mediterranean had yet beheld. . . . But this titular ascendancy was soon converted by her into practical and arbitrary dominion . . . [19]

Athenian power was smashed—by hubris?—at Syracuse, and with it went Athens' ambition for political and military domination of the Mediterranean. Sparta's resolute resistance to Athenian expansionism emboldened the other Greek city-states across the Med, and while Sparta—having intimidated even Alexander, thus preserving its independence—faded from history after the Roman conquest in 146 B.C., it was the Spartan martial spirit, far more than the philosophy and poetry of Athens, that influenced the legions of the budding Roman Republic. The Roman civil war, after all, was fought largely in Greece,

19. Creasy, *Fifteen Decisive Battles.*

and the defeat at Actium by the future Augustus of the forces of the Ptolemaic Greek Cleopatra, ruler of Egypt, and her lover Mark Antony, ensured that Roman, not Greco-Macedonian, power would henceforth dominate the Western world.

And yet, the bones of Thermopylae never rested. They went with Alexander to India and Babylon, they ruled where the Pharaohs once sat in Egypt; they founded Alexandria, the greatest seat of classical and early Christian learning until the Muslim conquest of 641 A.D., which also saw, according to Koranic law, the destruction of the great Library the following year. "If those books are in agreement with the Quran, we have no need of them; and if these are opposed to the Quran, destroy them," said the conquering caliph, Omar, one of Muhammed's companions. Greek was also the language of Roman scholars and aristocrats, the language of poetry and science. Greek was even, to a certain extent, the language of the Roman court: the second-century emperor Marcus Aurelius wrote his famous *Meditations* in Greek.

The Greeks also went to Italy itself, where they populated the boot and the island of Sicily with Greek cities, among them Naples, Syracuse, Agrigento, and Taranto: the Romans called the area Magna Graecia.[20] They spread across the Mediterranean, populating much of Asia Minor to the east, parts of the North African coast to the south, and what today we call the French and Spanish Rivieras. The Greeks also were among the first to be Christianized by St. Paul and the other early apostles, and indeed the New Testament of the Christian Bible was originally written in demotic Greek.[21]

---

20. In *A Study of History,* Toynbee attributes some cultural progression to geographic causes: "If it is true, as our evidence suggests, that new ground provides a greater stimulus to activity than old ground, one would expect to find such stimulus specially marked in cases where the new ground is separated from the old by a sea voyage. . . . It appears, for instance, in the degree to which the two greatest of these colonial foundations, Syriac Carthage and Hellenic Syracuse, outstripped their parent cities, Tyre and Corinth. The Achaean colonies in Magna Graecia . . . became busy seats of commerce and brilliant centres of thought, while the parent Achaean communities along the northern coast of the Peloponnese remained in a backwater until after Hellenic Civilization had passed its zenith."

21. *Es ist eine Feinheit, daß Gott griechisch lernte, als er Schriftsteller werden*

After the Fall of Rome in 476, Byzantine Greek–speaking Romans became emperors at Constantinople. Eventually the Greek influence and ethnicity overwhelmed the Eastern Empire's Romanness: once Charlemagne proclaimed himself the successor to the Western emperors, Byzantium was no longer considered the continuation of the Empire but rather an empire of Greeks. The religious schism of 1054, which broke Christendom into Latin and Eastern Orthodox rites, finished the transformation. A millennium later, the split still has not been fully reconciled. "The Greeks," notes Ernle Bradford in his 1955 study of the battle, *Thermopylae: The Battle for the West*, "[are] the only people in history who have made four major contributions to human culture and civilisation (the spring of Minoan Crete, the summer of fifth-century Athens, the golden autumn of the Alexandrian empire, and the wintry splendour of Byzantium)."

The Greeks had another influence, perhaps less expected and more surprising, and that was upon Russia. In emulation of the Greeks, the Christianized Slavs adopted the Cyrillic alphabet and many Greek names as well, such as Alexander and Olga. Moscow became "the Third Rome"—the inheritor of a Christian religious and cultural tradition that began with the Eternal City, was transferred to Constantinople, and, after the Muslim conquest, removed itself to Moscow. As we shall see later, this in part accounts for the ferocity with which the Russians resisted Napoleon and Hitler during their respective invasions: indeed, after Operation Barbarossa in 1941, Stalin abandoned any pretense that the *Rodina* (motherland) was fighting to defend atheistic Marxism-Leninism, but rather made the Great Patriotic War into a defense of hearth, home, and Orthodox culture against the German barbarians. With the defeat of Army Group South at Stalingrad[22] in 1943, it worked.

Thermopylae, then, is not simply the first great last stand of which Western history has taken notice but also the model for many that

---

wollte—und daß er es nicht besser lernte, wrote Nietzsche in the Apophthegm 121 of *Beyond Good and Evil*: "It's a particular refinement that God learned Greek when he wanted to become a writer—and that he didn't learn it better."

22. See Chapter XII.

followed. A noble cause—the protection of the Greek homelands, and therefore of the West—but a militarily hopeless situation. A barely defensible position exploited for every conceivable advantage. Most important, the will to fight on, to the end, when at least for a time retreat was possible but thought shameful. Scholars have noted that, unlike the Athenians, the Spartans left behind nothing of archaeological significance, instead choosing to bequeath as their legacy the awe and fear they inspired in their enemies, as well as their utter devotion to discipline, and the way they died in their finest hour.

Bradford writes, "The invasion of Greece made the turbulent, brilliant people of this mountainous and largely inhospitable land aware that they shared one thing in common: a belief in the individual human being's right to dissent, to think his own way, and not to acknowledge any man as a 'monarch of all I survey.' Curiously enough, the state of Sparta, which was to play a large part in the campaign, was the only one where men had evolved a constitution in which the individual was trained and disciplined to be totally subordinate. The difference was that the Spartans were indeed subject, although not to a 'Great King,' but to the concept of the State itself."[23]

To put their epitaph into the words in which it is best known in English:

Go, tell the Spartans, stranger passing by
That here, obedient to their laws, we lie.

The Spartans may be gone, but their example will live on until the West crumbles into dust—or, as seems more likely, loses its belief in itself and the rightness of its cause. To paraphrase Xerxes at Salamis, with the men of the West having turned into women, will the women of the West turn into men?

---

23. Any resemblance to the current geopolitical struggle between the forces of personal liberty and those of state power should come as no surprise.

CHAPTER II

"VARUS, GIVE ME BACK MY LEGIONS"

CANNAE (216 B.C.) AND THE TEUTOBURG FOREST (9 A.D.)

SPARTAN, AND INDEED GREEK, MILITARY SUPREMACY DID NOT LAST long. Across the Ionian Sea, another superpower soon arose, one that had, according to its foundational myth, sprung from the ruins of Greece's mortal enemy, Troy. Whether merely poetic or historical, the triumph of the defeated Trojans was born in the ashes of Ilium, whose "topless towers" had fallen to the subterfuge of wily Odysseus and the wooden horse whose pregnant belly had disgorged the Achean troops who rampaged through the city, avenging the wronged honor of the Peloponnesians of Mycenae.

Plus ça change: the Macedonian military genius, Alexander, had transformed the Spartan infantry into an irresistible threshing machine that had chewed its way across Asia Minor and all the way to Afghanistan and India. But Alexander's vast empire had essentially died with him in Babylon in 323 B.C., to be split among his generals—one (Ptolemy) in Egypt and, eventually, the Byzantines at Constantinople: the expansionist, syncretic Romans quickly enough learned military tactics from their former antagonists, transforming the phalanxes of their enemies into the more flexible and lethal legions who were able to confront the Macedonians at Cynoscephalae in 197 B.C. and defeat them on their home turf, exposing the weakness of the phalanxes on rough terrain by flanking and then enveloping them from the rear.

Still, the Greeks' lasting influence came at Rome, their bastard offspring and greatest successor. Without the Greeks, there is no Rome—no philosophy, no learning, no drama, no architecture, no sculpture, no literature. Countries—civilizations—are not simply the sum total of their military conquests or their judicial systems (countries can exist without lawyers; lawyers cannot exist without countries), but are, at root, the essence of their people. Rome could not have existed without Greece, from whom it took wholesale its legends and its gods. Without Rome, there is no West. And without the military traditions of both cultures there is only barbarism. Force of arms, and the willingness to use them, is the sword and shield of Western civilization. *Arma virumque cano*[1]—"I sing of arms and the man"—are the most potent words in the history of pre-Christian Western civilization, rooting our society squarely in the history of untrammeled masculine bellicosity.

And yet not even the Romans, who forged a civilization out of ruthless willpower in the face of opponents of far greater physical size but less discipline and determination, almost always won. Except when they didn't. And even then, they did—for reasons that might at first blush seem nonmilitary but were profoundly sexual and cultural.

From the beginning of Rome, from the time of the "rape" ("abduction" is a better word) of the Sabines in the eighth century B.C., in which the Romans exchanged sexual access to the Sabine women for peace with their menfolk, and thus incorporation into the new city, Rome relied on the patriotic fertility of its women to supply the warriors of the future. When the vengeful Sabine men later returned to try and conquer Rome, it was the abducted women—now mothers and wives of Rome—who made the peace. And thus the Sabines became Romans.

This fecundity enabled the Romans to resupply the ranks of their military almost at will; martial sexual potency played as important a role in the creation of "armed men" as did the boudoirs of peacetime. And, at pivotal moments in the history of the Republic, it proved to be decisive—even (or perhaps especially) when the Romans suffered a crushing defeat.

---

1. The opening lines of Virgil's *Aeneid*.

The Battle of Cannae, fought on a hot August day in 216 B.C. on an Apulian plain near the Adriatic coast southeast of Rome, was one of the greatest disasters in military history. Never had Republican Rome fielded an army of such size, nor would it; neither would Imperial Rome. Never again would it suffer such an epic disaster. In all, more than 55,000 (some estimates run as high as 70,000) legionaries went to their deaths in a battle against Hannibal Barca and his invading but numerically inferior army of Carthaginians, Numidians, and Celtiberian and Gallic mercenaries; by the time the slaughter had ended, the cream of Roman society, including consuls, senators, equestrians, and commanders, lay dead, and Rome herself lay open to invasion and conquest.

The engagement was the centerpiece of the Second Punic War, a struggle for supremacy in the Mediterranean basin between the Romans and the Carthaginians, descendants of the seafaring Phoenicians who had moved beyond the eastern Mediterranean to establish colonies in Sicily, North Africa, Spain, and elsewhere. Talk about a clash of civilizations: between Rome and Carthage, there could be only one winner. The Romans, whose armies were largely Roman, worshipped their multiple gods, who derived largely from the Greeks; the Semitic Phoenicians principally worshipped the fertility god, Baal, practiced child sacrifice, and generally preferred that mercenaries under Carthaginian command fight their wars.

Cannae wasn't just a rout, for a rout might imply that many of the Romans fled and escaped. Rather, it was a slaughter, an abattoir, as the legions, pressing forward as was their wont, were sucked into a trap, attacked on both flanks, and finally surrounded and killed to nearly the last man. Think of Cannae—warfare's textbook example of a double envelopment—as the panic of a very large crowd that suddenly finds itself hemmed in on all sides and, in its frenzy to escape, begins trampling itself. At the end, the exhausted Romans, penned in and unable to fight or even move, simply consigned their spirits to the gods and went under African swords—or their own. If ever there was a time when the fall of the axe was welcome, Cannae was surely it.

How could this have happened? How could the best-outfitted and best-trained army of the ancient world have come to such a pass? And how and why did Rome recover and not only go on to win the Second Punic War but also to utterly destroy Carthage in the Third?

> It may be asked how seventy thousand men could have let themselves be slaughtered, without defense, by thirty-six thousand men less well-armed, when each combatant had but one man before him. For in close combat, and especially in so large an envelopment, the number of combatants immediately engaged was the same on each side. Then there were neither guns nor rifles able to pierce the mass by a converging fire and destroy it by the superiority of this fire over diverging fire. Arrows were exhausted in the first period of the action. It seems that, by their mass, the Romans must have presented an insurmountable resistance and that while permitting the enemy to wear himself out against it, that mass had only to defend itself in order to repeal assailants.
>
> But it was wiped out.
>
> —Col. Ardant du Picq, *Battle Studies* (1880/1902)

The simplest explanation of what happened on that awful day was that the tactical (but not, as we shall see, strategic) genius, Hannibal, raising hell throughout central Italy after twin victories over the Romans at Trebia in 218 and Lake Trasimene in 217, lured the impatient Romans into the jaws of a trap they all too willingly rushed into. The people of Rome were embarrassed by the Carthaginian's rampage through Italy and impatient with the long-term strategy of Fabius Maximus, a consul who had been dictator (a temporary, exigent position) precisely in order to deal with Hannibal. But Maximus sought to avoid direct combat with the Barcid, instead relying on time and attrition to bleed the invaders, far from home and living off the land. So a vast army was raised and given over to the two new consuls, Lucius Aemilius Paullus and Gaius Terentius Varro who, in the Roman tradition, each commanded in the field on alternate days.

Hannibal's path to Italy remains one of history's greatest logistical feats. Taking his forces—which included at least 40,000 men and some 40 North African war elephants—from Spain, through the Pyrenees, across the Rhône, over the snowy Alps, and finally down into Cisalpine Gaul (Northern Italy), Hannibal caught the Romans completely unawares. Along the way, they were harried by Helvetian "mountain men," lost many troops to the weather and accidents, and had to pull off several major engineering feats as they made their way up and down narrow mountain paths that often hugged the cliffs, with rock on one side and death on the other. In his riveting account of the Punic Wars in *The History of Rome*, the historian Livy describes Hannibal's inventiveness when confronted with a seemingly insuperable obstacle[2]:

> They next came to a much narrower passageway on the rock face, where the cliff fell away so steeply that a soldier free of baggage could barely make it down by feeling his way and clinging with his hands to shrubs and roots projecting round about him. The spot had been naturally steep before, but it had now also been sheared off by a recent landslide, which had created a drop of fully one thousand feet. . . . The slippery path afforded no foothold, and on the incline it made the feet slide all the more quickly. . . . The men were then taken off to make a road down the cliff, which was the only possible way to go on. Solid rock had to be cut. They felled some massive trees in the area, stripped the branches from them, and made a huge pile of logs. This they set on fire when a strong breeze arose suitable for whipping up a blaze, and as the rocks became hot they made them disintegrate by pouring vinegar on them. After scorching the cliff-face with fires in this way, they opened it up with picks and softened the gradient with short zigzag paths so that even the elephants, not just the pack animals, could be brought down. Four days were spent at the cliff, during which the pack animals almost starved to death.

And so the Romans marched out to meet Hannibal at Cannae, smarting from their string of defeats and determined to put an end to the Barcid interloper once and for all.

---

2. See Extract 2.

Ironically, it was the Roman way of war that got the legions under Varro (who was commanding that day) into such trouble. Each soldier was armed with a *pilum* (spear), *gladius* (short sword), and *scutum* (shield). Troops were deployed in formations that echoed their Greek antecedents, but with greater flexibility so as to be able to adapt to rapidly changing battle conditions. Classical armies preferred to fight on level plains, where the geography of their formations mirrored that of the landscape; hills and valleys meant exposed flanks, and exposed flanks meant casualties and defeats. Major battles were intended to be decisive.

In his magisterial—and still, to the modern reader, sprightly written (despite its vast length)—*The Decline and Fall of the Roman Empire*, the eighteenth-century British historian Edward Gibbon[3] describes the making of a Roman soldier:

> On his first entrance into the service, an oath was administered to him, with every circumstance of solemnity. He promised never to desert his standard, to submit his own will to the commands of his leader, and to sacrifice his life for the safety of the emperor and the empire. The attachment of the Roman troops to their standards was inspired by the united influence of religion and of honour. The golden eagle, which glittered in the front of the legion, was the object of their fondest devotion; nor was it esteemed less impious than it was ignominious; to abandon that sacred ensign in the hour of danger . . . it was an inflexible maxim of Roman discipline, that a good soldier should dread his officers far more than the enemy . . .
>
> The recruits and young soldiers were constantly trained both in the morning and in the evening, nor was age or knowledge allowed to excuse the veterans from the daily repetition of what they had completely learnt. . . . The soldiers were diligently instructed to march, to run, to leap, to swim, to carry heavy burdens, to handle every species of arms that was used either for offence or for defence, either in distant engagement or in a closer

3. See Extract 3.

> onset; to form a variety of evolutions; and to move to the sound of flutes,[4] in the Pyrrhic or martial dance. [It] is prettily remarked by an ancient historian who had fought against them, that the effusion of blood was the only circumstance which distinguished a field of battle from a field of exercise.

Gibbon was writing from the perspective of the Age of the Antonines, at the moral and political apex of the Empire under Marcus Aurelius.[5] For a more detailed description of the Roman tactics at the time of the Second Punic War, we must rely on both Livy and Polybius, a Greek historian (c. 208–125 B.C.) taken hostage by the Romans, who wrote forty volumes of *Histories*, of which five and some fragments survive. Fortunately for us, Polybius's account[6] of the Roman military system in the Republic has been preserved:

> The youngest soldiers or *Velites* are ordered to carry a sword, javelins, and a target (*parma*). The target is strongly made and sufficiently large to afford protection, being circular and measuring three feet in diameter. They also wear a plain helmet, and sometimes cover it with a wolf's skin or something similar both to protect and to act as a distinguishing mark by which their officers can recognize them and judge if they fight pluckily or not. The next in seniority called *hastati* are ordered to wear a complete panoply. The Roman panoply consists firstly of a shield (*scutum*), the convex surface of which measures two and a half feet in width and four feet in length, the thickness at the rim being a palm's breadth. Besides the shield they also carry a sword, hanging on the right thigh and called a Spanish sword. In addition they have

---

4. Music has long played an important part in military exercises, from trumpets and drums to regimental bands. It kept the march rhythms, sounded triumphs and alarms, and acted as a signalling device for combat orders.

5. Whose *Meditations* were forged from Stoic philosophy and also contain many elements we would recognize as Christian today, even though the Empire did not formally become Christian until Constantine a century and a half later.

6. See Extract 4.

> two *pila* [spears], a brass helmet, and greaves. Each [*pila*] is fitted with a barbed iron head of the same length as the haft. This they attach so securely to the haft, carrying the attachment halfway up the latter and fixing it with numerous rivets, that in action the iron will break sooner than become detached . . .
>
> Finally they wear as an ornament a circle of feathers with three upright purple or black feathers about a cubit in height, the addition of which on the head surmounting their other arms is to make every man look twice his real height, and to give him a fine appearance, such as will strike terror into the enemy. The *principes* and *triarii* are armed in the same manner except that instead of the *pila* the *triarii* [the most seasoned troops] carry long spears (*hastae*).

It was a mighty, tripartite military machine—the mightiest the world had ever known. With the cavalry protecting their flanks, the highly trained legions, organized into fluid units called maniples, could group and regroup as conditions necessitated. In the Grecian lands, the Romans time and again defeated the Greeks with their superior version of the Greeks' contribution to military history. But at Cannae, Hannibal was waiting for them. Not with better arms or braver soldiers. But with, on that day and in that place, superior tactics that turned the Roman strengths into weaknesses and ensured their destruction in one of history's bloodiest battles, one that would not be rivalled in butchery until the mechanized destruction of the First World War.

The staggering loss of life makes modern readers, especially Westerners, squirm. It's not just the waste of human capital, as bad as that was. Rather, in an increasingly pacifistic and irreligious age, nothing today seems worth the sacrifice of the Self, which has replaced the gods, or a God, as the highest deity of the household, its very own *lares* and *penates* all rolled into one. We abhor the use of violence, even as we live it vicariously in films and literature. Rarely, if ever, are we forced to ask ourselves: Faced with certain, violent death, what would we do? How would we react? Would we cry, break down, beg for mercy—or fight, and sell our lives as dearly as we could, if only for the satisfaction of seeing our enemy's eyeballs in our palms and his nose in our mouths?

Which was precisely the choice facing the surrounded, doomed, Romans at Cannae.

"Yet it cannot be denied that a fearful and wonderful interest is attached to these scenes of carnage," writes Creasy from his mid-nineteenth-century vantage point, when England had conquered Bonaparte and had made the world safe for the Congress of Vienna in 1814/15. "There is undeniable greatness in the disciplined courage, and in the love of honour, which make the combatants confront agony and destruction. . . . Catiline was as brave a soldier as Leonidas, and a much better officer. . . . We thus learn not to judge of the wisdom of measures too exclusively by the results. We learn to apply the juster standard of seeing what the circumstances and the probabilities were that surrounded a statesman or a general at the time when he decided on his plan: we value him not by his fortune, but by his *Προαρεσς*,[7] to adopt the expressive Greek word, for which our language gives no equivalent."

No matter their generalship, what the legions could not do was fight in quarters so close that their *pila* were useless and their *gladii* unable to be drawn from their scabbards. And that was precisely what Hannibal intended to make them do. Placing his valiant but sometimes skittish and unreliable allies, the Iberians and the Gauls, at the center of his line where he could personally command them, he allowed the approaching legions, marching forward in three deep columns, to collide with him head-on. This should have been an easy battle for the Romans, for one on one they were superior to the barbarians in tactics, discipline, and armaments, if not in physical size. But as the battle unfolded, Hannibal led his center troops (who took the brunt of the 5,700 Carthaginian deaths that day) in a controlled retreat, luring the Romans ever forward.

Confronting Hannibal's army, the Romans might have observed how unlike their own it was. Whereas the legions during the Republic were almost exclusively Italian, the Carthaginian mercenary forces were as polyglot an army as could be imagined. The German military historian Arnold Heeren (1760–1842), described them as follows:

7. *Prohairesis,* roughly meaning "a principled moral choice," found in the Stoic philosophy of Epictetus and in Aristotle's *Nicomachean Ethics.*

> It was an assemblage of the most opposite races of the human species, from the farthest parts of the globe. Hordes of half-naked Gauls were ranged next to companies of white clothed Iberians, and savage Ligurians next to the far-travelled Nasamones and Lotophagi. Carthaginians and Phoenici-Africans formed the centre; while innumerable troops of Numidian horse-men, taken from all the tribes of the Desert, swarmed about on unsaddled horses, and formed the wings; the van was composed of Balearic slingers; and a line of colossal elephants, with their Ethiopian guides, formed, as it were, a chain of moving fortresses before the whole army.

As the Romans, sensing victory over their hated foe, rushed forward, Hannibal unleashed his two cavalry wings on the outnumbered and inferior Roman horsemen. Under Hasdrubal (not to be confused with Hannibal's brother of the same name) some 10,000 horsemen, including 2,000 Numidian (North African Berber) light cavalry, overwhelmed the undermanned and overmatched Roman cavalry, thus allowing the Carthaginians to assault the legions at their vulnerable flanks and to get behind them and attack from the rear. Unable to move forward and unable to retreat, the legions became a pitiful, helpless giant, ripe for the slaughter that followed.[8] Pushing and shoving like a panicked crowd in a burning building, the troops trampled each other in their rush to flee certain death, colliding in their frantic haste to escape the horns of their tactical dilemma[9]—but had nowhere to go except straight into its Barcid jaws. Ducks in a shooting gallery, fish in a barrel—that was the Roman plight.

---

8. The Roman position was somewhat analogous to that of the Persians on the first two days at Thermopylae, who were similarly unable to bring the brunt of their army to bear on the limited front the Greeks controlled. Once surrounded, however, they more resembled the Greeks.

9. For a similar conundrum, but with a vastly smaller defensive force, see Chapter XI to learn how the British at Rorke's Drift solved it versus the Zulu warriors. Flexibility, superior armaments, steadfast, unwavering courage, and cool-headed leadership turned out to be the solution.

The historian Livy—not always accurate, but a magnificent storyteller—writes of the battle in Book 22 of *The Second Punic War*:

> Here and there amidst the slain there started up a gory figure whose wounds had begun to throb with the chill of dawn, and was cut down by his enemies; some were discovered lying there alive, with thighs and tendons slashed, baring their necks and throats and bidding their conquerors drain the remnant of their blood. Others were found with their heads buried in holes dug in the ground. They had apparently made these pits for themselves, and heaping the dirt over their faces to shut off their breath. But what most drew the attention of all beholders was a Numidian who was dragged out alive from under a dead Roman, but with a mutilated nose and ears; for the Roman, unable to hold a weapon in his hands, had expired in a frenzy of rage, while rending the other with his teeth.

By the close of battle, thousands of legionaries lay groaning, bleeding, or already rotting on the field, and thousands of others were taken captive, to be dispersed as slaves across the Mediterranean. The mightiest army Rome would ever field, fighting a battle for the survival of the Republic, was ignominiously destroyed in a defeat so humiliating that the few survivors, mostly reserves—called the *legiones Cannenses*—were for years shunned as outcasts, not paid their wages, and exiled to Sicily.

For his part, Hannibal followed up his stunning triumph by doing . . . nothing. To the west, Rome lay prostrate and vulnerable, nearly undefended. To use a contemporary term, it had been decapitated, its leadership class bloating in the sun. Considering the relatively minimal loss of life on the Carthaginian side, the question naturally arises why Hannibal—who as a nine-year-old boy, at the behest of his father, Hamilcar, had sworn a blood oath to the destruction of Rome—did not pursue his advantage and march on the city. Instead of striking at his mortal enemy at her weakest, however, Hannibal turned away.

He had many good reasons for doing so, primarily logistical. His foraging army was deep in hostile territory. He needed horses and pack animals, food for his soldiers; were he to undertake a siege, engines designed for just that purpose would have to be built. Against that, Rome had been living in terror since Hannibal's daring attack over the Alps upon Cisalpine Gaul in 218. He was seemingly invincible, inflicting three crushing defeats on the Roman army in a row, culminating with the annihilation at Cannae. Indeed, he was regarded as something of a superman and viewed by the ordinary Roman in much the same way that the rampaging Turk[10] would be by the Hungarians, Wallachians, Romanians, and Germans of Eastern Europe during the Ottoman-Habsburg Wars of the sixteenth and seventeenth centuries.

And yet, he did not attack. "In a single day Hannibal had decimated a substantial proportion of Rome's leadership, a blow that some might well have considered mortal," wrote Robert L. O'Connell in *The Ghosts of Cannae* (2010). According to Livy, his cavalry commander, Marhabal, upbraided him: "You know how to win a victory, Hannibal, but you don't know how to use one."

In the end, Cannae turned out to be a brilliant tactical victory whose strategic value was close to nil; over the course of the next thirteen years, the Second Punic War devolved into a stalemate, during which Rome won some battles and lost some as Hannibal scurried around southern Italy. Owing to its superior manpower, and the fecund wombs of its women, however, Rome gradually grew in strength. Unlike the Carthaginians, the Romans were able to steadily replenish their armies via population growth; as in the Greek and Phoenician myths (Cadmus and Jason), new soldiers (called the *spartoi*) continually sprang up from the ground from a slain dragon's teeth to worry and harass the enemy.

The hesitation to finish Rome eventually proved fatal. Among the patrician survivors of Cannae was the young Publius Cornelius Scipio, still in his early twenties, a scion of one of the noblest families in Rome

---

10. Reflecting and addressing the fears for the Christian West, Martin Luther published his pamphlet *On the War Against the Turks* in 1529. He regarded Muslim depredations as God's punishment on errant Christianity. He regarded Islam, however, with extreme distaste: "*Ego usque ad mortem luctor adversus Turcas et Turcarum Deum*," he wrote. "I will always struggle to the death against the Turks and the god of the Turks."

and the son and nephew of two celebrated military commanders. Upon returning to Rome and hearing that some of the nobility were ready to abandon the city and take up new lives abroad as mercenaries, Scipio is said to have drawn his sword, ordered them arrested, and forced them to swear an oath of allegiance to the Republic.

Hannibal's dilatory nature gave Scipio, later honored as "Africanus" after Rome's final revenge, time to mature and afforded him the opportunity he needed to put Cannae behind him and establish Roman superiority over the interloper. In 211 B.C., his father and uncle were killed in Spain while fighting Hannibal's brother, Hasdrubal, who was organizing his own transalpine crossing in order to reinforce Hannibal from the north. Scipio won stunning victories against the enemy in New Carthage, Spain (today called Cartagena—the name lives on), but in 209 B.C. Hasdrubal elided Scipio's trap and escaped across the Pyrenees and the Alps and into Northern Italy. The idea was for the two sons of Hamilcar to catch all of Rome in the jaws of a vice—Cannae but on a larger scale—with Hasdrubal coming down from the north and Hannibal up from the south.

It was not to be; in 207 Hasdrubal was confronted and killed at the Battle of the Metaurus, where he was defeated by a Roman army under the consul, Nero (not the later emperor).[11] His head was severed, brought south, and chucked into Hannibal's camp—when Hannibal saw his brother's head, he is said to have remarked: "Rome would now be the mistress of the world."

After the Metaurus, Hannibal spent the next four years in Bruttium (Calabria), in the toe of Italy, before being recalled to Carthage to mount a defense of the city against the resurgent Romans. In effect, the Metaurus was the last stand of the Carthaginians against Rome, although it would take years for the outcome to fully play out. In any case, the threat to Rome was over.

Hannibal's end was ignominious. He was elected to the leadership position of *suffete* of Carthage in 196 B.C., thus winning a temporary

---

11. "The infamy of the one has eclipsed the glory of the other," wrote Byron. "When the name of Nero is heard, who thinks of the consul? But such are human things."

victory in the Barcid family's struggle for political control of the city against rival aristocrats. Defeated by the Cannae survivor, Scipio Africanus, at Zama in present-day Tunisia and forced by political machinations, partly orchestrated from Rome, to flee, first to Tyre in the eastern Mediterranean (one of the foundational cities of the Phoenician Empire) and then farther east to Bithynia, in present-day Anatolia (Turkey), where he hoped to restore an eastern coalition against Rome, Hannibal was eventually run to ground at Libyssa (Gebze) and forced to commit suicide c. 183–181 B.C. His last words were, "Let us now put an end to the great anxiety of the Romans, who have thought it too long and hard a task to wait for the death of a hated old man." In 149 B.C., at the conclusion of the Third Punic War, Carthage was utterly destroyed; as Creasy observes, "An entire civilization perished at one blow—vanished, like a falling star." *O tempora! O mores!*

Taken in the abstract, the Punic Wars may sometimes seem a dusty bit of ancient history, an exercise in primitive Great Power politics fought over control of the Mediterranean. But as cultural history has shown, it was far more than that.

In the reign of Augustus, the first emperor, the poet Virgil composed his epic poem, the *Aeneid*, between the years 29–19 B.C. Its hero is the mythical Trojan leader Aeneas, and the poem describes the flight of the defeated Trojans at the hands of the Greeks (the subject of Homer's *Iliad*) across the Mediterranean, first to North Africa and thence to Latium, where the Trojans defeat the native Latins and establish the city of Rome. The *Aeneid* is the essential text of the Empire, but it's much more, of course. For in its most poignant and affecting Books (there are twelve), it dwells at some length upon the fatal attraction between Aeneas and Dido, the founder and queen of the Phoenician city of Carthage.

This doomed romance itself has had a resonant afterlife, most notably as the subject of Henry Purcell's baroque opera (c. 1689) *Dido and Aeneas*. But it is with certain elements of the poem with which we are here concerned. Dido's fury at her rejection by her lover—who must, according to the gods' commands, leave her to sail for his rendezvous with destiny in Italy—and her spectacular suicide atop a blazing funeral pyre that limns the vengeful roots of the Punic Wars still resonate as powerfully today as they did when first written:

What could my fortune have afforded more,
Had the false Trojan never touch'd my shore!"
Then kiss'd the couch; and, "Must I die," she said,
"And unreveng'd? 'T is doubly to be dead!
Yet ev'n this death with pleasure I receive:
On any terms, 't is better than to live.
These flames, from far, may the false Trojan view;
These boding omens his base flight pursue!"

—translation by John Dryden (1697)

Thus, the origin of the Rome-Carthage rivalry was transformed from a battle for economic supremacy in the Mediterranean into the most primal of human conditions, the angry reaction to a failed love affair, with Dido's curses echoing down the centuries. And it was in just this historical moment, during the ascension of Augustus, that Rome was to suffer another catastrophic defeat that would change the course of empire and affect the map of Europe for two thousand years to come: in the Teutoburg Forest in the dark barbarian heart of Germany.

THE *CLADES VARIANA*

The Teutoburg Forest (9 A.D.)

Our story begins a few years after it ended, with the defeat and annihilation of three Roman legions—XVII, XVIII, and XIX—under the command of Publius Quinctilus Varus, who led them into battle against the forces of Arminius (Hermann), a Roman knight and naturalized citizen honored today in Germany as the father of German independence. Leading a Roman expeditionary force to the site of the battle, between modern day Osnabrück and Detmold, the great Roman general

Germanicus[12] was conducting a search for the remains of the unhappy legions. The Roman historian Tacitus relates the tale[13]:

> The scene lived up to its horrible associations. Varus's extensive first camp with its broad extent and headquarters marked out, testified to the whole army's labours. Then a half-ruined breastwork and shallow ditch showed where the last pathetic remnant had gathered. On the open ground were whitening bones, scattered where men had fled, heaped up where they had stood and fought back. Fragments of spears and of horses' limbs lay there—also human heads, fastened to tree-trunks. In groves nearby were the outlandish altars at which the Germans had massacred the Roman colonels and senior company commanders. . . .
>
> So, six years after the slaughter, a living Roman army had come to bury the dead men's bones of three whole divisions. No one knew if the remains he was burying belonged to a stranger or a comrade. But in their bitter distress, and rising fury against the enemy, they look on them all as friends and blood-brothers. Germanicus shared in the general grief, and laid the first turf of the funeral mound as a heartfelt tribute to the dead. Thereby he earned Tiberius's[14] disapproval . . .

Germanicus, the son of Nero Claudius Drusus and the adopted son of his uncle, Tiberius, was not in Germany bent on conquest but rather on retrenchment. For Varus's defeat at the hands of Arminius halted the Roman expansion across the Rhine and into the territories of the most fearsome and warlike Germanic tribes, among them Arminius's own Cherusci. The ablest, and perhaps the noblest, Roman of the early Empire, the wildly popular Germanicus (as Tacitus notes above) eventually fell afoul of an increasingly corrupt and decadent Tiberius, who

---

12. Tacitus, *The Annals of Imperial Rome*, translated by Michael Grant.

13. See Extract 5.

14. Tiberius, the second of the five Julio-Claudian emperors, had succeeded Augustus upon the latter's death in 14 A.D.

very likely had him assassinated by poisoning in the year 19 A.D. while in the field at Antioch in the Roman province of Syria. And while Germanicus's appearance in our story is fleeting, it is crucial to the later history of the Empire. For after the death of Tiberius (smothered after a seizure at his imperial retreat on the island of Capri, where he spent his final years in increasing decadence), the throne went not to the rightful heir, Germanicus,[15] but to Caligula.

Therefore, the decline of the Roman Empire can well be traced to the Battle of the Teutoburg Forest, which may be viewed in retrospect as the moment Rome overreached. In the aftermath of this signal defeat of imperial arms, the Roman historian Suetonius[16] relates that Augustus "was in such consternation at this event, that he let the hair of his head and beard grow for several months, and sometimes knocked his head against the door-posts, crying out, 'O, Quinctilius Varus! Give me back my legions!'[17] And ever after, he observed the anniversary of this calamity, as a day of sorrow and mourning." As Gibbon notes in a footnote to the first chapter of *Decline and Fall:*

> *Footnote 3:* Augustus did not receive the melancholy news with all the temper and firmness that might have been expected from his character.

Although the Empire expanded to its farthest limits under Trajan[18] in 117, and was maintained largely intact through the reign of Marcus Aurelius, the failure to conquer Germany in the first decade of the first century[19] eventually spelled its doom, as it was the descendants of those

---

15. How different the history of Rome might have been had Germanicus lived. The "great man" theory of history was never more apposite.

16. In *The Twelve Caesars* (121 A.D.).

17. Of the three destroyed legions, only one—the XVIII—was ever reconstituted (under the Emperor Nero). It was disbanded under Vespasian, who ruled from 69 to 79.

18. Although erected centuries later, Trajan's Column in Rome vividly depicts how the legions looked and fought during the Empire period.

19. See Extract 6.

same Germans who later sacked and then conquered Rome in the fifth century. Fittingly, the last emperor—a fifteen-year-old boy, who reigned from 475 to 476—was derisively called Romulus Augustulus,[20] or "little Augustus."

The resonance of the Teutoburg Forest echoes to this day. Rome's failure to bring the Germanic tribes to heel and into the Empire, and to make citizens out of barbarians, not only led to the fall of the Western empire but also gave rise a few centuries later to the Holy Roman Empire, which eventually morphed into a loose alliance of largely German states and principalities in Central Europe and Northern Italy, in contradistinction to the emerging nation-states of France, Spain, and England to the north and west. This linguistic and cultural fault line endured into the Napoleonic era, recurred again in the Franco-Prussian War of 1870–71, and reached its awful culmination in the World Wars of 1914–18 and 1939–45. Indeed, the postwar push for a common market was meant to ensnare France and Germany in an economic alliance, one that has persisted and molted into the European Union, a Franco-German superstate with the other, smaller countries bent to their will.

Almost from the time they encountered them, the Romans were fascinated by the Germans, a people so unlike themselves and yet one of their most formidable adversaries. They were impressed by their height, their large frames, their physical strength, their blue eyes. Caesar had encountered them in his battle against the Celtic Gauls but never attempted to conquer them. Until the new Empire began another round of expansion, the west bank of the Rhine and the southern bank of the Danube were the rough borders between the Latin and German worlds, but the fascination of the other continued long after the Roman defeat in the Teutoburg Forest.

Writing in the year 98 A.D. during the second consulship of Trajan, who later became emperor and ruled from 98 to 117, Tacitus undertook a study of the Germans in his monograph, *Germania,* a

20. Romulus after the mythical founder of Rome, and for whom the city was named. The last emperor's very name summed up the life of the Republic, and adumbrated its destruction.

taxonomy of the various tribes and customs of the fearsome, bellicose savages who dwelled in the trackless woods north and east of the empire. Their sacred spaces were the groves of the forest; they hanged traitors and deserters but killed cowards and sodomites by burying them alive, face down, in a bog. They sacrificed animals and sometimes people as well. Valor on the battlefield was prized above all else. Some blackened their shields and bodies and attacked at night like a phantom army of ghouls. Yet they married for life, kept their women chaste, and gave them a significant role in their social organization. Generosity and hospitality toward strangers was *de rigueur.*

The end of the Empire, however, was still far in the future when Varus's legions, auxiliaries, and camp followers—some 20,000 people in all—left their summer headquarters in Vetera and headed for their winter camp in the interior (Romans generally did not fight in the winter). Although their tortuous path took them through the swamps, marshes, and thick woods of Germany, the cordially loathed Varus did not think he had anything in particular to fear. Rome had already conquered about half the lands of the Germans, and the process of romanizing the tribes west of the Rhine was well underway. The young German nobles who might have given a thought to resistance were bought off with the perquisites of being Roman.

But not Arminius, a product of the romanizing system and one of Varus's most trusted advisers—and the man who led him into the ambush. Arminius had been taken to Rome as a hostage when still a child, a common Roman practice when dealing with the children of barbarian leaders. Selected from the highest levels of their societies, hostages were proof of a conquered people's fidelity to Rome, since any abrogation of treaty or revolt would result in their instant deaths; if the chief of a Gallic or German tribe dared to rise up, his children would surely die. Arminius rose to become a commander of one of the auxiliaries, fighting forces attached to the legions and consisting mostly of foreign-born soldiers, and then was seconded to Varus's staff as Rome prepared the full conquest of Germania east of the Rhine. It was there he would take his long-awaited revenge.

Bent on defeating the restive tribes the way his predecessor,

Tiberius,[21] had done, Varus—a lawyer by trade, not a military man, and one who owed his position to the happy circumstance of his marrying Augustus's grand-niece, the felicitously named Claudia Pulchra—was persuaded by Arminius to thread a narrow path through the forest, hemmed in on one side by a large bog and on the other by a hill. Strung out in single file roughly ten miles long, marching in the September rain in unfamiliar terrain, the Romans were attacked on the first day of the battle from all sides, with German spears—many aimed at the Roman horses—raining down on them as they tried to make camp and construct some kind of shelter.

But Arminius knew that this is what the Romans would do. As the Romans attempted to break out from their improvised camp—already having sustained heavy losses—the surrounding Germans struck again against the legionaries, who were unable to get into proper formation; further, the heavy rains had rendered much of Roman equipment, especially their shields, waterlogged and useless. In essence, by falling on the rear of the Roman column first, the Germans had sectioned the Roman centipede, rendering communication among the legions and centurions impossible. That night the Romans attempted to escape in a night march, but this time they were literally caught between a rock (the Kalkriese Hill) and the hard place of a large bog. With nowhere to run, they were doomed. Some of the Roman cavalry attempted a breakout, but they were quickly hunted down and killed or captured for later torture. Rather than be taken alive, the humiliated Varus committed suicide.

For these were not the legions of the old Republic, manned by ethnic Romans with a personal stake in the military outcome; rather, their ranks were filled with slaves and foreigners, whose numbers were already about half the population of the Italian peninsula. The carnage of the civil wars had taken its demographic toll in the field; meanwhile, back home, flattery and courtiership had replaced republican virtues. Outwardly, Rome appeared as strong as ever—but appearances were deceiving.

Teutoburg was in its way as crushing a defeat as Cannae—a last stand that would later find its closest historical analogue in what

21. Who succeeded Augustus on the throne in 14 A.D. As a commander, Tiberius had been the scourge of the Germans.

happened to the Seventh Cavalry under George Armstrong Custer at the Little Bighorn in 1876. Savages against the mechanized forces of civilization. Tribes against trained soldiers. A daring and ruthless general, much despised by his opponents, versus natives defending their home turf, with some knowledge of the tactics and weapons of their invaders. Indeed, the way the entire battle played out is more akin to the Indians' guerrilla tactics against the British and the Americans in the French and Indian War[22] than to conventional Roman maneuvers from Caesar on.

The Romans got no mercy, nor did they deserve any. The legions, like the Roman people themselves at the time, viewed mercy as weakness and quarter as cowardice. They dealt with the enemies, however gallant and honorable, in the cruelest possible way: having been defeated by Caesar at the Battle of Alesia in 52 B.C., the Gallic leader Vercingetorix surrendered himself in order to stop the bloodshed. He was rewarded with five years' imprisonment in Rome, and then, in 46 B.C., he was paraded through the streets of the city in celebration of Caesar's triumph[23] and strangled to death.

So when the Germans fell upon the hapless legionaries in the mud and blood of Teutoburg, the outcome was never in doubt. Like the battlefield tactics, the butchery was also reminiscent of the American Indians' treatment of wounded soldiers and captives—prolonged torture of the direst nature, dismemberment, mutilations that beggar description. As Arminius knew it would be, the loss of the eagles—the standards that marked each legion—was especially keenly felt back in Rome,

---

22. The Battle of the Monongahela in 1755, in which a British and colonial regiment (which included George Washington, then a lieutenant colonel in the Virginia militia) under Gen. Edward Braddock was soundly defeated by a combined French-Canadian-Indian force. Braddock was killed, and Washington organized the retreat, thus beginning his rise to national fame.

23. A *Triumphus* was the highest Roman civic and military honor, a public declaration and celebration of a signal Roman foreign victory, declared by the Senate. The general so feted rode through the streets in a quadriga, leading his army, his captives, and followed by the spoils of war. According to tradition, a slave stood behind the general, holding a laurel wreath over his head and whispering in his ear, "Remember, thou art only a man."

perhaps as much as the loss of the legions themselves. Rome could take defeat, but it could not stomach humiliation.

Another advantage the Germans had over their Italian counterparts was their size and strength. Shorn of their armor, weapons, discipline, and superior battlefield tactics, the average Roman soldier (who weighed about 130 pounds) was no match physically for his barbarian counterpart. When the Roman lines broke, their aura of invincibility vanished into the mist and rain. When the legions realized they were trapped and unable to defend themselves, what went through their minds? Fear? Anger? Resignation? Shame?

It's impossible for us, at this historical remove, to tell. We do know that the Romans, spiritual descendants of Sparta, not Athens, but with Lucullan appetites for the pleasures of the flesh and a pre-Christian lack of guilt about same, regarded life as fleeting, as well as, in the main, nasty and brutish. Death could come to anyone at any time—by disease, by the sword, at the behest of the Senate or the emperor, by your own hand or at another's, in war, in peace. When condemned, Roman nobles generally met their demises with equanimity—Petronius's final dinner party, at which he had his surgeons open his veins and those of his mistress in order to fulfill Nero's command, talking and dying as wittily as possible before his gathered guests, comes to mind—if not actual aplomb. As pagans, their notion of the afterlife was the gloomy confines of the underworld, to which were headed the good and the bad alike, to live eternally in eternal shadows, shades of the past, their earthly powers and glories stripped and gone, and visited only upon occasion by an intrepid traveler such as Aeneas in Book VI of the *Aeneid* (who encounters both his father, Anchises, and, rather less happily, the late Dido, as he learns of his destiny as the founder of Rome).

But fear, at least as we understand it in the modern sense, probably played little role in the emotions of the warriors. Death became the ancients, which is why our history is written with their bones dipped in their blood and the blood of their enemies. A good death, not eternal salvation, not even *la pace de la tomba*, was the goal of every man (women didn't figure into this equation). Gibbon, correctly, ascribed some of the late Empire's weakness to its Christianization, but this is a partial misreading of Christian bellicosity—*in hoc signo vinces* was, after all, the battle cry of the first Christian emperor, Constantine, and the Crusaders who wrested Jerusalem from the Muslims in the last year of the eleventh century cried *Deus lo vult* as they put the Jews and Mohammedans to the sword in the name of the Lord Jesus. By the early Middle Ages, everyone's God, it seems, was sanguinary.

One suspects, therefore, that there was not a lot of weeping, wailing, and gnashing of teeth as a man's fate was confronted at the point of a sword, a spear, or battle-axe. As we know from Cannae, many of the soldiers went unresisting to their deaths, dropping their arms and embracing the sweet bloodletting of the sword as it plunged into their entrails, their throats, or at their collarbones with a killing thrust. True, most soldiers went down fighting, selling their lives as dearly as they could, but faced with the inevitable there was no shame in resignation and submission. All men fall: mighty Caesar, the conqueror of Vercingetorix, the greatest man of the ancient world, was struck down by the knives of cowards like Brutus and Cassius, and history since is replete with great men felled by pipsqueaks.

In short, the word the ancients used was *honor*. In the post–World War II era, "honor" has become risible, an archaic insult, the taunt of the atheist and the weakling against the strong. A hero goes to his death willingly; we moderns call that man a chump. Which is correct?

The contradiction of Eros and Thanatos is that men will die for Eros, but they will seek out Thanatos in its pursuit and embrace it when that is the price to pay for sexual satisfaction. It is impossible to read of Cannae, whether in Polybius or Livy, without a thought for the brave Roman soldiers, ambushed in the columns, who died without being able to deliver so much as a sword thrust or an ear chaw. No real man dies without a fight. No real man deems his death a willing sacrifice without collecting as dear a price as he can.

There is one hero in the Teutoburg Forest, and that is Arminius, or Hermann,[24] to give him his proper, unromanized name. Like Hannibal, Arminius is something of a tragic figure, conqueror of Varus but victim of tribal machinations, largely having to do with which leader—to make

24. The city of Hermann, Missouri, originally a German settlement, is named after him.

matters more complex, they were often related by blood—was or was not an ally of Rome in the battle along the German front. After battling Germanicus to a relative standstill and thus permanently keeping the Romans out of *Germania Magna*, Arminius was assassinated in 21 A.D. by members of his own tribe, who feared his will to power; like Caesar, he went under his own people's knives.

It is hardly surprising that the Teutoburg Forest does not loom large in Roman history. The defeat at Cannae at the hands of a genius like Hannibal and the perfect execution of the double envelopment[25] was one thing. It was also avenged by Scipio Africanus, who brought the Punic Wars to their definitive conclusion. But annihilation at the hands of barbarians in the German forests? For centuries, the misadventure across the Rhine was referred to by the Romans as the *clades Variana*—the Varian disaster.

For such an epochal struggle, the Teutoburg Forest has not entered the realm of myth and legend in the same way as Thermopylae or the Little Bighorn. In one of the most disastrously expensive sword-and-sandal movies ever made, *The Fall of the Roman Empire* (1964), there is a visual allusion to the battle early on, when the forces of Commodus are set upon in the woods by German barbarians—who, however, are soon routed by the timely arrival of General Livius and his troops. But this film is set at the end of the second century, not the beginning of the first. Indeed, its real story, which essentially was reworked for Ridley Scott's 2000 epic *Gladiator*, focused on the struggle for power after the death of Commodus's father, the emperor Marcus Aurelius (121–180 A.D.), ending with a fictional duel in the arena between Commodus and Livius. This film, which came on the heels of such similar epics as *Cleopatra* and *El Cid*, cost about $20 million to make, grossed less than $5 million, and effectively spelled the end of producer Samuel Bronston's career.

The battle, however, did resonate culturally in one particular place—Germany. In 1875, four years after German unification under Prussia and in the aftermath of the German victory in the Franco-Prussian

---

25. Emulated, however coincidentally, by the Zulus with their "horns of the bison" strategy against the British garrison at Rorke's Drift in 1879. But not successfully, as we shall see in Chapter XI.

War, the new German nation-state commemorated Arminius and his struggle for independence from Rome with a large monument, 53 meters high, near the site of the battlefield. Atop a *monopteros* stands a large statue of Hermann, holding aloft a sword that bears the inscription "*Deutsche Einigkeit: Meine Stärke / Meine Stärke: Deutschlands Macht*," which means: "German Unity is My Strength. My Strength is Germany's Might."

Around the same time, the Cologne-born composer Max Bruch began work on his heroic oratorio *Arminius*, which was premiered in early 1877. Composed for vocal soloists, chorus, and full orchestra, it's an earnest but strangely uninvolving work—the battle itself comes as an anticlimax in the fourth and last part of the piece—musically, little more than a blending of Brahms and Wagner but without the distinctive genius of either. Even the obligatory choral anthem to German martial glory that closes the piece comes off as more dutiful than inspirational, despite the words: *Gross ist der Ruhm der deutschen Söhne / Gross die Ehre der gefallenen Helden!*—"Great is the renown of Germany's sons / Great is the glory of the fallen heroes!"

But the real reason that both Arminius and *Arminius* have been consigned to the European attic has to do with World War II. With German militarism decisively defeated, and the jingoistic underpinnings of National Socialist Germany in complete disrepute, the world was in no mood for odes to Nietzsche's all-conquering Blond Beast.

And so Arminius—Hermann of the Cherusci—is largely forgotten today, although the legacy of his admittedly treacherous victory over Varus and Augustus lives on. Is a denatured and clawless Germany preferable to one that, with a proper moral compass, can contribute to the defense of Western civilization? Ferocity has long been a hallmark of the German character. But so has a love—a worship—of nature, which explains the success of its contemporary Green Party. The soldiers of Arminius nailed the heads of the Romans to the trees in order to propitiate their arboreal gods. A chilling thought occurs: What if German militarism is once again wedded to a primitive naturism (the Nazis made significant steps in this direction), with the will and the power to enforce a radical environmentalist agenda? Stranger things have happened, especially in the homeland of Hansel and Gretel, and Faust.

As Tacitus observed, "Assuredly [Arminius] was the deliverer of Germany, one too who had defied Rome, not in her early rise, as other kings and generals, but in the height of her empire's glory, had fought, indeed, indecisive battles, yet in war remained unconquered. He completed thirty-seven years of life, twelve years of power, and he is still a theme of song among barbarous nations, though to Greek historians, who admire only their own achievements, he is unknown, and to Romans not as famous as he should be, while we extol the past and are indifferent to our own times."

Today's West has precisely the opposite problem. We seek to bury our past for having the effrontery for not living up to the moral standards of the present—but what else do we inter with it?

This, needless to say, was not the Roman way. Even in their two most shattering defeats, at Cannae and in the Teutoburg Forest, they took their beating and, in many ways, came back the stronger for it. Hannibal never repeated his triumph at Cannae, and it would not be for another 467 years that the German barbarians would, finally, come through the Roman gates for good. History may not have an arc, but it does have a very long reach.

CHAPTER III

"WE HAVE IT IN OUR POWER TO DIE HONORABLY AS FREE MEN"

MASADA (73/74 A.D.) AND WARSAW (1943)

At first reflection, last stands would appear to be exclusively the province of doomed cultures. What could be more final than a last stand? And yet, they often signify precisely the opposite: that the culture that expends its all in one final act of military resistance, and is then subdued, can often emerge the ultimate victor should it be culturally and religiously strong enough to survive the ensuing oppression. The history of the Jewish people offers us just such an example. In two great battles, millennia apart, the Jews were not only defeated but killed nearly to the last man. And yet, less than a century after the second of these existential struggles, they not only have regained their biblical homeland but also boast one of the world's most efficient militaries, devoted solely to the concept of Never Again.

The Siege of Masada and the Battle of the Warsaw Ghetto both mark ends. Masada signified, along with the destruction of the Second Temple, the end of Jewish political autonomy at the beginning of the Roman Empire; the physical annihilation of the Warsaw Ghetto in 1943 spelled the end of Poland's once-thriving Jewish intellectual, legal, and commercial community and the beginning of the horror known as the Final Solution. That the Jews have overcome both is a testimony to the power of culture and faith in the teeth of two of the mightiest and most ruthless military machines the world has ever known.

The story of Masada, as we know it, has come down to us through the writings of the historian Titus Flavius Josephus. A member of an aristocratic, romanized Jewish family, Josephus lived and worked in the first century A.D. during the reigns of the last three Julian emperors and the Flavians who ruled between 69 and 96 A.D.—a remarkably turbulent time in Roman, Jewish, and Christian history. He was the son of a priest and, on his mother's side, descended from the Hasmonean dynasty that had ruled Israel until Herod in 37 B.C., and throughout his life—no matter which side he was on—he traveled in high circles. A diplomat, a politician, a warrior, a rebel, he began his career working for the Romans, switched sides during the first Jewish-Roman War, was captured and enslaved by the Romans but was granted his freedom by the general Vespasian in 69 A.D., after prophesying correctly that the military commander would become emperor of Rome. Josephus was with Titus—another future emperor—during the Siege of Jerusalem and witnessed the fiery destruction of Herod's Temple in the year 70. He wrote extensively about his own times, producing his magnum opus around 75 A.D., *The Jewish War*, a work whose most riveting section contains the only known account of the Siege of Masada in the year 73 A.D.

The question is, can we believe him?

The Masada story itself is as stirring and tragic as any in the literature. A small group of about 960 Jewish rebels, known as the *Sicarii*, took refuge after the fall of Jerusalem in a hilltop fortress called Masada overlooking the desert and the Dead Sea, about 33 miles from the city. Led by the charismatic Eleazar Ben Yair, they were an offshoot of the Zealots, who opposed Roman rule in the province of Judea. The *Sicarii* were especially deadly assassins—a *sica* was a dagger—who would strike down their victims, whether Romans or imperial sympathizers, in public, and then melt away into the crowd. In short, hit men.

After the fall of Jerusalem, the Romans continued to mop up Jewish resistance around the province. One by one they rolled up the strongholds until at last there was only Masada—a forbidding and majestic mesa rising some 450 meters out of the desert[1] and topped by a fort

1. But only 58 meters above sea level, because its base near the Dead Sea is so low.

and an opulent palace, terraced into the hillside, built by Herod himself as a last refuge in case the Jews tried to depose him and restore the Hasmoneans. After Herod's death in 4 B.C., the Romans enlarged the province of Judea to include Samaria and Idumea and took possession of Masada with a small garrison, but the *Sicarii* overwhelmed and slaughtered the troops and occupied the redoubt as they prepared for a millenarian last stand. And so it was toward the nearly impregnable fortress of Masada that the Roman general Flavius Silva and the legendary Tenth Legion (one of Caesar's own), numbering about eight thousand fighting men, marched out and prepared to lay siege.

Everybody knows the ending: after three months or so, the Romans managed to construct a broad ramp and roll a huge siege engine up to the walls.[2] Upon breaking through, they found nearly every man, woman, and child in the fort lying dead on the ground. The Jews had chosen death by their own swords rather than at the hands of the Romans.

It's come down to us as a tale of good vs. evil—as indeed, representationally, it is. The Siege of Masada, which ended, as best we can reckon, in April of 74 A.D., is part of the foundational mythos of an independent Israel and a source of national pride. Upon completion of basic training, some new members of the Israel Defense Forces' Armored Corps complete their swearing-in atop the fort, vowing, "Masada shall not fall again." Masada is the alpha as the Holocaust is the omega to Israel's defiant existential motto.

History, however, is never quite as tidy as we would wish it to be. In every human conflict, both sides think they are in the right; both sides fight for something that matters deeply to them, whether in retrospect noble or base. In *Othello*, Iago thinks himself the good guy; on the Ides of March, the plotters who killed Julius Caesar called themselves the Liberators, believing they were acting in the best interests of the Roman Republic. History may indeed be written by the victors, but sometimes the losers have the last laugh after all. Context is everything.

The first century was a particularly complex and vexatious time for

---

2. One of the principal reasons the Romans were so successful in war was not just that they were good fighters, but they were great builders as well. Roman engineers made the Empire possible.

the inhabitants of the Roman Empire. The forty-year reign of the former Gaius Octavius had put an end to the Republic, mostly by avoiding the question of whether it would ever return, but no one was quite sure what was going to come after him. The first Roman emperor had never quite formally assumed the title—being "dictator for life," as his great-uncle Caesar had been, ensured that Augustus's patron's own life had been immediately cut short. So Imperator Caesar Augustus he became.

The bloody transition from Republic to Empire, however, was only the second most important event of the period. At the eastern edge of the Mediterranean, the carpenter's son known as Jesus of Nazareth came into the world and changed it far more significantly than did Augustus. If the historical Jesus was born in Bethlehem during the reign of Herod, he would have had to have been born before 4 B.C. Luke 2:1 specifically states that Jesus was born when Caesar Augustus issued a call for an empire-wide census for taxation purposes. Augustus died in the year 14, to be succeeded by Tiberius, who reigned until 37 A.D., after the death of Christ. Both Josephus and Tacitus write that Jesus was put to death by the Roman governor of Judea, Pontius Pilate, which places the Crucifixion somewhere between the years 26, when Pilate assumed the governorship of Judea, and 36/37.

It's a historical confluence of immense moral, political, and literary significance: the birth of the Roman Empire and the birth of the Christian Redeemer occur practically simultaneously. By the time Tiberius died (or was strangled) at his home on Capri—he hadn't lived in Rome for a decade—Jesus had also died, and so two great antithetical forces, the new Roman Empire and the fledgling faith of Christianity (then regarded as a Jewish sect) were now set upon each other. There could be, as it turned out, only one.

Messianic prophecies were in the air[3]; the promise of Jesus was one of many. In the midst of this theological turmoil, the destruction of the Temple was another signal event: the beginning of the Jewish Diaspora. Surely the end was nigh. Most Jews in the Empire had been content with Roman rule; the Romans were, after all, liberal in their attitude

3. As we shall see in our account of Custer's defeat at the Battle of the Little Bighorn in Chapter X, such prophecies often precipitate last stands, on one side or the other.

toward religion (having co-opted and accommodated many native religions in the conquered provinces to foster secular harmony). But a sizable minority of Jews continued to be exercised not only by theological fine points but by issues of nationalism.[4] Even though this was not in their best interests, politically speaking, it didn't matter. In the first century, with Rome expanding and Jesus preaching the new Kingdom of Heaven, there could be nothing but trouble ahead.

As the eminent British historian Paul Johnson[5] notes in *A History of the Jews*, "There is no parallel to this sequence of events in any other territory Rome rules. Why were the Jews so restless? It was not because they were a difficult, warlike, tribal and essentially backward society, like the Parthians, who gave the Romans constant trouble on the eastern fringe. . . . On the contrary, the real trouble with the Jews was that they were too advanced, too intellectually conscious to find alien rule acceptable. The Greeks had faced the same problem with Rome. They had solved it by submitting physically and taking the Romans over intellectually. Culturally, the Roman empire was Greek, especially in the East.[6] Educated people spoke and thought in Greek, and Greek modes set the standards in art and architecture, drama, music and literature.[7] So the Greeks never had any sense of cultural submission to Rome. Therein lay the difficulty with the Jews . . ."

In considering the history of the Romans, the Greeks are often regarded as an afterthought, who bequeathed their phalanxes and priapic

---

4. Richard Strauss's first great operatic success, *Salome* (with a German libretto based on Oscar Wilde's French-language play), features a number of contentious Jewish figures. One of them sings: "*Niemand kann sagen wie Gott wirkt. Seine Wege sind sehr dunkel. Es kann sein, daß die Dinge, die wir gut nennen, sehr schlimm sind, und die Dinge, die wir schlimm nennen, sehr gut sind. Wir wissen von nichts etwas . . .*" (Nobody can say how God works. His ways are very dark. It's possible that the things we call good are very bad, and the things that we call bad are actually very good. Therefore, we know from nothing . . .")

5. Who dismisses Josephus as "tendentious, contradictory and thoroughly unreliable."

6. Byzantium, which survived into the fifteenth century at Constantinople. Alexandrian Egypt was also Greek, culturally and politically, from the time of the Seleucids, through the arrival of the Romans, to the coming of Islam.

7. And, one might add, in things military.

gods to the Romans and then wandered off the pages and into obscurity. But such was not the case. The Romans had first encountered the Greeks on the Italian peninsula, where cities planted by the seafaring Greeks dotted the coastlines not only of Italy but of the entire Mediterranean. Via Alexander, the Greeks had founded Alexandria and ruled Egypt as the pharaohs of the Ptolemaic dynasty.[8] Greek was the language of the intellectuals, the tongue of poets and philosophers. If you wanted to influence the course of events during the early Roman Empire, you wrote, and thought, in Greek.

The problem was, the Greeks and the Jews did not get along. Although the two populations were roughly equal, it was the Greeks who controlled the intellectual currents of the Roman Empire, and they had little use for Hebrew language or culture: "The culture-contempt on the Greek side, and the love-hate which some educated Jews had for Greek culture, were sources of constant tension. In a way, the relationship between Greeks and Jews in antiquity was akin to the dealings between Jews and Germans in the nineteenth century and the early twentieth, though that comparison should not be pushed too far . . ."

As Johnson notes, the Greek texts were celebrations of honor and virtue; the Jewish texts were "plans of action." The Greeks tried to understand the world; the Jews wished to transform it into what they thought it should be, whether through education or revolution and, if need be, martyrdom. The Greeks had many gods, the Jews had one. It was a Jewish culture into which fit comfortably the Maccabees'[9] revolt against the Hellenistic Seleucids—an empire that stretched from Asia Minor throughout the Levant and into Mesopotamia, Persia, and Afghanistan and Pakistan. The Seleucid imperial line was descended from one of Alexander's generals, Seleucus, the commander in chief of the Companion cavalry that had destroyed the Achaemenid Persian Empire under Darius III in 330 B.C.

---

8. Which would end, fittingly, with Cleopatra, the lover of both Julius Caesar and Mark Antony.

9. Which temporarily liberated Judea in 167 B.C. This was the foundation of the Hasmonean dynasty, from which Josephus was descended. Handel wrote an oratorio, *Judas Maccabaeus,* on the subject in 1746.

It would be wrong, therefore, to see the principal cultural conflict of the time as being between the Jews and the Romans. Compared to the Jews and the Greeks, the Romans had no culture to speak of, other than militarism. The greatest example of Roman literature, Virgil's *Aeneid*, did not come along until 19 B.C., as a celebration of Rome's foundational myth and presented to Augustus. Even then, Virgil stole his main character from Homer's *Iliad*.

The Romans, true to their custom, were also religiously indifferent to the exotic deities of conquered peoples. They made room for foreign gods in their own religion when and as needed, and largely left matters of theology to the locals. Jesus, in Pilate's eyes, was merely a civil troublemaker, not the Son of God. But in the eastern Mediterranean the real conflict was between the Greeks and the Hellenized gentiles, on one side, and the monotheistic Jews who believed in the God of Israel; neither could accommodate the beliefs of the other. Both groups made up sizable portions of the population of Alexandria, the foremost city of learning in the world at that time, and their battles were fought out both in the streets and within the famous Library itself. They were also in conflict elsewhere across the province of Judea, in Hellenized cities such as Caesarea. When the Great Revolt began in 66 A.D., it began in Caesarea, spread to Jerusalem, and ended at Masada.

The Jews rose against the Greco-Romans on multiple occasions during the latter half of the first century and into the first couple of decades of the second, resulting not only in the destruction of Herod's Temple but also in the Diaspora—those who were not killed or Hellenized during and after the sack of Jerusalem by Titus were sold into slavery around the empire; the long history of the Jews as outsiders begins here. These uprisings came in the wake of millenarian prophecy, which resulted in divisive theological squabbling among various Jewish factions, not only about apocalyptic visions of the end of the world but also regarding the coming of the *Moshiach* (Messiah). If the end was near, why not fight, whether to hasten its coming, end the misery of the present, or both?

Thus, the popularity of the Book of Daniel, which exercised an enormous influence on Jewish thought of the time. For many, if not most, Jews, Judaism was destined to be a minority faith—a light unto the Gentiles, perhaps, but still reserved for the select. Jewish Jews were believers, not proselytizers, Hellenized and romanized Jews, such as Josephus, were what today we might characterize as liberal or Reform Jews, culturally Jewish but happy to live and even worship under non-Jewish rule, such as that of the Romans, who didn't much care about the Jews unless they revolted.[10] Daniel, however, promised not only the restoration of an earthly Hebraic kingdom but future immortality via the Resurrection, with the dead directed either to Heaven or Hell at the last trump, and the martyrs for the faith given their eternal reward. The Pharisees in particular seized upon the concept of the afterlife (denied by the Sadducees), in which the arc of history finally terminated in divine justice—the scriptural basis, it might be argued, for the contemporary Jewish trust in the ultimate rule of law.

The Zealots,[11] who traced their history to the year 6 A.D., and in particular to the *Sicarii,* took the Pharisaic belief in immanence a step further, into the here and now. Not only Romans but Jewish collaborators (the forerunners of the *kapos* who manned the German extermination camps during World War II) went under their knives, in order to bring about the Kingdom of Heaven. Thus, the historical Jesus was not a one-off, a malcontent, an outlier, but a figure squarely within radical Jewish movements of the time. When Pilate, the governor of Judea, consigned Jesus's fate to the whim of the Passover crowd that chose the murderer Barabbas[12] over the pacifist insurrectionist Jesus for commutation,[13] the choice was a matter of supreme indifference

---

10. Imperial Rome was called the "Kingdom of the Wicked" by the Jews. See also Anthony Burgess's 1985 novel of the same name, about the early days of Jewish Christianity, as the original disciples were eclipsed by the Hellenized Jews, such as St. Paul, and the persecuted Nazarene sect become the largest religion on the planet.

11. Josephus was no fan of the Zealots. "They copied every crime there was, and zealously reinvented for their own purpose each and every previous horror remembered in the tradition . . . each of them came to an appropriate end, and God awarded them all the penalty they deserved."

12. *Bar-Abbas*, or the "son of the father." Some biblical sources give his full name as "Jesus bar-Abbas," adding to the literary irony.

13. The "Paschal Pardon." In some quarters this is, alas, the locus of Christian anti-Semitism.

to the Romans (to their later regret) but something with theological, political, and cultural resonance to the crowd.[14] Barabbas might live to kill again, but Jesus was an existential menace—which, in historical fact, proved to be true.

The *Sicarii*, therefore, were less a threat to the Roman religion (expansionist and accommodationist) than to the political order of a minor province, far less important militarily and politically than Syria, which was on the front lines of combat and would remain so throughout the Empire, past its fall, into the Byzantine period, and up through the Crusades. The Romans could not have Jews killing other Jews—or Roman officials, especially for liberationist aims. It was Roman policy to put down any revolt, and so all aspects of Jewish rebellion, whether for religious or political reasons, had to be eliminated. The Crucifixion was just another exercise in capital punishment for non-Romans.[15]

From the Roman point of view, Herod[16] had been installed as king of the Jews in order to replace the Hasmonean dynasty with a client regent and to thus eliminate any threat of Hasmonean revanchism; Josephus himself was living proof of that, a scion of the Hebraic dynasty transformed into a Roman official in Judea. That Josephus—turned rebel, turned Roman slave, turned Roman official again—found a place at the Emperor Vespasian's side was unusual but hardly surprising; that the Empire lasted as long as it did was a testament to the wisdom of this approach of co-opting potential foes.[17]

And so Josephus was there, at the Siege of Jerusalem, to record its appalling bloodshed. Vespasian had begun the campaign to pacify restive Judea in the spring of 67 A.D., but had turned over command of

---

14. Not exclusively Jewish, as Pope Benedict XVI observed in his book *Jesus of Nazareth* (2007); in Catholic doctrine, the sole blame for Jesus's condemnation and execution is laid on the Romans, in the form of Pilate, not upon the Jews.

15. A citizen of Rome could not be crucified.

16. Herod was neither of royal blood, nor a priest; indeed, he came from Idumea, south of Judea, whose population had been forcibly converted to Judaism a century earlier.

17. Until Arminius and, a few centuries later, Odoacer.

the operation to his son, Titus, during the Year of the Four Emperors two years later, following the death of Nero—a year which saw Galba, Otho, Vitellius, and finally Vespasian himself seize the vacant throne. Titus invested the Holy City and reduced its inhabitants to a starving, helpless rabble before launching his final attack in the year 70. Jerusalem had long been protected by its formidable walls—actually three concentric walls, with the innermost Old Wall, dating from the time of David and Solomon, being the sturdiest—but the Romans knew both how to build walls and how to reduce them to rubble with their massive siege engines. With the city on the verge of not simply capture but annihilation, Josephus claims he addressed the Jewish leaders in Hebrew:

> . . . adding his own insistent appeals that they should spare their country, beat out the flames that were ready to lick round the sanctuary, and restore the sacrifices which they owed to God. There was no response from the people, cowed into reticence as they were, but the warlord heaped abuse and curses on Josephus and ended his rant by saying that he would never fear capture of the city, as it belonged to God. At this Josephus shouted back: "And of course you have kept it so immaculate for God, haven't you? No pollution of the holy place—oh no! No insults to the God you hope will fight for you, no interruption to his accustomed sacrifices! You impious wretch, if anyone starved you of your daily sustenance you would take him as an enemy—so how can you expect the God you have robbed of his ever-continuous worship to be your ally in this war? And how can you blame your own sins on the Romans? They have carefully respected our traditions throughout, and are now pressing you to restore to God the sacrifices which you, not they, have cut off. Who would not groan and lament for the city at this absurd inversion of roles—aliens and enemies rectifying the effects of your own impiety, while you, a Jew, a child of the laws, treat it with more cruel contempt than anything coming from them?"

The Jews refused to surrender to the turncoat, and so Titus, in true Roman fashion, decreed no mercy.[18] The Temple was fired and the wholesale annihilation of the mostly Jewish inhabitants began:

> As the temple burned anything found was looted and anyone caught was killed. The slaughter was massive—no pity shown for age, no regard for rank: children, old men, laymen, priests were killed indiscriminately, and war extended its grip to encompass people of every class and condition, no matter whether they were begging for mercy or trying to resist. As the fire spread ever further, the roar of the flames mingled with the groans of the dying. The height of the hill and the mass of the burning edifice made it look as if the whole city was on fire: and as for that noise, it would be impossible to imagine anything more dominant or more terrifying. There were the war cries of the Roman legions as they went into action; the yells of the rebels surrounded by fire and sword; the screams of the civilians trapped up there as they ran panic-stricken straight into the enemy and met their fate. The clamour on the hill was duplicated by the crowd in the city below, and many who were too wasted by starvation to retain the power of speech now gathered enough strength to moan and wail when they saw the temple on fire. The din was intensified by the booming echoes sent back from Peraea and the surrounding mountains.
>
> Yet more terrible than the noise was the human suffering. The temple hill, one huge mass of fire, seemed to be boiling over from its very roots, but you would also have seen rivers of blood outrunning the flames and the killed outnumbering the killers.

---

18. Titus is the main character in Mozart's last opera, *La Clemenza di Tito*, written alongside *The Magic Flute* and commissioned for the crowning of the Holy Roman Emperor, Leopold II, as the King of Bohemia in 1791. In the opera, Titus is nothing but merciful toward various plotters and mistresses who would overthrow him. He ruled Rome for only two years before his death in 81 A.D., and was succeeded by his brother, Domitian. The Empress Maria Louisa, who was in the audience in Prague for the premiere of Mozart's work, called it *una porcheria tedesca*—"German swinishness."

> Nowhere could the ground be seen for the corpses covering it, and the soldiers had to clamber over piles of bodies to pursue those still trying to escape.

While Josephus was not present at Masada—he composed his account based on reports of the Roman commanders and centurions who were there—he did have access to contemporaneous Roman reports of the battle and its aftermath. He wrote his narrative of the final struggle between the Romans and the Jews with a profound sympathy for his own people and determination to present their heroism in the best possible light. In the spirit of Jewish millenarianism and cultural heroism, that is exactly what he did. His audience may have been Roman, but his truth was Jewish, whether it was literally true or not.

And so in Josephus we read of several examples of Jewish mass suicide rather than Roman murder or enslavement. For example, in his description of the Siege of Jotapata (Yodfat) in 67 A.D., in which Josephus was fighting on the side of the rebels against the Romans, the defenders of the small hilltop fortress drew lots, then killed their comrades until there were only two left, one of whom was Josephus. At that moment, Josephus related a dream he'd had earlier, which indicated that God was now rooting for the Romans as punishment for the sins of the Jews.[19] Accordingly the two of them surrendered to an acquaintance of Josephus, who happened to be a member of Vespasian's general staff. It was the luckiest break of his life—not to mention an adumbration of the historian's account of Masada as well.

By cheating the Romans of a victory, Josephus elevated the deaths of Jews—and by extension, all oppressed peoples—above the actual circumstances of their demises into something universal, heroic, and archetypal, thus linking them directly to the Spartans at Thermopylae; losers transformed, in an act of both defeat and defiance, into winners. Better dead than the red of the Empire.

---

19. The notion of apocalyptic divine retribution for the loss of faith is a common element throughout the history of last stands. One is reminded of the beginning of the narrative epic poem *The Siege of Sziget*, in which God punishes the Hungarians and Croats for their sinful ways by loosing the Ottoman Turks upon them. See Chapter VII.

The particulars of the Siege of Masada are well known; if Josephus is essentially the only source of our information, his basic account has been both backed up and, in spots, challenged by extensive archaeological work on the site. But we know something extraordinary happened there. The Jews did not perish from starvation or from lack of water. Excavations have unearthed coins and weapons, and perhaps even shards of the lots used to decide who would be victim and who the executioner. Remains of biblical scrolls and other literature in Aramaic as well as in Hebrew and Greek testify to the literacy of the defenders and their fervent belief in their cause. But they were up against the cream of the legions, and once the Romans had managed to roll a siege-engine-cum-battering-ram up and along a man-made path erected by filling in a chasm, their fate was sealed.

Masada, in fact, was less a battle than an engineering feat that only the Romans of the time could have pulled off. As Caesar had done in the Siege of Alesia, his final triumph over the Gauls of Vercingetorix in 52 B.C., the Romans built a circumvallation wall around the base of the fortress, both to prevent external reinforcements and to keep the besieged locked up. They constructed forts and placed the legions and auxiliaries around the site. The only footpath up to the top was known colloquially as the "snake path," a single-file footway that zigzagged its way for two kilometers up the eastern side of the mountain, from the level of the Dead Sea to the top four hundred meters above.[20] There was no way the Romans could get their legions up that way. So they decided to attack from the west.

The problem was how to elevate themselves in order to roll the siege engines into place and breech the walls. The solution they devised was to design a wide ramp built on a foundation of dirt and crushed stone. It took them nine months, but when it was finished, up the ramp trundled a 90-foot siege tower equipped with a battering ram to pound the walls to pieces and the garrison into submission. At one point, the Romans

---

20. Josephus: "Anyone using this route has to proceed crabwise, transferring his weight from one foot to the other, with a fatal plunge a manifest possibility—at every point there yawns below him an abyss frightening enough to daunt the most courageous."

shot flaming arrows into the wooden parts of the Masada walls, but the wind shifted direction and briefly ignited the siege engine itself before changing direction once more, igniting the defensive walls. Seeing that reversal as a sign of divine favor, they returned to camp and planned their final attack for the morrow.

So the Almighty had cast his lot with the Romans. This was the end, and the leader of the Jewish forces, Eleazar Ben Yair, knew it. In back-to-back long speeches, undoubtedly invented by Josephus in the historical tradition of Livy and other earlier Greek and Roman historians, he urged the Jews to die by their own hands rather than fall into the clutches of the Romans, who could only bring torture, slavery, and death.

> I think it actually a favour from God that we have it in our power to die honourably as free men, unlike others who have met an unexpected defeat. We face certain capture tomorrow, but we still have the free choice of a noble death for ourselves and our loved ones. The enemy, for all their hopes of taking us alive, can no more prevent this than we can now defeat them in battle . . . we have lost all prospect of survival—that is manifestly the hand of God. . . . There is a penalty for these crimes. But let us not pay it to our mortal enemies the Romans, but to God, and at our own hands.

Speaking for Eleazar, Josephus reminds the Jews of the sack of Jerusalem and the destruction of the Temple: "Where now is that great city, the mother-city of the whole Jewish race, secure behind all those rings of walls, protected by all those guard-posts and massive towers . . . ? Where has it gone, that city of ours which was believed to have God as its founder? It has been torn up by the roots and swept away."

It was time to die.[21] First, each man killed his wife and children. Then they piled up their possessions and set fire to them. They chose ten of their number by lot to kill the survivors. Finally, they chose one of the ten to kill the other nine: "The one last survivor first checked that in the whole spread of bodies in this massive carnage there was no one still

21. See Extract 7.

needing his hand to finish them: satisfied that all were dead, he set the palace ablaze, and then with all the force of his hand drove his sword right through his body, and fell dead alongside his family."

When the Romans entered the fort, they found no resistance, just hundreds and hundreds of dead bodies. "There was none of the usual sense of triumph over an enemy: instead they could only feel a wondering admiration for the nobility of their collective decision and for the disregard of death which so many had resolutely taken to its conclusion."

Perhaps anticipating that his veracity would be challenged by future historians, Josephus[22] somewhat defensively concludes *The Jewish War* with these words: "We promised to set down a completely accurate history for the information of those who want to know the detail of how this war between Romans and Jews was fought. The success of its literary expression must be left to the judgement of its readers, but as for its accuracy, I would not hesitate to claim with confidence that throughout the whole narrative I have aimed at nothing but the truth."

One thousand, eight hundred and sixty-nine years later, another small group of embattled Jews would find themselves facing an even more hostile military machine, this one backed up by a dictator with even greater powers and far more malicious intent than the Roman emperors. While the ending would substantially be the same, how it came about would be vastly different—and what emerged from it would change the world.

"DON'T ADJUST! REVOLT AGAINST THE REALITY!"

The Warsaw Ghetto, April–May 1943

The mightiest counterpart to the Aryan is represented by the Jew. In hardly any people in the world is the instinct of

---

22. Josephus, writes Johnson, "was an example of a Jewish phenomenon which became very common over the centuries: a clever young man who, in his youth, accepted the modernity and sophistication of the day and then, late in middle age, returned to his Jewish roots. He began his writing career as a Roman apologist and ended it close to being a Jewish nationalist."

> self-preservation developed more strongly than in the so-called "chosen." Of this, the mere fact of the survival of this race may be considered the best proof. Where is the people which in the last two thousand years has been exposed to so slight changes of inner disposition, character, etc., as the Jewish people? What people, finally, has gone through greater upheavals than this one—and nevertheless issued from the mightiest catastrophes of mankind unchanged? What an infinitely tough will to live and preserve the species speaks from these facts!
>
> Adolf Hitler, *Mein Kampf*, Chapter 11

At first glance, Adolf Hitler appears to be paying the Jews a compliment, admiring their cultural and religious tenacity, the maintenance of their Jewish character throughout the Diaspora, their sheer instinct for survival in the face of the "mightiest catastrophes." To anyone else, they would seem admirable and worthy of emulation.

But not, of course, to Hitler. Throughout his public career, he had never made any secret of his antipathy for the Jews. During his time in Landsberg Prison, in which he was incarcerated for 264 days in 1924 for his role in the failed Munich Beer Hall Putsch, Hitler dictated *Mein Kampf* (*My Struggle*) to his secretary, Rudolf Hess. It is the most heartfelt testament of a born loser ever committed to paper, and certainly the most influential; in it, the aspiring *Führer* defended his role in trying to overthrow the Weimar Republic, indulged his animus toward both the Jews and the Communists by lumping them together as Bolsheviks and linking them as enemies of "Aryan" civilization, and planted the seeds of his political and social programs that would bear such poisonous fruit just twenty years later.

There are many ways in which to view Hitler, one of the most written-about figures in world history. There is Hitler the failed landscape painter, his sociopathic watercolors strangely devoid of people and all human feeling. There is Corporal Hitler the doughty war veteran and Iron Cross honoree, gassed at Ypres in 1918 by the British and temporarily blinded. There is Hitler the firebrand politician and spellbinding orator (although today we find him merely histrionic;

German speakers surely noticed his hayseed Austro-Bavarian accent, sounding like the Central European equivalent of Gomer Pyle). There is Hitler the paramilitarist, Hitler the political theoretician, Hitler the early member of the German Workers Party, which he joined in 1919 and transformed into the National Socialist German Workers Party, with himself as leader, by 1921. By 1933, he was chancellor of Germany. Six years later, the world was at war. Six years after that, he was dead.

Hitler's political program was always clear. As the Weimar Republic collapsed, two major ideological groups battled for supremacy both at the ballot box and, crucially, in the streets. They were the Communists, or "reds," and the brownshirted National Socialists, both movements of the German political left. The Communists and their offshoots looked to the new Soviet Union, the flagbearer of international Socialism, while the National Socialists sought their cultural roots in German prehistory, which they called "Aryan." In today's terms, neither could be called either "conservative" or "right-wing," although the National Socialists—who generally called themselves exactly that, *Nationalsozialisten*[23]—shared some nationalist traits with the real conservatives, the landed aristocracy of the *Junkers* (*jung Herr*, or young nobleman), the group from which Hitler's deadliest domestic enemies would eventually emerge.[24]

For Hitler, the Jews and the Communists were almost interchangeable. There were many Jews in the front ranks of the early Bolsheviks—Trotsky, Sverdlov, Zinoviev; even Lenin had a Jewish great-grandfather,

---

23. The term *Nazi*—an abbreviation of *Nationalsozialisten*—was largely a term invented by the party's opponents, both a cognate to the term *Sozi* (a shortening of *Sozialdemokrat*—and a colloquial play on the Christian name *Ignaz*, a Bavarianism best translated as "bumpkin." The National Socialists rarely referred to themselves as "Nazis." The promiscuous use of the word today is ahistorical and inaccurate.

24. Our contemporary notions of "right" and "left" are not particularly useful in analyzing the politics of post–World War I Germany. As in Fascist Italy, the industrialists and the Prussians had no problem making common cause with various forms of state socialism. Bismarck, the Prussian under whom Germany was united, was by our measure a socialist. Hitler, who despised the representative democracy of the Weimar Republic, was never an ally of Britain or the United States, but he was an ally of the Soviet Union.

Moshko Blank, who had converted to Russian Orthodoxy in 1844—so the opportunity to tar the Jews with the sins of the Bolsheviks was too easy to pass up. After all, even Karl Marx was of Jewish origin, descended from a long line of rabbis on both sides of his family; like many German Jews of the nineteenth century, Marx's father had converted to Lutheranism to improve his prospects, changing his first name from Herschel to Heinrich. Marx himself addressed religion and Jewishness in his 1843 materialist tract, *Zur Judenfrage* (*On the Jewish Question*).

Hitler saw Jewish influence everywhere. The Jews were the hidden forces behind all of society's ills, a rootless, cosmopolitan population of cultural appropriators. He believed wholeheartedly in the tsarist forgery, *The Protocols of the Elders of Zion,* which portrayed the Jews as incorrigible schemers against temporal authority and the architects of a vast conspiracy to control the world.[25] "If, with the help of his Marxist creed, the Jew is victorious over the other peoples of the world," wrote Hitler in *Mein Kampf,* "his crown will be the funeral wreath of humanity and this planet will, as it did thousands of years ago, move through the ether devoid of men."

But Hitler's animus against the Jews ran deeper, into outright, irrational, and all-consuming loathing. Naturally, there was a sexual component:

> With satanic joy in his face, the black-haired Jewish youth lurks in wait for the unsuspecting girl whom he defiles with his blood, thus stealing her from her people. With every means he tries to destroy the racial foundations of the people he has set out to subjugate. Just as he himself systematically ruins women and girls, he does not shrink back from pulling down the blood barriers for others, even on a large scale. It was and it is Jews who bring the Negroes into the Rhineland, always with the same secret thought and clear aim of ruining the hated white race by the necessarily resulting bastardization, throwing it down from its cultural and political height, and himself rising to be its master.

25. The *Protocols* were exposed in 1921 as a forgery, largely plagiarized from other sources (one of them satirical).

> For a racially pure people which is conscious of its blood can never be enslaved by the Jew. In this world he will forever be master over bastards and bastards alone.
>
> And so he tries systematically to lower the racial level by a continuous poisoning of individuals.
>
> And in politics he begins to replace the idea of democracy by the dictatorship of the proletariat.
>
> In the organized mass of Marxism he has found the weapon which lets him dispense with democracy and in its stead allows him to subjugate and govern the peoples with a dictatorial and brutal fist.

This is thoroughly nasty stuff, made all the nastier by its contemporary recrudescence. But there is no way to sugarcoat it: identity politics was the essence of National Socialism as articulated by the *Führer* and as put into practice by the National Socialist German Workers Party upon their seizure of power—democratically, to be sure—in 1933. Whereas the Romans had largely been indifferent to the Jews as a race (as the term was used at that time), took little or no interest in their One God, and only intervened when there was a military threat to the Empire, the National Socialists made Jew-hatred a principal tenet of their new and terrible paganism.[26]

There is no disputing the centrality of anti-Semitism in the Nazi cosmology. From the Nuremberg Laws to beginnings of the continuous deportations to the east, the course of Jewish persecution in the *NS-Staat* (National-Socialist State, as it was frequently termed by Germans themselves) was clear. The railroads from the principal cities of the Reich ran all the way to the end of the lines, at Auschwitz, Treblinka, Sobibor.[27]

---

26. Although the National Socialists would occasionally pay some lip service to "God," they viewed Christians as little better than Jews, viewing the followers of the Jew Jesus as a very large and successful sect of Judaism. Many pastors and priests died in the death camps.

27. The main *Vernichtungsläger*, or extermination camps. Others, such as Buchenwald, not far from the capital city of German culture, Weimar, contained a large number of Soviet prisoners of war, as well as Jews and other political prisoners. The effect, however, was the same: some 43,000 people died at Buchenwald, with another 10,000 shipped off to the death camps.

In each city, the Jews were at first confined to their quarters—the Jewish ghettoes—organized and systematically stripped of their belongings and their rights by Germans acting through the agencies of the Jewish Councils, the *Judenräte*.[28] Later, as the German fortunes of war waned, particularly after the failure of Operation Barbarossa at the end of 1941 and the long rollback of Hitler's assault on the Soviet Union throughout 1942, the pace of deportations from the ghettoes to the death camps increased. If Hitler could not take out his maniacal ire on the Bolsheviks—who, after all and much to his surprise, could fight back—then he would take it out on the near-helpless Jews, the vast majority of whom lived in Poland and the Soviet Union.[29]

And so we come to Warsaw at the beginning of 1943, a city Hitler particularly loathed, for multiple psychological reasons. For one thing, Hitler, like many Germans, despised the Poles as *Untermenschen*, Slavs occupying valuable *Lebensraum* to the east and fit only for slavery to their Teutonic masters. For another, the largest Jewish community in Europe (3.5 million people) resided in Poland, with some settlements dating back to the Middle Ages, their inhabitants eking out a living in small *shtetlekh* (Yiddish for "villages") as traders and merchants. Poland has the geographic and historical misfortune of being sandwiched between Germany and Russia, and down the centuries its periodic bouts of independence were more than offset by its domination by one or the other. In Hitler's eyes, Poland offered ripe lands for settlement for an expansionist Reich, but was burdened with an enormous Jewish population that needed to be removed by any means necessary.

---

28. The United States Holocaust Memorial Museum describes them in this way: "These Jewish municipal administrations were required to ensure that Nazi orders and regulations were implemented. Jewish council members also sought to provide basic community services for ghettoized Jewish populations. Forced to implement Nazi policy, the Jewish councils remain a controversial and delicate subject. Jewish council chairmen had to decide whether to comply or refuse to comply with German demands to, for example, list names of Jews for deportation."

29. The number of German Jews killed in the Holocaust is estimated at between 160,000 and 180,000. Between 1933 and 1939, approximately 304,000 German Jews had already fled the country—more than half the original population of about 522,000.

On April 19, 1943, on the eve of Passover, the German authorities under Hans Frank,[30] Hitler's personal lawyer and the Governor-General of Poland, ordered the emptying of what was left of the Warsaw Ghetto and the immediate deportation of the roughly 60,000 Jews who were still there. Most of the Jews had already been shipped off to the death camps, including some 265,000 dispatched to Treblinka and thousands more simply shot or sent to forced-labor camps elsewhere, to be worked to death.

By this point, it was impossible for the remaining Jews not to know what was happening in the outside world (20,000 of the Jews still in the ghetto were in hiding, their presence unknown to the Germans). Reports had filtered back all over Europe: that when the transport wagons arrived, those deported would never be seen again. Sometimes Jews themselves had helped the Germans with the deportations while acting in reasonable—or unreasonable—self-interest.[31]

Accordingly, by mid-1942 the Warsaw Jews had organized themselves into two paramilitary units, the Jewish Combat Organization and

---

30. At Hitler's request, Frank was authorized to investigate the ethnic origins of his grandmother, Maria Schicklgruber, who had been a *shabbos goy* in the prosperous Jewish home of the Frankenberger family in Graz when she became pregnant and was sent home. Frank advised Hitler that Maria had very likely been impregnated by one of the Frankenbergers, but modern scholars dismiss this and argue it's far more likely that Alois Schicklgruber, Hitler's father, was most likely the product of Austrian hill-country incest. Maria eventually married Johann Hiedler, whose name was recorded as "Hitler" (the pronunciation can be very similar, depending on the dialect), and the rest is history.

31. The terrible moral dilemma was illustrated by the case of *The Attorney-General of the Government of Israel v. Malchiel Gruenwald* in Israel in 1955. Gruenwald, a Hungarian Jew who had survived the Holocaust and who was living in Israel, accused Rezső (Rudolf) Kasztner, a fellow Hungarian Jew, of having collaborated in July 1944 with Adolf Eichmann and SS officer Kurt Becher in Budapest in order to save some 1,700 friends and members of his own family at the expense of thousands of others, who were sent to the camps. The Israeli government sued Gruenwald on Kasztner's behalf. Gruenwald was acquitted of libel at trial—Kasztner, one of the judges wrote, had "sold his soul to the devil"—and Kasztner was assassinated in 1957. Shortly thereafter, the Israeli Supreme Court overturned the original verdict, preferring to see Kasztner as a man who did the best he could in an impossible situation.

the Jewish Military Union; at first adversarial, they eventually began to work together. Their combined numbers totaled about 750 fighting men, which at the height of the conflict swelled to about 1,500. Their weapons came from members of the Christian Polish underground, who had been putting up a separate, heroic resistance against the Germans practically from the time of the initial invasion in 1939. The Polish Resistance eventually culminated in its own Warsaw Uprising in the summer of 1944, while the Wehrmacht was busy trying to hold back Red Army on the outskirts of Warsaw. But as the Poles rose to attack the retreating Germans, the Russians halted their advance, giving the Germans time to temporarily regroup, crush the last vestiges of the Polish resistance, and to raze the city.

That, however, was still in the future as the Warsaw Jews planned their defense of the Ghetto. Of course, they knew it was hopeless. With the Germans still in full control of the city, their living conditions nearly impossible, their sources of armaments uncertain, and their men largely untrained, they stood no chance against the Wehrmacht. But they didn't care. Like the Jews at Masada, they were going to die to the last man if need be; unlike the Jews at Masada, they were going to take as many Germans with them as they could.

Their leader was Mordechai Anielewicz, just 24 years old but actively engaged in the resistance from the moment of the German invasion. Roman-style, the Germans had begun the circumvallation of the Ghetto in 1940, segregating it from the rest of the city and confining the Jews in cramped quarters to let disease and starvation do their dirty work for them.[32] Armed basically with hand grenades, Molotov cocktails, and pistols (there were few rifles and no heavy weapons, such as mortars or bazookas), the Jews created a system of underground bunkers

32. Something similar happened in far-off Shanghai, where between 1941 and 1945 the Germans leaned on their Japanese allies to herd the city's sizable Jewish population, many of them refugees from the Soviet Union, into the restricted Shanghai Ghetto, where they shared living quarters with the Chinese. The Japanese, however, were uninterested in killing the Jews or turning them over to the Germans. Among the "Shanghai Jews" who eventually came to America are Harvard professor Laurence Tribe, Hollywood producer Mike Medavoy, and concert pianist Misha Dichter.

in which the air was so close, one man recalled, that you couldn't light a candle for lack of oxygen.

The first battle came on January 18, 1943, as the Germans tried to resume deportations. Jewish fighters infiltrated a column of Jews being marched away for "resettlement" and they attacked the German guards. In the melee, some of the prisoners got away but most of the warriors were killed; Anielewicz managed to escape. It was a minor victory—but a huge moral one.

In the German language, in part because of the determinism of its grammatical structure, what should not be possible therefore *will* not be possible. If it is against the law, it will not happen. If it is permitted, then nothing untoward can occur. To this day, Germans will drive their fast cars on the autobahn at unlimited speeds straight into a fogbank because there are no signs to forbid them from doing so. Their faith in the letter of the law is touching, but too often the result is an 80-car pileup with multiple fatalities. At first, many of the German Jews subscribed to that notion, refusing to credit Hitler's animus against them, relying on their service to the German army during the First World War; in their minds, they were every bit as "German" as the ethnic Germans. It took *Kristallnacht* and the Nuremberg Laws to finally disabuse them of that fatal delusion.

In the time of Caesar and Augustus, the reputation of the Germans had been that they were brave but undisciplined warriors; like the Gauls, they were prone to cut and run at the first sign of trouble. On the battlefield they lacked a supreme commander, and even when they had one, such as Vercingetorix, they still ran from a reversal of fortune, especially once their commanders fell. But first under Bismarck and the Prussians and later under the National Socialists—who sought explicitly to evoke ancient Rome with their massed ranks of *Soldaten* marching under an imperial eagle—they had learned how to fight. In fact, they had learned it so well, and had been rewarded with such easy victories over the exhausted French in May 1940 and the other victims of the *Blitzkrieg*, that they had almost forgotten how to lose.

The Eastern Front had rudely reminded them of human fallibility. But in that case, they were up against a Red Army they had drastically underestimated, a foe capable of absorbing maximum casualties thanks to its nearly limitless manpower. The Soviets' tactical retreat along the broad front of Operation Barbarossa—shades of Hannibal at Cannae, but on a gigantic scale—sucked the three invading Army Groups into the maw of Mother Russia in winter; suddenly the Germans felt a great affinity with Napoleon, whose own ill-advised attack on Russia had been defeated by General Winter in 1812. But to take casualties from a Jewish rabble destined for Treblinka and annihilation? It was impossible.

There was a lull as the Germans, occupied across the Eastern Front, decided how best to make Warsaw *Judenrein*. The first indication came on April 16, when a Gestapo lieutenant called a meeting with the Warsaw *Judenrat* to discuss the health of the Ghetto children and their need for fresh air (a particular German obsession). Why not build a playground in the courtyard of the *Judenrat*? With Passover coming up, he'd even throw in some *matzos*.

It was a trap. Two days later, the Germans mobilized at 2 a.m. and cordoned off the Ghetto at six o'clock in the morning. Anielewicz promised his men a guerilla war to the death. The Battle of the Warsaw Ghetto was underway. The Germans made little headway on the nineteenth, but late that evening the newly arrived German commander, SS general Jürgen Stroop, got a telephone call from none other than Heinrich Himmler, who informed Stroop that, as April 20 was Hitler's birthday, he expected a *Grossaktion*[33] in celebration, and thus an expeditious end to the Jewish problem in Warsaw.

In fact, the battle raged for nearly a month. The Germans turned their artillery on the houses and set them alight with flame throwers. They tunneled under buildings to destroy the bunkers; for their part, the Jews moved underground, through the sewer systems that were still connected to the city beyond the Ghetto, to bring in what information and supplies they could. The Germans killed the resistance fighters wherever they found them. Despite the heroism, however, it was just a matter of time.

---

33. "*Aktion*," in German, does not simply mean "action" but violent action; the American student radicals of the 1960s adopted it in their phrase, "direct action."

In his last letter, Anielewicz wrote, "The most difficult struggle of all is the one within ourselves. Let us not get accustomed and adjusted to these conditions. The one who adjusts ceases to discriminate between good and evil. He becomes a slave in body and soul. Whatever may happen to you, remember always: Don't adjust! Revolt against the reality! Peace go with you, my friend! The dream of my life has risen to become fact."

Anielewicz was killed in action on May 8, 1943, buried in the rubble of his headquarters at 18 Mila Street, where his bunker was located. The Germans had finally located the lair of their tormentor and were drilling through the earthen roof, dropping grenades below. When Anielewicz and his companions refused to come out, the Germans began piping in gas. One of his men recommended that, like the Jews at Masada, they should kill themselves. Anielewicz argued against it. Author Dan Kurzman in *The Bravest Battle* (Da Capo Press, 2009) writes:

> As at Masada, where 2000 years earlier a group of Jews decided to kill themselves rather than surrender to the Romans, most of the 120 fighters at Mila 18 chose the same solution, though it was not imposed on anyone. The more than eighty civilians who remained would either surrender or die of asphyxiation in the bunker.

No one is sure what really happened in the end. We don't know whether Anielewicz and his girlfriend, Mira Fuchrer, shot themselves or died of the poison gas. Ironically, one of the Jewish commandos discovered an escape route that no one had known existed and got away. But it was too late.

On May 16, with the resistance extinguished, General Stroop ordered the city's main synagogue, built in 1877, demolished. As the engineers laid the charges, the German statisticians totaled up the numbers: 56,065 Jews killed or captured since the uprising began. Around 8:15 p.m., Stroop pressed the detonator button, and the synagogue vanished. That evening, he sent a cable to his superiors in Krakow: "The former Jewish quarter of Warsaw no longer exists."

Two years later, in another underground bunker, Adolf Hitler lay dead as well, shot by his own hand, preferring death[34] to capture by the enraged soldiers of the Red Army. Perhaps he would have found it (fleetingly) ironic that both he and the Jewish fighters should have chosen the same setting for the same end—he for reasons of fear and cowardice, they for their nation and their faith. Hitler's obsession with the Bolsheviks had led him first to make a sham alliance with them, via the Molotov-Ribbentrop Pact of 1939, and then to launch a surprise attack on them less than two years later. And his obsession with the Jews turned not only into the Holocaust but also an *auto-da-fé* for himself and Germany as well. Hatred, it seems, has consequences for everybody. The last stands at both Masada and Mila Street eventually spelled doom for both the empires that afflicted them.

Jürgen Stroop was captured in Germany at the end of the war, tried and convicted by the Allies of murdering American prisoners of war, and then extradited to Poland, where in 1952 he was convicted of crimes against humanity and hanged. Today, Mila Street is not only Anielewicz's grave but a memorial to the resistance fighters who died rather than submit.

From the arid hilltop of Masada to the fetid sewers of the Mila Street bunker, the long journey of the Jewish people had taken many a tragic turn. But on May 14, 1948, just five years later, the State of Israel was born. The Romans are gone, Hitler is gone, the National Socialists are gone—but Jews are free to worship in the Nożyk Synagogue, and once again, Masada is in Jewish hands.

Perhaps this is not the sweetest revenge the Jews have taken on their former tormentors. One of the strongest weapons in the Jewish arsenal has been humor, the surgical use of ridicule—not from a distance, either, but up close, personal, and in your face. The great Jewish comics and filmmakers, born in the first half of the twentieth century, did not flinch when turning even the enormity of the Holocaust, Hitler, and National Socialism to their advantage. In his 1967 comedy *The Producers*, Mel Brooks (b. 1926) put a *Führer*-like figure on stage in the middle of a mock-musical, *Springtime for Hitler*. He lampooned the Nazis again in 1983 with his remake of Ernst Lubitsch's *To Be or Not to Be* (Lubitsch was also Jewish), about an acting troupe in prewar Warsaw planning

34. See Chapter XII.

a production of *Hamlet* on the eve of the occupation. Amazingly, Lubitsch's original was made in 1941 and released early the following year.

In 1962, the musical *A Funny Thing Happened on the Way to the Forum* appeared on Broadway and became a film four years later under the direction of Richard Donner. With both music and lyrics by Stephen Sondheim, the show takes aim at Rome under the Emperor Nero, pitting slaves such as Pseudolus (Zero Mostel, the pride of New York's Yiddish theater) and Hysterium (Jack Gilford) against the patrician Senex and a Roman general, Miles Gloriosus, on behalf of Senex's dim-witted son, Hero (played by a very young Michael Crawford[35]). Few can miss the resonance.

The most audacious confrontation between Jews and their German antagonists came in Stanley Kubrick's 1964 blackest of black comedies, *Dr. Strangelove.* The Jewish Kubrick co-wrote, produced, and directed the film, which took a gimlet-eyed look at nuclear Armageddon and cast the brilliant British comic actor Peter Sellers in three roles: as the balding American president, Merkin Muffley[36]; as the stiff-upper-lipped British officer, Group Captain Mandrake; and as the unrepentant Nazi scientist, Dr. Strangelove. Sellers, whose mother was Jewish, brought an especial gusto to Strangelove (formerly Dr. Merkwürdigliebe—"He changed it when he became a citizen"), whose paralyzed right arm and prosthetic hand periodically shoot up in an uncontrollable Nazi salute, maniacally cackling even as the world goes up in flames.

It is doubtful today that the culture of victimhood would tolerate such shenanigans; almost everything now is too serious for comedy. But, more than anybody, the Jews of the war generation understood that it is precisely because some things are so horrible that they should not be joked about that they *must* be joked about, lest we all go mad.[37] It doesn't matter, from Josephus to the present, whether the stories really happened. What matters is that they are true.

---

35. Who two decades later created the role of the Phantom of the Opera for Andrew Lloyd Webber.

36. The double double-entendre was entirely intentional.

37. As my friend James Levine, the greatest conductor in the history of the Metropolitan Opera, once said to me in Salzburg: "There are some Jews who won't go to Germany. I'm one of the ones who *has* to go to Germany."

CHAPTER IV

"WE HAVE COME TO RUE YOUR PROWESS, ROLAND!"

THE BATTLE OF RONCEVAUX PASS AND *LA CHANSON DE ROLAND* (778/1115)

In John Ford's classic western *The Man Who Shot Liberty Valance*, a distinguished American politician named Ransom Stoddard, played by Jimmy Stewart, is asked by a group of newspapermen to recount the story of how the frontier town of Shinbone was saved 25 years earlier from the predations of the outlaw Liberty Valance. Stoddard—a former governor, senator, and ambassador to the Court of St. James, now being tipped for vice president—suddenly confesses that he didn't fire the shot that killed the notorious gunslinger, as everyone believed he had. Rather it was his friend Tom Doniphon, a local rancher who was also his rival for Stoddard's fiancée's hand, who shot Valance from the shadows because he knew the mild-mannered lawyer would have no chance against a ruthless killer.

With the interview that could destroy Stoddard's political career completed, one of the reporters stands, recounts Stoddard's exemplary career—and then tears up his notes. "You're not going to use the story, Mr. Scott?" asks Stoddard. "No, sir," replies Scott. "This is the West, sir: when the legend becomes fact, print the legend."

Among the most famous Western last stands in history—that of the brave Christian knight Roland and his men at the Roncevaux Pass—is one that is entirely untrue in its most important particular. Granted, it occurred during Charlemagne's return from his campaign against the

Moors in Spain, and it seems likely that the emperor's rear guard, which included a historically obscure knight named Roland, was indeed wiped out in 778 A.D. during an ambush in the Pyrenees, most likely by Basque tribesmen angered over the destruction of their city of Pamplona. And yet, this relative footnote to medieval history was transformed some three centuries later (c. 1040–1115) into one of the cornerstones of French literature and, as the Crusades were getting underway, into the French national epic and the foundational artistic treatment of the conflict between Islam and Christianity. The Basque *Gascones* (or *Wascones*) became the Saracens, thus blending the historical setting of the battle with the fervor of European Christianity after Pope Urban II's rousing call at Clermont on November 27, 1095, to assist the Eastern Roman Empire at Constantinople in its battle against the Seljuk Turks, to protect the Christian pilgrims on their way to Jerusalem, and to reclaim the Holy Land for Christendom.

If Helen's was the face that launched a thousand ships, Urban's speech, which has come down to us in multiple versions, was the event that set in motion one of the most extraordinary logistical and military feats in history. A warring collection of various European dukes and princelings raised and transported an army from modern-day France and Germany, marched or sailed it across the known world, and, in just three years, conquered Jerusalem and established Crusader states in the Levant that would survive for almost two hundred years. The high-water mark of the Church Militant, the Crusades forged the nation-states of Europe, stymied Islamic expansionism for nearly four hundred years, and drew the rough, if often contested, borders between Christendom and the *ummah* to this day.

A taste of Urban's speech, in the transcription of one Robert the Monk[1]:

> Oh, race of Franks, race from across the mountains, race chosen and beloved by God as shines forth in very many of your works set apart from all nations by the situation of your country, as well as by your Catholic faith and the honor of the holy church! To you our discourse is addressed and for you our exhortation is

---

1. Five different versions of the speech, all of them written down after the fact, have survived. They differ widely.

intended. We wish you to know what a grievous cause has led us to your country, what peril threatening you and all the faithful has brought us. From the confines of Jerusalem and the city of Constantinople a horrible tale has gone forth and very frequently has been brought to our ears, namely, that a race from the kingdom of the Persians, an accursed race, a race utterly alienated from God, a generation forsooth which has not directed its heart and has not entrusted its spirit to God, has invaded the lands of those Christians and has depopulated them by the sword, pillage and fire; it has led away a part of the captives into its own country, and a part it has destroyed by cruel tortures; it has either entirely destroyed the churches of God or appropriated them for the rites of its own religion. They destroy the altars, after having defiled them with their uncleanness. They circumcise the Christians, and the blood of the circumcision they either spread upon the altars or pour into the vases of the baptismal font. When they wish to torture people by a base death, they perforate their navels, and dragging forth the extremity of the intestines, bind it to a stake; then with flogging they lead the victim around until the viscera having gushed forth the victim falls prostrate upon the ground. Others they bind to a post and pierce with arrows. Others they compel to extend their necks and then, attacking them with naked swords, attempt to cut through the neck with a single blow. What shall I say of the abominable rape of the women? To speak of it is worse than to be silent. The kingdom of the Greeks is now dismembered by them and deprived of territory so vast in extent that it cannot be traversed in a march of two months. On whom therefore is the labor of avenging these wrongs and of recovering this territory incumbent, if not upon you? You, upon whom above other nations God has conferred remarkable glory in arms, great courage, bodily activity, and strength to humble the hairy scalp of those who resist you. Let the deeds of your ancestors move you and incite your minds to manly achievements . . . [2]

---

2. See Extract 8.

Few saw this coming. As the English historian Steven Runciman notes in the opening section of his magisterial three-volume *A History of the Crusades*, despite the ongoing battles between the Byzantines, the Persians, and, later, the Fatamid Arabs who had conquered Jerusalem, "in the middle of the eleventh century the lot of the Christians in Palestine had seldom been so pleasant. The Moslem authorities were lenient; the [Byzantine] Emperor was watchful of their interest. Trade was prospering and increasing with the Christian countries overseas. And never before had Jerusalem enjoyed so plentifully the sympathy and the wealth that were brought to it by pilgrims from the West."

This state of affairs was due largely to Byzantine military and cultural potency, with the imperial capital of Constantinople, the seat of the Eastern Roman Empire, the most important city of the West. But succession troubles—the Achilles's heel of monarchies—were hollowing out the empire, and it began shedding pieces of territory not only to Islam but to lackland Normans invading from the north as well. The Normans, the bastard sons of the Vikings, had conquered much of Italy and wrested back Sicily from Muslim hands. Worse, there was pressure from the east, from the Turks, who had been converted to Islam in the tenth century and conquered much of central Asia and Persia, which worried both Byzantines and Arabs.

In 1071, the Byzantine emperor Romanus Diogenes led a polyglot army eastward to attempt the re-conquest of Christian Armenia from the Turks.[3] On the road to Manzikert, he was ambushed by the brilliant Seljuk Turkish commander, Alp Arslan. Romanus's mercenaries, which included Turks, Franks, and Normans, deserted him. The Byzantines were decisively defeated, and the wounded Romanus was taken prisoner. Ransomed by the Byzantines, he was soon enough deposed, blinded, and exiled to the island of Proti in the Sea of Marmara near Constantinople, where he died.

Manzikert was the effective end of Byzantine regional hegemony; their great capital city was now ripe for conquest, whether from the west or the east. The Turks began the process of rolling back the Byzantines

---

3. Throughout nearly a millennium of Muslim rule, the Armenians had stayed resolutely Christian.

from Asia Minor, thus creating the territorial foundation of modern Turkey, which meant the Byzantines could no longer protect the Christians of the Holy Land. Pilgrims traversing Anatolia, the seat of early Christianity, who had once enjoyed relatively free passage, found themselves under assault, caught in the struggle among Byzantines, Turks, and Fatamid Egyptian Muslims.

This, then, was the geopolitical context of Urban's mighty speech just 24 years later. And yet the call to militancy posed a problem for the faithful. As Runciman put it, "The Christian citizen has a fundamental problem to face: is he entitled to fight for his country? His religion is a religion of peace; and war means slaughter and destruction. The earlier Christian Fathers had no doubts. To them a war was wholesale murder. But after the triumph of the Cross, after the Empire had become Christendom, ought not its citizens to be ready to take arms for its welfare?"[4]

The answer was yes, and thus a thousand years of Western military inventiveness and, later, supremacy was born. The Byzantines regarded warfare as a necessary evil and a poor substitute for diplomacy, but the rude men of Europe who responded to the pope's call almost immediately took on the fervid hallmarks of the Muslim holy warriors. After all, as far back as the fifth century, St. Augustine had outlined the conditions for a Christian "just war" in *The City of God.* "They who have waged war in obedience to the divine command, or in conformity with His laws, have represented in their persons the public justice or the wisdom of government, and in this capacity have put to death wicked men; such persons have by no means violated the commandment, 'Thou shalt not kill.'"

And so the French-born Urban, having finally won his struggle in Rome against the antipope Clement III with the help of King Henry IV, was visited at the Council of Piacenza in March of 1095 by a Byzantine ambassador, requesting aid from the Christian West in repelling the advance of the Turks into the historically Christian lands of Anatolia. At the Council of Clermont that November, therefore, he issued his public call to action. A chance for adventure, plunder, and lands of one's own,

---

4. A dilemma brilliantly elaborated upon by Tom Holland in his 2019 book, *Dominion.*

plus a complete remission of sins if you were killed in battle—what was not to like?

Even at the reserve of nearly a millennium, it is impossible to overstate the effect the pope's words had on the assembled listeners. The Europe that Charlemagne (a Frankish German, whose mother tongue was German, despite his place in French history[5]) forged from the ruins of Rome had become the Holy Roman Empire[6]; indeed Charlemagne himself had been crowned "Emperor of the Romans" by Pope Leo III in the year 800. At the same time, the fledgling French and Spanish languages were beginning their evolution from Latin into their modern counterparts, often through the medium of popular literature derived from songs and legends. In France, these took the form of the *chansons de geste*—"songs of heroic deeds"—which themselves had evolved from the oral traditions of the *jongleurs* and then codified in written form; in Spain, the outstanding example of the form is the twelfth-century *The Poem of the Cid,* which deals directly with the *Reconquista* of Spain from the Muslims as well. These texts (generally sung to music) in turn became the foundational texts of the French and Spanish states, shaping their national characters.[7]

The Song of Roland, the first surviving work written in Old French,

---

5. Even today, radical revanchist Muslims refer to Westerners collectively as "Franks."

6. Voltaire famously and derisively observed that the kingdom was neither holy, Roman, nor an empire, but that is not true. At a time when there were still pagan tribes in Europe, it was Christian; it was founded—literally, as in the case of Charlemagne's capital of Aachen/Aix-la-Chapelle—on Roman towns; and it was indeed an empire, lasting in one form or another until its formal dissolution in 1806. That was two years after Napoleon became emperor of the French, wearing a gold laurel wreath on his head and holding aloft a replica of Charlemagne's crown at his anointment by Pope Pius VII, thus explicitly inheriting the mantle of both the Roman emperors and Charlemagne. The ceremony was held at the Cathedral of Notre-Dame in Paris.

7. According to *Roland* scholar and translator Gerard J. Brault, "Writing about 1125, William of Malmesbury relates that a *cantilena Rolandi* was sung before the Battle of Hastings [1066] to incite William the Conqueror's men to emulate the French hero. It is not certain that this work was the *Song of Roland*. However, other evidence also suggests that the poem had the power to stir up combatants and was composed with the warrior class in mind."

is the best-known segment of the so-called Carolingian Cycle of literature revolving around Charlemagne, a literary work known as "the Matter of France." (There are also "Matters" of Britain—the Arthurian tales—and of classical Rome, thus emphasizing the unity of European history.) Like the other *chansons*, and as its name implies, it was originally sung by a *jongleur*, accompanied on a medieval fiddle called a *vielle*. As we might say today, it was a smash hit, almost immediately becoming part of the French patrimony, where it remained for centuries. Indeed, it became required reading in French schools following the Franco-Prussian War (which France lost), to much *esprit de corps* but little martial avail.

The plot of this epic is simple but effective: the Breton knight Roland, together with his best friend, Oliver (to whose fair sister, Alda, Roland is engaged), a group of ten other noble Companions, and 20,000 Frankish warriors are assigned to bring up the rear as Charlemagne—*Karl der Grosse* to the Germans—conducts his main force back to Aix from his wars against the Umayyad Muslims occupying Spain.[8] Betrayed by the evil Ganelon, Roland's stepfather, they are ambushed by a Muslim force headed by King Marsile. Roland, Oliver, and the fighting Bishop Turpin hold out to the end, but it's no use: they're overwhelmed.

Charlemagne returns with aid, but too late. Marsile, who has lost his right hand in combat with Roland, is routed and dies of his wound, but not before he summons help from the Emir Baligant of Babylon. In a *battle royale*, Baligant is personally killed by Charlemagne, who captures Saragossa and returns to Aix with Bramimonde, Marsile's widow, who converts to the True Faith. Ganelon is tried for treason and is almost acquitted—he pleads self-defense, since Roland had originally suggested him as leader of the rear guard, which he felt was

---

8. Although the *Reconquista* was not completed until 1492, it was well underway by the ninth century, when the most significant remaining Muslim stronghold was centered on the modern city of Saragossa near the Ebro River, which at the time of Hannibal had been the border between the Carthaginians and the Romans. The Ebro was also a crucial battleground during the Spanish Civil War of the twentieth century. The myth of a prolonged and beneficent Muslim "golden age" in Spain is exactly that.

a trap—when the issue is decided via trial by combat. An unprepossessing knight, Thierry, challenges Ganelon's henchman, the ferocious Pinabel, to a duel, in which Pinabel is miraculously killed. The guilty Ganelon is executed by quartering, his four limbs tied to horses and his body yanked apart. Thirty members of his family are hanged.

What makes *La Chanson de Roland* more than simply a revenge tale, however, is the moral complexity at its center: for, truth to tell, Roland is not a particularly attractive hero. Through his pride and stubbornness, he gets himself and all his men killed thanks to his adamant refusal to sound his famous horn, the *oliphant*, to summon help from Charlemagne, insisting that to call for assistance would be tantamount to cowardice. Not only does he prefer death before dishonor, he wills it. Roland would rather rely on his noble steed, Veillantif, and his trusty sword, Durendal, to kill as many Muslims as he can, than evince fear. His friend Oliver begs him to call for help, but not until it's too late does Roland finally relent, sounding the *oliphant* so lustily that is bursts a vein in his head, and he dies, surrounded by the bodies of his friends.[9]

Told that the pagans are on their way to attack him, Roland seems to welcome the coming fight. In *laisse* (stanza) 81, we read:

The noise is great and the French heard it.
Oliver said: "Companion, sir, I believe
We may have a battle with the Saracens on our hands."
Roland replies: "May God grant it to us!
We must make a stand here for our king:
One must suffer hardships for one's lord
And endure great heat and great cold,
One must also lose hide and hair.
Now let each see to it that he employ great blows,
So that no taunting song be sung about us!

---

9. In this ending, as we shall see, Roland was not unlike George Armstrong Custer. And in his stubborn refusal to summon help, he is the spiritual father of General Gordon at Khartoum—as we also shall see.

Pagans are in the wrong and Christians are in the right.
I shall never be cited as a bad example."[10]

—translation by Gerard J. Brault

As the Saracens approach, Turpin, the archbishop of Rheims, promises them martyrdom in the sight of God should they die in battle, blesses them, and absolves them of their sins. Turpin is the archetype of the warrior monk,[11] as extreme as Roland in his desire for glory and his loathing of cowardice. As it becomes clear to the French troops just how dire their situation is, they implore the bishop to summon help, but he sides with Roland: "My lord barons, don't harbor base thoughts! For God's sake I beg you not to flee, so that no worthy individual sing bad songs about it. It is much better that we should die fighting."

Both Franks and Musselmen understand that this is an existential fight to the death, and that no quarter will be given. As the unknown poet observes, "Anyone who knows no prisoners will ever be taken puts up a stout resistance in such a battle. That is why the Franks are fierce as lions." The French give a good account of themselves, but at last it becomes clear even to Roland that either they recall Charlemagne to the field or they die. In *laisse* 128, he turns to Oliver:

Count Roland sees the great slaughter of his men.
He calls his companion Oliver:
"Dear sir, dear comrade, in God's name, what do you make of this?
You see so many good knights lying on the ground!
Sweet France, the fair, is to be pitied, how impoverished she is now of such knights!
O dear King, what a shame you're not here!

---

10. To provide a flavor of the Old French, the last two lines read: "*Paien unt tort e chrestiens unt dreit / Malvaise essample n'en serat ja de mei.*"

11. "No tonsured person who ever sang mass / was personally responsible for so many meritorious deeds" (*laisse* 119).

Dear Oliver, how shall we do it,
How shall we break the news to him?"

Now he asks. Roland announces he will sound the horn—and Oliver reproaches him:

Oliver said: "that would be dishonorable
And a reproach to all your relatives,
The shame of it would last the rest of their lives!
When I told you to, you did nothing at all,
Don't expect my consent to do it now.
If you sound the horn, it will not be a brave act.
See how bloody both your arms are!"
The Count replies: "I have struck mighty fine blows!"

Oliver's retort is cruel, and cuts to the erotic/thanatonic quick: "By this beard of mine, if I manage to see my fair sister Alda again, you shall never lie in her arms!"

The central conundrum of *Roland* is summed up in the next stanza (131), when Roland asks Oliver why he is so angry with him:

The other replies: "Comrade, you brought it on yourself,
For heroism tempered with common sense is a far cry from madness;
Reasonableness is to be preferred to recklessness.
Frenchmen have died because of your senselessness.
We shall never again be of service to Charles.
If you had believed me, my lord would have come,
We would have fought or won (?)[12] *this battle,*
King Marsile would be captured or slain.
We have come to rue your prowess, Roland!
Charlemagne will not have any help from us.
There shall never be such a man again until Judgment Day.

12. The Oxford text here is unclear.

You will die here and France will be dishonored.
Today our loyal companionage comes to an end.
Before nightfall, our parting will be very sad."

Roland finally blows his magic horn. His temple ruptures from the strain. Oliver and Turpin die fighting. Roland is the last to go; he even tries to smash his indestructible sword rather than have it dishonored by falling into enemy hands. Charlemagne weeps over his dead nephew. It's a bleak poem, intensified by the latter half of the epic, which goes on to describe Charlemagne's nightmares, his sanguinary defeat of Baligant, and the gruesome execution of Ganelon. The concluding stanza (291) ends on a note of weariness and near-despair:

When the emperor has dispensed his justice,
And his great wrath has been appeased,
He has Bramimonde christened.
The daylight fades away, night has fallen,
The King has gone to be in his vaulted room.
Saint Gabriel came from God to tell him:
"Charles, summon the armies of your Empire!
You shall invade the land of Bire,
You shall aid King Vivien at Imphe,
The city the pagans have besieged,
The Christians implore and cry out for you."
The Emperor would rather not go there:
"God!" said the King, "my life is so full of suffering!"
His eyes are brimming with tears, he tugs his white beard.
Here ends the story that Turoldus[13] *tells.*

Well might we weep with the emperor, for in this desolate world there is always another battle to be fought, more blood to be shed, more corpses to be buried. To read *Roland* today is to witness a sanguinary

13. Turold of Bayeux, a Norman poet and possibly the name of the poem's author; scholars are uncertain.

litany of individual combat: heads are lopped, bodies are cleaved in twain, limbs severed, brains spattered. Neither the poet nor his audiences recoiled from its graphic description of sanctioned violence. When Roland encounters the pagan Valdabron on the field, he strikes him "as hard as he can on his helmet, whose gold is wrought with gems, he slices through head, byrnie, and body, the good saddle, whose gold is wrought with gems, and deeply into the horse's back, he kills both of them, caring not a whit for blame or for praise." As the Muslims wail, the triumphant Roland mocks them: "I cannot brook you people, your side is evil and wrong."

This is about as blunt as the confrontation gets between Roman Catholicism and Islam. However politically incorrect this may strike us today, it is a vivid description of how seriously the West took the threat of Islam at the turn of the millennium: not as a political issue to be resolved by negotiation but as an existential threat that could only end with one side victorious and the other dead on the field or fleeing in fear. It would remain this way through the beginning of the twentieth century when, with the final destruction of the Ottoman Empire and thus the Muslim "caliphate," the West believed it had finally solved a problem that had bedeviled it for so long. The secular revolution of Kemal Atatürk in 1923, which deinstitutionalized Islam, seemed at last to have decided the conflict between Christianity and Islam in favor of the West. But as 9/11 so vividly demonstrated, this was not the case.

In considering *Roland,* the question of modern France necessarily arises. The French Revolution, which was even more anticlerical than antimonarchial, seriously damaged the position of the Catholic Church in France; Louis XVI went to the guillotine in 1793 but Napoleon was back on the throne by the end of 1804. The Church never recovered its primacy as France evolved into one of the first European states to become officially secular. Faith, however, is one of the things that made France great: it mobilized the Crusades, built the most magnificent cathedrals in Europe, and gave us some of the greatest sacred music, especially for organ, ever written. Today, however, the French have no spiritual resources within themselves to oppose their country's burgeoning Muslim population, which not only has no use for Catholicism but for the concept of *laïcité* itself. Will the French fight for their country, as Roland did? It seems, alas, improbable.

Whether actual combat was anything like that described in *Roland* is uncertain: the deeds celebrated by the *chansons de geste* were meant to inspire even as they horrified. In *The Poem of the Cid*, made into a memorable 1961 movie starring Charlton Heston and Sophia Loren, the Cid fights on past his own death, his corpse strapped to his horse, leading the Spanish and their Moorish allies in the victorious final charge against the North African Almoravids.

Roland, too, lived on—not on the battlefield, but in story and song for hundreds of years after his death, whether actual or poetic. Although the popularity of the *Chanson de Roland* had waned in France by the thirteenth century, it waxed in Italy, where the popular theater of the day seized upon Roland—now dubbed Orlando—and created, as it were, a backstory for him, detailing his life as a *paladino* (a solitary knight errant)[14] before the events at Roncevaux. Reflecting the growing taste for courtly romance in popular culture, the main character was transformed from Roland, the warrior knight, into Orlando, the Latin lover. In the late fifteenth century, the Italian poet Matteo Maria Boiardo published the epic poem *Orlando Innamorato* (Orlando in Love), set in the Carolingian period but blending elements of Arthurian romance as well.

The second coming of Roland/Orlando, however, really arrived with Ludovico Ariosto's poem, *Orlando Furioso* (Raging Orlando) completed between 1516 and 1532, which picked up where Boiardo's unfinished work had left off. Orlando's titular ire is occasioned by his traduced love for the pagan princess Angelica, who rejects Orlando's suit to run off with a Saracen instead. Orlando goes mad, laying waste to everything he encounters; he is finally cured when he flies to the moon aboard the prophet Elijah's chariot, where he finds his wits along with all the other items that had ever been lost on Earth. Cured of his passion for Angelica, he returns to Italy and kills the Saracen king, Agramante, in a battle on the island of Lampedusa.[15]

---

14. Older Americans surely recall actor Richard Boone as Paladin in the popular television series *Have Gun—Will Travel* (1957–1963).

15. In a bit of historical irony, the Italian island of Lampedusa—which lies just off the Libyan coast—has borne the brunt of the "migrant" crisis in Italy beginning

There have been many literary continuations of the Orlando myth, including echoes in Shakespeare's *Much Ado About Nothing*, and countless references to it elsewhere. Its best-known stage adaptations have come in the opera house, where Vivaldi, Lully, Rameau, Handel, Piccinni, and Haydn set the material to music, sometimes on more than one occasion. *Orlando* has also been a favorite source of inspiration for painters, including Delacroix, Ingres, Tiepolo, and Doré.

Like Arminius, however, Roland has faded from memory in the postwar period, and especially in the twenty-first century. The story strikes modern European audiences as jingoistic and possibly "racist," although there is no mention of race in our contemporary sense anywhere to be found in the source material; the conflict is strictly religious. Still, the idea of a bloodthirsty national hero offends contemporary pacifistic sensibilities; the Christian ardor of *Roland* is out of place in a France that is becoming palpably less Christian and French, and increasingly Muslim.

At the dramatic heart of the *Roland* myth is the dichotomy between the hero's choice to fight rather than to flee. "Death before Dishonor" is not only the motto of the U.S. Marine Corps, it also has been the warrior's credo for at least two thousand years. The Romans executed deserters; so did the U.S. military up until 1945, when Pvt. Eddie Slovik was shot by firing squad *pour encourager les autres* after the shock of the German offensive at the Battle of the Bulge had led to a serious desertion problem among U.S. forces in France and Germany.

Roland, however, makes dishonor impossible by refusing to take prudent measures once he knows his command will be overrun; accordingly, he sacrifices his life, those of the Companions, the bishop, and 20,000 men, to the misguided, supererogatory dictates of his conscience. It's hard for the modern reader not to think him a fool, a distant forebear of Colonel Nicholson in David Lean's *The Bridge on the River Kwai*, who lets his corrupted, impractical sense of duty and honor blind him to the aid he's giving to his Japanese captors until it's almost too

---

around 2011. In the constant conflict between the northern and southern sides of the Mediterranean, not to mention between the West and Islam, not much has changed since the Punic Wars.

late—and then (perhaps to his inner gratification) is redeemed only by his own death. Roland not only wipes out his own command and gets his best friend killed, but he also causes his fiancée, Alda, Oliver's sister, to die of a broken heart upon hearing of his heroic but unnecessary demise. Indeed, it's Charlemagne who emerges as the real, world-weary, but very modern hero of the *Chanson de Roland*, not the titular character, nor even the gallant, sensible Oliver.

What has kept the *Chanson* alive for a thousand years are its stirring battle scenes, among the goriest in Western literature, and the gallant way in which the knights confront their duty and embrace their mortality for a higher cause. The Saracens, too, are portrayed as fearless warriors in the service of a misguided faith; given a choice, the French would rather convert them all to Christianity than kill them, and in fact it is Marsile's false pledge to abandon the Crescent and embrace the Cross that precipitates the entire story. Post-Napoleon, during the many military reverses the French suffered in the nineteenth and early twentieth centuries, the nation re-embraced its flawed hero but, in the wake of its complete collapse in little more than a month against Nazi Germany in May and June of 1940, eventually abandoned him for good. In the end, it seems, Islam—imported from the former French colonies in North Africa, might win after all.

Unlike *El Cid*, there have been no major films about Roland, nor are the plays still in the repertoire; about his only dramatic reincarnation comes in revivals of Handel's *opera seria, Orlando.* His shade still wanders on in lesser-known poetry, principally by Victor Hugo in his three volumes of *La Légende des siècles* (The Legend of the Ages), which treats "*la mariage de Roland*" and fantasizes about a duel between Roland and Oliver as part of a prolonged, ambitious meditation on history and the fate of humanity.[16]

The most moving treatment of the Roland legend comes in Alfred de Vigny's poem, *Le Cor* (The Horn), published in 1826.

---

16. In this same long period (c. 1854–80, Hugo also wrote his stunning, unfinished epic poem, *Dieu et la fin de satan* (God and the end of Satan), originally intended as part of the larger work.

J'aime le son du Cor, le soir, au fond des bois,
Soit qu'il chante les pleurs de la biche aux abois,
Ou l'adieu du chasseur que l'écho faible accueille,
Et que le vent du nord porte de feuille en feuille.
Que de fois, seul, dans l'ombre à minuit demeuré,
J'ai souri de l'entendre, et plus souvent pleuré!
Car je croyais ouïr de ces bruits prophétiques
Qui précédaient la mort des Paladins antiques.

I love the sounding horn, of an eve, deep within the woods,
Whether it sings the plaints of the threatened doe
Or the hunter's retreat but faintly echoed
That the north wind carries from leaf to leaf.
How often alone, in midnight shadows concealed,
I have smiled to hear it, even shedding a tear!
I thought to hear sounding prophetic plaints,
Declaring the death-knell for knights of old.

—translation by Thomas F. Bertonneau with assistance from Susan D. Bertonneau

Death-knells indeed. Roland, the antihero, goes to his death willingly—it's inevitable once he refuses to sound the *oliphant*—but fruitlessly. The Battle of Roncevaux Pass is turned into a particularly bloody public suicide, a failure that, less than two hundred years later, would find its real-life counterpart in the Battle of Hattin in 1187, when the forces of the Crusader Kingdom of Jerusalem were crushed by Saladin. The Crusader chieftain, Raynald de Châtillon, was decapitated, possibly by Saladin himself, and several hundred of the defeated Knights Templar and Hospitaller also went under the sword. A few months later, the city fell, and while the Crusades would continue into the thirteenth century, the principal objective had been lost.

Let us give Vigny the last word:

Ames des Chevaliers, revenez-vous encor?
Est-ce vous qui parlez avec la voix du Cor?

Roncevaux! Roncevaux! Dans ta sombre vallée
L'ombre du grand Roland n'est donc pas consolée!

Souls of the knights, have you returned again?
Is it you who speak with the voice of the horn?
Roncevaux! Roncevaux! In your dark valley
The ghost of great Roland is not consoled!

Even the printing of the legend does not ensure immortality. All Western struggles are open-ended, and remain so to this day. We tend to view the West as not the sum of its art, faith, and culture, but simply its Enlightenment and even Napoleonic politics. But politics is transitory; parties sometimes tactically switch sides. Fundamental definitions change; our notions of "right" and "left" (which are derived from the anti-clerical French Revolution) become increasingly meaningless. In the end, all that is left is culture, which derives from faith, which itself derives from essential human nature. It is how we choose to interpret and immanentize that nature that lies at the heart of all human conflict. The ghost of proud, doomed Roland wanders still.

CHAPTER V

"LOOK AT ME. I AM STILL ALIVE."

THE BATTLE OF HASTINGS (1066)

In the fateful year of 1066, there were signs in the sky that something momentous was about to happen. Halley's Comet, although not known by that name then, flashed across the heavens on its once-every-75-years' journey past our planet. The undisputed English king, Edward the Confessor, had just died, leaving the question of who should succeed him very much in doubt. There were multiple rivals and claimants to the throne, some of whom the Confessor may have encouraged in their aspirations. Among them were Edward the Exile, son of the former King Edmund Ironside, deposed by Danish invaders under King Cnut (Canute) in 1016. But Edward had died in 1057, which left Harold Godwin(e)son, the Earl of Wessex and the king's brother-in-law, and William, Duke of Normandy, the king's first cousin once removed, whose lands lay across the English Channel in France.

The Confessor fell into a coma after Christmas 1065 but recovered a couple of days later and was able to speak: "He told of a dream about two monks he had once known in Normandy, both long dead. They gave him a message from God, criticising the heads of the Church in England, and promising that the kingdom within a year would go to the hands of an enemy: 'devils shall come through all this land with fire and sword and the havoc of war.'"[1] Contemporaneous chroniclers report that it was at this time that he bequeathed his kingdom to Harold,

1. Jim Bradbury, *The Battle of Hastings* (History Press, 1998).

and thus unleashed the devils with fire and sword and the havoc of war that he had foreseen. England and Europe, and thus America and the rest of the world, would never be the same.

Accordingly, Harold took the throne a week after Edward's death on January 6, 1066. Images of him depict a man who looked every inch a king, with finely chiseled features, blond hair, and a regal mien. Still, despite his wishes, Edward's demise set off a free-for-all for the throne. England, as its name implies, was at the time the object of contention between the Anglo-Saxons, the Norman French, and various Scandinavian Viking kingdoms, including Denmark and Normandy.[2] Almost from the moment of his coronation, Harold would have to fight for his throne. And for nine short months, he did, with skill and determination.

The first rival to be disposed of was Harold's own exiled brother, Tostig, who landed on the Isle of Wight, just off the south coast of England near Portsmouth and about 85 miles west of Hastings, in May 1066 with a fleet of an estimated 60 ships. That invasion was repelled, and Tostig fled, later to join forces with another claimant, the ruthless Harald Sigurdsson, known as Hardrada ("hard ruler"), the king of Norway,[3] who together with Tostig launched his own invasion, landing near York in September of 1066. A quick victory over the northern English earls at the Battle of Fulford got Harold Godwinson's attention, and the king organized a rapid response, moving his army from the south of England—where he had been anticipating an assault from William[4] the Bastard—to York.

The opening salvo in what became the Battle of Hastings in

---

2. According to Bradford, "in the *Roman de Rou* the twelfth century Norman poet Robert Wace has Harold demanding, 'Consent now that I shall be king,' to which Edward replies, 'Thou shalt have it, but I know full well that it will cost thee thy life.'"

3. Harold Godwinson's mother was the daughter of a Danish nobleman, Thorgil Sprakling.

4. The Benedictine monk William of Malmesbury, writing in the *Gesta Regum Anglorum* of 1125, has left us the following description of the unprepossessing William: "He was of a proper height, immensely stout, with a ferocious expression and a high bald forehead; his arms extremely strong. . . . He had great dignity

October 1066 turned out to be the Battle of Stamford Bridge on September 25—an all-important prelude to Hastings, without which Harold might well have defeated the Normans, and Anglo-Saxon England might have survived for centuries longer than it did. Before investigating both battles, let us pause for a moment to consider what would have been the ramifications of an Anglo-Saxon victory the following month.

For one thing, you would not be reading this book in this language—or even at all. The Norman Conquest changed not only the administration of England and Ireland (invaded by Strongbow in 1170, although not fully subjugated until the Act of Union in 1800 went into effect in 1801 and, in 1603, by the merger of the Scottish and English crowns), but also the nature of the English language. Without the infusion of the Latinate Norman French, English would be little more than a variant of Low German, something akin to Dutch or Frisian perhaps, and we would be without everything from *The Canterbury Tales* to Shakespeare to Dickens, and even *Harry Potter.*

Neither would our legal or political systems be the same, nor the immediate subsequent history of Europe, especially that of France and England. From our contemporary vantage point, it seems as if countries such as "England" and "France" have somehow always existed, and in their present forms. And yet the borders and boundaries of "England" and "France" remained fluid through the end of the Angevin empire of the Plantagenets of Richard the Lionheart (who spoke French), himself the son of Eleanor of Aquitaine, in the early thirteenth century. The enmity between England and France, reflected most recently in the British decision to exit the European Union, stems from the Battle of Hastings and the Norman Conquest.

How long the essential "Saxonness" of Britain resonated in English hearts and minds is clear from reading Creasy's *Fifteen Decisive Battles.* Writing in the middle of the Victorian era (Victoria, whose mother was German, married a non-English-speaking German in Prince Albert,

---

both seated and standing, although his prominent corpulence gave him an unshapely and unkingly figure."

and was fluent in German herself), Creasy repeatedly refers to Britain's Anglo-Saxon heritage and remarks how preferable it is to the Franco-Norman overlay that arrived with the Conquest—or indeed, in his opinion, to the "oriental" despotisms of Persia or the Semitic civilizations of Phoenicia, Carthage, and the Arab lands. Writing of the Punic wars, for example, he says:

> On the one side is the genius of heroism, of art, and legislation: on the other is the spirit of industry, of commerce, of navigation. The two opposite races have everywhere come into contact, everywhere into hostility. . . . It was clearly for the good of mankind that Hannibal should be conquered: his triumph would have stopped the progress of the world.

And, referring to the Teutoburg Forest:

> The narrative of one of these great crises, of the epoch A.D. 9, when Germany took up arms for her independence against Roman invasion, has for us this special attraction—that it forms part of our own national history. Had Arminius been supine or unsuccessful, our Germanic ancestors would have been enslaved or exterminated in their original seats along the Eyder and the Elbe; this island would never have borne the name of England, and "we, this great English nation, whose race and language are now over-running the earth, from one end of it to the other," [Arnold's *Lectures on Modern History*] would have been utterly cut off from existence.

Such jingoism—we might today term it "racism"—is today frowned upon. But "racism" is a comparatively modern notion, and one that is useless in a historical perspective. The Greeks would not have understood it, nor the Persians, nor the Romans. Encountering peoples different from themselves in culture, customs, and even physiognomy, the Romans would have seen, and called them, barbarians or foreigners. And this terminology would have been applied equally to Celtic Britons, Gauls, Germans, Scythians, or sub-Saharan Africans. The Romans treated all barbarians with equal cultural (not "racial") disdain. "It may sound paradoxical, but it is in reality no exaggeration to say . . . that England owes her liberties to her having been conquered by the Normans," writes Creasy. "As [John, 1st Baron] Campbell boldly expressed it, 'They high-mettled the blood of our veins.'" Hard to imagine any historian writing that today.

Anglo-Saxon Britons of 1066 were facing invaders from both Norway (their Viking half-brothers and cousins) and Normandy (land of the Northmen, descendants of the Vikings, intermingled with the Gallic French). In essence, the struggle for Britain that took place that year—twice—was familial as well as external. And yet . . . the English are correct in maintaining that modern Britain was forged at both Stamford Bridge and Hastings, setting the English forever apart from their Scandinavian and Frankish relatives. The inter-Scandinavian wars that saw first Denmark, then Norway, then Sweden battle for supremacy in the north are of great interest to the Danes, Norwegians, and Swedes but of little interest to the rest of Europe and the world. Because what emerged from the defeat of the Norwegians at Stamford Bridge and the Anglo-Saxon loss to the Normans at Hastings was not only a country, later a larger political entity known as "Britain," and later an empire, but also a language—the English language. Modern English, combining the Latinate French of the Normans and the sturdy Saxon tongue in a way that would never have been possible without the Norman Conquest, provided the linguistic mechanism for the eventual triumph of British notions of law, culture, colonization, and civilization. These sometimes took root by colonization, as in America, Canada, and the Antipodes; by force, as in Ireland and India; or withered, as in central and, latterly, South Africa, but English shows no signs of relinquishing its linguistic hegemony as the voice of literature, commerce, pop culture, air travel, and international finance.

And so, in the early fall of 1066, it was a fight to the death—a last stand not only for the Norwegian king Harald Hardrada at Stamford Bridge, whose rout and demise near York ended the Viking threat to the British Isles; not only for the English king, Harold

Godwinson and his *Huscarls* (housecarls, specially armed and trained fighting men attached to his person; a kind of Saxon Praetorian Guard) on Battle Hill, near Hastings, who left their bones but not their glory on the south coast; but also for Saxon England, which, by losing, enjoyed the fruits of the Norman victory for the next thousand years.

These twin battles are among the most written-about and analyzed in all of military history. From various primary sources—whose accuracy is, of course, much debated by scholars—beginning with the Bayeux Tapestry[5] and various contemporary or near-contemporary accounts by both Saxon and Norman historians, we have a fairly clear idea of the sequencing of events. We need not concern ourselves overmuch here with the lineal jockeying for position that preceded the conflicts of September and October. For the purposes of this study, two things in particular stand out.

The first is that, some thousand years plus after Cannae, how little the Western way of battle had really changed: death still largely came in hand-to-hand combat. The second is why Harold Godwinson, who had been expecting a challenge from William along his south coast for months, should have rushed exhausted from the fight against Harald Hardrada so quickly to meet his doom at Hastings.

To take the first issue first: in all of the descriptions of the Saxon battle lines, one element is of particular interest. Not their lack of cavalry, for armed equestrians had gone in and out of military fashion from the time of Alexander, but their use of what was essentially a defensive, static phalanx to repel invaders and then wait for an opening to counterattack.[6] The

---

5. An embroidered cloth, 20 inches high but stretching 230 feet, produced shortly after the Battle of Hastings, most likely for Odo, the bishop of Bayeux, who fought in the battle and became the Earl of Kent after the Norman victory, which forms an illustrated history of the Conquest. In 1944, with the Allies advancing on Paris, Heinrich Himmler tried to spirit it away from its safe resting place in the Louvre but was frustrated in the attempt by French partisans. It is now housed in the Musée de la Tapisserie de Bayeux, in France.

6. In this, Hastings somewhat resembles the Battle of Cynoscephalae in 197 B.C., fought between the Romans and the Greeks in Thessaly. The Romans, with superior flexibility and mobility, won.

Saxons on Senlac Hill fought with shields interlocked, their Dane axes at the ready, an immovable object facing the irresistible force of William's archers, foot soldiers, and heavy cavalry. And for the best part of the day, they held their ground. Again and again, William's forces crashed against the Saxon hedgehog, at great cost but to little tactical avail. Until, suddenly, whether through happenstance or circumstance, the Saxons made a fatal mistake.

The second point is one that has resonated down the millennium: why was Harold in such haste to confront William when he had just fought and won a resounding victory against the Norwegians several hundred miles to the north? The Norman invaders were isolated on the coast, still far from London, and would have had to live off the land and deal with a populace not kindly disposed toward them. And yet, marching at double time and raising a fresh force as he went, Harold could not wait to meet his appointment with destiny.

To understand this conundrum, therefore, let us begin near York, with the small but valiant last stand of a Viking warrior whose name has been lost to history, a giant of a man who, alone, held a bridge against Harold and his men until he was finally struck down by, literally, a low blow, thus opening the span across the River Derwent. The Viking host under Harald, allied with Harold Godwinson's disaffected brother, Tostig, had landed in Yorkshire and quickly defeated the northern earls, the brothers Edwin, Earl of Mercia, and Morcar, Earl of Northumbria. The city of York capitulated, and Harald had his foothold on English soil.

But in a brilliant feat of military logistics, Harold reacted to the news by moving his army quickly north—two hundred miles in a week—to counter the immediate threat from the formidable Viking king. He moved with such alacrity, in fact, that he caught the Vikings, their English allies, and some Flemish mercenaries on a warm early fall day on the side of the Derwent River with only half their army in camp, and minus their mail-shirt armor; the other half of their estimated 11,000 men were still at the Norse base camp at Riccall, just inland from the North Sea.

Godwinson knew he was facing a formidable opponent.

According to the Icelandic poet and historian Snorri Sturluson (d. 1241),[7] Harald Hardrada had been at Constantinople, where he became the commander of the Varangian Guard—the Eastern Empire's equivalent of the Praetorians—and served across Asia Minor and in Sicily before returning to Scandinavia to press his claim to the Norwegian throne in 1045. Two decades later, assured by Tostig Godwinson that the conquest of England would be a cakewalk, he assembled a fleet of some two hundred ships[8] and launched his invasion flying under his personal raven-emblazoned banner: "Landwaster."

The quick defeat of the earls and the warm reception Harald got from the largely Anglo-Danish nobles of York perhaps disarmed and encouraged him, which is why Hardrada was caught largely unawares by Harold Godwinson's rapid advance and assault. The lone crossing at the river was a simple wooden bridge, just about wide enough for two men to pass abreast. And it was at this bridge that our lone Viking warrior made the first of what would be a series of last stands that would decide the fate of England. Taken from one of the several extant versions of the *Anglo-Saxon Chronicle*, it relates

> a story, added in the twelfth century and repeated by several other writers, of how the English were for some time prevented from crossing the bridge over the Derwent by a single Norwegian warrior, apparently wearing a mail shirt, until at length an inspired Englishman sneaked under the bridge and speared the Viking in the one place where such armour offers no protection. This was supposedly the turning point of the battle: Harold and his forces surged over the undefended bridge and the rest of the

7. Author of *King Harald's Saga*. Some modern historians consider Snorri, like Livy, more of a storyteller and dramatist than a historian. His account of events is often at odds with that of the *Anglo-Saxon Chronicle*, a series of annals that began in the ninth century and continued through the Norman Conquest.

8. Other accounts put the number as high as five hundred.

> Norwegian army were slaughtered. Both Hardrada and Tostig were among the fallen.
>
> —Marc Morris, *The Norman Conquest: The Battle of Hastings and the Fall of Anglo-Saxon England* (2012)

With the Norse champion down,[9] Harold Godwinson's men rushed across the bridge and fell upon the Vikings. Harald toppled with an arrow to the throat, and Harold's brother Tostig was also killed.

The death toll has been placed at six thousand for the Vikings and around five thousand for the English, although the real tally is unknown. Contemporary sources report rivers of blood, the waterways choked with corpses, the shore spattered with "Viking gore." From our fastidious remove, it is tempting to discount such reports as overwrought. And, in truth (as we believe we know from Herodotus, among others), the estimates of troop strength and casualties in classical and medieval antiquity seem to be off by a factor of ten or more. Still, according to the *Chronicle*, the remnants of Harald's army were transported back to Norway in just 24 ships—a far cry from the hundreds that had started the journey.

That does not mean, however, that the accounts of the viscera are exaggerated. As we saw at Cannae, the slaughter of tens of thousands of men was not accomplished in the single blinding flash of an atomic bomb but one at a time, at the point of a spear or a sword. Our savage forefathers had a far greater tolerance for the sight and taste of blood. Heads were routinely severed and exhibited as proof of victory. If the only way to kill your man was to dismember him more or less alive, then so be it. Life was, in the memorable words of Hobbes, "nasty, brutish, and short"—and on the battlefield it was even worse.

By any standards, the Saxon housecarls—the word has a root meaning

---

9. In his retelling of the incident, Bradbury raises this question: "This story presents a problem: if the English had archers here, as generally accepted, why did they not shoot the man? If they did indeed have archers, the story would seem to be a fabrication. We are left with a doubt over both the presence of English archers and the tale of the defender of the bridge."

of "domestic servant" (*carl* became our English word *churl*, which acquired an added, invidious resonance)—were a frightening and deadly force. Long gone were the Roman arms of spears and short swords. Foremost among the English weapons was the Dane axe, a lethal armament that could halve a man from his skull to his groin and decapitate both rider and horse when swung with both hands. The Dane axe, however, was still light enough to be wielded with one hand while the other held the kite-shaped shield that formed part of the elite unit's protective carapace, along with a short mail coat, called a byrnie. A long, double-edged sword with a groove running down the blade on both sides, which made the weapon somewhat lighter to wield, rounded out their fighting kit.

Harold had little time to savor his victory. Almost immediately word came of William's landing at Pevensey Bay, west of Hastings, on September 28, 1066. The natural harbor protected his ships, while the landing site boasted an old Roman fort, which William fortified as he brought his men and horses ashore. The story goes that upon disembarking from his flagship, the *Mora,* and hitting the beach, the Bastard—soon enough to be the Conqueror—stumbled, fell, and came up with a handful of wet sand.[10] His men were aghast: surely this was a bad omen. But a quick-thinking Norman soldier nearby is said to have called out, "You hold England, my lord, its future king." To which (according to Creasy's account) William is said to have replied, "See, my lords! by the splendour of God, I have taken possession of England with both my hands. It is now mine; and what is mine is yours."[11]

Never mind the omens: William had landed unopposed. To this day, scholars and historians marvel at the fact that Harold Godwinson knew the Normans would invade and that they would naturally take a relatively direct route from Normandy across the Channel to the southern

---

10. Caesar did, and said, something very similar upon an arrival in Africa, as Suetonius reports in *The Twelve Caesars*: "And happening to fall, upon stepping out of the ship, he gave a lucky turn to the omen, by exclaiming, 'I hold thee fast, Africa.'"

11. During the battle itself, there was a second bad omen for William, when he donned his hauberk (a kind of protective undershirt made of mail) backward. He ignored it and proceeded.

English coast. (For his part, William didn't know until he arrived in England which of the two Harold/Haralds—Godwinson or Hardrada—he would have to fight.) And yet he had sent his fleet back to London and, in the wake of his victory at Stamford Bridge, disbanded his army[12] around September 8, although he still held his personal troops, his housecarls. Which meant that Harold, even while marching south to confront the Normans, needed to reassemble his army and so levied troops as he went. Today, we might term this an intelligence failure, but in the eleventh century, with its primitive means of communication, it was the bad luck that attended the accelerating pace of geopolitics and military strategy.

It was not that William had had an easy time of it. His naval force of some seven hundred ships had been ready to launch since early August, but unfavorable winds and bad weather in the channel prevented sailing well into the middle of September. Skeptics have charged that William's delay in leaving Normandy was a calculated gambit: he was just waiting for Harold to disband his forces so he could strike without fear. But, in warfare, one should never be too quick to attribute to skill what can be explained by luck or human error. As Marc Morris writes in his 2012 book, *The Norman Conquest*,

> The duke, it seems, was delayed by contrary winds. For once, William of Poitiers appears to have given us the unvarnished truth. The principal reason for believing Poitiers is that his testimony is corroborated by a new source—the so-called *Carmen de Hastingae Proelio*, or "Song of the Battle of Hastings."[13] . . . One thing that makes the *Carmen* especially interesting is that it was apparently written for the ears of William the Conqueror himself (the first 150 lines or so are written in the second person, i.e. "You did this, you did that") . . .
>
> "For a long time tempest and continuous rain prevented your

12. Unlike in ancient Rome, standing armies were almost unknown during this period, and needed to be put together on an ad hoc basis as crises erupted.

13. "An epic poem, 835 lines long, it was discovered in 1826 in the Royal Library in Brussels."

> fleet from sailing across the Channel. . . . You were in despair when all hope of sailing was denied you. But, in the end, whether you liked it or not, you left your shore and directed your ships towards the coast of a neighbour."

The Normans, it seems, couldn't wait to get at Harold and England. The reason, in large part, was due to the bad blood between William and Harold that had originated a year or two before, when Harold had been William's "guest"—possibly by shipwreck; the historical record is unclear—at his court at Rouen. At that time, perhaps under duress, Harold had been enticed to swear (without his knowledge) on the relics of saints that he would support William's claim to the English throne and would also become betrothed to William's daughter, in order to seal the deal. At which point, the story goes, Harold was allowed to sail back to England. (The episode forms an early part of the Bayeux Tapestry.)[14]

So when Harold renounced his sacred oath upon the death of the Confessor, and accepted the crown of England, William and the Normans were furious. They viewed Harold's perjury as not only perfidy but apostasy; and on the night before the battle, the Normans were saying their prayers and being absolved by their priests and bishops,

---

14. Creasy tells the story this way: "Before a full assembly of the Norman barons, Harold was required to do homage to Duke William, as the heir-apparent of the English crown. Kneeling down, Harold placed his hands between those of the Duke, and repeated the solemn form, by which he acknowledged the Duke as his lord, and promised to him fealty and true service. But William exacted more. He had caused all the bones and relics of saints, that were preserved in the Norman monasteries and churches, to be collected into a chest, which was placed in the council-room, covered over with a cloth of gold. On the chest of relics, which were thus concealed, was laid a missal. The Duke then solemnly addressed his titular guest and real captive, and said to him, "Harold, I require thee, before this noble assembly, to confirm by oath the promises which thou hast made me, to assist me in obtaining the crown of England after King Edward's death, to marry my daughter Adela, and to send me thy sister, that I may give her in marriage to one of my barons." Harold, once more taken by surprise, and not able to deny his former words, approached the missal, and laid his hand on it, not knowing that the chest of relics was beneath. The old Norman chronicler, who describes the scene most minutely, says, when Harold placed his hand on it, the hand trembled, and the flesh quivered."

determined to meet their maker shriven—while the English were getting drunk.

What a contrast the two armies made: the numerically larger Normans, with their archers and cavalry, short-haired and clean-shaven, versus the smaller English contingent of foot soldiers, who wore their hair long and whose faces bristled with fierce moustaches. The English blood was up—although mindful of Harold's oath to William, his brothers Gurth and Leofwine both advised him not to personally fight in a battle that probably should not have been fought where and when it was in the first place. No sense provoking the wrath of God. But the king was outraged at the despoliation of the countryside by the Normans as they had made their way eastward, and was not to be dissuaded.[15] After all, he and his men had just won a great victory at Stamford Bridge.

According to nineteenth-century French historian Augustin Thierry, a monk named Hugues Maigrot visited Harold in his camp to propose three alternatives to the wholesale slaughter that was sure to come. The first was Harold's withdrawal of his claim to the English throne. The second was to offer to present the situation to the pope for arbitration. The third was single combat. Harold rejected them all—there was no way he was going to resign his crown, and as far as the pope was concerned, he had already blessed William's claim, since Harold had sworn an oath on the relics of the saints. And single combat was out of the question—although in retrospect it might have been Harold's best option, especially against the porcine William.

According to Thierry, during the deliberations there came this poignant plaint, a question with contemporary significance that still resonates today: "We must fight, whatever may be the danger to us," said one of the English noblemen. "They come, not only to ruin us, but to ruin our descendants also, and to take from us the country of our ancestors. And what shall we do—whither shall we go—when we have no longer a country?"

---

15. According to the *Historia Ecclesiastica* by the twelfth-century English chronicler and Benedictine monk Orderic Vitalis, Harold's own mother tried to prevent him from leaving London to meet William, but he "insolently kicked her."

So to the death it was. Taking up a position atop Senlac (or Battle) Hill, and recognizing from the outset that he was fighting a defensive contest against mobile invaders, Harold Godwinson arranged his forces, on the trot from London and already both blooded and bloodied from their successful battle against the Norwegians under Harald Hardrada, atop a hillock where the Franco-Norman invaders would face an uphill climb. For although William could boast of cavalry and a fleet of archers, both of them were at a tactical disadvantage when charging and shooting uphill. This was not to be a classical battle, fought on a plain. If the English could only weather the shower of arrows and the charge of horsemen, repelling the barrage with their shields and hamstringing the horses and mounted men with their halberds—a long pole with a spiked axe-head at one end—and with their Saxon battleaxes, they could win the day.

For six hours, from nine in the morning until three in the afternoon, they went at it, with the Franco-Normans trying to breach the near-impregnable Anglo-Saxon shield wall, and the Britons holding off assault after assault. After the initial archers' barrage, repelled by the Saxon shields—owing to the English position, the arrows were launched high in the sky in order to rain down against the enemy; but this reduced their penetrating power; like the Greeks at Thermopylae, the Britons were "fighting in the shade"—and despite taking casualties, the English were getting the better of it.

All might have been well had the English held their lines. But, early in the fight, a rumor spread among both French and English that William had been killed. The French left—on the English right—turned and fell back. Fatally, the English broke ranks and pursued. Although the struggle would continue for hours, it was in this instant that the battle was lost, and the fate of England was sealed.

Whether the apparent Norman retreat was feigned has been the subject of analysis and dispute for more than a thousand years. Such tactics were not unknown in classical times. By moving his center back in a controlled retreat at Cannae, Hannibal had suckered the Roman legions into his double envelopment; Caesar had used his numerical weakness against Pompey at Pharsalus to his advantage, employing a regiment of hidden infantry wielding pikes to turn Pompey's superior cavalry on the right flank and force victory as Caesar's legions destroyed his rival's center and left. Indeed, Harold Godwinson had used this same ploy against Harald Hardrada at Stamford Bridge.

According to one account, during the first attack the Norman cavalry had foundered on the English shields and swords. The English line pressed forward and, when they saw their foes fleeing, ran after them. Their haste was amplified by the thought that William had fallen: medieval armies generally did not survive the loss of their generals, and often broke ranks in panic. But William came forward on horseback, tearing off his helmet to show his face to his men and shouting: "Look at me. I am still alive. With God's help I shall win. What madness is persuading you to flee?" (The scene is illustrated in plate 68 of the Bayeux Tapestry.) Seeing their king alive and unarmed, carrying only a baton as the insignia of his command—though he'd already lost two horses that day and needed a third to finish the fight—the Normans rallied.

A second version, as related in the *Carmen*, says the retreat was feigned at first but then turned suddenly real in the face of the ferocious English onslaught, at which point William rallied the troops and the battle was rejoined. In either case, and upon regrouping, the French cavalry fell upon the exposed English soldiers and slaughtered them. Once broken, the English line was no match for William's far more flexible three-pronged force of soldiers of foot, bowmen, and heavy cavalry. It was in this moment that the contest was decided.

Late in the afternoon, with the English line buckling—both of Harold's brothers had likely fallen at this point—William ordered his archers to fire another volley, high in the sky. One bolt struck Harold in his right eye, sending him to his knees in great pain, leaning on his shield. Fighting his way toward the center of the English line, where Harold had stood, cutting down Saxon after Saxon, William and three of his men, by some accounts, fell upon the dying and defenseless Harold, piercing him with a lance, beheading him, and disemboweling him with a spear. The *Carmen* reports that one of his thighs was hacked off and carted away; historians have taken this to mean his genitalia were severed and removed from the body. Nobody really knows: an English knight is shown on the Bayeux Tapestry receiving an arrow in the eye, but this may not be Harold. And the idea that William himself fought his way to the center of the battle to personally strike down Harold seems more dramatic than historical.[16]

In his somewhat melodramatic retelling of the battle, based on Robert Wace's *Roman de Rou*, Creasy paraphrases the Norman soldiers' reaction to their great chief: "Such a baron never bestrode war-horse, or dealt such blows, or did such feats of arms; neither has there been on earth such a knight since Rollant [Roland] and Olivier." In such ways can literature, even fiction, affect events.

What we do know is that, seeing their king fall, the English fled—all but the housecarls, who somehow fought their way back to the body to protect it with their lives, until they too went under the Norman swords. Sworn to protect Harold, they died to nearly a man, fulfilling their duty to their sovereign and their country until both had disappeared into history. Some of the Normans pursued the English past the top of the ridge and into a ditch known as the Malfosse, into which the Normans tumbled unawares, and were butchered by the remnants of Harold's army before grabbing their horses and riding away. But the victory had already been won.

As was customary, William and his men remained on the battlefield, dining and sleeping among the dead.[17] As the English came to identify and collect their naked dead,[18] one problem was how to properly identify Harold. The king's face and body had been so badly mutilated that he was unrecognizable—except to one intimate. Harold's mistress, known as Edith Swan-Neck, was brought to the field and was able to certify his corpse "by certain distinguishing marks" that only someone as intimate as a lover would know. William ordered Harold's body buried by the sea, but there is a tradition that it later was exhumed and interred at Waltham Abbey. There is even a legend that Harold somehow

16. An altar was later erected to mark the spot where, as best history can tell, Harold died.

17. Grisly, but such was the custom.

18. Bodies of a defeated foe were generally stripped, both for practical reasons (collecting weapons and useful items of clothing) and as one final humiliation. This custom, celebrated in Roman times with special honors, was nearly universal and lasted well into the nineteenth century: the bodies of Custer and his men were similarly treated by the Plains Indians at the Little Bighorn.

survived the battle, was hidden away in a cellar for two years, and then spirited off to Germany.

If so, he never returned. Anglo-Saxon England did not die with Harold and the housecarls but instead was subjugated to the Normans and, as we have seen, was elevated by its contact with them. Within a few hundred years, the Norman and Saxon lineages had fused to form a new tongue, a new country, and a new civilization—one that, a millennium later, would spread far and wide beyond its island origins to encompass the world.

And yet it began simply, in rage over an unfulfilled oath, and ended when the loving eye of a mistress steeled herself to inspect the corpse of her lover and, with the secret knowledge of a woman's heart, pronounce the words: *ecce homo*. If the purpose of war is for men to defend their homelands, their women, and their children, even those as yet unborn, then the final act at Hastings, however tragic, stands as its epitome. For there is victory even in defeat. That is the nature of humanity.

CHAPTER VI

"I MUST PERFORM SOME ACTION WORTHY OF A MAN"

THE LAST STAND OF THE SWISS GUARD (1527)

It didn't have to happen. The pope might not have made an alliance with the king of France against the Holy Roman Emperor, to his eternal regret. He might have kept his hired mercenaries to fend off any possible attack on the Holy City instead of discharging them. He might not have trusted his belief that Christian soldiers would not pillage and plunder the Holy See and instead made provisions for his safety and that of the people of Rome. But he didn't—and the rest is one of the least-known but most significant chapters in Western history: the sixteenth century Sack of Rome, far worse than anything the Gauls or the German barbarians ever wrought. We are paying the price for it still.

It is instructive to observe, in our survey of mostly Western military history, how large in our annals and imagination looms Rome and its sociomartial tradition. From the Greeks, the Romans learned the phalanx and, with refinements, turned it into the matchless offensive machine of the manipled legions. Despite their losses at Cannae and the Teutoburg Forest, the Romans demonstrated that high fertility and an indomitable will to win could handle most any reverses. The end of the Empire taught other lessons as well. It illustrated the folly of a declining native birth rate and generous immigration from inimical lands and peoples; and, mostly, it gave the lie to the notion of, in author Roger Kimball's words, "the fortunes of permanence": that what is here today, assuredly will still be tomorrow. It never is.

Even after Rome fell, however, it remained the ideal for centuries: Charlemagne attempted to restore the Caesars under the rubric of the Holy Roman Empire ("Holy" because the Catholic Church had effectively become pagan Rome's successor supra-state), and both the Germans and the Russians named their supreme leaders after them: *Kaiser* and *Tsar*. For Rome has never died. Long after the Western Empire fell in the fifth century, its legacy lived on—in the East for another millennium—in both the manners and mores of the barbarians, principalities, and emergent nation-states that followed in its mighty wake. Its military tactics, its weaponry, its administrative skills, and, most of all, its engineering feats ensured its survival for centuries. Even today, Roman roads and Roman aqueducts still function.

But most of all, what lived on was the idea of Rome: the ideals of the Republic, combined with the might and majesty of the Empire, however degraded it became. Caesar, in history's ultimate irony, was at once its redeemer and its destroyer. Ideals that were at first opposed to those of the minor Jewish sect of Christianity, until the Christians ultimately triumphed by their preaching and, even more, by the bravery with which they faced the most violent forms of torture and persecution from Nero to Constantine, who finally converted on his deathbed.[1] And though the Empire lasted for less than a century after Constantine, in the end it was the popes who really succeeded to the throne, not the barbarians. The discipline, the sense of honor, and duty, and country, lived on long after Rome fell. The word "colonialism" is in much disrepute these days, but who can deny that Rome was the greatest colonial power that ever existed? Therefore:

How splendid they look, these Roman Vatican cognates of the guards at Buckingham Palace, sporting their striped Medici tricolor dress uniforms of red, blue, and yellow, flaring pantaloons, knee stockings and all, and armed with pikes, halberds, and swords. They are the world's smallest army, first mustered for Pope Julius II in January of 1506, and the papal bodyguard ever since, recruited from the ranks of Swiss-born Catholic men all, between the ages of 19 and 30,

---

1. It was Theodosius who made the faith the official religion of the Empire in 380.

with at least secondary-school attainment and having completed basic training with the Swiss military. Both the Romans and Hannibal feared their forebears, the wild but disciplined men of the mountains, whose valor was beyond question, and whose dedication to country has kept Switzerland safe and free of foreign occupation since it won independence from the Holy Roman Empire in 1499. The Swiss are the hedgehogs of Europe, and even today, despite their theme-park appearance, the Swiss Guard is not to be provoked or trifled with.

When Harry Lime (Orson Welles) disparages the Swiss in his famous speech from *The Third Man*—"In Switzerland, they had brotherly love, they had five hundred years of democracy and peace—and what did that produce? The cuckoo clock"—he sums up the conventional wisdom about the Swiss. It's certainly true that in the realm of high culture, they have significantly underperformed: aside from watches—and cuckoo clocks!—what fine international goods do they still manufacture? The "gnomes of Zurich" mind the world's hidden money, which is squirreled away behind the facades of the buildings along the Bahnhofstrasse. In Geneva, the striped-pants set disports itself at taxpayer expense along the shores of Lac Léman, while in Chiasso, just over the Italian border from Como, wealthy Italian families maintain refuges just in case Italy finally collapses. It never quite does, but one never knows.

There is the Swiss Army knife, of course: at once practical, useful, multipurposed, and, when necessary, lethal—much like Switzerland itself. And the Swiss Army, which comprises nearly the whole young male population of the country. Weapons are mandatory, and are stored in the home for easy access.[2] Like the Americans, the Swiss take their tradition of an armed citizenry seriously, and the fact that neither Hitler nor Mussolini invaded them during World War II speaks to the respect the Swiss have won over the past half-millennium. It hardly matters whether the men speak German, French, Italian, or Romansch,

---

2. Since 2007, and with some exceptions, ammunition must be kept in central arsenals. In a country of 8.5 million people, there are an estimated 1.5 million military-grade weapons in private hands.

a linguistic descendant of Latin—they are all Swiss. It is one of the few "diverse" countries in the world (unlike, say, Belgium or Canada) that actually works, despite its religious division between Protestant and Catholic, because every Swiss is a Helvetian first. The country is known as the *Confoederatio Helvetica* (CH is the national designation on European bumpers) for a reason.

Modern Switzerland began to come together as early as 1291, after the fall of both halves of the Roman Empire, as three of the mountainous, isolated cantons joined together in a confederacy for mutual protection against the expansionist Habsburgs. The Swiss defeated the Habsburgs in several pitched battles during the fourteenth century; thereafter their reputations and worth as mercenaries grew. Adapting military techniques from their Roman conquerors, the Swiss updated the phalanx with the addition of the pike and the halberd, which the Swiss Guard still uses today. With the coming of gunpowder, the traditional Swiss way of war was rendered suddenly obsolete in the face of the *arquebus*, but they adopted the musket readily enough and continued to fight on.

The Papal States were a considerable land power in the early sixteenth century, so Pope Julius II—born Giuliano della Rovere; he took the name in honor of Julius Caesar, making the link to early Rome explicit—recruited Swiss mercenaries to form the papal army. At that time, the Papal States occupied much of what is now central Italy as well as the territory around Avignon, and Julius had big plans for the temporal expansion of papal power. In this sphere the "warrior pope," during his ten-year reign on the throne of St. Peter, ended the power of the Borgias, began the Christianization of the newly discovered Americas, and battled the French for control of Italy.

In the arts, he is perhaps most remembered today as the man who tore down Old St. Peter's in Rome (built, tradition has it, on the spot where Peter was crucified, upside down, by Nero, the last of the Julio-Claudian dynasty) and replaced it with a newly commissioned grand basilica designed by Donato Bramante; as the patron of both Raphael and Michelangelo, Julius also commissioned the latter's adornment of the ceiling of the Sistine Chapel,[3] one of the most stunning achievements in the history of Western art.

In 1507, Julius II authorized the sale of indulgences, and thereby set in motion a series of events that would rock the Christian world and irrevocably alter the course of European history. For ten years, the sale of indulgences—basically, time off in Purgatory in exchange for money—bumped along, surviving Julius's death in 1513, until Pope Leo X renewed the decree. Among the young members of the radical clergy in Germany was one Martin Luther, ordained a Catholic priest the same year Julius began his exercise in mixing the sacred and the profane. But it was only after Leo's continuation of the practice that Luther was outraged enough to write and post his famous *Explanation of the Ninety-Five Theses* of 1518 on the doors of the *Scholosskirche* (Castle Church) in Wittenberg—his seminal *j'accuse* against the Roman faith that triggered the Protestant Reformation, the Counter-Reformation, the Thirty Years' War, and a host of other significant historical and religious developments—in which he directly attacked the sale of indulgences.

"Indulgence" was a key word. Many of the most conservative Catholics, especially in the north, were outraged by the lavish lifestyles of the Latin senior clergy, with their sumptuous lodgings, Lucullan appetites, exotic sexual practices, bastard offspring, and publicly displayed mistresses[4]; Julius II wasn't the only true Julian scion among them. No wonder, the thinking went, the hypocritical clergy is so intent on lessening time in Purgatory: they need an escape clause more than anybody. Indeed, "Latinate" became a synonym for voluptuary excess. The Reformation was its perfectly understandable, northern reaction. The Alps

---

3. Memorialized on film in 1965's *The Agony and the Ecstasy*, starring Charlton Heston as Michelangelo and Rex Harrison as the pope, and directed by the British director Carol Reed, back when "Carol" was still a boys' name.

4. The homosexual, youth-molesting scandals of the contemporary Catholic Church are an inverted echo of this period, and may well result in a similar schism, this time between observant Catholics who reject the "reforms" of Vatican II and the current *curia*. Sedevacantism looms.

are not only a climatological but an intellectual, moral, and emotional barrier as well.[5]

The Reformation sundered European Christendom. The split was religious, of course, but it went deeper. The Alps were the old demarcation between Rome and the German barbarians east of the Rhine and north of the Danube. There was a linguistic element as well, with the Germanic languages dominant to the north and the Latin tongues to the west and south. The Alps also profoundly affected the European weather, setting off the warm countries of the Mediterranean south from the cold, rainy, snowy, and dreary Gallic, German, and Scandinavian provinces to the north. Lutheranism was simply the division made visible, and dogmatic. To this day, the austere interiors of Protestant churches stand in stark contrast to the ornate sanctuaries of Italian and Spanish Catholicism.

As a glance at any map will show, the fault line ran directly through Switzerland. Luther was German, but the revolution he began quickly spread, not only through much of northern Germany (Bavaria stayed Catholic) but to the Lowlands (and, eventually, Britain) and into the German-speaking cantons of Switzerland, where men such as Huldrych Zwingli preached and fulminated so effectively that by 1523 the city of Zurich was officially Protestant.[6]

Out went celibacy—Luther was an avid heterosexual and fully enjoyed the perquisites of married love. "Kiss and rekiss your wife," he wrote to his friend Nikolaus Gerbel, a Strasbourg jurist. "Let her love and be loved. You are fortunate in having overcome, by an honorable marriage, that celibacy in which one is a prey to devouring fires and to unclean ideas. That unhappy state of a single person, male or female, reveals to me each hour of the day so many horrors, that nothing sounds in my ear as bad as the name of monk or nun or priest. A married life is a paradise, even where all else is wanting." In other words,

---

5. Viz, Thomas Mann's short story "Death in Venice."

6. The inciting incident was Zwingli's 1522 sermon in favor of eating sausages during Lent, "Von Erkiesen und Freiheit der Speisen" (Regarding the Choice and Freedom of Foods), which became known as the "Affair of the Sausages." Moral: never come between a German and his *wurst*.

Protestantism—in Germany, Switzerland, England, and elsewhere—was founded upon sexual freedom, if not to say license.

Sexual dysfunction fascinated Luther, and he advocated what we would consider very modern solutions to issues involving female sexuality, including the impotence of her husband (the wife should have sex with her husband's brother, with any children as rightful heirs) and a woman's right to a divorce, although he preferred bigamy as a more family-friendly solution. The pope, he declared, had no right to judge the God-given nature of human sexuality: "Let him set them up for himself and keep hands off my liberty." Celibacy could only lead to "division, sin, shame, and scandal to be increased without end." Rome-enforced clerical celibacy, nowhere to be found in the Bible, Luther regarded as "the Devil's own tyranny." For the early Protestants, "the Whore of Rome" had a very specific sexual connotation.

The other Swiss cantons were encouraged to convert to the new faith by John Calvin, a Frenchman, born Jehan Cauvin, who moved to Francophone Geneva, aligned himself with the German-speaking Lutherans, and fathered the Huguenots[7] in France. Determinist in outlook, Calvin preached predestination, the paramountcy of scripture,[8] and the moral evil of idols, including all church ornamentation. Soon enough, Switzerland, like the rest of Europe,[9] was split into Catholic and Protestant denominations. The division would fester for nearly a century until it broke open into murderous hostility with the Thirty Years' War.

Rome under Pope Julius still hovered among the ghosts of ancient Rome, the fragmenting Holy Roman Empire (largely German, or at least Frankish), and the emerging political realities of Europe. From the final

---

7. The subject of a spectacular opera by Giacomo Meyerbeer, first presented in Paris in 1836. After the St. Bartholomew's Day Massacre in 1572, and continuing into the early eighteenth century, thousands of French Huguenots fled to South Africa.

8. One of the principal divisions between Catholics and Protestants, even today. Catholics, who regard the New Testament as the fulfillment of the Old (Hebrew) Testament, tend to regard the Jewish Bible as prologue; Protestants continue to revere it as Holy Writ.

9. Henry VIII brought the Reformation to the British Isles via the Act of Supremacy of 1534, which made the monarch the head of the Church of England.

defeat of the Western Roman Empire in 476 and the beginning of the line of barbarian emperors, the relations between the Germanic tribes and the Italians had been complicated and fraught. Some of the trappings and offices of Imperial Rome remained, including the consuls, but they were largely ceremonial; the real power was held by leaders such as Theodoric, the king of the Ostrogoths (the eastern Goths), who ruled in Rome while the Visigoths (the western Goths) dominated Spain, while the Vandals established kingdoms in North Africa, Sicily, and Sardinia.

As Western Rome fell, the power of the popes swelled. Prior to the end of the Western Empire, in 452, Leo I had ridden out to meet Attila the Hun, whose invasion of Europe had been checked by the Roman general Aetius and allied barbarian fighters at the Battle of Châlons, in Gaul, just the year before. Attila was still itching for a decisive fight as he approached the Eternal City, but Leo the Great somehow managed to talk him out of it. Whether through threats (unlikely), superstition (possible), or outright bribery (plausible), Leo, a native of Tuscany, got the Huns to spare the city. They withdrew, to be decisively defeated in 454 at Battle of Nedao in the Roman province of Pannonia (largely, present-day Austria and Hungary) by a coalition of Germanic warriors—many of whom had been settled inside the Empire as a reward, and who enthusiastically contributed to the Empire's demise two decades later.

Still, even in its diminished state, Rome was always the big prize. To conquer Rome was the barbarian's highest goal, and even after it was conquered, and yet still survived as the center of Christianity and Catholicism, it remained a potent symbol of Western power, cultural majesty, and religious veracity. To sack and rape Rome was to illustrate the West's impotence; to eradicate her was proof of military and, to one subsequent faith, religious superiority.[10]

In the tumultuous aftermath of Julius's death, the political, religious, and cultural divisions of Europe were stronger than they had ever been. The conflicts that had broken out all over the powder keg that was Western

---

10. Even today, Islam, in its ongoing battle against Christianity and Judaism, fantasizes about destroying and occupying Rome, to complete its conquests of Constantinople and Jerusalem. That the Eternal City still survives is a source of constant frustration.

Europe—the region was in a near-perpetual state of war—demanded shifting alliances among the Habsburgs, the Papal States, and the Holy Roman Empire, which ofttimes crossed spiritual borders to advance temporal interests. When Clement VII was elevated to the papacy in 1523, he not only became the 290th pope, he also inherited a profoundly unstable geopolitical situation. Clement was caught between the demands of Francis I of France and the Holy Roman Emperor, the Habsburgian Charles V[11]—both Catholics. Clement threw in with the Kingdom of France to form something called the League of Cognac,[12] hoping to rid Italy of foreign occupation. At the same time, Suleiman the Magnificent, the Turkish sultan, was beginning his rampages across Central Europe; the Ottoman Turks were pushing their way deep into Christendom from the east.

Matters came to an unexpected head in May 1527.[13] Charles's troops had defeated the French forces in Italy at the Battle of Pavia in 1525, even capturing the French king and forcing him to cede Italy, Flanders, and Burgundy to the Habsburgs. The problem was, the Habsburgian monarch had no money with which to pay his restive troops still in Italy. This was a common problem, not only in renaissance Europe but all the way back to the time of the Romans, when generals like Caesar sometimes raised, borrowed, or stole money in order to keep their soldiers happy. No matter how magnificent the emperor, monarch, or potentate, it seems that money was somehow always in short supply; accordingly, soldiers were often given a share of the proceeds of victory, via plunder, booty, and rapine.

Charles could not prevent his forces under the Duke of Bourbon from sacking Rome in order to pay his soldiers. While Charles himself took a dim view of Lutheranism, his imperial forces included many German Protestants (known as *Landsknechte*, and under the command of Georg von Frundsberg), as well as a sizable contingent of Spaniards

---

11. A prominent, but never seen, character in Verdi's opera *Don Carlos*, the deceased emperor makes an implausible but dramatically decisive return from the dead at the opera's end.

12. Other members included England, independent Venice, the Duchy of Milan, and the Florentine republic.

13. That same year, Henry VIII demanded a divorce from his first wife, Catherine of Aragon, thus precipitating the split between Canterbury and Rome.

and Italians, including the powerful cardinal Pompeo Colonna, the scion of a patrician Roman family with considerable temporal interests and a man who bore Clement, a Medici, little love. With his troops on the verge of mutiny, the Holy Roman Emperor turned them loose on Rome itself.[14]

Renaissance Rome may have been the center of an emerging cultural movement that would soon enough sweep over France, Germany, and England—not to mention the seat of the Vatican and the locus of the Papal States—but in the face of the armed might of the Habsburgs, it was essentially defenseless. By this time, the Romans had become lovers, not fighters. There was no one to stop the 34,000 imperial troops, including some 14,000 Germans and 6,000 Habsburgian Spaniards, from rampaging through the Holy City, stealing or destroying just about everything they could get their hands on. Art, artifacts, buildings, treasure, women—everything and everybody was fair game. The slaughter was tremendous, the wreckage appalling. Churches were desecrated, wealthy Romans held for ransom.

Rome had been sacked before, of course. The Celtic Gauls were at the gates of the city after the Battle of the Allia, just north of Rome, in 387 B.C., a defeat so humiliating that Livy concludes what we have of his *History of Rome* with this account[15] of the defeat of the Republic before it had developed the Roman way of war:

> The Gauls for their part were almost dumb with astonishment at so sudden and extraordinary a victory. . . . Presently the yells and wild war-whoops of the squadrons were heard as they rode round the walls. All the time until the next day's dawn the citizens were in such a state of suspense that they expected from moment to

---

14. Religion usually finished second in the political wars of the sixteenth century; in 1536, the French even made a formal alliance with the Ottoman Turks, which lasted off and on until Napoleon—how quickly *Roland* had been forgotten. The political situation in France today, with its surging Muslim immigrant population, is not entirely without precedent. In 1947, the Swiss historian and diplomat Carl Jacob Burckhardt called the Franco-Muslim alliance "the sacrilegious union of the lily and the crescent."

15. See Extract 9.

> moment an attack on the City. . . . Finally, the approach of the next day deprived them of their senses; the entrance of the enemy's standards within the gates was the dreadful climax to fears that had known no respite.

Utter panic reigned in Rome. The able-bodied spirited away as many sacred objects as they could and fled the city, leaving the elderly behind. When the Gauls entered the undefended city, they at first suspected a trap. They couldn't believe no one was raising a hand to stop them, and looked in awe upon the old men sitting peacefully in the porticoes of their homes, awaiting death. "So they stood, gazing at them as if they were statues, till, as it is asserted, one of the patricians, M. Papirius, roused the passion of a Gaul, who began to stroke his beard—which in those days was universally worn long—by smiting him on the head with his ivory staff. He was the first to be killed, the others were butchered in their chairs. After this slaughter of the magnates, no living being was thenceforth spared; the houses were rifled, and then set on fire."

With the city in flames, and afflicted by famine and plague, the Gauls moved on the citadel. With no hope, the surviving Romans struck a humiliating bargain and ransomed themselves. "Woe to the vanquished," cried the Gauls as they collected at least a thousand pounds in gold, and then attacked again. The Roman general, Camillus, who had been living in exile in Ardea, was named dictator, raised an army, and counterattacked while the drunken Gauls were sleeping off their despoliation. They fled, and Rome survived.

Rome remained safe from invasion for more than half a millennium. But a weakened Empire fell victim to the Visigoths in 410, presaging the coming end.[16] Muslim Arab raiders appeared in 846 and sacked Old St. Peter's basilica, but were stymied by the Aurelian Wall of the city proper, which had been built between 271 and 275 A.D. The Normans took the city shortly after the conquest of Britain, and this time the monuments of ancient Rome were not so lucky. But nothing

---

16. The Visigoths under Alaric, having been Christianized, did a great deal of damage but spared the people who took refuge in St. Peter's and other churches.

approached the destruction visited upon the city in 1527—perhaps the least-remembered but most consequential event of the Renaissance. It was, in its way, as consequential as the Sack of Constantinople by the Crusaders in 1204.

Everybody knew it at the time. "What more criminal thing can be imagined than that those who had once been pledged to the Christian religion should exert themselves to destroy Her," wrote the priapic Henry VIII in July 1527, when he was still "Defender of the Faith." Others predicted that "there will be no business done at Rome for a long time and the city itself is so destroyed and ruined that until 200 years hence, it will not be Rome again." In fact, this Sack of Rome brought an abrupt end to the Italian Renaissance, to the world of Michelangelo and da Vinci and Julius II that had existed just a few decades before. It would take the Italians another three centuries to recover. Rome's barbarian chickens had come home to roost at last, destroying the remnants of a two-thousand-year-old civilization in their baleful wake.

Why was Rome, at this point, so easily conquered? The reason lies in the complexity of alliances and self-interests that characterized Europe in the sixteenth century as the nation-states began to rouse themselves, as the Holy Roman Empire began to disintegrate, as the conquest of the Americas (especially by the Spanish, who were developing a brutality in the Old World that they would soon transfer to the New) got fully underway, as papal temporal authority began to crumble, and as Europe hurtled toward the Thirty Years' War. According to contemporary accounts, most of the moral onus rests upon Pope Clement VII himself, who never saw the danger coming.

An eyewitness and combatant during the struggle for Rome was none other than Benvenuto Cellini, the very definition, along with da Vinci, of a Renaissance man. Sculptor, goldsmith, soldier, poet, Cellini[17] was manning the walls of Rome when the renegade army of Charles V attacked. As the Germans and Spaniards breached the walls, Cellini,

---

17. The subject of an 1838 opera by Hector Berlioz, seldom performed today. It is not from the composer's top drawer. The composer's "Roman Carnival Overture" (1844) repurposed some of the opera's more vigorous principal themes and manic energy to much greater effect.

as a member of the Medici papal household, was ordered to fall back across the Tiber to the safety of the Castel Sant'Angelo[18]:

> I ascended to the keep, and at the same instant Pope Clement came in through the corridors into the castle; he had refused to leave the palace of St. Peter earlier, being unable to believe that his enemies would effect their entrance into Rome.

The nineteenth-century British writer T. Adolphus Trollope (younger brother of the novelist Anthony), who lived in Rome much of his life, was particularly harsh in his assessment of Clement. With Charles's renegade troops making their way south through Italy, he wrote, "Pope Clement, with his usual avarice-blinded imbecility, had, immediately on concluding a treaty with the Neapolitan viceroy, discharged all his troops except a bodyguard of about six hundred men."

> The fate of Rome was no longer doubtful. Clement, who by his pennywise parsimony had left himself defenceless, made a feeble and wholly vain attempt to put the city in a state of defence. The corrupt and cowardly citizens could not have opposed any valid resistance to the ruffian hordes who were slowly but surely, like an advancing conflagration, coming upon them, even if they had been willing to do their best. But the trembling Pope's appeal to them to defend the walls fell on the ears of as sorely trembling men, each thinking only of the possible chances of saving his own individual person. Yet it seems clear that means of defence might have been found had not the Pope been thus paralyzed by terror. Clement, however, was as one fascinated. Martin du Bellay tells us that he himself, then in Italy as ambassador from Francis I, hurried to Rome, and warned the Pope of his danger in abundant time for him to have prepared for the protection of the city by the troops he had at his disposal. But no persuasion availed to induce

18. Originally built as the tomb of the Emperor Hadrian, it was completed in 139 A.D., a year after the emperor's death. In Puccini's opera *Tosca*, the eponymous heroine leaps to her death from its ramparts.

> Clement to take any step for that purpose. Neither would he seek safety by flight, nor permit his unfortunate subjects to do so.

In short, the pope was paralyzed, by his own weakness, his inability to understand the strategic situation, and his foolhardiness in prematurely dismissing his mercenary troops, some of them the very Swiss who would soon battle so fiercely to save him and the papacy. At the last minute, he and his retainers fled across the Tiber via the Passetto di Borgo, a raised, covered passageway from the Vatican to the fortified Castel Sant'Angelo,[19] overlooking the Tiber on its northwestern bank. Cellini describes the scene:

> Night came, the enemy had entered Rome, and we who were in the castle—especially myself, who have always taken pleasure in extraordinary sights—stayed gazing on the indescribable scene of tumult and conflagration in the streets below. People who were anywhere else but where we were could not have formed the least imagination of what it was.

In short, thanks to papal malfeasance and Roman pusillanimity, on May 6 the nearly defenseless capital of Christendom—in the end, there were only about five thousand *condottieri* (militiamen) to defend it—had been overwhelmed, followed by an orgy of rapine and plunder that ultimately went on for ten months. Literally nothing was sacred to the invaders, especially to the German Lutherans, who had prepared for just this moment. Writes Trollope:

> As for Frundsberg, he was a mere soldier of fortune, whose world was his camp, whose opinions and feelings had been formed in

---

19. The Eastern Empire general Belisarius had holed up in the fortress while retaking Rome and much of Italy from the Ostrogothic emperor in 537. According to the Byzantine Greek historian Procopius, who traveled with Belisarius, much of the statuary that adorned the mausoleum, however, was destroyed when the defending Byzantines smashed them and threw the rubble down upon the heads of the besiegers, who fled.

> quite another school from those of his fellow-general; whose code of honor and of morals was an entirely different one, and whose conscience was not only perfectly at rest respecting the business he was bound on, but approved of it as a good and meritorious work for the advancement of true religion. He carried round his neck a halter of golden tissue, we are told, with which he loudly boasted that he would hang the Pope as soon as he got to Rome; and had others of crimson silk at his saddle-bow, which he said were destined for the cardinals!

Typically, those on the losing side saw their discomfiture as a sign of God's displeasure; surely, they must have done something to deserve all this death and destruction. "The reader who bears in mind what Rome was—her vileness, her cowardice, her imbecility, her wealth, her arts, her monuments, her memories, her helpless population of religious communities of both sexes, and the sacred character of her high places and splendors, which served to give an additional zest to the violence of triumphant heretics—he that bears in mind all these things may safely give the reign to his imagination without any fear of overcharging the picture," writes Trollope. "That it would have been better for Rome to have been taken by the Turks, when they were in Hungary, as the infidels would have perpetrated less odious outrages and less horrible sacrilege."[20]

The carnage was described in vivid detail by Luigi Guicciardini (1478–1551), a Florentine and, like Clement, a Medici, whose memoir, *The Sack of Rome*,[21] was written shortly after the events he describes in often vivid, authentic detail; his brother, Francesco, commanded the pope's military.

---

20. Cardinal Wolsey, in a letter to Henry VIII, noted, "This day there is come letters from Venyce confyrming the same tydinges to be true. They write also that they have sackyd and spoylyd the town, and slayne to the nombre of 45,000, *non parcentes nec etati nec sexui nec ordini*; amongst other that they have murdyrd a marveillous sorte of fryars, and agaynst pristes and churchis they have behavyd thymselfes as it doth become Murranys and Lutherans to do."

21. Translated by James H. McGregor from the Italian edition of 1867.

> But after some insincere negotiation with the pope's representative, the Spanish and Germans, who had conferred by then, decided that they wouldn't waste any more time or worry about being tired and hungry. Once they had discovered how confused and vulnerable the city was, they decided that they would take the rest of it immediately. Killing anyone they encountered, they began a terrifying slaughter. But since there was no one who resisted their fury, in a short while they became masters of this ancient, noble city, full of all the riches that the greediest and hungriest army could desire.
>
> Here again the example of our predecessors puts us to shame, since nowadays four, six, or twelve thousand untrained foreigners, poorly armed and lacking leadership, harass, consume, and overpower this country of ours. And in response the wise give up hope and join the ignorant in declaring that there is no way for us to head off this scourge sent by the wrath of God, and that for our horrible sins we deserve such punishment and worse.

Worse is what Rome got.

Plunder, however, was not enough: this time the invaders had another objective: the capture of the Pope himself. And this is where the Swiss Guard comes in. As it happened, the Duke of Bourbon, the rabble's nominal commander and a man much despised by historians,[22] was killed in the initial assault. In his memoir, Cellini credits himself with firing the shot that killed the black sheep of the Bourbons:

> "Since you have brought me here, I must perform some action worthy of a man"; and, directing my arquebuse where I saw the thickest and most serried troop of fighting men, I aimed exactly at one whom I remarked to be higher than the rest: the fog prevented me from being certain whether he was on horseback or on foot. . . . I discovered afterward that one of our shots had killed the Constable of Bourbon; and, from what I subsequently

22. "A disgraced and ruined man beyond redemption," says Trollope.

> learned, he was the man whom I had first noticed above the heads of the rest.

Von Frundsberg was also absent, incapacitated by a stroke on the way to Rome while trying to tame his mutinous *Landsknechte* and hence *hors de combat* (he died, never having fully recovered, in 1528). Leaderless, the soldiers quickly turned into a vengeful mob.

After the death of Bourbon, there was some semblance of negotiation, but the stiff-necked Clement treated the army camped on his doorstep with supercilious contempt, curtly dismissing the Portuguese ambassador who was representing the Spanish investors. Blaming the cruel Spanish for the worst of the depredations, Guicciardini notes that at first the Germans were much more respectful of the articles of war—which, alas, involved "cutting to pieces anyone they came upon (an act that is very necessary in the first hours of a victory)." The Germans were also more respectful of women, unlike the "lustful" Spanish. But soon enough they, too, got into the spirit of things and an orgy of torture and plunder began, unequaled in the Renaissance and, likely, modern history as well.

> How many courtiers, how many genteel and cultivated men, how many refined prelates, how many devoted nuns, virgins, or chaste wives with their little children became the prey of these cruel foreigners! How many calixes, crosses, statues, and vessels of silver and gold were stolen from the altars, sacristies, and other holy places where they were stored. How many rare and venerable relics, covered with gold and silver, were despoiled by bloody, homicidal hands and hurled with impious derision to the earth. The heads of St. Peter, St. Paul, St. Andrew and many other saints; the wood of the Cross, the Thorns, the Holy Oil, and even consecrated Hosts were shamefully trodden underfoot in that fury.

As might be expected, the Roman Catholic clergy were special targets; for the Germans, they represented the archenemies of budding Lutheranism; for the Spanish and the Italians fighting on the side of Charles V, it was payback time for the louche, hypocritical lives so many of the holy men had led. There was also an element of internecine Italian squabbling between the Guelphs and the Ghibellines,[23] as well as between the Medicis and everybody else. It was all taken out in blood:

> Many were suspended by their arms for hours at a time; others were led around by ropes tied to their testicles. Many were suspended by one foot above the streets or over the water, with the threat that the cord suspending them would be cut. Many were beaten and wounded severely. Many were branded with hot irons in various parts of their bodies. Some endured extreme thirst; others were prevented from sleeping. A very cruel and effective torture was to pull out their back teeth. Some were made to eat their own ears, or nose, or testicles roasted; and others were subjected to bizarre and unheard of torments that affect me too strongly even to think of them, let alone to describe them in detail . . .
>
> When in the midst of such horror these savages wanted to amuse themselves, using similar tortures, they would force the prelates and courtiers to confess to their infamous and criminal habits. The obscenity and filth of their actions not only amazed and stupefied the foreigners, but forced them to admit that they would never have imagined that the human intellect could conceive of such shameful and bestial things, let alone do them. . . . I will not describe what happened to the noble and beautiful young matrons, to virgins and nuns, in order not to shame anyone. The majority were ransomed, and anyone can easily imagine for himself what must have happened when these women found themselves in the hands of such lustful people as the Spaniards. Since they devoted such energy and skill to the task of making their prisoners pay incomparable sums of money in order to escape from their hands, it is probable that they applied the same methods in order to insure the satisfaction of their hot and intemperate libidos.

---

23. The Guelphs sided with the pope, the Ghibellines with the Holy Roman Emperor.

> One cannot imagine therefore an unbearable form of torture that their prisoners did not experience and endure many times for the sake of cruel and insatiable greed. How patiently these torments were borne by refined and delicate prelates and effeminate courtiers, is easy to imagine, if one realizes with what difficulty in good times, they bore, not the ills of the body, but the bite of a fly. And because many of these barbarians feared that their prisoners had not revealed to them all the money and valuables that they had hidden away, they forced their prisoners, even if they were high-ranking nobles, to empty with their own hands the sewers and other disgusting places where human excrement and the like were disposed of. Anyone can imagine how much pain and suffering that must have given to those who had always been accustomed to having their houses, their clothes, their bodies, and especially their boots perfumed with sweet and alluring scents.
>
> The immense riches of the Roman nobility, preserved in their families for many centuries, were destroyed in an hour. . . . The sumptuous palaces of the cardinals, the proud palaces of the pope, the holy churches of Peter and Paul, the private chapel of His Holiness, the Sancta Sanctorum, and the other holy places, once full of plenary indulgences and venerable relics, now became the brothels of German and Spanish whores.

As a force of about 20,000 Spanish Bourbons and German *Landsknechte* approached the Vatican, the only thing between them and Clement were 189 members of the Swiss Guard, prepared to die rather than let the pope be captured. A pope would be worth a fortune in ransom, and besides, it was payback time for the Vatican's alliance with the defeated French. But the Guard cared little for the political events swirling around it. The men had sworn a blood oath to guard the person of the pontiff with their lives, and they intended to keep it. Under the command of Capt. Kaspar Röist, they fought a prolonged, pitched last stand on the steps of St. Peter's against the invaders.

It must have been one the bloodiest and most brutal battles since Cannae. The men of the Guard could not retreat; the Pope's troops had to stand and fight and die, which most of them did. Of the original company, only 42 managed to survive long enough to conduct a fighting retreat[24] into the Castel Sant'Angelo. Although we lack eyewitness descriptions of this battle itself, it is possible to reconstruct what might have happened from what we know of the Swiss military tactics of the time.

For one thing, the Swiss hated the Habsburgs; indeed, Swiss independence grew out of the Helvetian resistance to them,[25] so it's no wonder that the Guard would resist so fiercely. The idea of the Swiss citizen-soldier, with every man pledged and armed to fight for the defense of his landlocked, mountainous country, created as well a supply of mercenaries, who rented out their endurance, ferocity, and battle-hardened tactics to the highest bidders in Europe. The same people who had harassed the mighty Hannibal on his way to Cisalpine Gaul and Italy had little fear of anybody else. It was part of their code to take no prisoners, to kill or be killed, and everybody knew it.

Additionally, the Swiss were defensive fighters. As early as the Roman period, but certainly from the thirteenth century on, they had barricaded their mountain passes to create *Letzinen* (fortifications), and the Swiss soldiers were never happier than when the odds were against them. At the Battle of St. Jacob-en-Birs (1444), about a thousand Swiss held off a Habsburgian force of about 15,000 for four hours; they died to a man, but took twice their number with them. Armed with halberds, pikes, and swords, the Swiss in formation could repel any form of cavalry (horses would not charge into a rank of eighteen-foot-long pikes), and their other weapons were lethal at close range.

By 1525, though, the Swiss were already fading as an offensive fighting force. France's defeat at the Battle of Pavia was caused by the

---

24. A forerunner of the Marines at Chosin: see Chapter XIII.

25. Albrecht Gessler, the villain of the William Tell legend, was an Austrian Habsburg. Tell's refusal to salute Gessler's hat, his feat of crossbow marksmanship in splitting the apple atop his son's head, and his subsequent killing of Gessler are all part of Switzerland's origin story. They date from the late fifteenth century.

failure of the Swiss pikemen to stop Charles V's Spanish brigades on the French flank, in part due to the withering fire of the Spanish *arquebusiers*. The old pike squares—a descendent of the phalanx and the legions—could not compete with the combined firepower of the attackers.

So with the Germans and Spaniards pouring into St. Peter's Square, the Guard did what it did best: starting at the Teutonic Cemetery and moving to the steps of St. Peter's, it fought off the invaders by forming a moving square that could escort the pope to safety from the Vatican through the Passetto di Borgo and into the nearly impregnable Castel Sant'Angelo. The Helvetians managed to escort the pope into the old mausoleum, to join some cardinals and prelates who had had the good sense to escape to safety early in the battle. The rest, including Röist, died, but they took hundreds, if not thousands, of the invaders with them and thus ensured the pope's survival.

Despite their heroics, Clement surrendered on June 6; the price was a ransom of 400,000 ducats and the concession of various papal territories. Charles thus won a free hand to expand his empire in Italy while strengthening his hold on Spain and Central Europe. The League of Cognac effectively collapsed. The freed but humiliated pope now toed the imperial line, crowning Charles the Holy Roman Emperor in 1530; he also refused the request of his erstwhile ally, Henry VIII, to annul the king's marriage to Catherine of Aragon—who happened to be Charles's aunt—thus precipitating the Reformation in England. Clement's reign is one of the great disasters in papal history.

Guicciardini concludes his account with this doleful, but fully deserved, image:

> One can easily imagine the anguish and torment of the pope, constantly seeing and hearing such a scourge of punishment raised against himself and against Rome. Like the rest of those under siege, he is suffering in fear that he will soon fall into the hands of cruel enemies, obviously thirsting for his blood. And though he enjoyed great honors and sweet pleasures in the past, now he is paying for them with humiliation and pitiful distress. If he ever considered himself a wise and glorious prince, now he

> must acknowledge himself to be the most unfortunate and the most abject pontiff who ever lived. And since it is his fault that the Church, Rome, and Italy all find themselves in such extreme danger, we can easily imagine that he often looks toward the sky with tears in his eyes and with the bitterest and deepest sighs demands: "Wherefore, then, hast thou brought me forth out of the womb? Oh, that I had died, and no eye had seen me!" [Job 10:18]

In short, the Sack of Rome was an unmitigated cultural and military disaster of the highest magnitude. It ushered in the wars of religion that plagued Europe for a century and more, and its ramifications are with us still, including the division of Europe along a north-south religious axis, and is currently reflected in the history and makeup of the European Union. It is not so *ancient* as we might suspect.

Today, new members of the Swiss Guard are sworn in on May 6, to honor the valor of their comrades of five hundred years ago; the ceremonies begin with an early Mass, a wreath-laying service, the taking of the oath, and conclude with a private audience with the pope. In the light of modern history, who is to say their services will not someday be needed again? One of the fallacies of modern historical interpretation is that what's past is past, that it dies along with its protagonists. But does it? History has a longer arc than modernity might suspect. And it may not always bend toward "justice."

Just ask the Romans.

CHAPTER VII

"TODAY WE BRING DIGNITY UPON OUR NAMES"

THE SIEGE OF SZIGETVÁR (1566)

On the last day, with nearly all their resources exhausted, food supplies running low, ammunition and other military capabilities nearly expended, the six hundred or so remaining Hungarian and Croatian soldiers, out of an original force of 2,300 fighting men still holed up in the castle of Szigetvár's keep, gathered around their prince, the Count Miklós Zrínyi. In two languages—for the Zrínyi family was of Croatian origin, the name rendered as Nikola Zrinski—he explained the situation. The Turkish forces under Suleiman the Magnificent, numbering at least 100,000 and perhaps twice that, had destroyed two previous redoubts within the city walls, having pounded those same walls to rubble with the most fearsome weapons of the age, Turkish cannons. The outnumbered Christian forces in the small fortress had no chance of either victory or survival. There was only one thing left to do—and that was to open the last gate, charge across a narrow wooden bridge, and die to the last man.

If anyone demurred, his voice was not recorded. And so they did.

Szigetvár—the name in Hungarian means the "fortress of Sziget"—is the name of the small town in what is now Hungary, but which at that time fell within that large portion of Hungarian territory occupied by the Ottoman Turks as they pressed their expansionist wars of conquest against the Christian Hungarian and Croatian kings (often united in one kingdom) and the Habsburg Empire. Then, as now, Hungary was on the front lines of the conflict between East and West, with the Habsburg royal seat of Vienna the ultimate prize—the overland gateway into the heart of Christendom and thus a trophy of enormous symbolic importance to the Muslims, who had conquered the Eastern Roman Empire's capital of Constantinople[1] little more than a century earlier, in 1453. With the defeat of the Hungarian forces at the Battle of Mohács in 1526, the Turks under Suleiman had taken command of a huge swath of the Kingdom of Hungary (effectively bisecting it), including the city of Buda[2]; had killed the Hungarian king Louis (Lajos) II; and had dealt a terrible blow to the forward defenses of Christian Europe, which now quaked in terror at the oncoming, all-conquering Turk. Indeed, in 1529, Suleiman had laid siege to Vienna itself, lasting two weeks before ending in failure and withdrawal.

Three years later, Martin Luther published *Vom Kriege wider die Türken* (On the War Against the Turks), in which he sounded the tocsin against the moral, religious, political, and territorial threat of metastasizing Islam. Originally, Luther had viewed the Turks as God's punitive justice against European Christians who had fallen from their faith, and a welcome corrective against the impiety he had so recently excoriated in his *Ninety-Five Theses.*

The spiteful Luther, a man motived by a Luciferian rage against his real and perceived enemies[3]—particularly the pope (the "anti-Christ") and the Jews—had finally awakened somewhat to the Muslim threat, partially rearranging his "we had it coming" attitude[4] to one a bit more prudential, although, dogmatically, he still regarded orthodox Catholics and Jews as far greater sinners. Luther dove into the Old Testament, particularly the apocalyptic Book of Daniel,[5] to find the biblical prophecy he needed in the account of Daniel's vision of the four terrifying beasts: "I saw in my vision by night, and, behold, the four winds of the

1. The name of which became corrupted as "Istanbul."

2. The hilly western half of Budapest, across the Danube from Pest.

3. Luther would not be rivaled in this animus for three centuries, until the arrival of the composer Richard Wagner and then Adolf Hitler.

4. An attitude reflected in the epic poem *Siege of Sziget*, as we shall see.

5. See Chapter III.

heaven strove upon the great sea. And four great beasts came up from the sea, diverse one from another." They were a lion with eagle's wings, a bear, a leopard, and then a fourth monster, "dreadful and terrible," with iron teeth, "diverse from all the beasts that were before it; and it had ten horns."

Belatedly, Luther had become alarmed by the ease with which some conquered Christians had adopted Islam,[6] whether by choice or under duress, and so the necessity of stopping the Turks as a matter of cultural and religious self-defense had become evident. Accordingly, he devoted his writings to providing theological counterarguments to what he viewed as the Islamic heresy, issuing one of the first Western translations of the Koran in 1543.

In other words, the Christian West was finally beginning to see the arrival of Islam on its doorstep as an existential threat, both religiously and politically. Even the loss of the Holy Land in the late twelfth century to Saladin and the Ayyubid Sunnis (Saladin was not Arab, but Kurdish), the ceding of formerly Christian Anatolia, the Islamic crossing of the Bosphorus—the traditional boundary between Europe and Asia, the subjugation of Constantinople, and the conversion of the Cathedral of St. Sophia into a mosque—the Islamic signal of permanent conquest—had not alarmed the West in the same way that Mohács, or the near-fall of Vienna, had done.

Now something had to be done—but the Habsburgs were not the people to do it. Nor were any of the other emerging European nation-states, most of which would soon enough be (in large part thanks to Luther) embroiled in one of the deadliest and costliest wars in European history, the destructive and, in retrospect, pointless Thirty Years' War of religion between 1618 and 1648.

So in this instance it was left to the Hungarians and Croats, peoples of what today we term Eastern Europe, to defend the West. Ironically, both the Hungarians—who traced their lineage back to Attila

---

6. Indeed, Islamic armies of the time often featured elite warriors called Janissaries, composed largely of captured and converted Christians but also including some Christian allies of the Turks.

the Hun[7]—and the Turks, who arrived on the fringes of Europe in the eleventh century, were of non-European derivation. But Attila was defeated at Châlons in 451 by the Roman general Aetius, whereas the Turks had been Islamified in Central Asia as early as the seventh and eighth centuries, a faith they brought with them westward, still very much fueled by its homicidal missionary zeal.

Zrínyi's is a name almost unknown to Americans in particular and to Westerners in general, unless, heading east from the Danube in downtown Pest, they are suddenly motivated by a desire to visit St. Stephen's Basilica, in which case the *Zrínyi utca* is the road that will deliver them directly to Szent István's doorstep. The lone statue on the street is not one of Zrínyi but rather that of the Fat Policeman stationed at the intersection of the *Oktober 6 utca*, next to which tourists from all over the world take selfies after rubbing his shiny, ample belly for good luck before deciding where to dine among of the many restaurants that dot the neighborhood.

And yet, in Central Europe, where the struggle against recrudescent Islam continues to this day, Zrínyi lives on, principally through the epic poem by his great-grandson—a splendid military man in his own right who spent most of his life battling the Turks as well. The poem is *The Siege of Sziget,* by the hero's namesake, Miklós Zrínyi (1620–64), written in just one month while the poet was wintering on campaign against the Ottomans and published just short of a century after the battle that took the life of his famous great-grandfather, but which, in the words of Cardinal Richelieu, "saved civilization." While the subsequent repulse of the Turks at the Gates of Vienna in 1683 turned out to be the decisive defeat that finally halted Muslim expansionism into the West, historians have long noted the crucial importance Szigetvár played in Christendom's survival in the mid-millennium.

For one thing, the battle itself took the life of Suleiman, the most potent Mohammedan commander since Saladin four centuries earlier. The tremendous casualties inflicted by the Croat and Hungarian forces

7. "Attila" remains a popular boys' name in Hungary today.

upon the Muslims during their resistance severely weakened the sultan's army and made an attack upon Vienna at that point unfeasible. Finally—and something easily discounted today but of huge importance at the time—was the symbolic victory of the Christian God over Mahomet and Allah. Just as we saw in *The Song of Roland*, clashes between Christian and Islamic armies were seen as not merely military but theological Armageddons as well.

Szigetvár had all the elements necessary for an epic struggle, and one worthy of being immortalized in a poem in the manner of Homer's *Iliad*, Virgil's *Aeneid*, and the *Chanson de Roland*. That it is not nearly as well known in the West can be explained by the course of Islamic, Napoleonic, Habsburgian, and Soviet European history, the impenetrability of the Hungarian language to outsiders, and the political developments that have afforded both Hungary (though territorially a rump of what it formerly was) and the Croatian nation-state a greater prominence in European affairs.

The Siege of Sziget is one of the touchstones of Hungarian literature,[8] and a valuable, eyewitness account of what the Turkish wars were like, told from an authoritative military perspective. With deliberate echoes, including one major character name, of Virgil's *Aeneid*, it is also an adumbration of not only the moral principles of Milton's *Paradise Lost* but also some of its incidents, especially Book II, the satanic debate in Pandemonium. In this instance, it is the scene from Part Eight, set among the Muslim commanders as they discuss how best to attack the fortress of Sziget and kill the insolent Christian prince who dares oppose them—a man they both hate and fear, just as Lucifer hates God, fears St. Michael,[9] who defeated him and the rebellious third of the heavenly host under his command in the War in Heaven.

---

8. The poem also contributed to the enlargement—often by classical or foreign loan-words—of the Hungarian vocabulary, which the poet himself lamented in the poem's foreword: "Latin words I have mixed into my verses, for I thought it more pleasing thus, and then the Hungarian language is impoverished . . ."

9. St. Michael even makes an appearance early in the poem, unleashing one of the *Erinyes*, Alecto, to appear to the Turkish sultan, Suleiman, in the guise of his dead father to inspire him to go to war against the faithless, strayed Hungarian Christians.

Indeed, in the poem's second quatrain, Zrínyi the poet strums Virgil's heroic lyre:

Arms and heroes I sing! The might of the Turks.
Him who was willing to undergo Suleiman's wrath–
That same Suleiman's mighty arm,
He at whose saber Europe trembled.

So the poet invokes, as did Virgil, Homer the Muse. To us, four hundred years later, *The Siege of Sziget* may seem merely a talisman of a bygone age, much like *The Song of Roland*, featuring dead heroes expiring nobly in a lost cause, but not before a great deal of mayhem, limb-severing, and bloodshed, as two antithetical faiths battle each other for doctrinal and military supremacy.[10]

But it would be to misread the situation by applying evanescent contemporary standards of ideology to the very real emotions, beliefs, and practical lives of the people of the sixteenth century. Few, if any, counseled diversity, tolerance, or peaceful coexistence with the Turks. There was no American tradition of secularized democracy (however historically false that notion of the Founding actually is) which conflated, and confused, the idea of political citizenship with national identity according to the *jus sanguinis*, as opposed to the *jus soli*. Rather (as we have seen with Luther), the Islamified Turk was considered a double existential threat, both militarily and religiously, no matter which lands he had conquered. He was someone who would, if he could, expunge Christianity and the emerging nation-states of Europe in favor of the Islamic *ummah* under a caliph holding court in the conquered, formerly Christian, capital of Istanbul—the City of Constantine, the first Christian Emperor.

In short, no one advocated a negotiated settlement with the Turks, except on a provisional or compulsory basis. Alliances and even surrender, of course, occurred—but as the Christians learned to their dismay,

10. Judaism is lacking in such apocalyptical artistic expression.

the Turkish word was nearly worthless; the Muslim doctrine of *taqiyyah*[11] saw to that. Time and again in *The Siege of Sziget*, Zrínyi remarks upon the faithlessness of the Turks and on the dire consequences that befell those Christians who trusted them. Let one example, among many, suffice:

Foolish is he who believes the Turk's oath,
Especially if he entrusts his life to the Turks.
A Turk considers it a sin to hold to his word,
Especially if it is given to a Christian.

And yet the poet Zrínyi—again, writing from his personal experience on the battlefield—does not disparage or underestimate the Turks' military prowess. Instead, like all the Christians of the time, he evinces a healthy respect for Muslim military might, especially regarding their expert development and employment of siege cannons against walled cities such as Szigetvár, and even of the moral caliber of their greatest leaders. In Christian eyes of the time—as exemplified both by Luther and Zrínyi—the Turks believed fervidly in their Mahometan faith and considered their zealotry worthy of emulation by Christians who had often wandered far afield from the tenets of their own devotions. The Turk—the exemplar of Islam—was everywhere to be feared, cleft in twain, beheaded, extirpated, but respected as a worthy adversary, and one sent by God to chastise errant Christians. He was, in short, the ultimate beneficial bogeyman.[12]

I must write the truth, listen to me now:
Though Sultan Suleiman was our enemy,

11. Lying to an "infidel" for religious or, more usually, political or military gain.

12. It was a sign of Christian confidence, and relief, after the Western victory at Vienna in 1683, that the vanquished Turk could be lampooned in popular culture by Mozart—in *Die Entführung aus dem Serail* (The Abduction from the Seraglio, 1782)—and Rossini in both *L'Italiana in Algeri* (The Italian Girl in Algiers, 1813) and *Il turco in Italia* the following year.

Only his faith being pagan aside,
Perhaps never was there such a lord amongst the Turks.

Indeed, throughout the poem, the Christians and Muslims are evenly matched in fortitude, military skill, bravery, and adherence to the faith. Only the numbers were in favor of the Turks. Preparing for the siege with skill and expertise, Zrínyi musters (according to the poem) not only his men but their rations and their armaments: wine, bread, meat, salt; picks, ladders, shovels, materials for starting fires, and even primitive fire extinguishers. And more: lumber, barrows, flammable wood, saltpeter, sulfur, burnt charcoal, grenades made from hard oak—"In one word, everything that is needed for a fort, he had brought." The pitiless Turks meant business.

The determinative factor, of course, is the Turks' superior manpower, the number of their powerful siege cannons, their sappers, Janissaries, and multiethnic squadrons of Believers from all across the *ummah*, which allows them to draw on a wider variety of military skills and specialties than the Hungarians and Croats have at their disposal.

From the start, Zrínyi knows his is a lost cause, and that his brave last stand will cost him his life. And yet, like a true Christian martyr, he goes to his death willingly, even joyously (he even has a conversation with God about it), certain that his redeemer liveth, and that this day, like St. Dismas,[13] he will be with Jesus in Paradise. For their part, the Muslims also credit the rightness of their faith, believe they are on a holy quest to destroy the heretical Christians (and, by extension, their spiritual fathers, the Jews), and thus fulfill their prophet's final revelation from the Almighty.

Today, we fight over politics and seek political solutions to problems so academically intractable that, thanks to political correctness, we can no longer give them either tongue or voice. For at root, war is not about ideology—no one dies for an abstract, impersonal concept, no matter how motivated or animated he was at first by its tenets—but by the most personal and elemental emotions to which the human animal is given: home, hearth, country, faith, leader. When the Muslim and Christian

13. The "good thief," who dies alongside Jesus on the cross, and whose soul is saved.

heroes clash at Szigetvár, they may have been mustered there by faith, however described, but equally they meet on the field of honor because of their tribe and their sex. When the fearsome Saracen general Demirham and the Christian knight Deli Vid (married to a Turkish girl who converted to Christianity) collide for the second time, they both fell each other, each dying a hero's death:

Vid, however, makes [Demirham] to fall further,
For his breast with his gleaming sword he forces open,
Then his weeping soul he spews below the earth,
By a terrible shadow his life is darkened.
Deli Vid himself can struggle no further,
Just barely he manages to hold in his spirit,
Close to Demirham, he too fell there,
The sky sees his soul, the grass drinks his blood.

Szigetvár was a battle about both faith and blood and language and home: all that is elemental in man. Faith is what drives the men on both sides—but blood (lineage) alone accounts for the burning desire not to dishonor their families' names (the flip side of their desire for glory or even salvation). As in *La Chanson de Roland*, *The Siege of Sziget* is about fighting and killing, wallowing in its own bloodthirstiness, expecting its audience not to be appalled by the carnage but to vicariously revel in it. Not to fear the onslaught of death but to welcome it as the ultimate proof of manhood. Not to fear for the safety of the men on either side but to admire them for their *sangfroid* in the face of their unknown, but most likely lethal, fates. It is a battle of hero against hero, of the Hungarians and Croats against the mightiest warriors drawn from across the sultan's lands. It is, in the end, a war of heroes against heroes. Indeed, as in *Roland*, the *Aeneid*, *The Iliad*, and every other classical epic, it is a story of superheroes—the foundational origin story of all subsequent origin stories.

In one of several echoes and callbacks to the *Aeneid*, *The Siege of Sziget* features a prominent female character named Cumilla.[14] Here,

14. "Camilla," the Lycian warrior princess in the *Aeneid*.

she is a Muslim princess, the daughter of the sultan himself, married to the impotent Rushtan but in love with the mighty Tatar warrior Deliman, who slaughters the cowardly Rushtan in his tent and, poisoned by love's arrows, rudely takes the princess in her bed. Writes the poet:

What shall I say about their union:
Romantic youths' many romances?
They redouble their kisses around each others' mouths,
Their hearts rejoice over Venus's victory parade.
As ivy enwraps a tree
As a snake winds about a pillar,
As Bacchus's vine leans on a post,
In so many ways did the two phoenixes, entangled, sway.

It's been noted that the only love story in this fifteen-part epic occurs on the Muslim side, another example of the poet Zrínyi's empathy even for a mortal enemy. For there can be no doubt, whether reading *Roland* or *Sziget*, that the Christian poets viewed their Islamic enemies as fully worthy of both respect and fear, even as they girded their loins to combat and kill them in the cruelest and most violent ways possible. Both sides were confident in the righteousness of their causes; all's fair in love and war.

For these were also wars for women—to protect them from the unequal physical struggle against an armed masculine warrior, fueled by zealotry, greed, anger, revenge, and lust. Everyone in a besieged city knew what his or her fate would be should the walls come tumbling down: the men and boys were to be slaughtered or enslaved, and the women and girls to be raped into concubinage or sold into sexual and domestic slavery.[15] There was no contemporary "moral" element in any of this; these were simply the spoils of war, the bonus pay due a victorious army.

But there is another element; in defending their women, the warriors were also defending their families and, most important, the sons who would carry on their bloodlines—or another's. *The Siege of Sziget* has several examples of sons wishing to stay and fight beside their fathers,

15. The number of Western women abducted into Muslim harems by the North African Barbary pirates between 1530 and 1780 is estimated at one million.

only to be sent packing because for their fathers, the preservation of the bloodline is more important than a moment of foolish, youthful, transient glory. The boys will grow up to become men and, like the Zrínyis themselves, will continue the fight until the fight is either won or lost, for as long as it takes.

This philosophy and cultural attitude strikes us today as absurd, even barbaric (how the Romans would have laughed), and certainly as "sexist," a word, as well as a term of opprobrium, entirely unknown to our ancestors. Indeed, some of the noblest words in the English language, deriving from Latin, contain elements of masculinity in their roots, including *virtue* (from the Latin for "man") and *testimony,* from the Roman practice of holding one's testicles while swearing an oath. Absent the Bible, there was nothing more sacred that a man could swear upon than his own masculinity and the lives of his male progeny.

And so, poetically and dramatically, *Roland* first boils down to a contest among and between men—between the French champion and the villainous Marsile of Saragossa, and, later, between Charlemagne and the pasha Baligant. Therefore must *Sziget* also end with a confrontation between the Christian hero Zrínyi and the Muslim commander Suleiman, even if such a duel never actually happened.[16] There are many others stories of single combat—for war at this time was a series of single combats, some brief, some epic—but in the end, like any good movie, the story comes down to the hero and the villain, face-to-face at last.

There is something elemental in this form of storytelling. Achilles must meet his Hector for the *Iliad* to have dramatic shape and impact; and though we might root for Hector, who after all is simply defending his homeland from the invading Greeks, Hector must die that the Greeks might win—and the morally flawed Achilles must also die. It is significant that in this, one of the earliest examples of the Western way

---

16. There is, of course, no way to know for sure. Zrínyi, the great-grandson, was obviously far closer in time to Suleiman's death, although he does have a vested interest in giving his distinguished ancestor a noble martyr's death. Then again, neither would it serve Muslim hagiography to have Suleiman cut down while fleeing the battlefield.

of storytelling about the Western way of war, Achilles is not vouchsafed a hero's death because, in violation of the rules of war and in rejection of the Trojan hero's dying plea, Achilles desecrates the body by dragging it behind his chariot around the walls of the city. His death at the hands of the cowardly Paris, shot from behind by an arrow in his one vulnerable spot, is thus fully deserved, and dramatically right. Heroes are, after all, heroes.

Audiences hate to see the final confrontation—which is invariably between good and evil—occurring offstage. If it does, they feel cheated of the necessary catharsis the Greeks instinctively understood as essential to proper drama. Real life may not always be able to shoehorn itself into a three-act structure (beginning, middle, end, according to Aristotle), but its dramatic retelling or foretelling most certainly can, and must be. And even when we know the ending and the outcome—Leonidas dies, Roland dies, Zrínyi dies—we nonetheless watch, look, and listen raptly right to the ordained, immutable end. Even when evil triumphs over good, as it so often does, we want to see it—and then see good return for the rematch.

One of the aspects of heroism that so often goes unremarked, but which emerges so clearly from epics like *The Siege of Sziget*, is that the heroes know that their self-sacrifices are simply tiles in the great, ongoing mosaic of history. Zrínyi understands that unless the Habsburg emperor Maximilian comes to his aid, he has no chance of staving off Suleiman's forces. Accordingly, he sends out two scouts to try and hack their way through the Turkish lines by night (most of the Turks are drunk and insensible); they almost make it, and then are caught and chopped to pieces. At that moment—their demises are reported to him in the night by one of his most heroic warriors, Deli Vid, who saw their deaths in a dream—Zrínyi knows that help will not arrive in time[17] and that he and his Hungarian and Croatian warriors are doomed.

And yet the Christians fight on, somehow relieved that relief will not come and that their deaths, while foreordained, can only result in ultimate glory. Thus freed of fear, they determine to sell their lives as

17. His own death is an adumbration of Gordon's at Khartoum, more than three hundred years later. See Chapter XI.

dearly as possible, to take as many Turks with them as they can, and to let history sort things out. In Part Five of the poem we read, "*Because fear falls not upon the unmovable / He who with a true cause and a good heart is armed.*" The temptation of a coward's way out, through flight or suicide, is no longer available, and it comes as great relief.

And here we arrive at a key element in all our accounts of last stands, which is the cultural confidence it takes to relate these stories. History is generally written by the winners, but sometimes—as in the case of the last stands under discussion here—it takes a crushing loss in order to inspire the winning side to victory.

In his soul, every boy understands that, on some level, he must test and measure and weigh himself against not only his father, but also the other boys of his generation: to compete with them as men, to fight with them, to ally or struggle with them. There is among males an unconscious sizing up, whether of moral, technical, or physical prowess, something that every boy who's ever had to wait to be picked for a sandlot game understands. There is no test, no curriculum, no set of laws that determines the pecking order among males; only an unspoken but widely acknowledged obeisance to the instinctive masculine chain of command.

At Szigetvár, Zrínyi and Suleiman are the top dogs, and everybody knows it. They stand at the apogee of their respective armies by dint of their military prowess, their wisdom, their faith. Whether they are "good" or "bad" is immaterial; what matters is that their men respect, obey, and follow them to the death. Their soldiers heed their personal examples and willingly carry out any orders they are given. There is little or no discussion (and then only among senior officers); there is no democracy, no committees, few if any meetings, and no plebiscites. Feminine emotions do not figure into the discussions. There is only willpower, to be put to the test in order to answer the question: Whose is greater? For all the bloodshed, all battles are, in the end, contests of wills.

Thus the graphic descriptions of the combats we find in these epic poems. As at Hastings, heads roll, skulls are cleft, limbs are lopped off and fly through the air. More poignantly, life is often described as "escaping" through the gaping and grievous wounds the warriors suffer; their blood is "tasted" by their opponents' swords and spears and even the Earth herself; their deaths are not something lived briefly in agony but instead are presented as an almost welcome reward after the fear and pain of the battlefield. Everyone must die, and this is how these men choose to die. Turk or Christian alike, they believe their souls will go elsewhere, and thus their faith animates them in a way an unbeliever's agnosticism cannot. If there are no foxholes in these battles, neither are there any atheists.

As in *La Chanson de Roland*, we might perhaps dismiss these descriptions as poetic license. But that is our weakness, not the poets'. The younger Zrínyi was as much a veteran of the Turkish wars as was his great-grandfather. He knew what single combat was like. He knew the wounds swords, arrows, spears, and, especially, cannonballs could make. To get hit was a statistical improbability, but once hit, death was nearly an inevitability. Few soldiers recovered from their wounds, and when the armaments did not kill them, infection and disease did. From each individual combat, there could emerge only one winner.

The advent of gunpowder hastened fate. By the sixteenth century, the Turks were fighting not only with arrows but also muskets (mostly wielded by Janissaries, who were, unlike the Turks, excellent shots) and deadly siege cannons. So also were Zrínyi's men, although not to the same extent. During the Siege of Malta the year before, the Knights Hospitaller[18] under Jean Parisot de Valette had held off the Turkish fleet under Suleiman for four bloody months, during which the two thousand or so Hospitallers—who had been evicted in 1522 from their prior stronghold of Rhodes, only to occupy the more strategic island of Malta, in the middle of the Mediterranean—fought to the end, finally repelling the Turkish host.[19] To this day, the name of the Maltese capital, Valletta, commemorates the Hospitaller who defeated Suleiman's Turks.

Nonetheless, whether by sea or by land, the Turks were the most

---

18. The Knights, a remnant of the fighting crusader orders (the other was the fearsome Knights Templar, who were destroyed on Friday the thirteenth 1307 on the orders of the French monarch, Philip IV), facilitated the pilgrims' journey to the Holy Land across two thousand miles of dangerous territory.

19. Destroyed completely by a European alliance under the Spaniard Don Juan of Austria (the bastard son of the Holy Roman Emperor, Charles V) at Lepanto, in the Ionian Sea in western Greece, in 1571. Cervantes, the author of *Don Quixote*, fought at Lepanto.

formidable enemy the Christian Europeans of that time could possibly face. Awaiting the arrival of Suleiman's army, Zrínyi looks out from his tower to see, approaching from a distance, "a dark cloud in the air . . . as if a mountain were moving on a level plain." The sight must have been at once terrifying and definitive. As the poem relates, Suleiman at first tries direct hand-to-hand combat with the Christians who sally forth to engage his forces before the walls of the city. But the Croats and Hungarians get the best of that battle, sending the Turkish commanders scurrying back into camp to debate how best to take the city. Their solution is a classic siege: they dig trenches around the fort to prevent the soldiers from emerging, they excavate the moats and drain them, they atomize the walls of the citadel with cannon fire—"shovels and ammunition take forts."

To visit Szigetvár today is only to glimpse, as through a glass darkly, what happened there almost five centuries ago. The old town is gone, and the waterway on which it was built is gone as well; the modern town of Szigetvár lies a short distance from the battlefield, as do the homey residential neighborhoods. What remains is a restored version of the castle keep, the redoubt from which Zrínyi and his remaining men sallied forth in their final stand against the swarming Turks. The narrow wooden bridge, over which they passed and on which they fought and died, has been replicated, and there are statues of the armored Christian warriors on the grounds, serried in ranks and ready to march again if need be and when called forth from their graves. There is also an informative museum as well as a reconstruction of the mosque with which Suleiman's forces temporarily memorialized their conquest. It is quiet now, the reports and cannonades, shouts and screams long since stilled.

How different it was back then! It is hard for modern people to grasp the noise of war. In the sixteenth century, Turkish cannons in their plentitude could pound a city's walls to rubble in a matter of days—indeed, in the poem, the Turks decide to crush Sziget in exactly this way, after losing early pitched battles to the Western knights. The guns on both sides, manned both by the Christians and the Muslim Janissaries, were (as guns are today) startlingly loud, especially in an age in which there was no man-made ambient noise to inure the ear. The clang of metal on metal, the thump of spears and arrows into shields, and, above all, the screams of the wounded and the dying, which lingered on long after the guns had been silenced, formed the aural backdrop to the warfare of this period.

It was only natural that some good had to be found in this, and that good was to be found in innate ideals of bravery, martial skills, physical prowess, moral courage and endurance, and a willingness to fight to the death, which after all was the only option, other than flight, a soldier had back then. The body counts of modern warfare are terrifying, especially involving the usage of powerful bombs and even nuclear weapons, but as we have seen, the Greeks and Romans would have regarded long-range rifles as they did bows and arrows—as the weapons of cowards not man enough to stand toe to toe with their opponent, to either kill or be killed.

In short, warfare was elemental, in the same way that life of that time was. The fundamental things applied: birth, life, sex, war, progeny (whether born or unborn), and death. No one expected to live very long in any case, certainly not by contemporary standards; death, in fact, was the whole point of life, its foregone conclusion, and the only question was how it would come and how a man would meet it. A good death elevated a life; a noble death enshrined it. Disease and accidents killed far more people than warfare, but only warfare held out the promise of territorial and personal gain, the slaking of a lust for money, women, or power, and the promise of a better future, even if it took place over the corpses of others. Given human nature and the verities of the human condition, war was not only inevitable but desirable.

As the French army officer and influential war theoretician Ardant du Picq writes in *Battle Studies* (1880)[20]:

> Centuries have not changed human nature. Passions, instincts, among them the most powerful one of self-preservation, may be manifested in various ways according to the time, the place, the

---

20. Du Picq died in 1870 at Metz of wounds suffered during the Franco-Prussian war; his book was published posthumously.

> character and temperament of the race.[21] Thus in our times we can admire, under the same conditions of danger, emotion and anguish, the calmness of the English, the dash of the French, and that inertia of the Russians which is called tenacity. But at bottom there is always found the same man. It is this man that we see disposed of by the experts, by the masters, when they organize and discipline, when they order detailed combat methods and take general dispositions of action. The best masters are those who know man best, the man of today and the man of history.

The men who emerge from the stanzas of *The Siege of Sziget* are not so very different from the men of today—or at least the men of the day before yesterday. Neither steroid-fueled behemoths nor bewhiskered, chestless boys, they were ordinary in size and stature (we would be surprised by how small yet physically strong they actually were) but outsized in courage and resolve. Their fighting worth came via discipline and a profound knowledge of human nature; for proof of that, we can reach back to Caesar and his *Commentaries* on the Gallic wars and the events leading up to the Roman civil war and the fall of the Republic. His views of the Gallic temperament—that the Gauls were crazy brave but also undisciplined, prone to discouragement, and ready to flee at a sudden reversal of fortune—were spot on, and help to account for his victories, perhaps most spectacularly during the siege of Alesia in 52 B.C. when, outnumbered as much as four to one at times and threatened both by the Gallic forces within the city and those rallying to their support from the outside, the Romans defeated Vercingetorix and his men by means of superior siege craft.

At Szigetvár, of course, the strategic situation was the opposite. Zrínyi and his men were occupying a castle that stood squarely in Suleiman's path to Vienna; turned back once before at Eger, the sultan needed Szigetvár to fall. Having failed the previous year to take the Crusader island of Malta by sea, Suleiman had no choice but to proceed overland to sack the capital city of the Habsburgs and thus not only

21. By "race" du Picq means what today we might call ethnicity: French, English, German, Italian, Russian, etc., or, in a larger sense, a "people."

complete his conquest of the Christian outpost of Hungary but also open up all of Europe to the Crescent.

This Zrínyi and his men knew all too well. One by one, Christian strongholds such as Byzantium, Albania, Bulgaria, Bosnia, and Serbia had fallen to the Turks. The sacking of Vienna, like the taking of Rome, had been a goal of Islam for centuries. Should Vienna[22] fall, there was nothing standing between Suleiman and the German lands of the Holy Roman Empire, or what used to be Cisalpine Gaul south of the Alps into Italy. The defenders at Szigetvár had no choice but to fight: stopping Suleiman by any means necessary was the overriding objective.

Clio, the Muse of History, strums unusual melodies upon her lyre. The mass migration of more than a million Muslims from all over the *ummah* in 2015 was first felt in Hungary as they marched through, new cell phones in hand, new trainers on their feet, on their way to the former Christian heartlands of Germany, France, and England. Hungary was also one of the first nations of Central Europe to barricade its borders with some of its neighboring states, including Croatia and Serbia, through whose lands Syrians, Afghans, and Arabs proceeded unmolested. Once again, the Hungarians and the Croats found themselves on the front lines of the cultural, political, and religious confrontation between historic Christendom and Islam. Who knows how the latest civilizational clash will turn out?

With Szigetvár's walls crumbling before the Turkish mortars and cannons, who could have foreseen that the Suleiman the Magnificent would die while the siege was still in progress—indeed, on the verge of success? To this day, no one knows why or how. His death, of possibly natural causes (he was, after all, 72 years old), occurred in his tent the night before the final sack of Sziget and was immediately concealed by his grand vizier, who strangled the physician who had pronounced Suleiman dead. What is certain is that the Siege of Szigetvár was also an Islamic last stand. For all his "magnificence," Suleiman died unmourned at first and unburied as well, just another oriental satrap

---

22. During the Cold War, it was interesting and sobering to note that Vienna, in "neutral" Austria, lay considerably to the east of Soviet-occupied Prague—a wedge into the heart of the Soviet empire.

who departed his life with an enemy still holding out in the fortress of Szigetvár who knew his life was also expendable, and with a result that even the Magnificent could not have foreseen.[23]

In the poem's retelling—or reimagining—Zrínyi does not die in the last heroic charge across the bridge but slashes his way through the Turkish horde, unstoppable, dealing death with every blow. Eventually he comes upon Suleiman; the emperor is surrounded by guards and bodyguards, but Zrínyi hacks his way through them as well. Terrified, Suleiman rushes to mount his horse, but Zrínyi is too quick for him:

Ten of the emperor's aides he cuts down there,
And then to emperor Zrínyi thus began:
"Bloodsucking selendek,[24] *despoiler of the world,*
The hour of your greed has come;
God your sins no longer pardons,
You must depart, ancient cur, to eternal damnation."
Thus saying, at his waist he splits him in two,
His blood and his life he spills onto the earth;
Cursing, the emperor releases his soul,
Which his body held so proudly in life.
This was the end of the great emperor Suleiman . . .

The poet Zrínyi's account of Suleiman's death is implausible, but like any good Hollywood dramatist, the great-grandson saves the final encounter for a *mano-a-mano* duel between the two antagonists. Having literarily established both as worthy adversaries—just as, according to Aristotelian dramatic principles, the contest cannot really be decided until protagonist and antagonist come face-to-face—the fate of Christendom and the *ummah* comes down to single combat.

Zrínyi meets his own fate in short order. Afraid of confronting the fearsome *bán* (governor) directly, the Janissaries instead bring him

23. A historically reliable and accurate account of Suleiman's death would be most welcome, from a Western perspective.

24. "Hunting dog" in Croatian—canines are *haram* (forbidden, unclean) to Muslims.

down in a hail of missiles, Leonidas-like, Harold-like, one shot hitting him in the chest, the other in the forehead; his soul is immediately transported to Heaven by angels. Zrínyi's death, however, is not quite the end of the battle. With all the defenders dead, the victorious Turks rush into what's left of the castle keep. But Zrínyi had booby-trapped the powder stores by lighting a slow-burning fuse. The resulting explosion takes the lives of an additional three thousand Ottoman soldiers, making the Siege of Szigetvár one of the costliest victories in Muslim history.

Before the last charge, Zrínyi exhorts his troops to fight and die like men. He cannot sugarcoat the truth: they have no chance, except to go down swinging and then receive their reward in Paradise. He says:

Let us not recoil, then, from going to our deaths,
Which will give us a path to eternal joy;
Today, soldiers, we must lose our lives,
And today all our trials end.
We have lived nobly, let us die nobly,
Give the entire world an example by it;
Today we bring dignity upon our names,
This gilds all past actions.

Does anyone in the West still think and talk like this? Do we still have a concept of what it is like to live—and die—nobly? Do we even have family names upon which to bring dignity instead of notoriety or celebrity? Who still believes in going to eternal joy? Or is self-sacrifice a fool's errand, a suicide charge into oblivion, which the world will little note and not long remember? If nothing is worth dying for, then what are we living for?

The Ottomans won the month-long battle, but at a very great cost—upwards of 20,000 men—so great, in fact, that they abandoned their push toward Vienna. Further, the long delay in subduing Szigetvár meant that time had effectively run out on their military campaign before winter arrived; and there was also the matter of the delicate transition of power to Suleiman's son, Selim II, who had survived Suleiman's purge of two of his brothers and the natural deaths of two others. With the Treaty of Adrianople in 1568, a fragile truce was agreed to, along with the payment by the Habsburgs of an annual monetary tribute[25] to the sultans, a peace that lasted a quarter of a century before another generation of Zrínyis would rise once more to Hungary's defense. Never giving up is part of the masculine way of war, as sure as victory or defeat. The last trump never sounds, until it does.

It would not be for another 120 years that the Ottomans would be capable of trying to take Vienna again, and this time they were decisively defeated before the city gates in 1683 by a largely European military coalition led by John Sobieski of Poland and his famed "Winged Hussars." The Turks would not be gone from Hungary for good until 1699, when, in the Treaty of Karowitz, they ceded most of their conquered territory in the region back to the Habsburgs and other powers. But their baleful memory lingers on in the minds of every Eastern European from now-vanished Wallachia to the western banks of the Danube.

Such a future, however, would not have mattered to the defenders at Szigetvár, even had they been able to foretell it. For them, as for all soldiers, the battle was in the here and now, and it was in that eternal present that they fought, died, and now live on.

Today, at Szigetvár, there is a Hungarian-Turkish Friendship Park, constructed in 1994 on the outskirts of the city, featuring gigantic busts of Suleiman and Zrínyi. The heart and viscera of Suleiman are said to be buried nearby. Zrínyi's remains are nowhere to be found, but the fact that Szigetvár lies in Hungary, and not in Turkey, bespeaks the success of his last stand—and perhaps once again, given the course of Western and Islamic history, the need for another.

---

25. Thirty thousand gold ducats, worth about $4.5 million today.

CHAPTER VIII

"THESE AREN'T MEN, THEY ARE DEVILS!"

THE ALAMO (1836) AND CAMARÓN (1863)

CAN A LAST STAND BE POLITICALLY INCORRECT? AS TERRITORIES EXPAND and contract, as countries change from within and without, as peoples lose their self-confidence, moments in national history once viewed as prototypically heroic take on a different hue.

Central Europe, especially around the Balkans, is filled with such battles. In 1389, for example, the Serbs under Prince Lazar Hrebeljanović confronted the invading Ottomans at the Battle of Kosovo, a clash in which the Christian and the Muslim commanders were killed and both armies effectively destroyed. The Serbian losses, however, prevented any further effective defense against the Turks, and much of Serbia fell under Islamic domination. To the Serbs, the date of the battle, June 15 in the Julian calendar (June 28 in the Gregorian), is one of the most sacred days in Serbian national history.

When the restive and heavily (96 percent) Muslim Serbian province of Kosovo broke away from Serbia in 1999 following the dissolution of Yugoslavia a few years earlier, the Serbs fought to maintain control but were on both the wrong side of history and of the forces of the United Nations. Kosovar self-determination won out over Serbian history, although even today the territory is the subject of considerable dispute in the region. Still, Serbian history counted for little in the teeth of democratic zeitgeist.

On the American continents, the great divide has never been

Christianity versus Islam, but the legacy of Spanish colonialism against the Anglo-Saxon tradition of territorial settlement. The voyages of discovery to the New World in the fifteenth and sixteenth centuries were dominated by Spain, then at the height of its military and naval power, as well as Portugal. With the Treaty of Tordesillas (1494), the two Catholic powers essentially divided South America into spheres of influence between themselves. They followed up this diplomatic effort with the Treaty of Zaragoza in 1529, which sorted out Asia, thus accounting for the Portuguese colonies along coastal Africa, India, and China, including Mozambique, Goa, the Spice Islands (the Moluccas), and Macau. For their part, the Spanish made the Philippines, the Marianas, Guam, and even parts of Formosa (Taiwan) constituent elements of the Spanish East Indies.

Portugal never threatened the British colonies in North America, but the Spanish did—or perhaps it was the other way around. Spain claimed much of what today is the United States, from Florida, through Texas, to California, as well as New Spain, in the form of Mexico, and continued to do so well into the nineteenth century; the final acquisition of Mexican territory occurred with the Gadsden Purchase of 1854. Before that came the Mexican War of 1846–48, one of the most consequential and yet least considered wars in American national history. As issues of Hispanic immigration into Anglophonic America loom ever larger in contemporary political discussion, the fraught and antithetical history of England and Spain needs to be taken into account.

The defeat of the Spanish Armada by British forces under Good Queen Bess in 1588 broke Habsburgian Spanish dominance of the high seas and, despite the Treaty of Tordesillas, opened the way for British colonization of the Americas. The war continued to be contested in the New World, especially in the Caribbean (birthing the romantic notion of pirates and privateers, celebrating cutthroats and criminals depending on whose side they were on), where a rough demarcation between the Latin Catholic and English Protestant powers was established. Europeans generally established themselves in areas that most closely resembled their continental homelands: the Spanish in New Spain and Mexico, the English in what became New England, the Germans in

Pennsylvania, the Scandinavians in the upper Midwest and, later, the Pacific Northwest.[1]

What a difference between the British and Spanish/Portuguese approaches to colonization: the British sent settlers, the Iberians sent *caudillos*.[2] It was a cultural mind-set that resonates to this day. Whereas the British were determined to "make the world England,"[3] the Spanish under Hernán Cortés de Monroy y Pizarro Altamirano, Marquis of the Valley of Oaxaca, were content to defeat the natives and thus do Western civilization a signal service by destroying the Aztec Empire in what is now Mexico. And yet the Spanish never followed up on their victory in Mexico or the rest of Latin America. To this day, the political class of most of South America is, or has been, largely white descendants of the Spanish aristocracy, with administrative and ethnic bona fides that keep the largely *mestizo* and/or former slave/mulatto populations in subordination. If there is any "racism" in the Americas, look to south of the border for its origins.

The fact is that the Spanish model[4]—the imposition of colonial governorship by Spaniards eager to return to the mother country after their tour of duty in the Americas, and an exploitation of the peoples and the natural resources of the colonies—was the worst possible model for

---

1. The dispossessed peasants of Ireland, Italy, the Jewish Pale in Czarist Russia, and, later, Greece were the exceptions. They went to the cities, where political power was to be fought for and won, often in the streets.

2. In contrast to the British, who exported people steadily to the New World, the French and, even more so, the Spanish sent the lackland sons of the minor aristocracy across the Atlantic to seek their fortune, accompanied by Jesuit and Dominican missionaries to solicit souls. Most of the former returned home; others stayed to sire the military and political families—the *caudillos*—who ruled over the Indian and *mestizo* peasants while mingling with them socially as little as possible.

3. As the memorable line from Michael Mann's *The Last of the Mohicans* has it, written by Christopher Crowe.

4. The fictional character of Zorro, created in 1919 by the American writer Johnston McCulley, battled the grandees of Spanish California; with the twin identities of the foppish aristocrat, Don Diego de la Vega, and Zorro, the man of the people, he was the forerunner of Batman.

the Americas. In Mexico, the Spaniards subjugated the Indians and, by interbreeding, created a class of mixed-race *mestizos* to occupy the large middle, along with the unslaughtered Indians. In Argentina, they annihilated the native population, imported few African slaves,[5] but opened up the country to large-scale European immigration, especially from Italy, Germany, and the British Isles.[6]

The United States sits uneasily between Mexico and Canada—a huge geographical entity with the population of California, a former British colony, and largely Anglophone, the first anti-American country, owing to its Tory origins during the Revolution and the War of 1812. Aside from a few brief flurries of belligerence between the United States and Canada, the border between the two largely Anglophonic North American states has been mostly peaceful.

True, there was some unpleasantness about "54-40 or fight," a winning campaign slogan for President James K. Polk of Tennessee in his 1844 victory over the heavily favored Whig candidate, Henry Clay. At the time, both Britain and America had claimed the Oregon Territory, which included the present U.S. states of Oregon, Idaho, and Washington as well as the now-Canadian province of British Columbia. The numbers referenced the latitude of the boundary that Polk was demanding, far into what is Canadian territory today. In 1846, the two nations settled on the 49th parallel, thus largely establishing the current border. No blows were exchanged—and besides, the United States was also embroiled in considerable difficulty with its troublesome southern neighbor, Mexico—a historical conflict that would eventually (if, in retrospect, temporarily) be settled by the Mexican and Spanish-American wars, both of which the Americans won.

Polk's expansionism was part of his larger program of Manifest Destiny, the notion that the United States was determined by fate to occupy the entire midriff of the North American continent, from the Atlantic

---

5. Unlike Brazil, which took the bulk of the African slave trade to the New World—40 percent by most estimates. By contrast, what became the United States took about 3.5 percent.

6. Pope Francis, the first Jesuit pontiff, was born in Argentina but is of pure Italian heritage.

to the Pacific, "from sea to shining sea." Never mind that the American Indians, as well as European powers and their colonial offspring, often stood in its way: the westward migration of the American population was not to be denied. Polk—a one-term president known as the "Napoleon of the Stump," owing to his small stature—was more flatteringly termed "Young Hickory," in homage to his fellow Tennessean[7] and presidential forerunner Andrew "Old Hickory" Jackson. Often lost among the mediocrities occupying the White House during the run-up to the Civil War, Polk was one of the most consequential of presidents, who, next to Jefferson, territorially created the country we know today.

By the time the Oregon Treaty was ratified and hostilities with Britain thus averted, war was already raging south of the Rio Grande: the Mexican War of 1846–48. It's a war not much remembered today, but it was to have immense significance for the United States less than two decades later. The Mexican territory of Texas had been annexed under Polk's immediate predecessor, John Tyler, during his last week in office in March 1845, and would be admitted to the Union during the first year of Polk's presidency. The seeds of the *Reconquista*—the notion that formerly Mexican territory, ironically, rightfully belongs to the remnants of New Spain—were born here.

The loss of Texas rankled the newly independent Mexican government, but in many ways it only had itself to blame. As noted, the Spanish colonized but did not settle. Instead, they sailed across the Atlantic for plunder and booty to be spent on advancement back in the mother country. Like the huge area known as Alta (Upper, as opposed to Baja, or Lower) California, Texas itself, for all its vast territory, was sparsely populated by whites, and Mexico needed more people in order to secure control of the lands contested by the Comanche Indians, who freely raided Mexican outposts. The Mexican government, therefore, not only turned a blind eye to the influx of American settlers moving into the northern territories but also encouraged them at times. It was a decision that by 1829 the Mexicans had come to regret, as the Americans quickly began annexing large swaths of Texas and coastal California in their

---

7. Polk was born in North Carolina but like Andrew Jackson and Andrew Johnson, whose birthplaces are obscure, considered himself a Tennessean.

push westward. In response, Mexico closed Texas to American immigration, although the Americans kept coming and, in 1836, proclaimed the Republic of Texas. Mexican forces under General Antonio López de Santa Anna, a descendant of a prominent Spanish colonial family and one of the principal figures in Mexican history,[8] were sent northward to sort things out.

And thus we come to the Alamo.

Few battles on the American continent, not even that between Wolfe and Montcalm at Quebec, have affected the course of North American history as has the Alamo. And none has turned out to be, in retrospect, more controversial. For a century and a half, the Alamo has been celebrated as the throwing off of the yoke of Spanish/Mexican oppression. Today, in large part as a result of the aspirational *Reconquista*, it is seen as another vestige of colonialism, the seizure of sovereign Mexican territory by Anglo interlopers.

The truth, as usual, lies somewhere in between. There is no doubt that the American settlers, called Texians, essentially seized Mexican territory by force of eminent domain; the Mexicans were in no position to contest Manifest Destiny. Thanks to the lackadaisical Spanish attitude toward colonization, the turf was ripe for taking. The Mexicans could not effectively combat the warrior tribes of North America, especially the fierce Comanches, who were as feared in their day as the Lakota Sioux along the Canadian border would be a few decades later. As military history from the Greeks on demonstrates, to the victor go the spoils, a notion much contested today.

The battle of the Alamo is one of the most famous last stands in history, certainly in American history, where it is rivaled only by Custer's Last Stand. Like "54-40 or fight," or "Remember the *Maine*" (which in part provoked the Spanish-American War), "Remember the Alamo" became a rallying cry for the American public, but to even greater effect. Without the loss of the Alamo and its small garrison (about 250 men) of Texians and other American immigrants, the Mexican War itself might

8. Santa Anna was president of Mexico multiple times between 1833 and 1855, but is today largely remembered as the man who conquered the Alamo but lost Texas.

never have happened just a decade later. Without the Mexican War, a whole generation or two of American military officers, including both Robert E. Lee and Ulysses S. Grant, would not have been blooded in actual combat. Indeed, the complex tangle of personal and professional relationships among the officers fighting in the Mexican War (James Longstreet, Winfield Scott, Stonewall Jackson, William T. Sherman, George McClellan, George Meade, Zachary Taylor, among others) gave not only the Union and Confederate forces their leadership in the Civil War but also the United States several future presidential candidates and presidents, among them Franklin Pierce, Scott, McClellan, Taylor, and Grant.

The principal defenders of the Alamo, all of whom died during the 13-day siege, are no less prominent; some have even entered the mythos of the American West in a way most of the famous generals have not:

* Davy Crockett, the "King of the Wild Frontier," a Tennessean who had served in the U.S. House of Representatives and whose artistic afterlife included a popular Disney television series in the 1950s starring Fess Parker (who also played frontiersman Daniel Boone in the 1960s).
* Jim Bowie, an artist with the "Bowie knife" (and perhaps the forerunner of the character played by James Coburn in the 1960 film *The Magnificent Seven*); his fame soared when, shot and stabbed in the middle of a Louisiana brawl, he killed the sheriff of Rapides Parish with his eponymous blade. Upon moving to Texas in 1830, he had become a Mexican citizen and had taken to wife a Mexican girl from a prominent family.
* Lt. Col. William B. Travis, the co-commander of the garrison, who died holding the fort at the age of 26. His famous "Victory or Death"[9] letter to the people of Texas and "all Americans in

9. "I am besieged, by a thousand or more of the Mexicans under Santa Anna. I have sustained a continual Bombardment and cannonade for 24 hours and have not lost a man. The enemy has demanded a surrender at discretion, otherwise, the garrison are to be put to the sword, if the fort is taken. I have answered the demand with a cannon shot, and our flag still waves proudly from the walls. I

> the world," written during the siege and smuggled out by courier, cemented his reputation in the panoply of American heroes.

The Battle of the Alamo, a former Franciscan mission[10] in what is now San Antonio, in some ways resembles the Siege of Szigetvár. It was a contest between rebels (the Texians) and an investing, superior force (the Mexicans). It was, like Szigetvár, in part a conflict of faiths, the Americans being primarily Protestant and the Mexicans Catholic. The ratio of attackers to defenders was wildly lopsided. The defenders, as in all sieges, were running low on everything—food, water, ammunition, men. But their spirit was unbroken and their heads unbowed. They died for those most abstract and yet most fundamental of concepts: duty, honor, country.

Still, it took the Hungarians more than a century after Szigetvár to finally liberate the heart of their kingdom from the Turkish yoke, whereas the Texians under Gen. Sam Houston polished off the Mexicans two months later in just 18 minutes at the Battle of San Jacinto, capturing Santa Anna and effectively forcing Mexican acknowledgment of the reality of Texas independence.

What was it about the Alamo that changed the history of the American southwest? Militarily, its importance was minor; just another fort to be conquered and re-subsumed into sovereign Mexico. The Mexicans had made the fatal mistake—as the Romans had a millennium and a half before—of inviting in foreigners from an antithetical ethnicity, faith, language, and culture and allowing them to flourish and supersede the natives in population and thus overwhelm them by sheer force of numbers—enhanced, of course, by considerable cultural and political animosity.

---

shall never surrender or retreat. Then, I call on you in the name of Liberty, of patriotism and everything dear to the American character, to come to our aid, with all dispatch. The enemy is receiving reinforcements daily and will no doubt increase to three or four thousand in four or five days. If this call is neglected, I am determined to sustain myself as long as possible and die like a soldier who never forgets what is due to his own honor and that of his country. VICTORY or DEATH."

10. Surprisingly small, especially to first-time visitors, it hardly seems the appropriate site for such momentous events. But such is history.

Diversity, it seems, was of as little use to the Mexicans as it was to the Romans in the fifth century. There was no "strength" in it, only trouble.

One thing that distinguished the Alamo from other famous last stands, however, was that the Texians were clearly in the wrong and the Mexicans clearly within their rights to put down the rebellion. Perhaps this is why the Alamo is to most Americans, outside of Texas, relatively uninvolving, its heroes having morphed briefly into Disney action heroes and coonskin-cap merchandizing mechanisms and then retired into the cultural woodwork, like so many other television icons of the midcentury. In which context today could they ever be politically correct? Having failed in 1836, the current Mexican attempt at *Reconquista* is proceeding with armies of illegal immigrants wielding sick children as weapons and responding, whether consciously or not, to the "Aztlan"[11] movement, which holds as a strategic objective the reclamation of formerly Mexican or Spanish lands within the current territorial United States.[12]

Additionally, the rapid growth of the American population into east Texas (where "Texas" began) was fueled by a number of factors, one of them slavery. Many of the settlers came from the slave state of Louisiana, and the expansion of slavery into the new western territories was very much the hot political topic of the day. The Missouri Compromise had been effected in 1820, when Missouri entered the Union as a slave state but was balanced by the creation of Maine out of part of Massachusetts and admitted as a free state. Southerners wanted to stake a claim to Texas as potential slave territory, and possession at that time was still very much nine-tenths of the law.

Further, the Texians under Stephen Austin and Sam Houston were born troublemakers, as wandering expats can often be. In 1825, Austin had brought the first of three hundred American families into the area

---

11. A mythical Aztec nation, vaguely located in what is now the American Southwest, invented in order to give Latino territorial ambitions a patina of historical legitimacy and to foster and nurture a sense of resentment against Anglophone America. That the Aztecs were among history's most bloodthirsty savages, and whose conquest by Cortés was aided by other Indian tribes, goes unremarked.

12. The colonialist irony, of course, is obvious.

under a Spanish land grant that had been honored by Mexico; among them were slaveholders. More arrivals quickly followed; what had begun as a kind of garrison program, with the Anglos defending the northern precincts of Mexico against the Indians, had morphed into outright colonization. Too late did the Mexicans realize the error they had made in admitting so many Anglos, and Santa Anna's revanchist war was designed in large part to sweep them out of Mexican territory forever.

Still, the Texians at the Alamo under Travis may have been fighting for an illegal and perhaps even immoral cause, as we have the luxury of believing today. But they did not regard it so at the time. They were not at the Alamo because they loved slavery or hated Mexicans but because they loved freedom and self-determination, and were willing to die for it—archetypal revolutionary American traits still being evinced 60 years after the Revolution.

It is noteworthy how many last stands take place on frontiers. Thermopylae blocked the Persians' way west. Roncevaux was fought, poetically, on one of Islam's bloody borders, as was Szigetvár. The Romans collided with the Germans in the Teutoburg Forest, near the Rhine, the border between the two cultures. It is perhaps one thing to fight and even lose a battle well within your own turf (as the Romans did at Cannae) when you have the solace of knowing you can retreat and live to fight again another day. It is quite another when your back is to the wall, ammo is running short, you have nowhere to run and so therefore face near-certain death. In that situation, men become tigers, determined to sell every last drop of their blood as dearly as possible, whatever the modern "rightness" of their cause.

So when Travis, Bowie, Crockett, and the others made their final stand in the old mission, effectively at the spot where Mexico would become the United States, they epitomized the gallant spirit of all doomed warriors. It went without saying that, to the Americans, their cause was not simply just but heroic. Iconographically, it could be presented as mustachioed, superstitious Catholic Spaniards against the clean-limbed American pioneers who owed their allegiance to neither pope nor potentate—a visual dichotomy that would inform all subsequent iconographic depictions and retellings of the battle.

And so the legends sprouted: the wounded Bowie, abed, emptying a brace of pistols into the onrushing Mexicans until they overwhelmed and killed him. Crockett fighting until swarmed, then cut down where he stood. Travis falling, shot in the head as he rallied the dwindling defenders. Never mind that other accounts suggest that Bowie was hiding under his bed when he was killed, and that Crockett had surrendered and then was murdered on Santa Anna's orders, and that Travis (like Roland or, later, General Gordon at Khartoum) was too stiff-necked to surrender as he waited for reinforcements that came too late. Print the legend.

The final assault came at dawn on the morning of March 6, 1836. Like Suleiman, Santa Anna had ordered his men to make a decisive attack. At first, his men were repelled at the north wall by the defenders' cannons and muskets, but gradually the Mexican sappers breached the fort's perimeter while Mexican cavalry opened a salient at the southwest corner and pushed the Texians and the Americans back into the convent and the church itself. But there was no sanctuary to be found; Catholic or no, the superior Mexican forces moved from room to room, liquidating the resistance as they went with bullets and bayonets. Some defenders, perhaps as many as 60, managed to break out but were quickly cut down by the cavalry. Many of the civilians were spared, as well as a few of the couriers, but the fighting men died, to live on as martyrs for the cause of Manifest Destiny.

Just how much the resonance of the story of the Alamo has changed can be seen by a glance over the past 70 years or so of American popular culture. During the 1950s, it was the rare American boy who didn't have a Davy Crockett coonskin cap, buckskin jacket, lunch pail, or rubber Bowie knife. Fess Parker portrayed Crockett in a television miniseries in 1954–55, and the show's theme song—"Davy, Davy Crockett, King of the Wild Frontier"—could be sung by just about everybody under the age of ten. The series covered Crockett's past as an Indian fighter and a member of Congress from Tennessee, and his death, battling against the Mexicans to the last, at the Alamo.

In 1960, the battle got the full-scale Hollywood treatment in *The Alamo*, not only starring John Wayne as Crockett but being produced and directed by him as well. Running nearly three hours, shot on 70-millimeter film, and costing some $12 million to make, it was intended as an epic retelling of the story to rival the various swords-and-sandals historical extravaganzas then nearing the apex of their popularity. Starring alongside Wayne were Richard Widmark as Jim Bowie and Laurence Harvey as a stiff-necked Colonel Travis; even crooner Frankie Avalon shows up as the most youthful of Crockett's Tennessee volunteers. That said, the picture is almost unwatchable today. An hour or more of needless exposition, pointless subplots (the budding romance between Crockett and a Mexican beauty[13] goes nowhere), extended byplay between and among the minor characters, and long-winded speechifying for the principals make it a tedious slog. Widmark is wasted, Harvey steals the picture, and we look forward to the last act when they all finally get killed. The picture, into which Wayne himself put $1.5 million of his own money, was a modest success, earning about $20 million.

The Alamo was remade in 2004 in a big-budget ($107 million) production starring Billy Bob Thornton as Davy Crockett, Jason Patric as Bowie, and Patrick Wilson as Travis; it was produced by Ron Howard and Brian Grazer's Imagine Entertainment. As might be expected, this version was more politically correct, offering the Mexican side of the story and even featuring a major role for Emilio Echevarria as Santa Anna (who is only barely glimpsed in Wayne's treatment). But time had passed the Alamo by; a changing American demographic wasn't particularly interested in seeing a handful of Anglo interlopers hold off the entire Mexican army on what was, at the time, sovereign Mexican territory, and the film earned less than $26 million.

As a heroic legend, the battle of the Alamo now appears to be as dead as Davy Crockett. In late 2019, the remains of three people were unearthed during excavation for a renovation project at the tourist site, raising the issue (as the *New York Times* put it) of "how best to accommodate tourists while respecting the Alamo's complex history—and about whose stories have been venerated and whose have been forgotten." Some American Indians claim the battlefield as a burial ground. Further, as the *Times* noted, "before it became an artifact of Anglo expansionism, the Alamo was known as the Misión San Antonio de

---

13. In real life, Wayne married thrice, each time to an Hispanic woman.

Valero, a mission populated mainly by Spanish priests and Indigenous people who had converted to Christianity."

And so the battle rages on in the political arena. Texas won its independence and then, as we have seen, became a part of the United States—an acquisition cemented by the successful prosecution of the Mexican War by Winfield Scott, Zachary Taylor, Robert E. Lee, and Ulysses S. Grant a decade later. In that conflict, in a brilliant feat of logistics, the American army landed amphibiously at Veracruz, on the Gulf of Mexico, and marched inland to Mexico City, forcing surrender and the cession of the territory north of the Rio Grande.[14]

In his memoirs, Grant spends a good deal of time on the Mexican War, which was such a formative part of his military life and career. He had a great deal of sympathy for the Mexicans, as he would later have for the plight of the African American slaves (Mexico had abolished slavery in 1843), whom he rightly viewed as American citizens worthy of respect, dignity, and freedom. In fact, he regarded the Mexican War as fundamentally immoral. "To this day," he wrote, "I regard the war which resulted as one of the most unjust ever waged by a stronger against a weaker nation. It was an instance of a republic following the bad example of European monarchies, in not considering justice in their desire to acquire additional territory. An empire in territory, it had but a very sparse population, until settled by Americans who had received authority from Mexico to colonize. These colonists paid very little attention to the supreme government, and introduced slavery into the state almost from the start, though the constitution of Mexico did not, nor does it now, sanction that institution. . . . The Southern rebellion was largely the outgrowth of the Mexican war. Nations, like individuals, are punished for their transgressions. We got our punishment in the most sanguinary and expensive war of modern times."

By which Grant, writing near the end of his life in 1885, meant the American Civil War—a war that, as we shall see, produced the

---

14. Grant was a quartermaster in the Mexican War, during which he learned not only the importance of personal valor but also the crucial determinative factor of functioning supply lines. He also learned Spanish, and remained partial to the Mexican people throughout his life.

principal figure of the most electrifying last stand in our history, George Armstrong Custer. But that was still to come, eleven years after Lee's capitulation at Appomattox Court House, Virginia—at which, in one of history's consonances, Custer was present. The conclusion of the Mexican War, which Polk had effectively micromanaged from the White House, solved a political problem and allowed him to keep his campaign promise that he would be a one-term president—probably the most significant one-term presidency in the history of the Republic. He may also have been fatally ill. He returned to Tennessee and died in Nashville just three months after leaving office.

Polk was succeeded by Zachary Taylor, one of the heroes of the war (Grant was a great admirer of Taylor, and vastly preferred his informal leadership style to that of "Old Fuss and Feathers," Winfield Scott). Taylor, however, was destined to be one of our shortest-serving presidents, in office only 16 months before suddenly dying; he was succeeded for the remainder of his term by his vice-president, Millard Fillmore—the last of the Whigs, the party that would soon give way to the new Republicans. Slavery had become the most important political consideration of the day, and Taylor/Fillmore, Franklin Pierce, and James Buchanan (all one-term administrations) each attempted to find, and failed, a resolution to the intractable problem. With the election of the first Republican president—Abraham Lincoln, running on a National Union ticket—the conflict would now have to be settled militarily before it could be repaired politically.

"THE LEGION DIES. IT DOES NOT SURRENDER"

The Battle of Camarón, 1863

Meanwhile, Mexico was in the throes of a prolonged political crisis as well, brought on by its defeat in the war, which left it open to interference from its old colonial master, Spain, and the French Bourbons under the emperor Maximilian. The interplay and rivalry between France and Spain regarding Mexico is largely forgotten today, but Napoleon, during his Peninsular War, deposed the Spanish monarchy and in 1808 installed his elder brother Joseph[15] as the Iberian ruler for five years, until Joseph abdicated after Napoleon suffered a series of military reverses. The Spanish Bourbons were restored in 1813 and deposed again in 1868; and it is with this period in Mexican history we are now concerned.

In 1864, the Austrian archduke, Maximilian (brother of the Austrian emperor Franz Joseph I), accepted the position of emperor of Mexico from the French monarch, Napoleon III. This nephew of Napoleon had first been elected as president of France during the short life of the Second Republic, then, nearing the end of his term, seized power in an 1851 coup and reigned as emperor until the Franco-Prussian War, when the crushing French defeat toppled him in 1870 and sent him into exile in England, where he died in 1873. His principal legacy was the reconstruction of Paris by Baron Haussmann, who designed and gave us the Paris we know today.

The position came to Maximilian after a joint French-British-Spanish invasion of Mexico in 1861. The proximate cause was an attempt to collect debts from the government of Benito Juárez, a Zapotec Indian who had emerged as a reformist leader following the Mexican War. Juárez was a novelty, an indigenous Mexican rather than a scion of Spanish invaders, and was quickly recognized by the American government as the country's rightful head of state. Under pressure from the United States[16]—acting on the authority of the Monroe Doctrine, which forbade European interference in the affairs of the Western Hemisphere—the British and the Spanish soon withdrew, but Napoleon III sent a French force to take and occupy Mexico City. He proclaimed the Second Mexican Empire on June 10, 1864—at the same time Ulysses S. Grant was suffering one of his worst defeats[17] at the hands of Robert E.

---

15. An itinerant royal, Joseph had also been king of Naples and Sicily, and later lived in the United States, primarily at his estate in New Jersey, from 1817 to 1832. In Spain, he is credited with ending the Spanish Inquisition in 1812, although it lingered on in places until 1834. He died in Tuscany in 1844.

16. By then deeply embroiled in the Civil War.

17. See Extract 10.

Lee at the Battle of Cold Harbor during the ultimately successful Overland Campaign that eventually drove Lee to surrender.

So with America distracted, the French took the opportunity to expand their sphere of influence abroad. It could not, and did not, stand. With the war over in 1865, America put renewed pressure on France to withdraw and, in 1867, she did. Cut off from military support, Maximilian surrendered Mexico City to troops under Porfirio Díaz, and was executed. Juárez resumed control of the government.

All of which is prelude (and postlude) to one of history's greatest, and least-sung, last stands: the Battle of Camarón—Camarone, in French—in 1863. If Szigetvár is generally unknown in the West, then Camarón has been almost completely forgotten, even in the Western Hemisphere. It is, however, remembered in France, where it has become the foundational myth of one of France's most celebrated and potent fighting forces, the *Légion étrangère*, better known in English as the French Foreign Legion. And all—or at least in significant part—because of Captain Danjou's hand.

Jean Danjou was born in 1828 and attended the military academy of Saint-Cyr (the French West Point). In 1852, he was assigned to the Second Foreign Infantry Regiment, which later became part of the French Foreign Legion. Sent to Algeria, then undergoing French colonization, he lost his left hand when it was blown off by a musket malfunction. Rather than muster out, Danjou had a prosthetic wooden hand made for him, which he wore for the rest of his life. He served during the Crimean War, in central Europe, and in Morocco before being sent to Mexico in 1862, where he became (as Grant had been in the Mexican War) a quartermaster to Colonel Jeanningros, the commander of the Legion. With French forces besieging the critical town of Puebla, southeast of Mexico City, where the French had previously been defeated on May 5, 1862,[18] a convoy was on the way inland to supply money and ammunition to the besiegers.[19] Short of manpower, Captain Danjou de-

---

18. The origin of the Mexican holiday of Cinco de Mayo, which has evolved into the Mexican St. Patrick's Day in the United States, a day of ethnic pride and celebration.

19. The result turned out to be a French victory at the Second Battle of Puebla, a few weeks after Camarón.

cided to personally command a force consisting of three officers and 62 Legionnaires to protect the convoy. It proved to be his last command.

Guarding a 40-mile portion of the Royal Road that ran through tropical lowlands from the port city of Veracruz, occupied by the French, westward to Puebla and then on to Mexico City, the Legion's posting was one of the worst imaginable. As the Americans had discovered a few years earlier, conditions were primitive, and deadly diseases, such as malaria, typhus, and yellow fever, were rampant. (The majority of deaths during combat in Mexico were from illness.) They were also under occasional attack from guerillas loyal to Juárez.

Danjou's unit, the Third Company, First Battalion, Foreign Regiment, had only been in country a month but was hard hit by illness; a third of his command had already been stricken with yellow fever and had spent time in the hospital. This left him with the equivalent of two platoons, the men drawn from all over Europe. Among them were twenty Germans, sixteen Belgians, eight Swiss, and a smattering of others. Their principal weapons were a rifled musket called the *Minié*, for which they carried 60 rounds of ammunition (*minié* balls), and a sword bayonet. The makeshift uniforms consisted of a dark blue jacket with yellow or green epaulets, a red sash, beige trousers, and a Mexican sombrero instead of the standard *képi*.

On April 30, 1863, they were assigned to a reconnaissance mission to assess guerilla activity along a portion of the road that would soon see the artillery convoy heading toward Puebla. Resting along the way in the town of Palo Verde, Danjou and his Legionnaires were roused by the sound of hoofbeats. It was Mexican cavalry. Forming a hollow infantry square, bayonets fixed—the textbook response to a cavalry charge—Danjou led his men in a controlled, fighting retreat back to the small village of Camarón, where they shot their way into its farmyard and then sought refuge within La Trinidad Hacienda, a Spanish colonial villa fallen into desuetude but whose demesne was surrounded by a ten-foot wall.[20] Unfortunately, some Mexican troops were already

20. According to an English-language version of a Legion web page: "*La Trinidad Hacienda* was built in 1814–17 by Spanish Lord Ferrer. Later the property of the Alarcon family, it was abandoned in the late 1850s due to the Reform War in

occupying the upper floor of the residence (as was typical of this kind of structure, there was no interior staircase; stairs ran along the exterior of the building), which meant that their snipers had a clear field of fire into the enclosed farmyard and would be difficult to dislodge by return fire.

Taking shelter in the hacienda was a rational decision. At this point, Danjou had no idea of the strength of the Mexican forces chasing him, which ultimately turned out to be a combination of infantry and cavalry battalions that numbered around two thousand men. But mounted horsemen would find it difficult to assault the hacienda and would be at a disadvantage in the close quarters of the farmyard. If the Mexicans were going to defeat the Legionnaires, it would have to be on foot.

At about 9:30 in the morning, a Mexican emissary arrived to demand the French surrender. Just before he arrived, Danjou opened his last bottle of wine and gave each of the men a few drops to drink; having marched all night and fought their way into the redoubt, the wine was the first liquid they'd had that day. It would also be the last. Sending the envoy packing with the words, "We have munitions. We will not surrender!" the Legion braced for battle. Each of the men swore an oath on Danjou's wooden hand to fight to the finish. The first attack came 15 minutes later.

Danjou was among the first men killed, shot in the chest by one of the snipers while moving from the house to the men defending the two open gateways from behind the courtyard walls. Command was assumed by 2nd Lt. Jean Vilain, 27; normally the battalion paymaster, he had volunteered for the reconnaissance mission. With the house rapidly becoming overrun by Mexican troops, the French decided to abandon the villa and fight outside; of the original fourteen troops

---

Mexico (1858–60). The hacienda was a Spanish colonial building with a farmyard forming a square, with about 55 yards (50 m) long stone-built walls. The walls were roughly 10 feet (3 m) tall. The north side of the building facing the road had a raised, whitewashed facade with at least one entry/doorway (without doors) close to the western corner. On the other side of the facade, inside the farmyard, a three-room house of an unspecified length, comprising a first/ground floor + attic. On the western side, the wall was pierced by two large gateways. Both gateways were without gates, however. The legionnaires barricaded them and a group of 6–8 men was put to guard each gateway."

stationed inside, only five remained. Around noon, Mexican reinforcements arrived, adding three infantry battalions (about 1,200 men) under Col. Francisco Milan to the besieging force. Again, surrender was demanded; again, it was refused.

The bulk of the remaining Legionnaires, the reserve, was stationed between the two gateways, with other units at various corners of the farmyard. By this time, however, the Mexicans had blown huge holes in the walls of both the farmyard and the hacienda and were peppering the Legion, forcing it out of its defensive position and toward a couple of sheds near the southern gateway; one of the sheds was in serviceable condition, with good walls, while the other was a ruin. At about 2:30, Vilain was killed by a shot to the head, leaving only one other officer, 2nd Lt. Clément Maudet, a 15-year veteran of the Legion who had worked his way up from Legionnaire to junior officer. He was also the regimental standard-bearer.

It must have been clear to everyone at this point that the Legion had no chance. The surviving men hadn't eaten or drunk anything, aside from Danjou's wine, for the entire day. The Mexican sun was broiling them alive. Some of the men drank their own urine; others, driven mad by their wounds, lapped their own blood, the bodies of their comrades piled up all around them. Sometime after 3 p.m., the Mexicans fired the hacienda and then riddled the Legionnaires with gunfire.

Around five o'clock in the afternoon the Mexicans withdrew, expecting surrender this time for certain. The French took their count: only 12 able-bodied men left, including Maudet. A third surrender offer was made; it was greeted with silence. Outside the walls, the Mexican commander, Milan, exhorted his men to finish the job. In a sudden rush, the Mexicans eliminated the resistance at the gates. Holed up in the good shed, down to his last five men, out of ammunition, Maudet ordered a last volley, followed by a bayonet charge. Two of the men were killed outright; Maudet was badly wounded. Three—a corporal and two Legionnaires—were captured. The Battle of Camarón was over.

When the three remaining Legionnaires were brought to Milan—who had lost an estimated three hundred men in the fight—he exclaimed, "These aren't men, they are devils!" In all, including men previously wounded, there were about 12 survivors. (Maudet died of his wounds about a week after the battle.) They were imprisoned, cared for, and later exchanged for Mexican prisoners of war.[21] The regimental drummer, Casimir Lai, had been shot twice and run through by lance or saber seven times but had managed to crawl out from beneath the dead and escape into the brush. He survived.

In retrospect, Danjou's decision to fight seems suicidal, a display of Gallic bravado that would have done Vercingetorix proud, unwarranted by the military circumstances. But was it? The French, just 50 years past Napoleon, still had confidence in their military prowess (that would be destroyed seven years later when Bismarck's Prussians annihilated them at Sedan) and professional contempt for, as we might today term it, the Third World army they were facing. As we have seen from the Greeks at Thermopylae through Grant's remarks regarding the Battle of Cold Harbor, the notion that one soldier of *X* is worth five of *Y* is ingrained in the Western way of war. Sometimes, it is true; sometimes it is not. At Camarón, it probably was—but the Legionnaires still died, nearly to a man.

In the larger strategic sense, however, Danjou's resistance was important. Once Danjou realized he was engaging a large Mexican force, he knew he was fighting the units that had been sent to disrupt the convoy with supplies for the ongoing siege of Puebla. The longer he could keep the Mexicans tied down, and bloodied, the better chance the convoy would have to get through.

The Mexicans were fighting for their country; the Legionnaires were fighting for their honor and that of the Legion. "The Legion dies," Danjou is said to have shouted as the battle began. "It does not surrender." It may be argued that the Legionnaires were fighting for nothing but themselves. After all, the whole point of the legion was to take foreigners of likely dubious pasts and weld them into a fanatically loyal fighting force whose efforts would lead, if they survived, to French citizenship. But to this day Legionnaires swear their fealty not to France but to the Legion itself: *Legio Patria Nostra* is one of the Legion's mottos. Part of

---

21. There is a story that Maudet and his two surviving comrades demanded repatriation to France, along with their weapons, their flag, and Danjou's body, but this appears to be apocryphal or at least exaggerated.

their Code of Honor reads, "Each legionnaire is your brother in arms whatever his nationality, his race or his religion might be. You show him the same close solidarity that links the members of the same family."[22]

Some time after the battle, a Mexican farmer poring through the wreckage found Danjou's wooden hand and sold it to the French military authorities. The painted hand made its way back to the Legion's headquarters in Sidi Bel Abbès, Algeria. After the Algerian War, the Legion relocated its administration to France, Corsica, and other French possessions, and the hand currently rests in the Museum of the Foreign Legion in Aubagne, east of Marseille. It is paraded with honor before the assembled Legionnaires every year on April 30, known as Camarón Day.

The Alamo changed both Mexican and American history. The Mexicans would soon enough have cause to regret they had martyred the men at the Alamo, for vengeance was surely on the minds of many American soldiers and sailors during the Mexican War a decade later, when they blockaded the country on both coasts and then marched from Veracruz to Mexico City and forced a humiliating peace and loss of considerable territory on Mexico. What delusions of Spanish or Mexican military grandeur that might have been dancing in the head of Santa Anna vanished at San Jacinto, never to return. Mexican suspicion of, resentment of, and jealousy of *el Norte* grew from that day forward.

Camarón, meanwhile, changed nothing. The French were eventually forced out and had to abandon their revanchist notion of Empire under the Napoleons. Mexican dreams of a *Reconquista* of the American southwest were briefly rekindled when Wilhelmine Germany proposed an alliance with Mexico should the United States enter the First World War against the Kaiser: Mexico would recover Texas, Arizona, and New Mexico, the latter two having only become states in 1912. But the notion died in January 1917 when the British intercepted and decoded the Zimmermann Telegram from the German Foreign Office; the revelation that Germany and Mexico were plotting to seize American

---

22. *Chaque légionnaire est ton frère d'armes, quelle que soit sa nationalité, sa race ou sa religion. Tu lui manifestes toujours la solidarité étroite qui doit unir les membres d'une même famille.*

territory inflamed public sentiment against both countries[23] and possibly speeded America's entry into the war a few months later.

None of this, however, diminishes the gallantry shown by both sides in each battle. In each case, the Mexicans were up against extraordinary groups of men, if fighting for different causes. The fact that General Milan, near the end of the Battle of Camarón, had to exhort his men to one last great effort in order to destroy just a handful of Europeans signified both its moral and psychological significance to the Mexicans. Similarly, Santa Anna's impatience to get the siege of the Alamo over in one final assault bespoke the importance of the siege, not just to him—as president of Mexico and its top military commander—but to his young country, newly liberated from Spain.

The problem for the Mexicans in both fights, however, was that they weren't up against men, they were up against devils, fueled on hunger and thirst and anger and fear and hopelessness and courage. Both sides welcomed the final charges. The defenders knew they would die, in the hope that the Cause might live. Whether it was rational or just or worthwhile they have left for us to decide. On all sides, it certainly seemed to be.

---

23. Under Pancho Villa, Mexican forces had crossed the border and undertaken raids on American towns, the most notorious of which came at Columbus, New Mexico, in March 1916. There, Villa encountered the U.S. Army, which bloodied him badly and chased him back into Mexico. Outraged, President Wilson sent an expeditionary force under Gen. "Black Jack" Pershing into Mexico, although it failed to catch Villa. A year later, Pershing was the commander of the American Expeditionary Force in France during World War I.

CHAPTER IX

"LICK 'EM TOMORROW, THOUGH"

GRANT AT SHILOH (1862)

ANTIETAM WAS BLOODIER; GETTYSBURG WAS BIGGER AND LONGER. BUT no battle of the American Civil War was as important—as determinative of the preservation of the Union—as the battle of Shiloh, fought on April 6–7, 1862, when the Rebellion was still young and few on either side suspected that it would go on as long as it did, and at what terrible cost. Had Ulysses S. Grant lost the battle, with his past as a drunk, an army washout, and a civilian failure still haunting him, and with his reputation on the line, the defeat would likely have been the end of him, as well as of his most trusted lieutenant, William Tecumseh Sherman. Grant's rise would have been halted—indeed, his career would have been over (as it very nearly was anyway), the critical victory at Vicksburg the following year never achieved, and the final confrontation between Grant and Robert E. Lee postponed indefinitely. Worse, a crushing Union defeat might have encouraged England to enter the war on the Southern side. The stakes were higher than anyone knew at the time.

Shiloh is not often thought of as a last stand, since the Union troops escaped the trap the enemy had set for them, killed one of the South's ablest generals, and drove off the Confederate forces. But on the evening of April 6, with the Federals having been caught by surprise early that morning, their position rolled back more than a mile, their backs against the Tennessee River as they awaited a final onslaught by fired-up rebels sensing blood and victory, it certainly became one. In fact, over the course of the two-day battle, there were multiple last stands—not only Grant's but that of the Union troops at the notorious Hornet's Nest, where divisions commanded by Brig Gens. Benjamin Prentiss and W. H. L. Wallace, after some of the fiercest fighting of the war, were surrounded and two thousand soldiers were taken captive; Wallace was killed in action.

But in hindsight, it was also something of an early last stand for the South itself: its failure to destroy Grant's army, or even to dislodge him from his control of the waterways, led a year later to the fall of Vicksburg and with it any hope the Confederacy had of victory, or even survival. Rebel ferocity, heralded by the eerie, chilling "rebel yell," which sent shivers down the spines of the Union armies, and *élan vital*[1] would not, and could not, compensate in the end for the manpower and the productive factories of the North. But at this moment, at Shiloh, they almost did.

The Confederates' senior commander, Gen. Albert Sidney Johnston, understood that the South's only hope to defeat the Federals in the War Between the States was to knock them out of the war early and force Lincoln to sue for peace.[2] A Union loss would have meant not simply a transient defeat but the annihilation of the Army of the Tennessee[3] and with it, very likely, the permanent sundering of the United States itself. Instead, it was the South that was destroyed.

That Grant got to the battlefield late from his headquarters in Savannah, Tennessee, and spent the first day of the battle rallying his defeated and demoralized troops, many of them green recruits still familiarizing themselves with their weapons, very nearly spelled the end for him and his army. Taken unawares by the massed Confederate attack under Johnston and P. G. T. Beauregard, the unentrenched and unfortified Union positions along the Tennessee River were overrun and pushed

---

1. Grant wrote in his *Personal Memoirs*, "It was a case of Southern dash against Northern pluck and endurance."

2. The other alternative, which emerged later in the war, was for the South to hold on long enough for the Northern public to grow tired of the bloodshed, and offer a negotiated settlement.

3. As Grant's army had just come to be called.

back more than a mile and along a broad front, many of the unseasoned troops fleeing down the riverbank to hide. The men had come to see the "elephant"—a quaint expression of the times that implied confronting something novel, huge, and terrible—"something few if any of them had seen before," as Winston Groom explained it in his book *Shiloh, 1862*. What they found was less a tame circus animal than a rampaging mastodon fit for Hannibal.

In other words, the battle was well on its way to being lost in the first hours when Grant arrived. Sherman, whose troops were positioned on the Union's right flank, bore much of the brunt of the first day's fighting, especially in the early going; it was an embarrassment Grant never forgot, and very nearly did not survive. It was only near the end of the fight, after suffering more than 13,000 casualties, against the Confederates' loss of 10,700 killed, wounded, or missing in action,[4] that Grant came to the reluctant but implacable conclusion that the war was going to be—and would have to be—fought to the death, and to the complete destruction of both the Confederacy and the economy of the South itself if the Union were to endure. In that moment, Unconditional Surrender Grant was born.

Never was a place name—Shiloh, the Place of Peace[5]—more ironic.

The engagement began as Grant, flushed with early victories at Fort Henry on the Tennessee River and Fort Donelson on the Cumberland and eager to show his nominal superior, the martinet desk jockey Gen. Henry Halleck, that he was worthy of the trust that Lincoln was already investing in him, assembled his Army of the Tennessee along the rivers that ran through and connected several Southern states, among them Tennessee itself, Mississippi, and Alabama. At a time when the navy was very much considered the lesser of the two services, Grant instinctively understood the binding power of the South's riverways and

---

4. The combined casualties (killed, wounded, missing) at Shiloh alone exceeded all previous American wartime losses, from the Revolution through the War of 1812 and the Mexican War.

5. "The sceptre shall not depart from Judah, nor a lawgiver from between his feet, until Shiloh come; and unto him shall the gathering of the people be" (Genesis 49:10).

knew that to control the rivers would be to bifurcate the Confederacy. Accordingly, he early on made a friend of Adm. Andrew Foote, whose ships could not only transport his men through the western heart of the rebellion but also supply offshore firepower in a way the Confederates could not. The tactical alliance of Grant and Foote is one of the most crucial of the war, and oft unsung.

This, however, should not have been surprising to anyone who knew Grant's military past. From his early days as a quartermaster during the Mexican War, Grant understood the importance of not only men but also materiel. In this, he was emblematic of the North's innate advantage over the South, its ability to rapidly produce hardware and fighting men in a way the South could not match. What the South relied upon was its fighting spirit and, for the first three-quarters of the war, its superior tactical generalship. Most of the Southern generals had, as Grant had, attended West Point (Lee, James Longstreet, even Jefferson Davis, now the president of the Confederate States of America), as did of course many of the Union generals. But the Federals also had a high proportion of so-called "political" generals, men given command not for their military experience or acumen but for their civil connections in their home states.[6]

Grant and Foote had won signal victories at the forts, triumphs that were to the North as important psychologically as militarily. The Union needed some wins. Expecting an easy victory over Johnny Reb, the cream of Washington society had turned out at Manassas, Virginia, in July of 1861, just a few months after the outbreak of hostilities, to observe the first battle of Bull Run, only to see the Union forces under Irvin McDowell routed by Beauregard and Stonewall Jackson. A series of minor wins and losses plus a number of inconclusive engagements followed, until Grant successfully attacked Belmont in Mississippi, not

---

6. After failing to win recommission from George McClellan at the outbreak of the war, Grant received his command from the governor of Illinois, Richard Yates, as the leader of the Twenty-First Illinois Volunteer Infantry Regiment. Grant, however, was a retired army officer and West Point graduate, eager to return to the field.

far from his command center in Cairo, Illinois, then followed up with two more river conquests.

At Shiloh—also known as the battle of Pittsburg Landing, after the spot on the Tennessee River where the Union Army was encamped as it prepared to march on Corinth, Mississippi, a major railhead just 20 miles to the southwest—Grant was gathering his largest army to date, and was to combine the Army of the Tennessee with the forces of the Army of the Ohio under Gen. Don Carlos Buell to sever the South's control both of its western rivers and its railroad lines. Grant himself was at the Cherry Mansion in Savannah, a couple of hours along the river from Pittsburg Landing via his flagship, the steamboat *Tigress*. As luck would have it, two days before the battle he had badly injured an ankle when his horse fell in the mud (and Grant was a master horseman) and pinned his leg. Grant, therefore, was on crutches and in pain as the news of the surprise Confederate attack at Shiloh reached him, heralded by the distant sound of the guns that beautiful spring morning.[7]

The South's bold gambit was the brainchild of the Confederate general Johnston, a West Point graduate whose father was a native of Salisbury, Connecticut. Although Johnston had been born in Kentucky, he had spent much of his life in Texas and had even fought in the Texian army during its struggle for independence from Mexico in 1835–36. The role of rebel came naturally to him. Add to that his general appearance and bearing—he was six feet tall and, in the words of one of his soldiers, "looked like a Viking king"—and you had a Confederate commander who might have rivaled and surpassed even Lee had he lived.[8] As the Confederate president Jefferson Davis remarked upon learning of Johnston's death, it was the turning point of the South's fate.

The stupefying butchery on the field would quickly become a template for the course of the war. A gut shot was certain death. An arterial

---

7. Contrary to myth, Grant was entirely sober when the battle began. His hostess, Mrs. W. H. Cherry, later wrote that "[h]e was at my breakfast table when he heard the report from a cannon. Holding, untasted, a cup of coffee, he paused in conversation to listen a moment at the report of another cannon. He hastily arose, saying to his staff officers, 'Gentlemen, the ball is in motion; let's be off.'"

8. As an overall strategist, he was surely Lee's superior.

nick (such as happened to Johnston) was fatal unless a tourniquet could be applied in time. Wounds to hands, arms, feet, and legs generally resulted in instant amputation, with the result that battlefields were littered not only with corpses, whitening in the elements, but also severed limbs. Cannonballs took off heads. Grant, surveying the carnage after the first day, said it was possible to walk across the field and never set foot on the ground, so many bodies lay there.

And yet, somehow, incredibly, the men and boys (for many boys fought and died as well) accepted it. Death came randomly—Grant was hit by a bullet that upended his scabbard and sent his sword flying, but spared him; Sherman was shot in the hand; Johnston didn't realize he had sustained a mortal wound until he bled to death from it. The Union general W. H. L. Wallace was shot through the back of his head, the exiting bullet blowing out an eye. It was up to Fate. Although at Shiloh there was cowardice enough to go around, most of the Union men took last-ditch defenses or near-suicidal charges as simply their lot, just as soldiers from Sparta and Rome had done long before them. To flinch from danger or to shirk one's duty was, to an honorable man, never to be preferred to death in the service of your country and your fellow soldiers. Self-preservation was never the better part of valor.

With the Cajun French popinjay Beauregard (the hero of Fort Sumter and First Bull Run) as his second-in-command, Johnston had conceived an audacious plan to attack Grant as he was marshaling his forces at Pittsburg Landing and smash him before Buell's forces could reinforce him. The Union position on the west bank of the Tennessee only appeared to be strong defensively. In reality, the Nationals had their backs to the river, where a few transport ships waited along with a couple of gunboats. If the attack could succeed swiftly, the Union army would be pushed back into the river and destroyed before Buell could arrive. Timing was everything.

And so, at dawn on April 6, it began. At first, the approach of the Confederates was shrugged off by Sherman[9] and others as merely

9. Sherman had only recently returned to active duty in the army, having spent the previous four months on leave for depression; the media obligingly reported that he was insane.

pickets and skirmishers. But as the day blossomed in bright sunshine, reality quickly set in. In short order, the entire Union front was under siege, with the Confederate right wing attempting to force Grant's left wing away from the river and Foote's protective gunboats, and instead to push the Army of the Tennessee north and westward, into the nearby swamps. At once, the Confederate troops moved forward to try and form a single front line that would hem in the Union between shot, steel, and water. In effect, Johnston's plan was an echo of Arminius's attack on the Roman legions at the Teutoburg Forest, with rebels, like the Germans, emerging from the woods to cut down the immobilized legionaries trapped between the woods and the water.

It very nearly succeeded. With the Federals struggling to regroup, Grant arrived from his headquarters a little after 8 a.m. and then, throughout that interminable first day, rode the line, pulling his shocked troops together and issuing orders right and left. Not only was he waiting for Buell, he was also counting on the three brigades of the Third Division under Maj. Gen. Lew Wallace,[10] who had been ordered to proceed south from his position at Crump's Landing near the Snake and Owl Creeks. But Wallace initially balked at the lack of a written order, and when he finally got one, he marched off in what turned out to be the wrong direction, effectively taking his troops out of the battle on the first day.

A famous anecdote, related by the Civil War historian Bruce Catton, recounts a meeting of Grant and Sherman, hard by the Tennessee River, on the night of April 6. The two generals, eventually to emerge as the principal architects of victory in the Civil War, encountered each other in the midst of a driving rainstorm. Grant, characteristically, was smoking a cigar in silence, his hat crunched down upon his head, as Sherman approached. "Well, Grant," said Tecumseh, "we've had the devil's own day, haven't we?"

---

10. There were two Union generals with the surname Wallace on the field; W. H. L. Wallace was shot in the head and mortally wounded near the Hornet's Nest, dying in his wife's arms three days later. Ann Wallace became an angel of mercy during the battle, tending to wounded soldiers aboard the steamboat *Minnehaha* in the river.

"Yes," said Grant. "Lick 'em tomorrow, though."[11]

But Grant said more. On the first day, in the fog of war and a Tennessee downpour, Grant was asked by Gen. James B. McPherson, his prized engineering officer, whether they should make plans to retreat. "Retreat?" exclaimed Grant. "No! I propose to attack at daylight, and whip them."

This is the essence of both Grant and the battle of Shiloh. As we have seen, battles in classical antiquity generally took place on a single day (Thermopylae was an exception), on a single field. The winner won the war, and the loser was either destroyed or enslaved. There were few second days. At Shiloh, however, Grant's will and ability to survive, pull his command together, deal with the vagaries and the vicissitudes of the contest (where was Lew Wallace? When is Buell arriving?) ensured that there would be a day two.

Shiloh was, by all accounts, a baptism by some of the most intense fire any human being had hitherto experienced. Fought on unforgiving terrain of woods, hills, creeks, swamps, marshes, and rivers, the battle was unprecedented in its rate of fire, bullets, shells, shot, and shrapnel whistling through the air, slicing the leaves of the trees to ribbons, and bathing the soldiers in the heavy metal of death. Some of the most intense fighting came in a place called the Hornet's Nest[12]—deep woods where Union troops held out most of the first day of the battle under hellacious conditions—and also at the bucolically and deceptively named Peach Orchard, where the ball and shot shaved the spring blooms and sent the petals showering down on the dying and wounded in satanic benediction. Green soldiers who just the day before were learning the disciplines of drill suddenly found themselves in one of the hottest shooting wars in history up to that time.

---

11. Despite a short falling-out during Grant's presidency, the two men were near-lifelong friends. "Grant stood by me when I was crazy," said Sherman, "and I stood by him when he was drunk." Neither man was drunk or crazy that day.

12. A private soldier, Corp. Leonard Houston, 26, of the Second Iowa, who was in the thick of it at the Hornet's Nest, wrote, "It seemed like a mighty hurricane sweeping everything before it when men and horses were dying; at this moment of horror . . . the little birds were singing in the green trees over our heads! They were as happy as if all were perfect calmness beneath them."

By chance, two accomplished journalists were present at the battle, fighting on opposite sides: the great explorer Henry Morton Stanley, a Welsh immigrant born John Rowlands, later to find immortality in Africa as the man who located David Livingstone by the shores of Lake Tanganyika in 1871 ("Dr. Livingstone, I presume?"), was there. So was the misanthropic American writer Ambrose Bierce, serving with an Indiana infantry regiment, whose short stories, some originally written for the *San Francisco Examiner*—including the oft-anthologized "An Occurrence at Owl Creek Bridge" and the terrifying "Chickamauga"—are some of the best and most horrifying descriptions of the brutality of the War Between the States, fully equal in intensity and emotional effect to Stephen Crane's short novel *The Red Badge of Courage.*

Stanley, in his 1909 memoirs, recorded a charming story of a young soldier, only 17, standing next to him in the line as the Confederates prepared their assault: "He drew my attention to some violets at his feet, and said, it would be a good idea to put a few into my cap." The reason? "Perhaps the Yanks won't shoot me if they see me wearing such a sign of peace." Stanley compared the sounds of the battle to "the roaring of a great herd of lions . . . the yapping of terriers . . . the swoop of eagles . . . the buzz of angry wasps." And yet, he added, "I thought it strange that a Sunday should have been chosen to disturb the holy calm of those woods."

Not that the soon-to-be-world-famous African explorer, sent to the Dark Continent at the behest of the *New York Herald*, couldn't be equally graphic when the need arose. Stanley himself had been knocked down by a spent bullet that ricocheted off his belt buckle and hit him in the stomach, which led to a short Virgilian odyssey into the living underworld of the soon-to-be-shades: "One man raised his chest as if to yawn and jostled me. I turned to him and saw that a bullet had gored his whole face and penetrated into his chest. Another ball struck a man a deadly rap on the head, and he turned on his back and showed his ghastly white face to the sky."

Bierce was, characteristically, more mordant.[13] The man who went

---

13. A typical entry from Bierce's *The Devil's Dictionary* (1906): "Gallows, n. A stage for the performance of miracle plays, in which the leading actor is translated

on to a stellar journalism career and, c. 1913, rode off to cover the Mexican revolution and was never seen or heard from again, wrote of Shiloh, day one: "The air was full of noises . . . distant musketry rattled smartly and petulantly, or sighed and growled when closer. There were deep shaking explosions and smart shocks. The death-line was an arc of which the river was the chord, filled with the whisper of stray bullets and the hurtle of conical shells; the rush of round shot. There were faint, desultory cheers. Occasionally, against the glare behind the trees, could be seen moving black figures, distinct, but no larger than a thumb; they seemed to be like the figures of demons in old allegorical prints of hell."

The roster of famous people at Shiloh doesn't end there. Commanding one of Grant's divisions was Lew Wallace, later the celebrated author of the novel *Ben-Hur: A Tale of the Christ*[14]; fighting on the Confederate side was John C. Breckinridge of Kentucky—the former vice president of the United States under James Buchanan, Lincoln's immediate White House predecessor. Another of the Confederate generals was Leonidas Polk—his first name evoked the Spartan king at Thermopylae, while his surname was shared with his more famous cousin, President James K. Polk; Leonidas Polk was also an Episcopalian bishop.

If the history of war tells us anything, it is that war is too important to be left to the generals. From the Greeks onward, great artists have recorded the events of their times, starting with Aeschylus (c. 500 B.C.), whose own tombstone reads: "Beneath this stone lies Aeschylus, son of Euphorion, the Athenian, who died in the wheat-bearing land of Gela;

---

to heaven. In this country the gallows is chiefly remarkable for the number of persons who escape it."

14. *Ben-Hur* (1880) became the best-selling American novel of the nineteenth century, avidly read in a single sitting by Grant himself. Wallace recovered some of his military reputation during the defense of Washington, D.C., in the summer of 1864, fought the last battle of the Civil War in south Texas a few days after Appomattox, served on the tribunal that tried Lincoln's assassins, and went on to become territorial governor of New Mexico and, later, ambassador to the Ottoman Empire.

of his noble prowess the grove of Marathon can speak, and the long-haired Persian knows it well."

Aeschylus was obviously not at Shiloh, but his spirit was. Where great events occur, there gather also great men. Aristotle taught Alexander of Macedonia. The poet Virgil instructed Augustus by means of the *Aeneid*, the heroic story of the founding of Rome. The author of *La Chanson de Roland* adapted historical events of the eighth century to contemporaneous political realities to comment upon, and effect, the political realities of the twelfth. When Napoleon finally encountered Wellington face-to-face at Waterloo, he celebrated the confrontation, to his ultimate chagrin.

Similarly, events can make the man, and Grant is perhaps the best example. What would have been his fate had the war not occurred when and where it did? He had resigned from the Army in semi-disgrace, dogged by accusations of alcoholism. He made a hash of his business affairs (and would continue to do so throughout this life, especially in his post-presidency), and came to rely on the kindness of a grateful nation to keep the wolf from the door. (Presidents did not get pensions in those days.) He might even have sold off his memoirs piecemeal as works-for-hire journalism had not his friend Mark Twain made him an exceptionally attractive publishing offer, including a 70 percent royalty, that kept Grant's widow, Julia, in style for the rest of her life. It also resulted in the finest wartime memoir since Caesar's *Commentaries*, rivaled later only by Winston Churchill's six-volume series, *The Second World War.*

While Grant's literary success may at first seem surprising, he had long evinced a love for literature and the theater and attended plays whenever he could, although he and Julia declined an invitation from the Lincolns to join them at Ford's Theatre for *Our American Cousin* on the fateful night of April 14, 1865, owing to the enmity between Julia and Mary Todd Lincoln. In the field, his written orders were clear and concise—another lesson learned at Shiloh. For decades, Grant never quite forgave Wallace for the confusion—one suspects he partly blamed himself for his lack of clarity in exigent circumstances—writing of the incident in his memoirs:

> Wallace did not arrive in time to take part in the first day's fight. General Wallace has since claimed that the order delivered to him by Captain Baxter was simply to join the right of the army, and that the road over which he marched would have taken him to the road from Pittsburg to Purdy where it crosses Owl Creek on the right of Sherman; but this is not where I had ordered him nor where I wanted him to go. I never could see and do not now see why any order was necessary further than to direct him to come to Pittsburg landing, without specifying by what route. His was one of three veteran divisions that had been in battle, and its absence was severely felt.

Grant later revisited his assessment of Wallace upon receipt of a letter from a war widow[15]: "My order was verbal, and to a staff officer who was to deliver it to General Wallace, so that I am not competent to say just what order the General actually received." He would never make that mistake again. In the field there is no time for excuses, but there is—in victory—plenty for magnanimity. A poor judge of character in his private life, Grant was a superb commander at both the tactical level (as Shiloh showed) and, more important, at the strategic level. Indeed, his partnership with Lincoln was a textbook example of the proper relationship between the president as commander in chief of the armed forces (a legacy of George Washington) and the general of the armies. For Lincoln's objectives were simple and direct: preserve the Union by any means necessary, and offer mercy to the defeated South only after the rebellion had been thoroughly crushed. Grant accomplished both.

The victory at Shiloh, however, was not at first viewed that way, especially by the Northern press. To be fair, no one was prepared for the butcher's bill. As the casualty toll mounted, the Union victory was savagely second-guessed by the newspapers.[16] Why was Grant late to the

---

15. See Extract 11.

16. "The American press," remarked Sherman years later, "is a shame and a reproach to a civilized people. When a man is too lazy to work, & too cowardly to steal, he becomes an editor & manufactures public opinion."

battle? Was he drunk? Why was he not entrenched? Was it true that the Nationals were so unprepared on the morning of April 6 that many soldiers were bayoneted in their tents? Why, on April 7, did not the Union forces pursue the beaten Southerners and finish them off? The clamor for Grant's removal eventually reached Washington, where Lincoln categorically rejected it. "I can't spare that man," said the president. "He fights."

At Shiloh, the Confederates under Johnston attempted to use Grant's defensive position on the river against him by rolling the Union troops northward; in fact, they drove them back to the river, where the men could shelter beneath the riverbank and take refuge in the gunboats. Their fatal mistake was not finishing the job. Toward the close of the first day, Beauregard called a halt to the attack and prematurely telegraphed Jefferson Davis in Richmond: "The day is ours!" It was not.

But Grant, while retreating, prevented Johnston and Beauregard from forming a solid line, and thus was able to counterattack in superior numbers the following day.[17] With Johnston dead, the all-out assault having failed to fully dislodge Grant from his position, and his army running low on supplies of food and ammunition, Beauregard packed up the remnants of his army and retreated to Corinth; an enraged Sherman gave chase but was turned back by the rebel cavalry under Nathan Bedford Forrest. What had been a soldier's war on the first day, marked by individual battles and vicious hand-to-hand fighting, turned into a general's war on the second, with Grant, bolstered by reinforcements from Buell and Wallace, easily besting the overmatched and now outnumbered Beauregard.

A few years later, Grant would employ a similar attack strategy against Lee in Virginia, this time successfully, consistently rolling to Lee's right while Phil Sheridan's cavalry (which notably included Custer, a media darling known as the Boy General) destroyed his sustenance in the Shenandoah Valley. This pushed Lee away from Richmond, to

---

17. The Confederates, like Harold's forces at Hastings, succumbed to the temptation of looting the Union camps as they overran them. This delay was critical later in their inability to form a solid line.

the south and west, and once the rail hub of Petersburg fell after a long siege, and with Richmond defenseless, Lee had nowhere to run.

The Battle of Shiloh has been largely ignored in popular culture, understandably. Gettysburg was the decisive, epic battle, played out on the national stage over three long days. But Shiloh matters. Bierce's chilling short story "An Occurrence at Owl Creek Bridge" takes its name from one of the battlefield's streams, although the story is set in Alabama. The battle was treated in the 1962 film *How the West Was Won* as part of a larger panorama; there is also a 1997 movie called *Shiloh*, but it is about a dog. A song written shortly after the battle, "Shiloh's Hill," is part of the canon of Civil War tunes but has never achieved the fame of, say, Stephen Foster's "We Are Coming, Father Abraham" or "The Battle Hymn of the Republic," sung to the tune of "John Brown's Body" to words by Julia Ward Howe. Because Shiloh came so early in the war and caught everyone by surprise, it has not taken on the historic sheen of inevitable victory that attends both Vicksburg and Gettysburg. Indeed, even among Civil War buffs, Shiloh remains a lesser-known step in the South's long and bloody capitulation to U. S. Grant.

And yet, near the start of the Civil War, a last stand resulted in the complete triumph of the Union cause and the unconditional surrender of the Rebellion. The lessons that Grant and Sherman learned in the Tennessee woods remained with both generals throughout the war, principally: never give up, no matter how steep the cost. It is instructive that in a battle that saw high-ranking generals on both sides killed in action, Grant and Sherman were in the thick of things, heedless of their own danger—a characteristic typical of all great commanders from Caesar to Wellington to Patton, a stance that is less death-defying than death-accepting as the price of victory. They were determined to win or die trying.

And perhaps this is the definition of true courage: the ability to function, as coolly as possible, not in the face of certain death but in the indifferent face of random uncertainty. Surviving Shiloh prepared Grant for the even greater horrors of all the battles that were yet to come, battles that had to be fought and won in order to end what is still the bloodiest war in American history.

Had Johnston not been killed, had the Confederates managed to close their vice, had Buell's Army of the Ohio arrived a day later, had either Grant or Sherman (wounded twice, with three horses shot out from beneath him) been killed, gotten drunk, or gone mad . . . how very different the history of the Civil War, and the American Republic, might have been but for one man's unwillingness to give in or give up, and his iron determination to lick 'em tomorrow. Shiloh was nearly Grant's unmaking, but his last stand on the banks of the Tennessee turned out to be the unmaking of the Rebellion instead.

CHAPTER X

"BIG VILLAGE"

CUSTER AT THE LITTLE BIGHORN (1876)

IT IS, WITHOUT A DOUBT, THE MOST FAMOUS LAST STAND IN AMERICAN history, superseding even the Alamo in its continuing resonance. Indeed, more has been written about this single battle in American history than all other engagements combined. The fight, which cost 268 American soldiers' lives and took place on what was then the final frontier, shocked a nation about to celebrate its first centennial. The news of the annihilation of a trained regiment of mounted soldiers, led by battle-tested and much-decorated veterans of the Civil War, rippled across the country within days of the disaster. Probably not until the Kennedy assassination nearly a century later has a single event so affected and afflicted the nation's psyche and its sense of itself.

For one thing, the country was bigger in 1876 than it had been 40 years earlier, bigger in every way—more people, more territory, more industry, more newspapers, more technology, more immigrants, more cities, more states, and yet still with plenty of room to grow in the push westward. The Plains and the Mountain West were the last places on the continent to be settled by the Americans. On the West Coast, California, Nevada, and Oregon had already been admitted to statehood. To the east, the rolling hills and the great river basins of the Midwest had been left behind for places of natural aridity, where rainfall was infrequent and the winters were long and harsh. It was not a fit country for man or beast, unless the men were farmers in the riper sections of Kansas and Nebraska and the beasts were cattle.

The farther north you went, the drier and stranger the territory became, populated by great roaming herds of bison and patrolled by the cream of the Indian warrior nations, the Sioux, forced into the Badlands by the relentless push of the Americans. It was into this country, the Dakotas and Montana territories, that George Armstrong Custer and the seven hundred men of the Seventh Calvary rode during the fateful month of June 1876, and from which so many of them never reemerged. And it was there, as well, that the American Indian, even in victory, made his own last stand.

"The Great American Desert" it had once been called, but to George Armstrong Custer[1] it was always "the Plains." In a series of articles for *Galaxy* magazine, he described it at some length when, as an American cavalry officer, flush with national renown from his exploits during the Civil War, he first encountered it in all of its austere, barren magnificence[2]:

> It was gradually discerned that the Great American Desert did not exist, that it had no abiding place, but that within its supposed limits, and instead of what had been regarded as a sterile and unfruitful tract of land, incapable of sustaining either man or beast, there existed the fairest and richest portion of the national domain, blessed with a climate pure, bracing, and healthful, while its undeveloped soil rivalled if it did not surpass the most productive portions of the Eastern, Middle, or Southern States. Discarding the name "Great American Desert," this immense tract of country, with its eastern boundary moved back by civilization to a distance of nearly three hundred miles west of the Missouri river, is now known as "The Plains," and by this more appropriate title it shall be called when reference to it is necessary.

---

1. Throughout his life, Custer—the surname is of German origin, Küster or Köster—was familiarly known as "Armstrong" or "Autie" for short by the whites, never "George"; to the Indians, he was Long Hair, Yellow Hair, and Son of the Morning Star.

2. See Extract 12.

It was also synonymous with Indian country:

> The Indian tribes which have caused the Government most anxiety and whose depredations have been most serious against our frontier settlements and prominent lines of travel across the Plains, infest that portion of the Plains bounded on the north by the valley of the Platte river and its tributaries, on the east by a line running north and south between the 97th and 98th meridians, on the south by the valley of the Arkansas river, and west by the Rocky Mountains—although by treaty stipulations almost every tribe with which the Government has recently been at war is particularly debarred from entering or occupying any portion of this tract of country.

So opens *My Life on the Plains*, a compilation of the *Galaxy* articles covering the years 1867–69, which Custer published in book form in 1874. A more perfect adumbration of a man's fate can hardly be imagined. The fascination the Plains—and the Plains Indians—had for this most misunderstood and controversial of American, and masculine, archetypes is right here. Like the beginning of some great drama of which we know the ending but can't help but watch, we are held spellbound every time we see it. Because, while we think we know the story, it cannot fail yet to surprise us.

About the last stand, which occurred on June 25–26, 1876, there is not so much mystery but misinterpretation. Many have wondered why Custer divided his forces, especially not knowing just how many warriors had gathered by the Little Bighorn River. Or why he pushed his troops so hard, ahead of the other two columns that were meant to converge on southeastern Montana, or what his greatest fear was heading into the battle. Critics attribute his actions to vainglory or buffoonery or a lack of military knowledge, yet in fact Custer was one of the finest tactical commanders of the Civil War, the darling of both the media and of his superior officer, Gen. Philip Sheridan, who wielded Custer as the instrument of his wrath upon the South. Custer was many things, but an incompetent glory hound was not one of them.

The proximate cause of the clash between Custer's mounted troops and the warrior tribes of the Plains is generally attributed to the discovery of gold in the Black Hills of South Dakota in 1874. It was an area not only sacred to the Sioux but expressly given to them by the Treaty of Fort Laramie, in the Wyoming Territory, just a few years before, in 1868. Nonetheless, fortune hunters quickly flooded the area, and the pressure was on, both in the West and in Washington, to open the area to miners, settlers, and the military.

But there was another cause, easily forgotten and ignored today but one that (as we have seen elsewhere in this book) resonates down the ages: religion. The fight between the Sioux and Cheyenne tribes and the settlers and soldiers of the United States was as much about faith as it was about greed or gold.

Faith today is something observed, generally on the weekends, but for the people of the nineteenth century it was something they lived. Faith informed every aspect of one's life, from birth to death, and at every stop along the way—from the stirrings of adulthood with the onset of sexual maturity, childbirth and child-rearing, through war, illness, triumph, and tragedy. That faith was not necessarily Christian, although it largely was. It could be Jewish or tribal; of agnostics or even freethinkers there were a few, although the notion of secular humanism as a kind of religion in itself[3] was still a few decades in the future. They were, however, all Americans, in the grip of Manifest Destiny, marching beneath an implicit and Constantinian guidon: *in hoc signo vinces.*

As it happened, many of the Indians who opposed the westward expansion in the Plains had been Christianized by Catholic or Protestant missionaries. These were not the conversions of the French Jesuits, made in the wilderness of the upper Mississippi or in French Canada and often at great personal risk. Rather, they were effected on the reservations, most of which included a military barracks, a trading post, a church or two, and Indian schools. The education of the Indians in the white man's ways was deemed essential, not only to the settlement of the West but for the advancement and well-being of the Indians themselves.

3. Best illustrated literarily in the character of Settembrini in Thomas Mann's masterpiece *Der Zauberberg*, which appeared in 1924 but was begun more than a decade earlier, as World War I approached.

Many Indians agreed with this notion, and as time went on the "reservation" Indians played an increasingly important role in policing and in part governing the reservations themselves.

Still, there was little love between the whites and the Indians, especially in the Plains. Just a decade or so earlier, in 1862, the bloody Dakota War had broken out around Mankato and New Ulm in southwestern Minnesota; tensions between white traders and the Sioux led to armed clashes and then to a general insurrection that saw nearly a thousand white settlers killed in especially brutal fashion. Lincoln, his hands full with the Civil War, nevertheless sent federal troops to the recently admitted (1858) state to pacify the tribes. But the memories of some of the bloodiest massacres in the history of white-Indian relations remained fresh. We have vivid accounts of the unpredictable brutality of the Indians from survivors such as Lavina Eastlick; awakened on the morning of August 20, 1862, by a neighbor announcing that the Indians were killing the settlers in their homes at Lake Shetek, she, her husband, and their five sons fled. Only Lavina and one of her children survived, as even the "friendly" Indians working the land turned on them.

> I could not find my children. I imagined they had gone to sleep somewhere among the dead and wounded. About nine or ten o'clock the Indians came back to where they had fought our folks. I heard them shooting. During the day I heard the children crying most of the time; sometimes I heard them screaming and crying. . . . No one can imagine my feelings. I wished I could die. I thought then, and think now, that they were torturing the children. It was a great punishment to me to hear the children crying and moaning under the cruel tortures of the Indians. . . . About four o'clock in the afternoon I heard three guns fired. The children then ceased crying. Poor, innocent ones!—they were now at rest.[4]

---

4. Mrs. Eastlick's story is anthologized in *Captured by the Indians: Fifteen Firsthand Accounts, 1750–1870* (Dover Books, 1961). Those who view the Indian Wars as one-sided will have their illusions quickly disabused.

Accordingly, military men such as Custer thought converting the Indians to be pointless. Not because he hated the Indians—he didn't, not the way his boss, Phil Sheridan did, when he reputedly said, "The only good Indians I ever saw were dead." Rather, Custer's proto-modernist view was that a civilized Indian was, in effect, a non-Indian: an unhappy, forced imitation of a white man. Custer, in fact and from personal experience (not all of it on the battlefield), regarded the sentimental, Rousseauian ideas of "noble savage" as empirically risible.

> If the character given to the Indian by [James Fenimore] Cooper[5] and other novelists, as well as by well-meaning but mistaken philanthropists of a later day, were the true one; if the Indian were the innocent, simple-minded being he is represented, more the creature of romance than reality, imbued only with a deep veneration for the works of nature, freed from the passions and vices which must accompany a savage nature; if, in other words, he possessed all the virtues which his admirers and works of fiction ascribe to him, and were free from all the vices which those best qualified to judge assign to him, he would be just the character to complete the picture which is presented by the country embracing the Wichita mountains. Cooper, to whose writings more than to those of any other author are the people speaking the English language indebted for a false and ill-judged estimate of the Indian character, might well have laid the scenes of his fictitious stories in this beautiful and romantic country. It is to be regretted that the character of the Indian as described in Cooper's interesting novels is not the true one. . . .
>
> It behooves us no longer to study this problem from works of fiction, but to deal with it as it exists in reality. Stripped of the beautiful romance with which we have been so long willing to envelop him, transferred from the inviting pages of the novelist to the localities where we are compelled to meet with him, in his native village, on the war path, and when raiding upon

5. Author of *The Last of the Mohicans* and the other four "Leatherstocking Tales."

> our frontier settlements and lines of travel, the Indian forfeits his claim to the appellation of the "noble red man." We see him as he is, and, so far as all knowledge goes, as he ever has been, a *savage* in every sense of the word; not worse, perhaps, than his white brother would be similarly born and bred, but one whose cruel and ferocious nature far exceeds that of any wild beast of the desert.

This was a commonly shared sentiment. One of the things that most frightened the Europeans was the sheer unpredictability of the natives, especially after they had been drinking. It was customary among the tribes, once the drinking had commenced, to finish every last drop.[6] The results could be horrific. Children were played with, then brained. Women went unmolested, or were suddenly taken to wife and made a member of the tribe.[7] Men were generally killed after prolonged torture and scalping. European savagery was something the immigrants from Germany and Scandinavia could understand and, in part, make some account for; Amerindian savagery was almost wholly inexplicable.

Indeed, to Custer, the white man's view of the Indian was naïve and sentimental. "The Indian, while he can seldom be accused of indulging in a great variety of wardrobe, can be said to have a character capable of adapting itself to almost every occasion. . . . This character is invariably paraded, and often with telling effect, when the motive is a peaceful one." Still, Custer was no "racist" in the contemporary sense of the word.

> Seeing them under these or similar circumstances only, it is not surprising that by many the Indian is looked upon as a

---

6. Similar in some respects to the Arabs whom the British explorer, Sir Richard Burton, encountered during his peregrinations among the Believers. In a footnote to his unexpurgated translation of *The Arabian Nights*, Burton notes: "Easterns, who utterly ignore the 'social glass' of Western civilization, drink honestly to get drunk; and, when far gone, are addicted to horse-play . . . which leads to quarrels and bloodshed."

7. The dramatic heart of John Ford's greatest movie, *The Searchers*.

> simple-minded "son of nature," desiring nothing beyond the privilege of roaming and hunting over the vast unsettled wilds of the West, inheriting and asserting but few native rights, and never trespassing upon the rights of others. This view is equally erroneous with that which regards the Indian as a creature possessing the human form but divested of all other attributes of humanity, and whose traits of character, habits, modes of life, disposition, and savage customs disqualify him from the exercise of all rights and privileges, even those pertaining to life itself.
>
> Taking him as we find him, at peace or at war, at home or abroad, waiving all prejudices, and laying aside all partiality, we will discover in the Indian a subject for thoughtful study and investigation. In him we will find the representative of a race whose origin is, and promises to be, a subject forever wrapped in mystery; a race incapable of being judged by the rules or laws applicable to any other known race of men; one between which and civilization there seems to have existed from time immemorial a determined and unceasing warfare—a hostility so deep-seated and inbred with the Indian character, that in the exceptional instances where the modes and habits of civilization have been reluctantly adopted, it has been at the sacrifice of power and influence as a tribe, and the more serious loss of health, vigor, and courage as individuals.

In other words, Custer viewed the Indians at once as a unique, alien people and as different from one another as they were from the white man. (In his books, he spends a great deal of time observing the linguistic and cultural differences between the tribes of the East and the Plains and gives some credence to the nineteenth-century belief that they were descended from the ancient Hebrews.) He knew, and made good use, of intra-Indian rivalries and squabbles, often employing in his war against the Sioux and the Cheyenne scouts and translators from other Plains tribes who bore the principal tribes no love.

In fact, many of the North American Indians sided with the *wasichus*—the white man. As in Mexico and Central and South America, the dominant tribes were often cordially loathed by the native peoples they conquered; the Aztecs, for example, used their fellow Indians as slaves and objects of human sacrifice to propitiate their bloodthirsty gods. Cortés could not have defeated the Aztecs quite as easily as he did or in such a short time were it not for help of his Indian allies,[8] who wanted to revenge themselves upon their tormentors. At the Battle of the Little Bighorn, Custer brought with him several scouts, most of them Crows,[9] including White Man Runs Him and Goes Ahead, but also including his favorite, Bloody Knife, who was the half-breed son of a Sioux father and an Arikara mother and raised in a Sioux village. As a youth, Bloody Knife had been abused by the Sioux for his mixed parentage—in particular by a warrior named Gall—and had fled to an Arikara village until he joined an American fur company as a trader and then became an army scout.

Like all captive or subjugated peoples, the American Indians of the Great Plains awaited a Messiah. Deliverance could come from within their native religions or from the white man's, or some combination thereof; the only essential was that he would elevate the Indians from the low estate into which they had fallen. Throughout the period of the Sioux wars, which lasted until January 1891, various "messiahs" sprang up and were given wide credence. One such was a man named John Johnson, also known as Quoitize Ow—the Messiah—a Paiute from the Walker River Reservation in Nevada who bore tattoos on both wrists as a sign of divine favor. (There was something supernatural about the place. Walker Lake was also said to be home to a giant sea serpent much like the Loch Ness monster, first sighted in 1868 and last seen in 1956.)

Some Indians believed that Jesus Christ himself had returned, this

---

8. Including his Indian mistress, La Malinche, who functioned as interpreter and adviser, as well as the mother of his son, Martin, considered one of the first *mestizos* (mixed European-Indian parentage) in America. Custer may have also taken an Indian mistress, Monahsetah, a pregnant woman captured at the Battle of the Washita in 1868 and who later bore Custer a son, Yellow Bird, who may have been present at the Little Bighorn. Against this, the priapic Custer was otherwise childless, perhaps due to a bout of venereal disease contracted at West Point.

9. Although the Sioux claimed the Black Hills and surrounding areas for themselves, in reality they had wrested them from other tribes; the Crows were among the disposed and therefore were natural enemies of the Lakota.

time with only eleven apostles, and that Johnson was the Christ ("I had always thought the Great Father was a white man, but this man looked like an Indian," observed one Indian witness). Johnson told the Indians he was the maker of the earth, that he had seen their dead relatives and had even encountered his own late father and mother. He chastised the Indians for the wicked ways that had brought them low[10] and said all men should live together in peace. If they obeyed him, they would all be returned to their youthful selves and would live forever.

A Sioux man named Masse Hadjo, or John Daylight, as he called himself, wrote an admonitory letter to the whites, published in the *Chicago Tribune* in December 1890, shortly before the Battle of Wounded Knee:

> You are doubtless a worshiper of the white man's Saviour, but are unwilling that the Indians should have a "Messiah" of their own . . . the Good Father of all has given us a better religion—a religion that is adapted to our wants . . . the code of morals as practiced by the white race will not compare with the morals of the Indians. We pay no lawyers or preachers, but have not one-tenth part of the crime that you do. . . . You are anxious to get hold of our Messiah, so you can put him in irons . . . the white man's heaven is repulsive to the Indian nature, and if the white man's hell suits you, why, you keep it. I think there will be white rogues enough to fill it.

But the real Indian Messiah was a Hunkpapa Sioux named Sitting Bull. It is perhaps ironic that the greatest leaders the American Indians ever had—not only Sitting Bull but also the tactical genius Crazy Horse of the Oglala tribe and the ferocious Gall—all appeared around the same time, as if called forth by some Great Spirit, and in their nations' hours of greatest need. That even their combined efforts were not enough is the tragedy of the American Indian.

Nobody really knew much about Sitting Bull. Some said he was

10. Shades of the opening of *The Siege of Sziget.*

half-white, that his name was "Charlie Jacobs" from Fort Garry, near Winnipeg, Manitoba, and that he had been educated at St. John's College there, a "remarkably intelligent lad, with ambition to become a 'big Injun.'" Shortly after the Little Bighorn, in August 1876, one Captain McGarry, who piloted a steamboat on the upper Missouri River, said, "Sitting Bull is a Teton-Sioux, and is thirty-five years old. He is a Roman Catholic convert, and said to be a firm believer in all the tenets of that church. He was converted by Father de Smet. By this priest he was taught French, and he is able to read and speak that tongue with fluency. Sitting Bull has read French history carefully, and he is especially enamored of the career of Napoleon, and endeavors to mold his campaigns after those of the 'Man of Destiny.'"

Other called him a Sac or a Fox, and not a Sioux at all. They said that he had once allied himself with Louis Riel, a mixed-breed of French-Canadian and Métis Indian origin who founded the province of Manitoba and was hanged in 1885 for treason for fomenting the North-West Rebellion, largely a revolt of the Métis and other First Nations Indians against the Anglo-Canadian government.

Still others were sure he had attended West Point in the mid-1840s under the name of McLean of Missouri. They described him as "above medium height, apparently between eighteen and twenty years old, heavy set frame, long, bushy hair, growing close to his brow and overhanging his neck and shoulders, his face covered with thin patches of fuzzy hair, the general get-up of this plebe was such as to cause the old cadets to hesitate in the heretical jokes usually played off on new cadets. Nicknames are often applied to cadets that they carry with them among their friends into the army, and even to their graves. The thick neck, broad shoulders, and long, bushy hair, caused the name of 'Bison' to be applied to this newcomer, and it adhered to him ever afterward." But "McLean" became drunk one night and got into a brawl, after which he was court-martialed and expelled in 1848.

Sitting Bull himself was quoted as saying, "I was born near old Fort George, on Willow Creek, below the mouth of the Cheyenne River. Cannot tell exactly how hold I am. . . . My father's name was The Jumping Bull, and he was a chief. At the age of fourteen I killed an enemy and began to make myself great in battle and became a chief."[11]

That, no doubt, was closest to the truth. The identity of "McLean" was proven to be that of a young man from Randolph County, Missouri, nephew of a former U.S. senator, and who entered West Point in 1846, the same year Stonewall Jackson graduated,[12] and was apparently killed by Indians in Arizona around 1870. The real Sitting Bull—Tatanka Yotanka—was a full-blooded Hunkpapa Lakota (Sioux), who was born around 1831 and died in 1890, effectively bringing an end to the last great conflict between the European settlers and the American Indians. And that conflict found its indelible expression and depiction in the battle of the Little Bighorn on June 25, 1876.

Like all great medicine men, Sitting Bull was a man of visions. Far more than the whites, the Indians were in touch with the divine via the ecstatic, principally dancing. The *wasichus* saw the tribal dances as savage customs that served no real purpose, but the Indians could approach African levels of spiritual and physical transformation as the warriors lost themselves in exhaustion and the pleasure that only great pain can bring. Although they never met, Custer's observation regarding the "red man" can pertain to the character of Sitting Bull as well:

> Inseparable from the Indian character, wherever he is to be met with, is his remarkable taciturnity, his deep dissimulation, the perseverance with which he follows his plans of revenge or conquest, his concealment and apparent lack of curiosity, his stoical courage when in the power of his enemies, his cunning, his caution, and last, but not least, the wonderful power and subtlety of his senses. . . . In studying the Indian character, while shocked and disgusted by many of his traits and customs, I find much

---

11. All quotations above from *Life of Sitting Bull and History of the Indian War* by W. Fletcher Johnson (1891). Johnson (1857–1931) was an editorial writer at the *New York Tribune*. He also wrote a biography of William T. Sherman.

12. By comparison, Grant graduated from West Point in 1839; George Armstrong Custer in 1861.

> to be admired, and still more of deep and unvarying interest. To me Indian life, with its attendant ceremonies, mysteries, and forms, is a book of unceasing interest. Grant that some of its pages are frightful, and, if possible, to be avoided, yet the attraction is none the weaker. Study him, fight him, civilize him if you can, he remains still the object of your curiosity, a type of man peculiar and undefined, subjecting himself to no known law of civilization, contending determinedly against all efforts to win him from his chosen mode of life. Civilization may and should do much for him, but it can never civilize him.

Dancing had always been part of the Plains Indian culture—there was the Grass Dance, which featured dog stew as part of the ceremonies (the Indians loved dog stew, and would kill and cook their most prized dogs in order to serve them up for honored guests), the Bear Dance, the Beggar's Dance, the Scalp Dance (which celebrated victory in war), the infamous Sun Dance, in which young braves were secured to poles by cords attached to skewers embedded in their naked chests and forced to stare at the sun for a full day, bringing on intense hallucinations. By 1890, as the last of the great warrior tribes were being rounded up and Sitting Bull himself was forced back onto the reservation at Standing Rock, the Ghost Dances were in full flower, a mass movement that eventually resulted, and ended, in December of that year with the death of the great chief at the hands of some Indian policemen, and the final confrontation at Wounded Knee two weeks later between the "hostiles" and men of the Seventh Cavalry bent on revenge for Custer and his doomed command.

This fervor, when combined with the visions of leaders like Sitting Bull and fueled by messianic fervor, could only mean trouble. In the days before the Battle of the Little Bighorn, Sitting Bull himself had a vision of uniformed soldiers falling from the sky. He related this dream to some of his warrior chiefs (Sitting Bull was too old to fight in 1876 and did not take an active part in the battle), assuring them of victory in a coming armed confrontation with the white man.

The news of the Little Bighorn, when it finally emerged a day or two after the battle, electrified the nation, not only by the magnitude of the defeat but by the horrors visited upon the corpses of the dead cavalrymen. Soldiers had been mutilated, stripped bare, and left to rot in the broiling sun, their bodies livid in the early stages of decomposition. They were discovered by the army columns with which they were to have rendezvoused, slain by their celebrity commander's famous impetuosity, a man who had hoped for a glorious entry at the Democratic convention in St. Louis at the end of June—his intention being to win the nomination and then run for president in the fall against his former commanding officer and current archenemy, Ulysses S. Grant, who had been widely expected to run for a third term.

Custer had envisioned a triumph on the order of ancient Rome, but it was not to be. From his position upriver, Capt. Thomas Weir heard shots in the distance and urged his superior, Capt. Frederick Benteen, to ride to the sound of the guns. While Benteen dawdled, Weir and others moved in Custer's direction but were turned back by counterattacking Indians moving southeast from Last Stand Hill. When Weir and the rest of the command finally got there three days later, the first sight of the slaughtered men caused him to exclaim, "Oh, how white they look! How white." The sight effectively drove him mad—Weir, one of the few heroes of the Little Bighorn who survived, drank himself insensible for the next five months and died alone in a hotel room in New York City on December 9, 1876. Such was the shock.

It's a shock that continues to echo. A trip to the Little Bighorn (formerly Custer) Battlefield is something every American ought to undertake, in order to get a sense of what sacrifice, bravery, brutality, and the immediacy of death in one of the loneliest places on earth feels like. The ghosts still speak there; the same wind that blew over the bodies blows still. Looking out over the barren landscape, one's first thought is, *What an awful place to die*. It is a place that turned men into animals and women into the worst kind of men.[13]

Both sides fought with every weapon at their disposal, not just firearms and bows and arrows but also knives (not swords, however—the Seventh was not carrying swords that day), clubs, bare hands,

13. An unconscious echo, perhaps, of the latter half of Xerxes's cry at Salamis: "My men have turned into women, my women into men!"

teeth.[14] And as the action swept up Last Stand Hill, the barren hillock on which its final and terrible denouement occurred, along came the Indian women to strip, hack, dismember, and eviscerate both the still-living and the freshly dead. There was nothing "noble" about the savagery on display that day but rather something elemental, and yet, at the same time, somehow sacred. It is impossible to spend even five minutes anywhere on the field—not just Last Stand Hill, but Reno Hill, Weir Point, Medicine Tail Coulee (down which Custer's men descended toward the river as they sought a crossing in order to attack the Big Village of the Indians at the start of the fight), and other places where men on both sides fought and died—without sensing the higher powers that make men mad. It is an open-air cathedral to the greatness and the futility of war.

The afterlife of the Little Bighorn was as close to instantaneous as the technology of the time allowed. Almost immediately, depictions of the brevet Boy General's[15] final moments sprang up across the land, on paintings, Anheuser-Busch beer posters, advertisements, and line drawings in the popular press. Hollywood got into the act with Errol Flynn's 1941 classic *They Died with Their Boots On*; there followed *Custer of the West* (1967), starring Robert Shaw, and *Little Big Man*, with Dustin Hoffman, in 1970. Custer has been the subject of numerous biographies and fictional depictions in literature. Even today, everyone has an opinion about Custer: Hero or villain? A tactical battlefield genius or an impetuous fool? A sexually voracious glory hound beloved by the newspapers and consumed by political ambition or a stone-brave cavalry commander who was always at the forefront of every battle, and whose men adored him?

The answer is all of the above and more. One of the most extraordinary men of the nineteenth century—at a time when the United States was positively brimming with them—he outshone nearly all his contemporaries, with the only exception being Grant himself. As with Grant, the Civil War made Custer's reputation; unlike with Grant, success came to Custer early, almost too easily. Despite finishing last in

---

14. Cannae was not a one-off in this regard.

15. At the time of his death, Custer's real rank was Lieutenant Colonel.

his class of 1861 at West Point (by comparison, Grant was twenty-first out of thirty-nine in 1843), "the goat" Custer distinguished himself as a dashing if often reckless cavalry officer during the Civil War,[16] and in particular on the third day at Gettysburg, where his Michigan Brigade repulsed Jeb Stuart's rebel forces at East Cavalry Field in the wake of Pickett's Charge, turning the tide of both the battle and the war. Custer was also present as Grant accepted Lee's surrender at Appomattox. If ever there was an American upon whom destiny, even Manifest Destiny, smiled, it was George Armstrong Custer, so much more dashing than the plodding but implacable Grant.

Indeed, the contentious rivalry between the two men, and their many points of comparison, is worthy of a book in itself. So opposite in temperament, so similar in results. On the one hand the older Grant had been beaten up by life and alcohol until man and moment met at Shiloh and he, alone among the Union commanders, grasped that the War Between the States was strategic, not tactical, and that the South was going to have to be crushed beyond its capacity ever to rise again if the Union was to survive. Grant, the immovable object, his uniform humble and mud-spattered, in demeanor the same in victory or defeat, always pushing forward, relentlessly, until Mr. Lincoln's objective of total victory was finally achieved at the village Appomattox Court House, Virginia, on April 9, 1865.

At the surrender, Grant kindly mentioned to Lee: "I met you once before, General Lee, while we were serving in Mexico, when you came over from General Scott's headquarters to visit Garland's brigade, to which I then belonged. I have always remembered your appearance, and I think I should have recognized you anywhere." Lee replied, "Yes. I know I met you on that occasion, and I have often thought of it and tried to recollect how you looked, but I have never been able to recall a single feature." The genteel contempt was mutual. Lee thought the inept George McClellan (whom Custer worshipped) to be the best Union general he'd faced[17]; Grant wrote of Lee, "I never ranked Lee as highly

---

16. Early in the war, he was a balloonist, sent aloft to scout enemy positions, a job he enjoyed immensely.

17. Easy for him to say, since he had repelled the timorous McClellan on several

as some others of the army—that is to say, I never had as much anxiety when he was in my front as when Joe Johnston was in my front. . . . He was treated like a demi-god. Lee was of a slow, conservative, cautious nature, without imagination. I could never see in his achievements what justifies his reputation."[18]

As senior commanders, Grant and Lee were of course present at the surrender of the Army of Northern Virginia, along with their subordinate generals and aides. So was Custer; you can see him in some of the pictures, the most junior man there, standing at one end of the Union lineup. At 23, he had become one of the youngest brevetted generals in the Union Army, taking his promotion to brigadier general with him onto the field at Gettysburg. He became Philip Sheridan's favorite cavalry officer, and was with Little Phil during the Shenandoah Campaign of 1864, which laid waste to the South's breadbasket and kept Lee bottled up in Richmond and Petersburg. By the time Fate brought him to Appomattox Court House, Custer was a brevet major general. In fact, it was Custer who first received Lee's surrender, and his widow, Elizabeth, even wound up owning the table upon which the terms of the capitulation were signed—a gift from Sheridan, who had purchased it from the owner[19] as a souvenir.

Both Grant and Custer hailed from Ohio. Both loved literature and the theater, and when in New York, or some other big eastern city, each saw every play he could attend. Both were soldiers and seekers of fortune—like Grant, Custer was always looking to make a killing on Wall Street and, like Grant, never did.[20] Grant habitually wore a private's

---

occasions earlier in the war.

18. Lee was a superb situational tactician, handing Grant several stinging defeats in Virginia during the last year of the war. But he lacked Grant's sense of objective, and in any case never commanded the full Confederate forces in the way Grant eventually commanded all the Union forces. Still, there can be no doubt which was the greater general, as the only thing that really matters in total war is the result.

19. Wilmer McLean, who abandoned his home in Bull Run, Virginia, during the opening days of the Civil War and resettled at Appomattox Court House: the Civil War began in his front yard and ended in his living room.

20. Custer invested heavily in the Stevens Lode Silver Mine in the Colorado

blouse, with the only signs of his rank on his shoulders. Custer dressed as flamboyantly as possible, in a navy blue shirt with a red collar, knee-high boots, buckskin breeches, and a wide-brimmed hat, from under which his long blond curls tumbled.[21] He was the star of his own legend.

The press lapped it up and ladled it out. "Future writers of fiction will find in Brig. Gen. Custer most of the qualities which go to make up a first-class hero," wrote the *New York Tribune* in August 1864 as the war ground on, but ground down as well. "Frank and independent in his demeanor, Gen. C. unites the qualities of the true gentleman with the accomplished and fearless soldier."[22]

Throughout the Civil War, from the first Battle of Bull Run (where, naturally, he also saw action), Custer was always the most visible target on the battlefield, and somehow never was hit. Part knight in shining armor, part Beau Brummell, he instinctively understood the nature of his appeal. Like Caesar, who was blessed by Mars, he was a celebrity general and war hero with his eye on higher office. As was, in his own halting way, Grant—but Custer looked and played the part. Upon being introduced by her husband to Grant, Libbie Custer observed: "Gen. Grant is quite inferior looking, so plain and not even a bright eye to light up his features."

They were both superb horsemen, and neither was afraid of anything on the battlefield. There was no point. Like soldiers throughout history, in combat they had no time to fear what *might* happen but only time enough to concentrate upon what *was* happening at that moment. If you died, you died, often so quickly—blown to bits by a cannonball, for example—that you were unaware of it anyway. There were things far worse than death, and being a coward was one of them. Waving his saber while charging the enemy lines, Custer killed without remorse, and with gusto. Near the end of the war, at Winchester, a rebel took

---

Rockies, and lost his money. He also applied for a leave of absence from the army in 1866 to fight with Juárez in Mexico against the French-imposed Emperor Maximilian, for a fee of $10,000 in gold. Grant approved it, but the idea was shot down by Custer's wife, Libbie, who didn't want him heading back into battle.

21. At the Little Bighorn, as we shall see, he was dressed quite differently.

22. Quoted in T. J. Stiles's sterling 2015 biography, *Custer's Trials*.

a near point-blank shot at him, but Custer reined in his horse, which reared, and the bullet missed. Then Custer brought his sword down on the man's head and split his skull, just the way Roland or William the Conqueror or Zrínyi would have done, and with even less afterthought.

The only thing on his mind, besides women, was victory, with himself leading the charge, laughing in the face of enemy fire and always returning safely. His men called it "Custer Luck"—"better to be born lucky than rich" he was wont to say—until one day it ran out.[23] And not just for him, but for his family as well: Custer was not the only Civil War hero on the battlefield that day. His brother Capt. Tom Custer, who had won two Medals of Honor during the war (one of only 19 men in American history to do so), died alongside Armstrong. So also did his other brother, Boston, a civilian; his brother-in-law, Lt. James Calhoun; and his 18-year-old nephew, Henry Reed. Tom's body had been so brutalized—his skull was crushed, his eyes were gouged, his tongue and genitals were missing, and he had been scalped—that he could only be identified by a tattoo of his initials on one of his arms. By contrast, Custer Luck held for the general even in death: shot in the chest and in the temple, his body (like all the others) had been stripped naked but, aside from a lacerated thigh, two punctured eardrums (to improve Yellow Hair's hearing in the afterlife), and an arrow shoved through his penis,[24] his body had not been molested as the others had.

Why it ran out know only the gods of war. For a century and a half, military men and historians have been second-guessing Custer's decision to divide his forces as they approached the Little Bighorn, unaware that the largest Indian village ever assembled, with at least two thousand warriors present, was waiting for him down the hill, across the winding

---

23. In *Son of the Morning Star*, his magisterial study of the battle, Evan Connell quotes the sketch artist and illustrator Theodore Davis, who rode with Custer for a time: "Endowed by nature with a confidence in himself which was never boastfully exploited, and a believer that the future would surely unfold a continuation of the successful past—Custer's luck, his talismanic guard was trusted by him all too blindly . . ."

24. Perhaps an acknowledgment of his paternity of Yellow Bird; some speculate the Indians might have considered him a honorary member of the tribe, which may also account for why his body was not desecrated.

river, and through the trees. A failure of intelligence, due entirely to impetuosity—but Custer was no stranger to the warfighting tactics of the Plains Indians. He had confronted them many times before, and experience told him that the Indians fled at the sight of approaching cavalrymen. Experience had also taught him, as it had at the Battle of the Washita in 1868, that by making for the women and children—the squaws and papooses, in the terminology of the time—he could force the braves to break off fighting and rush to protect their families. To quote Talleyrand (disputed, but still piquant), the Little Bighorn was worse than a crime, it was a blunder.

The tactics Custer used at the Little Bighorn had always served him well in the past. In a sense, they were the offensive version of Hannibal's double envelopment of the Romans at Cannae; by dividing his troops, he hoped to surprise the enemy with a pincers movement, with himself at the charge from the rear of the enemy's fighting forces. Custer is perhaps the most potent example of a man who learns a valuable life lesson early and then repeats it until it finally kills him; the price of fame and martial glory was a premature death on one of the most forbidding and forlorn battlefields on earth.

To gaze out across the largely treeless eastern Montana landscape from atop Last Stand Hill, the site of Custer's death, is to experience a desolation that is only emphasized by the national park buildings and few paved roads that meander from the indefensible hillock two or three miles east along the river until you get to another, more defensible promontory where Maj. Marcus Reno and Capt. Benteen—both of whom despised Custer—held off the Indians for another full day until help arrived. Many, perhaps most, of the men of the Seventh were immigrants, Irish, Germans, Italians, some of them barely able to speak English, men who had fled the strife and famines of Europe for what they hoped would be a more salubrious life in America. Instead, they had joined the army, learned to ride, been taught some discipline, and were sent west to die.

Imagine how it must have been. The weather was hot, the climate arid. Old Hard Ass, or Iron Butt, as Custer's men called him, had ridden them practically to exhaustion in his eagerness to get on with the fray. As one of three army columns sent to trap the restive Sioux, Cheyenne, and Arapaho fighters and force them back onto the reservation, Custer wanted to beat his brother officers to the battlefield. He was part of Gen. Alfred Terry's command, which was moving west from Fort Abraham Lincoln in Bismarck, North Dakota. Meanwhile, Col. John Gibbon's troops were arriving from the northwest, while Gen. George Crook's forces were forging north from Fort Fetterman in Wyoming. But there is no glory in being part of the herd.

Custer's relentless drive made Benteen and Reno hate him, practically to the point of open insubordination. Benteen was a Virginian raised in Maryland (a slave state that had stayed in the Union), and had joined the Union side during the war. Reno was a blackguard, a drunk, a coward, and (later, after the battle) an alleged seducer of other men's wives. In tandem, coupled with Custer's heedless propulsion, they proved a fatal combination.

Custer's last recorded words went to Benteen, in the form of a hand-scribbled message by his adjutant, Lt. W. W. Cooke, and delivered by Giovanni Martini (or Martino; in America he was known as John Martin), an Italian immigrant who had been a drummer boy for Garibaldi in Italy during the war for Italian unification, and who was now the regimental bugler: "BENTEEN. COME ON. BIG VILLAGE. BE QUICK. BRING PACKS.[25] P.S. BRING PACKS." The residue of Custer Luck must have rubbed off on Martini; he remained with Benteen and thus became the only man in Custer's immediate command who escaped the last stand.

Custer's Crow scouts had reported the presence of a huge Indian village on the west bank of the Little Bighorn River, so Custer divided his twelve companies into three battalions. As they approached the Indians, Custer sent Reno's battalion to ford the river and attack the village from the southeast while he rode the bluffs on the other side, looking to cross farther downstream and assault the village from behind. Benteen he left in the rear, ahead of the mule train, assigned to search for, and block, any possible escape routes for the Indians. (Custer's biggest worry was that the hostiles would try to elude him; he never expected them to

---

25. Ammunition.

turn on him and fight.) It was a plan that had worked for him in the past. But not today.

It was over fast. As he retreated back from the river, unable to find a ford and in the face of the advancing Indians (who knew exactly where the river ran shallowest), Custer again split his men, for defensive purposes, but it was no use. Maj. Myles Keogh, an Irish-born soldier of fortune, and his battalion were slaughtered en masse a short distance from Custer's final position; others died in the ravines.[26] Some tried to escape and were cut down. Some reportedly shot themselves rather than fall into the hands of the Indians, especially the Indian women, who they knew would brutally torture them to death. Some may have been drunk. The others were scattered along the ravines and buttes as the last stand unfolded.

Not only soldiers but also civilians died. One of them was Isaiah Dorman, a free black man, possibly of mixed African and American Indian parentage, who had married a Sioux woman named Visible and was on good terms with the Lakota; because of his curly hair, he was known to the Indians as "Buffalo Teat," or simply, "Teat." Shot from his horse during Reno's withdrawal from the initial attack, he was surrounded by Indians during the panicked retreat and begged for his life as the warriors approached. But they regarded him as a traitor and killed him anyway. As James Donovan recounts in *A Terrible Glory: Custer and the Little Bighorn*, the dying Dorman, shot in the chest, was first spotted by none other than Sitting Bull, who recognized Dorman and gave him a drink of water, and ordered the women who had accompanied him that he not be killed.[27] Then:

---

26. Keogh was the only other officer in Custer's immediate command whose body survived mutilation. He had fought with the papal armies during the wars of Italian unification, then joined the Union Army during the American Civil War; like Custer, he was a veteran of Gettysburg, and, like Custer, he had a taste for the ladies. He wore a papal medallion around his neck, which the Indians (many of whom had been converted to Catholicism during their time on the reservation) regarded as powerful medicine. His horse, Comanche, was the only survivor of the last stand, badly wounded but still alive. Comanche died in 1891 and was buried with full military honors.

27. This account is much disputed; other scholars place Sitting Bull in the village

> A Hunkpapa woman named Eagle Robe, mourning for her ten-year-old brother just killed by the *wasichus*, rode up and jumped to the ground. "Do not kill me, because I will be dead in a short while anyway," said Teat.
>
> "If you did not want to be killed," said the woman, "why did you not stay home where you belong and not come to attack us?" . . . Eagle Robe raised a revolver and shot Teat in the head.
>
> After killing him, Eagle Robe continued to the river, where she killed two more wounded soldiers. She shot one with her revolver and dispatched the other with her sheath knife. Behind her, other women began to mutilate Teat. They drove a picket pin through his testicles into the ground, slashed his body, and cut off his penis and stuffed it into his mouth.

They also killed Charley Reynolds, a white scout who fell near Dorman; Mitch Bouyer, a half-breed scout of mixed French-Canadian and Sioux background, was killed near Custer; and Mark Kellogg, a reporter for the *Bismarck Tribune,* whose dispatches were also running in the *New York Herald*, died early in the battle: "By the time this reaches you we would have met and fought the red devils, with what result remains to be seen. I go with Custer and will be at the death," read his final communication. When they found his body, he had been scalped and was missing an ear, presumably taken in trophy.

Since none of Custer's command survived (save the absent Martini), we have to piece together their deaths from the forensic evidence and from Indian accounts of the battle, which vary widely. According to a brave named Little Knife,[28] the American cavalrymen were poor riders and easily unhorsed (very likely, considering that some of them had never ridden a horse before they joined the army) as well as poor shots, sometimes firing wildly and killing their own men. Anyone who tried to surrender was immediately killed.[29] Long Hair, said Little Knife, had

---

throughout the battle.

28. In an 1879 interview, given while on the run in Canada, and published in the *Billings Gazette* a quarter-century later.

29. One soldier, Lt. James Sturgis, was apparently taken alive but killed later. His

been killed by a shot from a 15-year-old boy whose brother had been killed as they neared Custer's position on Last Stand Hill. The youth picked up his fallen brother's gun and shot Custer dead.

Other Indians later said that they did not know that the Son of the Morning Star was even on the battlefield. "Everything was in confusion all the time of the fight," said a brave named Low Dog. "I did not see General Custer. I do not know who killed him. We did not know till the fight was over that he was the white chief. We had no idea that the white warriors were coming until the runner [from the first engagement with Reno] came in and told us."

Many of the Indian witnesses agree that had Reno stood his ground during his initial attack on the village, they might have fled, exactly as Custer had expected them to do, rushing back to protect their families. Everybody agreed that had Custer taken, and deployed, the Gatling guns that General Terry had offered him back in Bismarck, they would have made a significant difference in the outcome. But Custer had declined the offer, and the guns went instead to Col. Gibbon's column. "I offered Custer the battery of Gatling guns," Terry later explained to Sheridan, "but he declined it, saying that it might embarrass him, and that he was strong enough without it."

Custer had no inkling what he was in for. Richard A. Roberts, the brother of Capt. George Yates's wife, who was one of Libbie's closest friends at Fort Abraham Lincoln, served briefly as Custer's secretary and was part of the "Custer Clan" at the fort; his account of the events immediately preceding the departure of the Seventh for Montana (written about 15 years after the Little Bighorn, in defense of his friend) gives us an intimate portrait of the Boy General and his circle. Before they left on their final mission, with the regimental band playing the signature songs, "Garryowen" and "The Girl I Left Behind Me," the officers of the Seventh used to gather at Custer's home to socialize.

> The evenings were generally spent in singing, piano playing and parlor games of all kinds, and many were the laughs and shouts

---

decapitated and burned skull was later found in the Indian village by the burial detail a few days after the battle.

> which would come across to the General's room, as the library was called, where he would often hide himself to jot down some remark or thought which came to him. He was composing his "Life on the Plains" at the time and spent a good deal of his time writing and reading aloud to Mrs. Custer, who was an able critic.

Custer, he wrote, was very fond of dogs, as well of his two horses, Dandy and the white-socked sorrel, Vic (for Victory), which he rode into the final fight. Custer was also an expert marksman: "General Custer was very fond of practicing shooting at marks, and was considered the best shot with a Creedmore rifle in the Cavalry branch of the service, and I doubt of any other branch could produce his equal." For sport, and to while away the hours, Custer would lead shooting parties on deer hunts. No one had the slightest inkling what would soon lay in store.

Certainly not Reno, who just a few days later in the midst of the battle's opening skirmish would utterly lose his nerve when a bullet struck Bloody Knife, Custer's most trusted scout,[30] in the head, spattering blood and brains all over Reno's face and causing him to order a headlong retreat. In a battle with at least a half-dozen what-ifs, what if Reno had continued his cavalry charge from the south, toward the Big Village? Had he continued, and had Custer been able to cross the river farther downstream to the north, they might have stampeded the Indians, no matter how many braves there were. Then Benteen would have been in place to block the Indians' principal avenue of escape and Custer's plan would have worked perfectly—and he might well have been heading the Democratic ticket[31] for president that fall instead of Samuel J. Tilden.[32]

---

30. Custer valued Bloody Knife's services so highly that he arranged to have him paid $75 a month, as opposed to the standard private's $13.

31. The Democratic convention that year was held from June 27 to June 29—just a few days after Custer's death. There were no primaries in those days; the nomination was secured at the convention. In effect, Custer's campaign in the west was also his campaign for president.

32. Tilden, the governor of New York, won the popular vote—meaningless, under the American electoral system—but eventually lost to Rutherford B. Hayes, a Civil War hero (like Custer, he was a brevet major general) and former governor

Another what if? What if Custer had not refused General Terry's offer of the Gatling guns? Had he not been in such a hurry, he might have deployed his artillery along the east bank of the river to sweep the field of fire before he crossed and attacked the village from the northeast. The Indians did not like heavy guns, especially when they were trained on their homes, and would have been demoralized; even with nearly two thousand fighting men, the likelihood is that they would have scattered in terror.

For Custer's greatest fear was not that he would be outfought but that he would be outrun—that the Indians would flee upon first sight of the cavalry, as they always had before, and he would be robbed of his triumph as the Caesar of the Plains, reduced to chasing them around the wilderness. Once he realized that he had likely been spotted by the Indians on June 25, he had to act. True, he had effectively violated General Terry's plan of a coordinated three-pronged attack (that, in any case, had already been frustrated when Crook's column, heading north from Fort Fetterman, was turned back at the Battle of the Rosebud on June 17), but he had not, strictly speaking, disobeyed any orders. Terry had given him the latitude to act as he saw fit under exigent circumstances, which he did.

And yet the Indians did not run. For that we have Reno's cowardice to thank. As he crossed the river, swung around the copse of trees growing by the water, and headed toward the southern end of the village, Reno encountered a superior force of braves riding out to meet him. Reno ordered his men to dismount and form a skirmish line—a fatal blunder, since dismounted cavalry are no cavalry at all. When the Indians saw *wasichus* leaping from their horses and thus becoming stationary, they also saw how few of them there were, which emboldened

---

of Ohio. The election was mired in confusion and marred by accusations of voter fraud. An independent commission was established, but the Democrats refused to accept its arbitration, which gave just enough disputed electoral votes to Hayes to provide him with the Electoral College majority, and began a filibuster. Ultimately a compromise was reached under which Hayes became president but was forced to remove Federal troops from the South, thus ending Reconstruction and restoring white Democrat rule across the former Confederacy. The effects of that bargain would last a century.

the warriors. Reno's prompt retreat into the trees might have afforded him a better defensive position (how quickly the Seventh went from offense to defense) but even then he panicked again, swimming for the hills across the river—and the battle became, in the word of the Indians, a buffalo hunt.

The men were clobbered by the mounted braves, clubbed, and scalped. As they dove into the breast-high water, they were shot. What moments before had been a cavalry charge had become a rout. As Reno's men scrambled for the high ground—the site now known to us as Reno Hill—the Indians were free to turn and rush back north, toward where Custer was trying to cross the river and attack their families. Joined by Crazy Horse[33] as they pushed across the river and chased down Custer and his men, they were as men possessed.

But this is what men do when pushed to the edge. It may not be the most attractive human characteristic, and our kinder, gentler age may recoil from what appears to be barbarity, but it is as vital and essential to masculinity—and thus, in tandem with femininity, to humanity. It may not be something we like to think about, but every little boy sees himself as a warrior, fighting, sacrificing if need be to protect the ones he loves. To rephrase the old saw about heroes—little boys die a thousand deaths, willingly, as they play at combat and war, just so that, in battle, they can die but once.

As Custer retreated but did not panic, he was likely cool to the end. Custer had the contradictions of many men, and many great men, of his age. He had fought to free the slaves during the Civil War and had had a close, practically familial, relationship with an escaped slave named Eliza Brown, who became his cook and major domo, and yet he did his best to undermine Reconstruction after the war. He had great respect for the Indians' ability to fight, and although he undercounted his enemy at the Little Bighorn, he never underestimated them. Yet he also had the Western man's disdain for other races and would not ever have

33. Observed Connell: "Crazy Horse tied a red-backed hawk on his head, wore magic pebbles, painted hailstones on his chest, and sprinkled his pony with dust. . . . Luck. Medicine. They were hatched in the same nest, these two."

thought of them as moral or political equals. He would not believe they could defeat him until he was shot through the heart.

At the end, what was going through his mind? As in all last stands, he didn't have time to be afraid. He already had no fear of death, convinced by Custer Luck that it had no power over him. Bullets had always missed him before. He seemed to have some magnetic field around him, dancing some private Ghost Dance against which the enemy's medicine held no sway. No doubt, once he realized that he was not going to be able to ford the river, and that Reno was not coming, and where the hell was that bastard Benteen, he did the best he could to maintain some semblance of order among his men—whose ranks after all included his own two brothers, Tom and Boston, and his namesake nephew, Autie. Up against the wall, the soldier needs not courage but discipline; he needs but to do what he has been drilled to do. Form the line. Pass the ammunition. Hold the line. Fight every battle hand to hand if need be. Never break, cut, or run. Keep firing, until the firing is done.

His entire life had led him to this spot. The best generals of antiquity spent days preparing the battlefields, choosing the correct terrain so as to afford themselves martial advantage. The fight was never joined until Caesar joined it. Now here was George Armstrong Custer, Yellow Hair without his hair, Iron Butt unhorsed, the Son of the Morning Star in the blazing Montana sun, nearly alone but firing until the first shot caught him in the chest, which spun him around and put him, for the first and last time in his life, on the ground.

Did he linger? The shot to his head came in the left temple but did not bleed, so it's possible an Indian delivered an unnecessary coupe de grace, still not realizing that the shorn Samson lying amid the bodies of his men was the great Long Hair himself. He was doubtless dead when the Indian women jammed the awls into his ears, dead when his formally issueless manhood was violated by an arrow. But his body was otherwise spared. Was it because that he really had fathered a child with Monahsetah—a child of six years, who even then might be staring across the river, toward where his father now lay dead—and was, therefore, a member of the tribe himself? Had the great Indian fighter, in facing death, finally come, however briefly, face-to-face with his Native American doppelganger, Crazy Horse?

No doubt there was no time to think about any of this. Custer did what he'd always done: fight fearlessly. So did most of his officers. They were veterans, after all. Tom was a Civil War hero twice over, if not a celebrity like his brother. Keogh, one of thirteen children from County Carlow, had been through the Italian wars, had seen Gettysburg, had even been a prisoner of war in the South before being exchanged in a swap, half dead from emaciation but ready to fight again; only a few months before he had visited Ireland, made his will, assigned his estate in Kilkenny to one of his sisters, and headed back to meet his fate in America. Custer trusted them, as they trusted him, with his and their lives.

And yet, in one great sweeping motion, here came Crazy Horse, turning what remained of Custer's right flank, preventing the men from consolidating on Last Stand Hill while completely surrounding them. The men were dismounted by then—they had shot some of their horses for breastworks, while the other mounts had been driven off. Through the smoke and the dust, they could barely see the Indians until the braves were practically on top of them, creeping through the tall grass—the Indian name for the Little Bighorn was the "Greasy Grass"—or suddenly appearing out of the haze aboard one of their fleet and nimble ponies, a captured rifle in one hand and a scalping knife in the other.

The few soldiers left with Custer were trapped. Custer was with them, of course, attired not in his flamboyant Civil War motley but in buckskin, his blond curls close-cropped, his broad-brimmed hat pinned back on one side, the better to sight a rifle—although, at the end, a rifle would hardly have mattered; like the Romans' *pila*, it was mostly useless at close quarters. The entire point of the mission had been to get the Indians back to the reservation, and the American Army felt it could accomplish that most effectively by destroying the nomadic lifestyle of the Red Man and forcing him to accept the new world order. Many of the Indians in the Big Village that day were "treaty" Indians, who had literally wandered off the reservation for the short summer months and had fallen in with the "hostiles" under the spell of Sitting Bull and his visions. And now here they were, with the soldiers falling, if not out of the sky, then from their horses, and going under the knives of the Lakota and the Cheyenne.

When the battle was over, the Indians did exactly what Custer had feared—they scattered. Some of them came in; some followed Sitting Bull into Canada, where they sat out the long and harsh winters. Eventually, broken and hungry, they came back; Sitting Bull surrendered in 1881 at Fort Buford in the Dakota Territory, the last of the Sioux to submit. The army didn't quite know what to do with him; they feared he would turn renegade again, or encourage other Indians to do so. For a time they held him in custody.

In 1884, he went into show business, touring with Annie Oakley, whom he dubbed "Little Sure Shot"; the following year, he joined Buffalo Bill (Cody)'s Wild West show, reenacting the drama of the Little Bighorn; he may or may not have said rude things in Lakota to his audiences and fellow performers, denigrating Custer and the *wasichu*. One likes to think that he would. He posed for pictures—with Annie Oakley, with his wives, with anybody—and charged for autographs. He became a thoroughly modern celebrity.

But it was the dancing that killed him. In 1889, the Ghost Dance movement swept the Lakota. It was one last gasp of religious fervor, a movement that promised the young warriors invulnerability against the white man, the deaths of unbelievers, and the return of Indian freedom if only they trusted in their medicine strongly enough and wore the magic shirts—their own version of Custer Luck. Mrs. J. A. Finley, the wife of the postmaster at the Pine Ridge Agency, described one such:

> In preparing for the dance they cut the tallest tree that they can find, and having dragged it to a level piece of prairie set it up in the ground. Under this tree four of the head men stand. Others form in a circle, and begin to go around and around the tree. They begin the dance on Friday afternoon. It is kept up Saturday and Sunday until sundown. During all this time they do not eat or drink. They keep going round in one direction until they become so dizzy that they can scarcely stand, then turn and go in the other direction, and keep it up till they swoon from exhaustion. This is what they strive to do, for while they are in swoon they think they see and talk with the Messiah. When they regain consciousness they tell their experiences to the four wise men under

> the tree. All their tales end with the same story about the two mountains that are to belch forth mud and bury the white man, and the return of the good Indian times. They lose all their enemies in the dance. They think they are animals. Some get down on all fours and bob about like a buffalo. When they cannot lose their senses from exhaustion they butt their heads together and beat them on the ground, and do anything to become insensible so that they may be ushered into the presence of the Messiah. . . . At the end of the dance they have a grand feast, the revel lasting all Sunday night. They kill several steers and eat them raw, drink, and gorge themselves to make up for their fast.

The Ghost Dancers naturally gravitated toward the great chief, Sitting Bull. Young warriors flocked to the native hero of the Little Bighorn. There were rumors that he was about to leave the reservation and join the hostile forces under Big Foot in the Badlands some 40 miles north of Fort Yates. On December 15, 1890, the agent at the Standing Rock Reservation ordered the old man arrested; there was trouble. One of his warriors shot one of the Indian policemen, who in turn fired at Sitting Bull, hitting him in the chest, while another shot him in the head. A larger fight broke out, in which both policemen and warriors died. The braves fled. The army went after them, itching for revenge for Custer. This time, they brought with them four Hotchkiss[34] mountain guns firing 1.65-inch shells weighing 2 pounds each, essentially a rolling rifled cannon with a range of 3,500 yards.

On December 29, 1890, the two sides confronted each other for the last time at Wounded Knee Creek on the Pine Ridge Reservation. There are conflicting accounts of what happened. The Indians were ordered to give up their arms. The dismounted men of the Seventh pressed in upon them, coming within 20 feet of the Indians, according to contemporary accounts. An army detachment rifled through the teepees, emerging with about 50 contraband firearms. The Indians, suspecting they were

---

34. The Hotchkiss School, a private prep school in Lakeville, Connecticut, was founded in 1891 by Maria Bissell Hotchkiss, the wealthy widow of munitions manufacturer Benjamin Hotchkiss. It is, of course, profoundly pacifistic today.

about to die, begin singing their death songs—which abruptly turned into war songs as they withdrew hidden rifles from beneath their blankets and opened fire on the soldiers; others charged with tomahawks and scalping knives. The soldiers opened fire with everything they had:

> The slaughter among the savages was terrible, despite the fact that the soldiers had to run them down in their ambuscades. When the fight had fully begun the troopers cheered one another with the cry, "Remember Custer." The regiment fought as only men with a revengeful grievance can fight.
>
> The manner in which Big Foot's band turned upon their captors, stood before the terribly raking fire and shot down so many soldiers, rivals anything that has accompanied the Indian wars of America. Though encumbered with their squaws and pappooses, they almost snatched victory from defeat, and displayed a degree of reckless daring and bravery that has rarely been equaled.[35]

And so the Sioux conducted their own last stand, this one in the snows of a frigid Dakota winter. Hundreds died, including women and children; some 25 soldiers lay dead as well. Far from dignifying it with the term "battle," the Indians called it a massacre[36]; others have termed it a "war of extermination," especially after the big guns opened up on the now-defenseless Indians, in the fulfillment of Sheridan's dictum. In his official report on the incident, Daniel Royer, the agent at the Pine Ridge Reservation, claimed that an Indian medicine man had started the fight, crying out, "Kill the soldiers, their bullets will not have any effect upon our ghost shirts," and firing a gun. History is written by the winners.

In 1973, activists from the American Indian Movement occupied the site at Wounded Knee, standing off the federal government for 71 days, during which two Indians were killed and a federal marshal shot and

---

35. *Life of Sitting Bull*, 438.

36. The case made by author Dee Brown in his 1970 bestseller, *Bury My Heart at Wounded Knee*, which began a wholesale reappraisal of the American military policy during the Indian Wars.

paralyzed for life. There was further trouble two years later, in which two FBI agents were killed in a gunfight with activists. The American Indian Movement leader, Leonard Peltier, was convicted and sentenced to life in prison.

In the immediate aftermath of the Little Bighorn, public sentiment was largely in favor of Custer, and against his officers Reno and Benteen, although Custer's posthumous reputational appeal was at first regional—the Republicans of the North hated him, while the Southern Democrats cheered him. Since then, the former "goat" has seen his morning star rise and fall, from hero and back to goat again; modern revisionism assigns him the role of feckless clown, the man who got what was coming to him, and how. Yet he was one of the bravest warriors America has ever produced, a man who won every battle he fought until the last, and that defeat was a failure of intelligence, not of nerve or battlefield skill.

Stung by accusations of drunkenness and cowardice, Reno asked for and was granted an official court of inquiry in 1879, and was acquitted. The public refused to credit the verdict, and all the evidence says the public was right. Reno panicked, conducted a disorderly retreat, losing many men in the process, and finally gained refuge atop Reno Hill while his commander was waiting for him near the Big Village. Benteen's behavior was, if anything, even worse. He deliberately lollygagged in bringing up the rear, even upon receipt of Custer's final, desperate order to Be Quick, and seemed perfectly content to leave Custer to his fate. Benteen did join Reno atop the hill and together they mounted a spirited and expert defense against the enraged Indians who had just dispatched Custer, surviving through the night of June 25 and throughout June 26, when the Indians broke off the engagement and disappeared. They were eventually relieved by the arrival of General Terry and Colonel Gibbon. But, oh, what might have been.

The remains of George Armstrong Custer were at first interred along with his brother Tom in a shallow grave on the battlefield, where they were scavenged by wild animals; what was left of the bones was exhumed and buried at West Point in October 1887.

As for Libbie Custer, she became America's most famous professional widow, her fame continuing to outshine even that of Julia Dent

Grant after the president's death in 1885. Libbie was a ferocious defender of her husband's memory, as well as the author of three books about his life and times, struggling out from underneath Custer's debts to become a national figure in her own right. Her literary works made her wealthy. She built a mansion in Bronxville, New York, and lived there until her death in 1933, just short of her ninety-first birthday.

She never remarried. Her greatest regret was that she never had any children, especially a son who would have carried on the Custer name. Whether that son was at the Little Bighorn no one will ever know. She forgave her Autie everything, including his womanizing, his financial irresponsibility, and his reckless, fatal, final act of bravado. She never stopped loving him. He was her hero.

CHAPTER XI

"TELL EVERYONE I DIED FACING THE ENEMY"

RORKE'S DRIFT (1879) AND KHARTOUM (1885)

Africa. In Roman times, it meant North Africa, and in particular the area around modern-day Tunisia: to be more precise, the Phoenician city of Carthage. Egypt was not "Africa" but rather an ancient kingdom, stretching back into prehistory, long before the Achaemenid Persians, Alexander's conquest and the establishment of the Ptolemaic dynasty, the Romans, the Byzantines, the Sassanid Persians, the arrival of the Muslim Arabs, the Kurds, and the Ottoman Turks. The Vandals had a kingdom in Africa, in the west, near Spain; the Berbers roamed the sands of the Sahara. What lay beyond the desert, up the Nile, and into the interior was largely a mystery except to a few minor Roman expeditions. As the European explorations began in the nineteenth century, Africa was known as the "Dark Continent"—not because of the race of the people who lived below the Sahara and beyond the reaches of even the peoples of Upper Egypt but because it was essentially unknown to all but its inhabitants: *terra incognita*.

And so it remained for centuries after the fall of the Western Empire. Until Muhammed arose in the old Roman province of Arabia Petraea, the Arabs were of little geopolitical or cultural consequence: the Western world revolved around the Roman *mare nostrum*: the Mediterranean Sea, its way of life, and its way of war.

During the Age of Exploration, from the fifteenth to the

seventeenth centuries, Portuguese and Dutch traders put in at safe harbors along the west coast of Africa, then rounded the Cape of Good Hope, founded ports and colonies along the east coast, and from there set sail to India and beyond. In 1497, five years after Columbus's first voyage to the New World in the west, the Portuguese explorer Vasco da Gama set off round the Cape to prove that a shorter route to India lay, in fact, to the east, and not toward the "Indies," which Columbus (an Italian in the service of the Spanish crown) had discovered. To this day, Portuguese is an official language in several African countries, on both coasts, exactly where we might expect to find it in da Gama's wake: Angola, Cape Verde, Guinea-Bissau, and the island country of São Tomé and Príncipe (all along the west coast, the closest lands, nautically, to Brazil), and Mozambique, on the east African coast.

The interior, however, lay unpenetrated by the West (or as today we might say, the "white man"). Until the mid-nineteenth century, there was no reason to send expeditions up the Nile or into the heart of the continent. For the ancient Egyptians, whose principal cities lay in the fertile plain of the Nile upriver from present-day Cairo or the Macedonian-founded Alexandria, downriver on the Mediterranean coast,[1] the interior of the African continent was of little interest. It was enough that the Nile, the sacred river, continued in its annual cycles of flood and remission that crops might grow and civilization might flourish. Once the Europeans had established trading posts along the coasts, however, it was only a matter of time before explorers would push inward. The Arab slave traders were active as early as the seventh century and became especially industrious after their conquest of Egypt around 641 A.D. With the Egyptians, the Romans, the Greeks, and the Vandals gone, there was no Western power to oppose Muslim expansion along the North African coast, and the birth of the international Islamic slave trade soon followed.

At the southern tip of the continent, the Dutch *Boers* (farmers)

1. Much of Greco-Roman Alexandria is now under water, due entirely to natural "climate change," but none of it owing to "man-made climate change."

followed in the wake of the Dutch East India Company in the mid-seventeenth century and began settling what later became known as the Cape Colony, which eventually came under British rule. Moving inland beginning about 1834, the Boers became *voortrekkers,* setting out by foot and covered wagon to establish their own colonies of Natal, the Transvaal, and the Orange Free State, which combined with the Cape Colony in 1910 to form the union of South Africa—but only after the bloody Second Boer War between the British and the Afrikaaners between 1899 and 1902.[2]

The "Scramble for Africa," however, was well underway by the mid-nineteenth century, led largely by the British, who via the Royal Geographical Society sent explorers Sir Richard Francis Burton[3] and John Hanning Speke on an expedition up the Nile in order to discover its headwaters. In 1858, they did just that; with the discovery (from a European perspective) of Lake Victoria, the source of the life-giving Nile was finally established. The British, however, were not alone: founding colonies in Africa as well were the French, the Germans,[4] the Italians, and the Belgians. Leading the Belgian expedition to the Congo on behalf of King Leopold II[5] was the Welshman Sir Henry Morton Stanley, who as a younger man had fought for the Confederacy at the Battle of Shiloh. Stanley had in 1871 also famously discovered Dr. David Livingstone, the Scottish-born missionary who had also been searching for the

---

2. The early histories of South Africa and the United States are strikingly similar: the flight from religious persecution, a war with the British, a push westward or northward, and the creation of a stable political entity in a region that had never known one.

3. Perhaps the greatest of the Victorian-era explorers, Burton, in mufti upon pain of death, was the first European to make the pilgrimage to Mecca, and also translated the *Arabian Nights* into unexpurgated English. An astounding linguist who was conversant in some 29 languages and dialects, he also spent time in India and Brazil. In many ways, Burton typified the kind of Englishman who made the British Empire not only great but possible.

4. German South-West Africa (1884–1919), now known as Namibia. It figures in the plot of Edgar Rice Burroughs's *Tarzan the Untamed* (1919).

5. Joseph Conrad's novella *Heart of Darkness* (1902) is set in the Belgian Congo. The story forms the basis for Francis Ford Coppola's 1979 film *Apocalypse Now.*

source of the Nile, in the village of Ujiji in what is now Tanzania while leading an expedition sponsored by the *New York Herald*, for whom he was a correspondent.

With Europeans engaging with Africa on all sides, there was bound to be trouble, and there was. Seeking new territory for their large farms, the Boers had pressed northward, defeating the Zulus at the Battle of Blood River in 1838, killing some three thousand warriors while suffering no—zero—deaths themselves (and only three wounded); they viewed their astounding victory as ordained by God.

The two most significant battles in nineteenth-century Africa between the Europeans and the natives, however, involved the British. By January 1879, the British were desirous of adding additional territory in South Africa, which meant expansion into Zululand. Accordingly, the high commissioner for Southern Africa, Sir Henry Bartle Frere, acting on his own initiative but in accordance with what he knew to be the Crown's wishes, had ginned up a crisis by delivering an ultimatum to the Zulu king, Cetshwayo, that the Zulus should disband their army and lay down their arms.

The Zulus were the foremost fighting force in Africa at the time, the Spartans of their day and somewhat akin to the Sioux in America. Although not members of a standing professional army, Zulu warriors began their martial training as early as age six, and were subject to being called into active service between the ages of 19 and 40, at which age they were allowed to marry but still remained in the reserves. (Zulu warriors as old as 70 sometimes took the field in times of need.) For the British to challenge them so directly was not only an affront to their manhood but also an act of extraordinary foolhardiness. It spoke of the condescension the Europeans had for the indigenous armies they encountered during the colonial period, and their inability to credit native fighting forces with command of tactics that had worked well for the Europeans themselves earlier in their military development.

In their confrontations with the Zulus—as with the Americans' experience with the warrior nations of the Plains Indians—an attitude the Greeks would recognize as hubris often took hold. In both instances, the

Anglo-Americans underestimated the ability of the locals to quickly adopt the weaponry and tactics of their enemies, however imperfectly.[6] The horse, for example, was not native to the Americas, but the Indians quickly became outstanding riders, to such an extent that the Americans had to catch up to them in horsemanship, if not in marksmanship. In Africa, the British (as they had been doing during the French and Indian War, the Revolutionary War, and the War of 1812) employed their forces as they would have against a European enemy, confident that the same formations and weaponry that had served them so well against Montcalm and Bonaparte would work equally well against red Indians and black Africans.

Such tactical derision was not only unfounded, it was often fatal. On January 22, 1879, a British army numbering about 1,800 men pressing into the Zulu Kingdom under the command of Maj. Gen. Lord Chelmsford[7] was effectively annihilated at Isandlwana by Zulu *impi* under Ntshingwayo kaMahole Khoza, King Cetshwayo's half-brother. It was the most decisive defeat ever suffered by the British Army in its colonial wars. Taken by surprise, the British lost more than 1,300 men killed in action—and this despite their overwhelming superiority in firepower, which included Martini-Henry rifles (then state of the art), two seven-pounder cannons, and a battery of Hale rockets.

But, as the British learned, modern weaponry was useless if it could not be deployed, and at the Battle of Isandlwana[8] there was no time. The irony was that this was a fight Chelmsford had sought. Confident as his well-trained troops marched into Zululand, Chelmsford had split his force of some 2,500—the same tactical mistake Custer had made at the Little Bighorn, and for much the same reason: he thought the Africans would flee, and wanted to trap them. Lacking adequate intelligence as to the whereabouts of the Zulu army, which numbered upward of

---

6. Neither the Indians nor the Zulus ever became very good shots with firearms.

7. Later, Frederic Augustus Thesiger, 2nd Baron Chelmsford, GCB, GCVO. His father, Frederick, the 1st Baron Chelmsford, was twice Lord High Chancellor of Great Britain; his sister, Julia, married Sir John Inglis, who commanded the British forces during the Siege of Lucknow during the Sepoy Mutiny in India in 1857. With friends in high places, Chelmsford largely escaped blame for the disaster.

8. *iSandlwana*, in Zulu orthography.

15,000 to 20,000 fighting men, and heedless of the need to establish a defensive perimeter in open country, Chelmsford made his *laager* at Isandlwana, a plain under the deceptive shelter of a small hillock about one hundred miles northwest of present-day Durban. Then he made another fatal mistake: he took more than half his men away from camp to hunt for the main Zulu army—and the remaining column at Isandlwana discovered too late that the Zulus had instead found them.[9]

It was all over quickly—not so much a last stand as a rout. Although the British attempted to form their traditional defensive positions by establishing firing lines, they were continually on the back foot throughout the four-hour battle. As it happened, there was a solar eclipse that day, around 2:30 in the afternoon; when the sun reappeared, the fight was essentially over. The British tried to form firing squares, but in the smoke and the darkness, it was no use. Down to their last rounds, the British—including in particular one big Irishman,[10] according to Zulu accounts—fought with bayonets, with primordial ferocity, until they went down. But it was no use. Back-to-back they battled but the numbers were against them. They were like the Romans at Cannae, crushed from all sides in an ever-tightening perimeter, fighting in the end with only teeth and fingernails against the black warriors, who pressed in like the Carthaginians, until there were no British left. Armed with shield and *assegais*, the Zulus executed perfectly their former king Shaka's[11] famous "horns of the bison" strategy, enveloping the British with the horns while the chest attacked head-on. Few African tribes could withstand it and, on this day, neither could the British.

And there the story might have ended, but for two complementary things. One, a small contingent of British soldiers had been left behind at a former farm known as Rorke's Drift, resentful at not being able to take part in the action; and two, there was still a sizable force of

---

9. Writing in 1878, Chelmsford had said, "If I am called upon to conduct operations against them . . . I shall strive to be in a position to show them how hopelessly inferior they are to us in fighting power, altho' numerically stronger."

10. A throwback, perhaps, to the Norse axman at Telford Bridge in 1066. History rhymes.

11. Sigidi kaSenzangakhona.

Zulu warriors who had been held in reserve at Isandlwana and who were just itching for a share of glory themselves. As Neil Thornton writes in his meticulous account of the battle, *Rorke's Drift: A New Perspective* (2016), "Both the British at the mission station and the Zulu reserve had, for circumstances out of their control, missed their much-craved chance to do battle at iSandlwana. Ultimately, they would lock horns at Rorke's Drift." And thus enter into the pages of military history.

> Rorke's Drift was situated at a prime crossing point by the river border and had quickly been identified as an ideal location from where the column could spring into action. The drift owed its name to Jim Rorke, an Irish trader who had purchased the land in 1849. On this piece of land, he had built his home and accompanying storehouse. Overlooking his abode was the Shiyane Hill, and just half a mile distant was the Buffalo (uMzinyathi) River, beyond which lay Zululand. Traders would visit Rorke before crossing into Zululand, and he became an established and popular figure among the Zulus across the border, who referred to his property as '*KwaJimu*' ('Jim's Place').
>
> Rorke died in 1875, aged forty-eight, and was buried a little way behind the storehouse by the Shiyane Hill. Shortly after his death, his wife sold the land. In January 1878, Rorke's Drift was purchased by Otto Witt on behalf of the Church of Sweden.[12] Witt and his family used Rorke's residence as their own and converted the storehouse into a chapel. That same year, talks took place between the Swedish government and the British regarding Rorke's Drift . . . it was agreed that Witt would rent out the mission station to the British government. The house would be used as a hospital and the chapel would revert back to its original use as a storehouse to hold supplies.

With Rorke's Drift as a base, the British under Chelmsford were able

---

12. Once again, the power of religion enters the *champs de Mars.*

to launch their unprovoked invasion of Zululand. The remaining garrison chafed at not seeing action. The surgeon James Henry Reynolds was detailed to remain with the hospital. As he noted later, his feelings were that of "disappointment when Lord Chelmsford marched away with his army and left me with about 100 other men to sit still and bite the bullet of inactivity at Rorke's Drift. There was no fighting for us, no doctoring for me; the army moved away to gain glory and we sat down in what Lord Halsbury would call a sort of base, to envy the other chaps their chances!"

But when Chelmsford's battalions were vaporized at Isandlwana, Rorke's Drift lay helpless and nearly defenseless; soon enough—a matter of hours—the men at the station would see all the action they could ever have desired. Until then, unaware of the disaster, they wrote letters, played cards, and generally whiled away the time.

The depiction of the battle in the movie *Zulu* is about as accurate as any motion picture that is not actually a documentary is ever likely to get. The 150 or so British and colonial troops, plus a handful of civilians, really did stave off an attack of somewhere between 3,000 and 4,000 *impis*. They really were led by a pair of junior officers, the military men John Chard (Stanley Baker in the movie) of the Royal Engineers, and the aristocratic Gonville Bromhead (Michael Caine), a scion of a military family whose great-grandfather had fought with Wolfe at Quebec, whose grandfather had fought against the Americans during the Revolutionary War, and whose father had served under Wellington at Waterloo. Both Chard and Bromhead were later awarded Britain's highest military honor, the Victoria Cross, along with nine of their men, at Rorke's Drift.

Trapped in a small but fortified *kraal*, with a main structure and some outbuildings surrounded by a wall, the British were in a similar position to that of the Foreign Legion at Camarón. Unlike the French, however, the British did not have to contend with fire from within their compound, which gave them some control over their position; they could thus direct their fusillades in whichever direction the attacks came. The Zulus, however, had captured a sizable cache of weapons from Chelmsford's brigade, and while they were not expert in firearms, some of their snipers were able to worry the British from their positions beyond the enclosure in the high ground near Shiyane Hill—the

Oscarberg, in Swedish—until the British riflemen were able to neutralize them.

From the moment they learned of Chelmsford's defeat from a couple of survivors who had staggered back into camp, the defenders at Rorke's Drift—the 2/24th Regiment of Foot, made up of English, Welsh, and Irish soldiers—knew the Zulus were en route: their prayers for action were soon to be granted, but not quite in the way—and with the degree of intensity—they expected. The delay in the Zulu army's arrival provided an opportunity for those colonials and civilians who wanted to leave to do so. Most did. The stragglers from Isandlwana had warned of an immense Zulu army heading their way and advised immediate retreat. But after some debate, the British soldiers decided to stay and not withdraw to the nearby British station at Helpmekaar, about ten miles away.

This was the moment of truth—to flee, retreat, regroup, or to stand and fight? Consider Chard's and Bromhead's position: the main force under Chelmsford had just been wiped out. An *impi* army was on its way, with God knows what armaments captured from the British. Against which stood a hundred and a half men, in the middle of Africa, cut off from any possible immediate assistance. Although flight was theoretically possible, a slow-moving column in open country, laden with sick and wounded (there were about 35 men in the camp hospital), would be easy pickings for the fleet Zulu army. The station, such as it was, offered the best possible defense. And then there were those pesky notions of duty, honor, and country.

One of the signal characteristics at Rorke's Drift was the low rank of both the commanding officers (both were mere lieutenants; the younger Chard slightly outranked Bromhead). There were no senior officers present: Rorke's Drift was not a prestigious assignment—the real action was with Chelmsford, a favorite of Queen Victoria—and in any case Chard was an engineer, there to look after the cable ferries (called "ponts") over the Buffalo River as the British planned their invasion of Zululand from neighboring Natal. Bromhead, then 33 years old and already going deaf, seemed not a patch on his heroic forebears. One of his commanders called him "hopeless," and upon arrival at Rorke's Drift he had had almost no command experience. Familially, he had a lot to live up to, and few expectations that he could—perhaps least of all from himself. But courage and heroism manifest themselves in the strangest places and sometimes among the least likely of men. To paraphrase Sherlock Holmes, masculinity in the blood is liable to take the strangest forms.[13]

Capt. William Penn Symons,[14] a Cornishman, served with Chelmsford and left an account of both Isandlwana and Rorke's Drift, the latter based on his interviews with the survivors. Of Rorke's Drift, he wrote in his diary:

> At 3 p.m. on the 22nd January [the same day as Isandlwana, in its aftermath], Lt. Bromhead received the startling news from two fugitives that the Generals' Camp was taken, and that the Zulus were on the way to attack his post. . . . The above warning gave the Officer at Rorke's Drift a short hour for preparation. It was badly needed as nothing had been done to prepare the place for defence. . . . The tents of the Company were pitched outside a farmhouse or rather houses, as there were two; one was used as a store, the other as a base Hospital and they were forty yards apart. . . .
>
> The tents were struck and the house loopholed[15] and occupied. They then managed to pile a few biscuit boxes and mealie sacks as a part of parapet towards the garden on one side, and along the other facing the hill, which completely commanded the houses and enclosures. They drew up three wagons and filled up the gaps with more boxes and sacks of grain. These "lines"

---

13. "Art in the blood is liable to take the strangest forms," observes Sherlock Holmes in the short story "The Adventure of the Greek Interpreter" (1893) by Sir Arthur Conan Doyle. Holmes's sidekick and amanuensis, Dr. Watson, served as a British Army surgeon and saw action in Afghanistan.

14. Killed in action during the Second Boer War in 1899. Gut-shot during the Battle of Talana Hill, near Dundee in northern Natal province, but refusing to admit his wound to his men, Symons died at age 56 three days later in the hospital, saying to one of the medical officers, "Tell everyone I died facing the enemy; tell everyone I died facing the enemy!"

15. Which is to say, the walls were punctured for rifle firing ports.

> connected the two houses and formed what we will call "the yard." It was a broken and imperfect barricade at the best; on the garden side nowhcre more than 3 ft high towards the hill they raised it in places to 4 and 4 ½ ft high.

As Grant had demonstrated, first as a junior officer in the Mexican War and later as commander of the Union forces during the American Civil War, logistics were crucial to the outcome of any conflict. The tip of the spear is naturally the focus of depictions of battle, but the effectiveness of the general lies in his skillful use of materiel and terrain. The French at Camarón, although they ultimately lost, had a wall, a hacienda, and some outbuildings from which to construct a defense; the British at Rorke's Drift had something even more defensible. They also had weapons and plenty of ammunition. But, as things turned out, it was the erection of an interior "mealie wall"—feed sacks of maize piled one atop the other like sandbags in a flood—that proved decisive in the defense of the compound.

Despite the Zulus' "buffalo" tactics, the Africans were never able to break what amounted to the center of the British lines. In front of and behind the mealie wall, they were able to stay organized and fire in three-rank volleys,[16] thus keeping up a continuous fusillade against the oncoming Zulus, who were defenseless against such a withering barrage. Although the Zulus were eventually able to overrun the hospital[17]—as with the hacienda at Camarón, not all its rooms communicated with one another, which meant the sick and wounded men had to break through the walls and run a gantlet to get to the safety of the British lines—they were unable to break the British position, no matter how brave the assault. By pulling back his forces behind the mealie wall, Chard was able to keep his defense intact; indeed, the tighter their formation necessarily became, the more lethal the British were.

---

16. A legacy of the three-tiered Roman maniples, with troops from the rear constantly moving forward to spell the men at the front.

17. "As in their dancing they stalked out of their concealment, pranced up with a high stepping action, and caring nothing for the slaughter, endeavoured to get over the barricade." Symons, ibid.

Rorke's Drift was that oddity, an afternoon, evening, and even night battle. Generally, in Africa, nobody wanted to fight after noon. Since most battles were waged during the summer and early fall, it often got too hot (January in South Africa, below the equator, is summer), and the position of the sun was often crucial, either to the attack or the defense. At Rorke's Drift, the heat of the day was intensified by the close-quarters nature of the battle; shots fired often at point-blank range; thrusting bayonets versus stabbing *assegais*.[18] Combat at its most elemental, exactly the way it was at the time of the Greeks and Romans.

And so the two sides fought on, the British maintaining as much order as possible and delivering volley after volley from the mealie wall (the functional equivalent of the rebuilt Phocian wall that partially protected the Spartans at Thermopylae), the Zulus coming in waves, fearless in the teeth of the white man's weapons, confident that their tactics, which had always worked in the past, would work again, and shouting their war cry: *Usutu!*

Dusk arrived, darkness fell. It didn't matter. The hospital's thatched roof caught fire; the two sides fought on by firelight. At close quarters, the Africans were unafraid to grab for the British rifles by the bayonet, heedless of the pain; had the soldier just reloaded, the warriors were blown apart, point blank. And still they came.

> The last of them left just before dawn. The number composing the [final] attack were estimated at 3,000. Many of the bodies by their shields and other distinctive marks, such as plumes, head gear, rings etc., etc., were identified as belonging to one of the King's chief and favourite regiments and one which bore a great reputation.
>
> Our loss was 13 killed and 10 wounded; three of the latter died soon after of their wounds. Of the enemy we buried 370 and after a few days found over 100 more skeletons lying here and

---

18. Pvt. Joseph Williams, a Welshman, killed at least 14 Zulu warriors until he ran out of ammunition and fought with his bayonet. He was eventually dragged out, killed, and mutilated. Others died in their beds.

> there in the long grass and bush between Rorke's Drift and the spot where they recrossed the Buffalo River . . . five out of six of the bodies found were those of old men, many of them quite wizened, and all spare and thin . . . we repeat that it was a fight at odds of one white man to twenty black savages and more, frenzied with success and slaughter [at Isandlwana]. Each individual soldier did his work and duty well. Ay, and right well.[19]

This was especially true of the men in the hospital, who were cut off from the main force behind the mealie wall. Many of them went down fighting; Bromhead himself risked his life several times over, running ammunition into the beleaguered building and ferrying the sick and wounded to safety.

As dawn broke on January 23, everyone braced for what he assumed would be the final assault, one in which they would all surely be overrun. Instead, they discovered that the Zulus had vanished. A few of the wounded African warriors played dead until the British approached them; then they attacked. After a struggle, they were put down.

About seven in the morning, the Zulus appeared once more, on a ridge line to the southwest of the compound. The men returned to arms and stations, but ammunition was now running low. They were instructed to make every shot count, and not to fire until the attackers came within 50 yards. Writes Thornton:

> The men waited silently for the enemy to come on, but they stayed by the hills around 1,000 yards away, ever growing in numbers as more and more warriors joined them. The garrison remained in a state of suspense. Although some Zulus moved a little closer to the defenders, the majority kept their distance. After an hour, another large body of men was spotted heading towards Rorke's Drift. A shout from a look-out on the storehouse roof alerted the garrison that there were thousands more black men closing in, and it was assumed this was the main Zulu impi coming to finish

19. Symons, ibid.

them off. However, this was not the case. The Zulus on the hill gradually retired out of sight.[20]

Chelmsford arrived later that morning, January 23, to briefly assess the situation. He left almost immediately to attend to other matters, but the next day requested that the following spare, characteristically unemotional message be delivered to the troops: "I wish to tell them how highly I think of their conduct. It was admirable, no troops could have been steadier or more collected especially during the night of constant alarms, the 22nd, and although their conduct might be equaled, it could not be surpassed."[21]

Stiff upper lips, indeed. Partly on the strength of Rorke's Drift, Chelmsford was promoted to lieutenant general in 1882; the heroic last stand had wiped away the stain of Isandlwana, rendering the larger and more important battle a footnote to the secondary conflict. He went on to become a full general and ended up as the Gold Stick in Waiting, one of the personal bodyguards of the British monarch on ceremonial occasions.

The shower of Victoria Crosses made the men of the Drift national heroes. Chard received a personal audience with Queen Victoria; he died of cancer in 1897, a full colonel. Bromhead had lived up to the valor of his famous forbears; he missed the audience with the queen, as he was fishing in Ireland and did not receive the invitation in time. He served overseas, in Gibraltar, India, and Burma, and died in India of typhoid fever in 1891 with the rank of major.

Neither could have expected that, just six years later, the most famous last stand in British history, superseding even theirs, would take place up north, down the Nile, in the Sudanese city of Khartoum.

---

20. Two of the most memorable scenes in the movie *Zulu* never occurred. The first was the choral battle between the African warriors as they steeled themselves for the fight and the defensive Welshmen singing "Men of Harlech" in response. The second was the final salute to British bravery by the departing Zulus on the ridge.

21. There is some doubt whether the message was, in fact, communicated to the troops at the time or, if it was, exactly when.

"MAY I BE GROUND TO DUST IF HE WILL GLORIFY HIMSELF IN ME"

KHARTOUM, 1885

The death struggles at Isandlwana and Rorke's Drift had been matters of state, not faith. The British, in the throes of their last desire for empire, had supplanted the Dutch Boers in South Africa and were expanding into Zulu territory for queen and country. For their part, the Zulus had no territorial aims, but were defending their traditional homeland against European incursion. The original black residents of what is today South Africa were not Zulus but Hottentots,[22] a nomadic people unable to put up much of a defense against the European invaders. There was nothing akin to the American sense of Manifest Destiny on the part of the British, just a fight for glory and honor.

A few years later, however, things had changed. Under the stewardship of William Gladstone, then in his second stint as prime minister, the British had become ever more concerned about African slavery, which had been abolished throughout the Empire in 1833 but which was still flourishing in Arab-controlled areas[23] where Islam met sub-Saharan black Africa. Into this cultural vortex had arrived one of the most remarkable men in British history, the enigmatic, deeply religious, mercurial, chain-smoking, heavy drinking, idiosyncratically Christian zealot, latently suicidal, and very probably chastely homosexual, Charles George "Chinese" Gordon.[24] During his first stint as governor of the Sudan in the 1870s, Gordon had worked vigorously to suppress the slave trade, making plenty of enemies along the way. Among them was one

---

22. Khoikhoi, in native parlance. They are related to the San, also known as Bushmen to the Europeans.

23. In the wake of their conquest of Roman Egypt, Muslim Arabs had attempted to subdue Christian Nubia—southern Egypt and the Sudan—but failed; however, under the terms of a truce, the Nubians were required to trade slaves for needed foodstuffs. By the early sixteenth century, the Ottomans had conquered Nubia. Henceforth, blacks were routinely captured and sold into slavery.

24. The Byronic echoes of his middle and surnames were wholly appropriate to his character.

Zobeir Pasha, an Afro-Arab who controlled the flourishing trade in black slaves in that part of Equatoria. When Zobeir's son, Suleiman, was arrested for slaving, Gordon ordered his execution. He meant business.

And then came the Mahdi.

Since the death of Muhammad in 632, Islam had been riven by a succession crisis, which is the origin of the present-day Sunni/Shiite split. The Sunnis believe that Abu Bakr, a friend of Muhammad, was his rightful heir, while the Shiites hold that only a direct lineal descendant of the "Prophet" should lead the emergent religion. Both sides, however—in a borrowing from both Jewish and Christian eschatology—believe that there would come a savior or redeemer to usher the Believers into the promised land of eternal justice under Allah.

Muslims held that, in the last days, this Mahdi would come together with Jesus (Issa)[25] to save the world from the *Al-Masih ad-Dajjal*, the anti-Messiah or Antichrist, who had to be defeated before the Day of Judgment. As in Judaism and Christianity, many false redeemers have arisen over the centuries and the millennia; that the world has not yet ended may be taken as proof of delusion or mendacity. Among the prominent false messiahs in Islam was one Muhammad Ahmad, a Nubian Muslim from Aba Island in the White Nile,[26] south of Khartoum, whose family, boat-builders along the river, could trace its lineage directly back to the Prophet. Anointing himself as the Mahdi, the Expected One, the Sufi mystic roared out of the Sudanese desert on June 29, 1881, proclaiming his *Madhiyya* and announcing his *jihad* to make the way smooth for the Second Coming of Jesus, and thus the beginning of the End Times. He demanded acknowledgment by all Muslims of his mission; high on his list of Unbelievers were the louche Ottoman Turk rulers of Egypt in Cairo, some of whose forces were holed up in Khartoum.

The British didn't much care what happened to the indigenous

---

25. Jesus is considered a major prophet in Islam; his mother, Mary, is mentioned more often in the Koran than in the Christian New Testament.

26. The White Nile is the main tributary of the mighty river, flowing north from its origin at Lake Victoria. The shorter Blue Nile arises in Lake Tana in present-day Ethiopia, but supplies most of the volume of the river downstream during the rainy season.

natives of the Sudan, but they did very much attend to the threat to the Egyptian Turkish garrison there, which was controlled by their fiscally bankrupt and wholly dependent ally, the Khedive of Egypt. There was only one man with the moral, political, and military authority to evacuate the Turks, and that was Gordon Pasha[27]—a man assured of the rightness of his ways and utterly unafraid of death.

Gordon was on the verge of accepting a commission from Leopold, king of the Belgians, to administer the Congo Free State,[28] Leopold's personal satrapy in central Africa, when Gladstone's government offered him his old gubernatorial post in the Sudan. His mission was carefully circumscribed: evacuate the beleaguered Egyptian force in Khartoum. That was all. Not to defend the city, which stood just south of the intersection of the White and Blue Niles. Not to defeat the Mahdists. Just get the troops out and back to Cairo. Surely, the hero of the Taiping Rebellion,[29] "Chinese" Gordon, whose command of the Ever Victorious Army had been instrumental in finally putting down the rebellion, could do that.

With some reluctance—and after a two-week visit to Ireland, where the appalling conditions among the Irish peasant farmers there provoked him to write a six-page memo to Gladstone urging much-needed reforms[30]—Gordon took the job. With Lt. Col. J. D. H. Stewart as his

---

27. As the emissary of the Ottomans—the real Egyptians, Greeks, Romans, and even Persians were all long gone from the area—and the newly appointed governor-general of the Sudan, Gordon was entitled to the honorific *Pasha*.

28. In this capacity, Gordon was to succeed Henry Morton Stanley, the veteran of Shiloh, at a greatly reduced salary. But money was never an object for Gordon. He also had offers to go to India as the private secretary to the governor-general of India (he briefly accepted, and quickly resigned), and then back to China, with war between Russia and China brewing. Against the wishes of the War Office, he traveled to Beijing (Peking) and even offered to resign his British citizenship before clashing with the Chinese authorities. The Foreign Office finally ordered him home.

29. A ferocious civil war in China, 1850–64, between the Manchurian Qing (Ching) dynasty and the Heavenly Kingdom of Great Peace, the latter led by a man proclaiming himself to be the brother of Jesus Christ.

30. The Land Wars were then at their height, as the dispossessed native Irish revolted against British colonial landlordism.

adjutant—Gladstone's personal check on the headstrong Gordon's famous willfulness—he set out for Egypt in January 1884.

Who was Gordon? One of the most complex and complicated figures of the high Victorian era, he was at the same time a product, even an avatar, of his era. A hero in his lifetime, he was soon enough a figure of derision among the Bloomsbury Group[31] that sprang to life during and after the First World War. In his quartet of character studies, *Eminent Victorians* (1918), the Bloomsbury writer Lytton Strachey left a dyspeptic but indelible portrait of Gordon:

> During the year 1883 a solitary English gentleman was to be seen, wandering, with a thick book under his arm, in the neighbourhood of Jerusalem. His unassuming figure, short and slight, with its half-gliding, half-tripping motion, gave him a boyish aspect, which contrasted, oddly, but not unpleasantly, with the touch of grey on his hair and whiskers. There was the same contrast—enigmatic and attractive—between the sunburnt brick-red complexion—the hue of the seasoned traveller—and the large blue eyes, with their look of almost childish sincerity. To the friendly inquirer, he would explain, in a low, soft, and very distinct voice, that he was engaged in elucidating four questions—the site of the Crucifixion, the line of division between the tribes of Benjamin and Judah, the identification of Gideon, and the position of the Garden of Eden. He was also, he would add, most anxious to discover the spot where the Ark first touched ground, after the subsidence of the Flood: he believed, indeed, that he had solved that problem, as a reference to some passages in the book which he was carrying would show.

---

31. A London-based group of intellectuals and writers, whose number included the writers Virginia Woolf and E. M. Forster, and the economist John Maynard Keynes; the name derives from their fashionable West End neighborhood of Bloomsbury. Dorothy Parker observed of them, "they lived in squares, painted in circles and loved in triangles." Andrew Lloyd Webber's finest musical, *Aspects of Love*, is based on the novella of the same name by David Garnett, another member of the group.

> This singular person was General Gordon, and his book was the Holy Bible. . . . For month after month, for an entire year, the General lingered by the banks of the Jordan. But then the enchantment was suddenly broken. Once more adventure claimed him; he plunged into the whirl of high affairs; his fate was mingled with the frenzies of Empire and the doom of peoples. And it was not in peace and rest, but in ruin and horror, that he reached his end. . . .
>
> What other nation on the face of the earth could have produced Mr. Gladstone and Sir Evelyn Baring and Lord Hartington and General Gordon? Alike in their emphasis and their lack of emphasis, in their eccentricity and their conventionality, in their matter-of-factness and their romance, these four figures seem to embody the mingling contradictions of the English spirit.

To Strachey, Gordon was a near-suicidal fanatic, exactly the kind of Briton that Britain was well rid of in the aftermath of the carnage of the Great War. To other eminent if fictional Victorians, he was a national hero. As every Sherlockian knows, the world's first consulting detective had only two images in 221B Baker Street[32]: an unframed picture of the abolitionist Henry Ward Beecher, brother of Harriet Beecher Stowe, of *Uncle Tom's Cabin* renown, which stood atop a pile of Dr. Watson's books, and a "newly framed" portrait of Gordon, which hung on the wall of the famous sitting room.[33]

---

32. As we learn in "The Adventure of the Cardboard Box," the action of which Holmesian scholars place in 1888–89. This passage was transferred essentially verbatim to "The Adventure of the Resident Patient," which takes place in 1886, after Doyle decided that "The Cardboard Box," first published in *The Strand* magazine in 1893, was too gruesome for inclusion in the anthology *The Memoirs of Sherlock Holmes.*

33. In the Sherlockian resurrection story (which occurs in 1894), "The Adventure of the Empty House," Holmes remarks to Watson that "I then passed through Persia, looked in at Mecca, and paid a short but interesting visit to the Khalifa at Khartoum, the results of which I have communicated to the Foreign Office." Since Sherlock's brother, Mycroft, often *was* the British government (as we learn in "The Adventure of the Bruce-Partington Plans," which occurs c. 1895), there

History, until perhaps recently, has come down on the side of hero. Gordon's active role in the abolition of black slavery by the Muslim Arabs in the Sudan cannot be disputed, nor can the fact that he gave his life, on Christian principles, for the Muslim Egyptians under his command at Khartoum. The stiff-necked Gordon was a man who, once returned to Khartoum, not only refused to evacuate the garrison as ordered but instead dug his stubborn heels into the desert sands, organized a spirited defense of the city—Gordon, like Chard, was a Royal Engineer—and stayed long past the opportunity for him to bequeath the city to the Mahdi's vengeful mercies. He died with the people he loved, a martyr to his faith and his cause, determined to show the pagan whose God was stronger, even though it cost him his life.

As with *Zulu*, the battle of wills between Gordon and the Mahdi was vividly dramatized in the 1966 film *Khartoum*, which features a restrained and understated portrayal of Gordon by Charlton Heston and a scenery-chewing impersonation of Muhammad Ahmad by Laurence Olivier, in full white-toothed blackface.[34] The son of a Scottish officer, Gordon was born in the military town of Woolwich[35] and grew up on various duty stations[36] until the family landed back in a flat in Woolwich a stone's throw from the famous military academy there; upon entering the school as a teenager, Gordon was ticketed for a commission in the Royal Artillery. But a couple of schoolboy pranks set him back six months, forcing him into the Royal Engineers instead.

Something else happened to Gordon during his school years, something never fully explained. It occurred while at school at Taunton, a

---

can be little doubt that Sherlock Holmes was actively involved behind the scenes in the entire Khartoum affair.

34. As in *Zulu*, some scenes were created out of dramatic necessity, including, notably, the desert colloquy between Gordon and the Mahdi; in reality, the two corresponded but never met face-to-face.

35. The British soldier Lee Rigby was shamefully butchered on the streets of Woolwich near the Royal Artillery barracks in that city in 2013 by African Muslim Nigerian "immigrants."

36. On the island of Corfu, in Greece, at age nine Gordon evinced his impulse to court danger by throwing himself off the rocks and into the sea, despite the fact that he couldn't swim, and thus had to be rescued.

boarding school in Somerset, where he excelled at map-making. He later wrote to a friend, "I remember a deep bitterness there, never can forget it, though I was only ten or twelve years old. Humanly speaking, it changed my life. . . . I never had a sorrow like it in all my life, therefore I love children very much. . . . I wished I was a eunuch at fourteen." As Robert Hardy noted in his BBC documentary film *Gordon of Khartoum* (1982), "Most have assumed that he had some sort of homosexual experience that scarred his soul. Whatever it was, it seems to have led to a repression of sexual desires for the rest of his life."

In his estimable biography *The Road to Khartoum* (1978), Charles Chenevix Trench addressed the issue of Gordon's homosexuality, or at least his tendency toward it: "It is possible that Gordon's nature was homo- rather than hetero-sexual; who can know this about a man who never mentioned the subject and died more than a century ago? That he was a practicing sodomite is, however, extremely improbable. The modern view of homosexuality as no more morally reprehensible than left-handedness is not one which he would have entertained: he would have been appalled by 'the sin of Sodom and Gomorrah,' and had he ever succumbed to this temptation, would have been tortured by a guilt of which there is nothing in his voluminous correspondence."

Whatever his sexual inclinations, Gordon was something of a prude. When Gordon first took up the governorship of the Sudan in 1874, he was received in state in Cairo, and a banquet was given in his honor. As Strachey notes, the banquet was "followed by a mixed ballet of soldiers and completely naked young women, who danced in a circle, beat time with their feet, and accompanied their gestures with a curious sound of clucking. At last the Austrian Consul, overcome by the exhilaration of the scene, flung himself in a frenzy among the dancers; the Governor-General [an Egyptian official, Gordon's nominal superior in his new post], shouting with delight, seemed about to follow suit, when Gordon abruptly left the room, and the party broke up in confusion."

After receiving his commission at Woolwich, Gordon was sent to Pembroke, in Wales, to construct fortifications along the riverbanks should they ever be needed. Naturally, this bored him—at the height of the Empire, with her navy ruling the waves, why would Britain fear invasion from the sea? While there, the man who would become intensely religious received his first Eucharist but remained unchurched. Instead, he began to delve deeply into the Bible, seeking to learn and understand its lessons for himself, and in his own way. Sent next to the Crimea, where Britain and Russia were fighting a difficult and dirty war, he saw action at Sebastopol and Balaclava while still searching for his faith and also evincing his first inclinations toward martyrdom. "I went to Crimea hoping, without having a hand in it, to be killed. I survived and lived, never fearing death but not wishing to be too closely acquainted with God, nor yet to leave Him," he wrote in a letter to his lifelong friend, the Reverend R. H. Barnes.

Following the Crimea, Captain Gordon was posted to Bessarabia in 1856 to map the now-settled frontier between Russia and the victorious allies of France, Britain, Sardinia, and Turkey. The war had broken out in part over a dispute between the French and the Russians over which Christian denomination—Catholic or Orthodox—should have the greater rights in visiting the Holy Land, which was then under Ottoman domination. Gordon spent two years surveying, returned home, and then, with the outbreak of the Second Opium War between Britain and China, was posted to China, arriving just after the cessation of hostilities. In China he contracted a mild case of smallpox, which he survived. "I am glad to say that this disease has brought me back to my Saviour, and I trust in future to be a better Christian than I have been hitherto," he wrote to his older sister, Augusta, his best friend and confidante, with whom he kept up a lively correspondence until his death.

In short order, the Taiping Rebellion broke out. It was led by Hong Xiuquan (Hong Siu-Tsuen, in the orthography of the time), who in 1837 had experienced a religious transformation, was converted to Christianity by an American Methodist missionary, and soon proclaimed himself the brother of Jesus Christ,[37] the son of God, and started calling

37. It speaks to the influence of Christianity that ethnic groups and races as distinct from each other as the Hungarians, the Sioux Indians, Arab Muslims, and the Chinese have all adopted or appropriated elements of the religion, either in whole or in part.

himself the *Tien Wang*, the Celestial King.[38] Revolting against the corrupt and indolent Manchus and demanding industrial development, land reform, famine and flood relief, and prohibition of infanticide, the ethnic Chinese under Hong launched a bloody civil war that lasted 14 years and took the lives of some 70 million people (estimates range as high as 100 million) and resulted in the wholesale destruction of the country. There were mass executions, beheadings, crucifixions, and live burials. The rebels, led by their very capable general, Chung Wang (the "Faithful King"), seized Nanking, Suzhou (Soochow), and Hangzou (Hangchow), and threatened Shanghai and Beijing. Something had to be done.

In March 1863, at the recommendation of his superior officer, Gen. Charles Staveley, Gordon took command of the native Ever Victorious Army in defense of the Manchus. It was one man of God battling another; Gordon at first had been sympathetic to the renegade Christians, but upon arrival in China had been horrified by the atrocities committed by the rebels in the name of Jesus and was determined to put them down. He trained the forces himself, encouraged discipline with a summary execution here and there, mounted a successful defense of Shanghai, and demolished the rebels at Quinsan, routing a force ten times larger than his own while only losing two killed and five wounded. "They never got such a licking before," he remarked.

Gordon returned to England in January 1865 and found himself a national hero: the celebrated "Chinese" Gordon. He was 32 years old and, as things turned out, leadership of the Ever Victorious Army, which was disbanded in 1864,[39] would be his last official military command. The Foreign Office never saw fit to put him in charge of any of the British forces who were at that time fighting all over the world, from South Africa to New Zealand. Why is hard to say. Perhaps it was due to his status in the Engineers rather than the regular army. Perhaps it was his personal eccentricity and borderline insubordination (a quality that would eventually get him killed at Khartoum); but, as Quinsan had

---

38. "Disobey the Heavenly Will and you will be ground to pieces with a pestle."

39. Gordon was offered a large sum of money by the Qings to stay in China and mop up, but he refused, although he did accept a gold medal, struck in his honor, from the emperor.

shown, he was personally brave, and his tactical abilities were formidable. More likely, it was simply because Gordon was utterly disinterested in capitalizing on his personal popularity; instead, he accepted a minor honor, Companion of the Bath, and spent the next six years constructing useless forts along the Thames estuary.

Or perhaps it was that his superiors had sensed what he often whispered in prayer to his special God: "May I be ground to dust if He will but glorify Himself in me." A man like that was dangerous.

While in England, he refined his notions of religion, developing (as Hong Xiuquan had, although far less sanguinarily) his own peculiar form of Christianity, in its way as syncretic as that of the Wangs in China. His visit to the Holy Land in 1883 put the finishing touches on his faith—a belief in the impermanence of earthly things, a desire not only to be with God but to earn his passage to the hereafter.

His first stint in the Sudan had established his reputation there, and so when the Mahdist revolt got underway in earnest around the same time Gordon was peregrinating through Jerusalem, he was just the man for the job. In fact, there was no one else. Once again in his life, religions were clashing, and Gordon, the man of God, would be forced to confront Muhammad Ahmad, the man of Allah. Like Zrínyi and Suleiman at Szigetvár, neither would walk away from the confrontation.

In November 1883, the Mahdi and his *Ansār* (followers) had destroyed an Egyptian force under a British officer, Col. William Hicks, at El Obeid, in circumstances very similar to Isandlwana. Egyptian control of the Sudan was now limited to the settlements along the Nile, which could be protected from the river by gunboats against the desert tribesmen. But the Mahdi laid siege to Khartoum, the principal city, and armed as he was with Hicks's guns and cannons, it seemed only a matter of time before the city fell, and along with it the trapped Egyptian garrison. In an interview with W. T. Stead,[40] the editor of the *Pall*

---

40. Stead was the template of the crusading, politically committed journalist, devoted to something called "government by journalism." In an 1885 series of articles about child prostitution, "The Maiden Tribute of Modern Babylon," he got Parliament to pass a bill raising the age of sexual consent from 13 to 16. In April 1912, he died when the *Titanic* sank on her maiden voyage to New York.

Mall Gazette, the normally reclusive Gordon[41] opined on the state of affairs in the Sudan, which set off a public cry for Gladstone's government to send Gordon back to the Sudan and *do something.*

Gordon viewed the deteriorating situation in the Sudan not as a localized conflict but as a geopolitical struggle:

> So you would abandon the Soudan? But the Eastern Soudan is indispensable to Egypt. It will cost you far more to retain your [hold] upon Egypt proper if you abandon your hold of the Eastern Soudan to the Mahdi or to the Turk than what it would to retain your hold upon Eastern Soudan by the aid of such material as exists in the provinces. Darfur and Kordofan must be abandoned. That I admit; but provinces lying to the east of the White Nile should be retained, and north of Senaar. The danger to be feared is not that the Mahdi will march northward through Wadi Halfa; on the contrary, it is very improbable that he will ever go so far north. The danger is altogether of a different nature. It arises from the influence which the spectacle of a conquering Mahommedan Power, established close to your frontiers, will exercise upon the population which you govern. In all the cities in Egypt it will be felt that what the Mahdi has done they may do; and, as he has driven out the intruder and the infidel, they may do the same. Nor is it only England that has to face this danger. The success of the Mahdi has already excited dangerous fermentation in Arabia and Syria. Placards have been posted in Damascus calling upon the population to rise and drive out the Turks. If the whole of the Eastern Soudan is surrendered to the Mahdi, the Arab tribes on both sides the Red Sea will take fire. In self-defence the Turks are bound to do something to cope with so formidable a danger, for it is quite possible that if nothing is done the whole of the Eastern Question may be re-opened by the triumph of the Mahdi. I see it is proposed to fortify Wadi Halfa,

41. Gordon was considered an expert on the Sudan, but he spoke little or no Arabic. Little matter: in China he had learned no Chinese.

> and prepare there to resist the Mahdi's attack. You might as well fortify against a fever. Contagion of that kind cannot be kept out by fortifications and garrisons. But that it is real, and that it does exist, will be denied by no one cognisant with Egypt and the East. In self-defence the policy of evacuation cannot possibly be justified.

In other words, Gordon was in agreement with the public: something must be done; he could see the *jihad* coming. Something, however, was the last thing the liberal Gladstone wanted to do. The canniest prime minister of his day, Gladstone wanted to preserve the Empire, keep his Downing Street residence—as things turned out, he traded it with the Tory Lord Salisbury several times—and keep the Ottomans both in Cairo and in Britain's debt. Britain had taken effective control of Egypt during the Anglo-Egyptian War of 1882, largely to control access to the French-built Suez Canal, a matter of vital geostrategic importance. Under pressure, Gladstone agreed to send Gordon and his deputy, Stewart, up the Nile to evacuate the garrison and come home.

Once there—he arrived in Egypt in January 1884—Gordon was named governor-general of the Sudan. He first tried to enlist the former slaver Zobeir as an ally, but Zobeir, still mourning the death of his son, turned him down flat. Gordon and Stewart sailed up the Nile and entered Khartoum on February 18, 1884. To cheering crowds, he declared he would not evacuate the Egyptians and leave the Sudanese to their fate, but instead—ever the engineer—he would organize the city's defenses and fight the Mahdi. Khartoum was eminently defensible, especially so long as the Nile remained open so the city could be resupplied by water. By digging a trench, he connected the White and Blue Niles to form a moat around the city, established a few forts around the perimeter, and figured he could hold out for at least a year; once the waters dropped, he would be vulnerable, but Gordon gambled that his stubborn refusal to leave would force Gladstone's hand, and a relief column would soon enough be on its way.

So now three strong-willed men collided: Gordon, Gladstone, and the Mahdi. But as Gordon dug in, so did Gladstone[42]; it became a contest of wills, fought out not only in the desert sands but in Whitehall and in the court of British public opinion. Gordon did not help himself with Gladstone in his early dispatches, assuring the prime minister he could manage, so as Gordon's tune changed and became more urgent, Gladstone was hard pressed to tell whether Gordon was serious or just being his usual dramatic and changeable self. Although the queen told her prime minister that Gordon must be saved, Gladstone was in no rush. He canvassed his cabinet at leisure; many of the ministers thought Gordon was just plain crazy, although none wanted to see him die. For a long time, nothing could be done. Nor was it.

In the meantime, the Mahdi's *Ansār*, whom the British called "dervishes," grew in strength. And once the Arabs had cut the river at Berber in May 1884 and destroyed the telegraph lines, the city was completely cut off, with the only remaining passage out for messengers north through the desert—extremely dangerous. If help did not arrive, it was only a matter of time before the city fell.

As with all sieges—Caesar would have recognized the situation immediately and probably wondered why it took the Mahdi the better part of a year to force the issue—the defenders can only hold out as long as their food and ammunition do. The food went first: by the end of 1884, there was not a live animal left in the city, including horses, donkeys, and dogs. They had all been eaten. With the civilians near starvation, Gordon opened the gates and allowed out any who wished to leave; half the population fled, leaving Gordon with about eight thousand troops armed with Remington rifles and a considerable cache of ammunition.

Like Custer, whom he resembles in some personal respects, Gordon tackled the problem of defending Khartoum with the characteristic energy, bravery, and technical skill he had always relied upon. He was also used to fighting non-Europeans, whose discipline and courage he found wanting. The problem was that at Khartoum, as Custer had been at the Little Bighorn, he was disastrously wrong. He overestimated his

---

42. Gordon, noted Gladstone, had "a small bee in his bonnet."

own moral and military resources and misjudged the ferocity of his opponent.

The rest of the story is quickly told. Gladstone had earlier succumbed to the pressure, sending the Irish-born major H. H. Kitchener to the Sudan with a small force as a sop to public opinion, but he failed to communicate any urgency. By August of 1884, however, the situation had grown dire enough for Gladstone to authorize a substantial force to Egypt under the command of Lord Wolseley, which landed in Egypt on September 9. But Stewart and other officials and civilians were killed that same month when their armored steamer, the *Abbas*, attempted to run the blockade, hit a rock in the river, and was beached in what had been considered friendly territory. Brought ashore, they were all murdered, and Gordon's dispatches fell into the Mahdi's hands. In effect, what had begun as a mission on which Gordon was to get the Egyptians out had become a mission to get Gordon out. And Gordon didn't want to come out.

His letters back to Augusta reflect what by now had become for him a death-before-dishonor situation. For a while, Gordon and the Mahdi exchanged letters and even gifts, but communications eventually broke off, and it became clear that the only thing that was going to settle the dispute between the Christian and the Islamic gods was going to be hot lead and bayonet steel. The fatalist Charley Gordon, who used to throw himself into the waters at Corfu without being able to swim, was about to take his biggest leap.

As Strachey notes in *Eminent Victorians*, "Whatever he might find in his pocket-Bible, it was not for such as he to dream out his days in devout obscurity. But, conveniently enough, he found nothing in his pocket-Bible indicating that he should. What he did find was that the Will of God was inscrutable and absolute; that it was man's duty to follow where God's hand led; and, if God's hand led towards violent excitements and extraordinary vicissitudes, that it was not only futile, it was impious to turn another way. . . . He was Gordon Pasha, he was the Governor-General, he was the ruler of the Sudan. He was among his people—his own people,[43] and it was to them only that he was responsi-

---

43. "The Soudanese are a very nice people," Gordon had told Stead in their interview. "They deserve the sincere compassion and sympathy of all civilized men.

ble—to them, and to God. Was he to let them fall without a blow into the clutches of a sanguinary impostor? Never! He was there to prevent that."

He held out as long as he could, having long since made his peace with his inevitable death. The only way out was feet first. By November 1884, he figured he had about six weeks. He knew Wolseley was on the way. What he didn't know was that Wolseley was operating on a somewhat more leisurely timetable, planning to reach Khartoum by January 31, 1885. The city was being peppered by potshots from the Mahdi's main force of *jihadis* across the river at Omdurman, but Gordon showed his contempt by sitting, illuminated, behind an open window at the palace. He refused to leave. If ordered to do so, he kept repeating, "I WILL NOT OBEY IT, BUT WILL STAY HERE, AND FALL WITH THE TOWN, AND RUN ALL RISKS."

The Mahdi, knowing the end was near, sent Gordon one final missive, offering to let him depart in peace and without ransom if he would only surrender the city. Like Gordon, the Mahdi was on a mission, and Gordon was in the way:

> Having seen what you have seen, how long are you going to disbelieve us? We have been told by God's Apostle, may God's blessings and peace be upon him, of the imminent destruction of all those in Khartoum, save those who believe and surrender; them, God will save. We do not wish you perish with those doomed to perish because we have frequently heard good of you. . . . In order that you should not abandon hope of God's mercy I say to you that God has said, "Kill not thyself for God is merciful to thee." Peace be upon you.

So now it was not simply Gordon versus the Mahdi, but deity against deity. This was a challenge Gordon relished, for either way he would win. Should the relief column arrive in time, the Mahdi would die or

---

I got on very well with them, and I am sincerely sorry at the prospect of seeing them handed over to be ground down once more by their Turkish and Circassian oppressors."

skedaddle; should the city fall, Gordon's death and transfiguration would be proof of the power of his God, who could turn defeat into Gordon's personal victory, his destiny finally fulfilled: "May I be ground to dust if He will but glorify Himself in me." Dust it would be, then.

On the night of the twenty-fifth, the Mahdi addressed his troops, ordering them to enter the city and slay every living soul, with the exception of Gordon and a few others. Shortly after midnight on the twenty-sixth, he attacked. Roused by the tumult, the sleeping Gordon put on his uniform, armed himself with a sword and a revolver, and stepped out onto the palace's external staircase.

Legend has it that Gordon died a Christian martyr's death on the staircase, calmly confronting the mob before one of the dervishes shouted: "O cursed one, your hour has come!" and plunged a spear into Gordon's breast; as he fell, he was hacked to pieces by the enraged *Ansār* of Allah.[44] But Gordon's bodyguard and manservant, Khalil Agha Orphali, who was battling alongside him as he fell, tells a more heroic tale: that upon stepping out onto the stairway, Gordon fired repeatedly with his revolver, was wounded in the shoulder by a hurled spear, and emptied his pistol into the mob before drawing his sword. He was wounded again, this time by a rifle round that hit him in the chest, but continued to fight, pushing the warriors back down the stairs. At the bottom of the stairs, he was wounded once again by a spear thrust in the side and then fell beneath the horde.[45] Gordon's long war with himself, with the army, and with God was finally over. He died the hero of his own, self-dictated last stand.

Gordon's corpse was decapitated and his head brought in a bag to the Mahdi, who was furious that his order had been disobeyed. Two days later the advance forces of the relief column arrived. Six months later, the Mahdi died of unknown causes, possibly smallpox or typhus.[46] Without their charismatic leader, the Mahdists faded as a religious, political, and military force. Although the British pulled out of the Sudan,

---

44. This is how Gordon dies in the film *Khartoum*.

45. As related by Chenevix Trench, *The Road to Khartoum*.

46. An echo, perhaps, of the mysterious death of Suleiman at Szigetvár.

they stoutly defended Egypt, and an attempted Mahdist invasion of Egypt in 1891 was crushed.

Thanks to Gordon's death, which inflamed the British public, the Gladstone government fell in June 1885 and the prime ministry was traded with the conservatives once more. But by 1898, with Salisbury back in power, the time was right to avenge Gordon. Kitchener—now General Sir H. H. Kitchener—mounted a punitive expedition[47] that engaged the Believers at Omdurman and annihilated a force twice his size with the latest rifles, dum-dum bullets, machine guns,[48] and artillery pieces. Twelve thousand Muslims were killed, another thirteen thousand wounded; Kitchener's casualties were forty-seven dead and three hundred and eighty-two wounded.

The Mahdi's ornate tomb had been damaged by British guns during the battle. Kitchener ordered it pulled down. He then had the body exhumed and the bones chucked into the Nile. The Mahdi's skull was presented to Kitchener for use as a drinking cup; Kitchener was of a mind to send it to the Royal College of Surgeons in London, but a public outcry and a stern condemnation from the queen eventually packed the skull off to be buried quietly in a local Muslim cemetery. The defeat was so decisive that there would be no further *jihad* for more than a hundred years, until on September 11, 2001, when the walls of the World Trade Center collapsed and the long, 1,400-year civilizational struggle between recrudescent Islam and the West commenced in earnest once again.

Osama bin Laden may not have seen himself as a new Mahdi, but his goal of restoring the caliphate and converting the world to Islam was very similar to Muhammad Ahmad's. If the West has a Kitchener or a Gordon, or a Roland or a Zrínyi to hand, he has not as yet evidenced himself. Islam still has plenty of need for heroes, but do the heirs of Rome? As the narrator intones at the conclusion of *Khartoum*, "A world with no room for the Gordons is a world that will return to the sands."

---

47. In which a young cavalryman named Winston Churchill took part, riding with the Twenty-First Lancers.

48. Prompting Hilaire Belloc's famous couplet: "Whatever happens, we have got / The Maxim gun, and they have not."

CHAPTER XII

"NOT ONE STEP BACK"

THE BATTLE OF PAVLOV'S HOUSE: STALINGRAD, 1942

THE GREATEST WARS DO NOT NECESSARILY PRODUCE THE GREATEST heroes. Achilles was the pride of the Greeks, but his honor was besmirched by his rage, while his hubristic desecration of Hector's body neither won the Trojan War nor redounded to his credit. At Cannae, the Romans died nearly to a man, and only scholars can name their leaders; Scipio's ultimate victory came years after the battle. The defenders at Masada died at their own hands. Aside from Kaspar Röist's, we don't recall the names of the individual Swiss Guards at the Vatican, but we know the pope escaped: they did their duty—which is the essence of heroism.

But some wars *need* heroes. Some battles are so outsized, so colossal, so important that they cry out for a personalizing moment, a story, or even, as we have seen, a legend. We require a man, or a few good men, to exemplify and embody the ideals of the nation: an avatar. Such a battle was Stalingrad, the crucial clash between two million-man armies in 1942–43 that would determine not only the course of World War II in Europe but the fate of the continent for half a century thereafter. The deadliest armed clash in history,[1] it was a battle on a classical scale, and with classical intentions: to decide the issue in one single, mighty engagement. Fought in the air, on the ground, with tanks, with troops, with gliders, with snipers, and

1. One million people, mostly men, were killed in seven months.

from house to house. Fought with clear battle lines, Germans to the west, Russians to the east. Fought by attacks and counterattacks; with breakouts and pincers and encirclements. Fought as both a clash and a siege. Fought to the death, not by great men but by common ones elevated to greatness. It was, in many ways, the ultimate last stand.

Such a hero was Yakov Fedotovich Pavlov, the junior sergeant[2] who led a "storm group" platoon into a German-held four-story apartment building overlooking the 9th of January Square, located between the rail lines and the Volga River in the heart of the city, and held it against the Wehrmacht from September 27 to November 25, 1942. Killing or driving off the rest of the Germans, Pavlov and his 24 men fortified the house, surviving multiple attempts by the Germans, sometimes with tanks, to retake the building. When the small garrison was finally relieved, the Soviet commander, Marshal Vasily Chuikov, bragged that Pavlov's men had killed more Germans than the Wehrmacht had lost in taking Paris in 1940. For his gallantry, Pavlov was named a Hero of the Soviet Union and awarded the Order of Lenin, among other honors. Joining the Communist Party, he was thrice elected to the Supreme Soviet of Russia, and died in 1981.

So . . . print the legend? First, some background.

In the summer of 1939, the world was poised on knife edge. The two great socialist powers of Europe, National Socialist Germany and the Communist Union of Soviet Socialist Republics, were eyeing each other warily across Poland and the rest of Central Europe. For centuries, Germany and Russia had battled over this territory. From time to time, other transitory powers had intervened, notably Sweden and Poland; the Grande Armée under Napoleon had invaded Russia and entered a burning Moscow in 1812. But the days of their territorial hegemony were long since gone, and now the only question between Russia and Germany was, who was to be master?

It was a critical moment. The Soviet Union had undergone a German-inspired revolution when Lenin was bundled aboard a sealed train from neutral Switzerland to Swedish Lapland and thence to the Finland

2. Before the war, he had been an accountant.

Station in Petrograd in 1917, with the expressed German intent to take Russia out of the First World War. Along with 29 other Russian exiles, a Pole, and a Swiss national, Lenin had been sent on an international Marxist mission of destabilization—a "plague bacillus," as Winston Churchill would later term him. Like the Ayatollah Khomeini returning to Tehran in 1979, but to even greater effect, Lenin was greeted by rapturous crowds as the old order trembled, tumbled, and fell.

Russia was already a mess. It had been defeated, embarrassingly, by a British-French-Turkish coalition during the Crimean War in 1853,[3] which forced the Russians (although they held on to the Crimean Peninsula, a crucial warm-water port) to the realization that the Potemkin Village that was czarist Russia was no longer sustainable. As the Grand Duke Constantine bitterly observed, "We cannot deceive ourselves any longer; we must say that we are both weaker and poorer than the first-class powers, and furthermore poorer not only in material terms but in mental resources, especially in matters of administration."

Worse, Russia had been thrashed by the Japanese during the Russo-Japanese War of 1904–5, in which its entire Baltic fleet was destroyed at the Battle of Tsushima, and it had been soundly whipped by the Germans during the Great War, knocked out of the global conflict after defeats at Tannenberg in East Prussia (today, part of Poland) and elsewhere along the Eastern Front. By February 1917 (March in the Western calendar), the first Russian revolution—the "February Bourgeois Democratic Revolution"—had deposed the Czar, and the opportunistic Lenin (whose turn to revolutionary socialism occurred in the wake of his elder brother Aleksandr Ulyanov's execution in 1887 for plotting an assassination attempt against Czar Alexander III) was returned by the Germans to stoke the flames of revolution.

---

3. Notable for the 1853 Charge of the Light Brigade, one of the more foolish last stands in history, and the subject of Alfred Lord Tennyson's 1854 poem. In the annals of British military blunders, it is rivaled only by Churchill's own contribution to the book of How Not to Do It at Gallipoli (1915) in the same part of the world, with the admirable goal of retaking Constantinople for the West—a kind of rerun of Crimea but with Britain and France this time on the side of the Russians. Once again, the Turks emerged victorious, although it was to be their last hurrah, as the Ottoman Empire dissolved after the war.

It's not often recalled that there were two Russian revolutions in 1917—the February Revolution, which resulted in the abdication of Czar Nicolas II,[4] the last of the Romanovs, and in the short-lived Alexander Kerensky[5] government, and the October Revolution, which brought Lenin and the Bolsheviks to power. Lenin's stuck, for nearly 75 years.

In the aftermath of the collapse of Soviet Communism on the day after Christmas, 1991, it's also easy to forget that czarist Russia, under the Orthodox Christian faith, had once regarded itself as the successor to Catholic Rome and Orthodox Greek Byzantium. This was one of the reasons that Lenin's atheist Communists were so intent on erasing faith from their newly conquered people's souls—to cut off the Russians from the wellsprings of their religious past in order to create the New Soviet Man, unbeholden to Christian principles and thus ripe for the reeducation or death camps, whichever came first.

In this annihilation of faith, the Soviets had much in common with their German socialist neighbors to the west, who were as dedicated opponents of Judeo-Christianity as the Russians were. Russia had gone Communist shortly after Lenin's arrival; after a brief civil war between the Reds (the Bolsheviks) and the counterrevolutionary Whites, which ended in a Bolshevik victory, the Union of Soviet Socialist Republics—essentially, the old czarist empire under another name—was proclaimed in 1922. Lenin died in January 1924 and was effectively succeeded by Joseph Stalin, who ruled the country until his death in 1953.

Germany lagged slightly behind in its own socialist revolution. For one thing, there were two forms of socialism on offer as the Weimar Republic disintegrated between 1919 and 1933. One was Marxist Communism, an international movement, which had already taken brief root in

---

4. Directly related to both King George V of Great Britain and Kaiser Wilhelm II of Germany through Queen Victoria; they were all cousins, and bore a striking physical resemblance to one another. The Romanov family was executed by the Bolsheviks in July 1918 at Yekaterinburg.

5. During my time as classical music critic of *Time* magazine, I often encountered Kerensky's grandson, Oleg, in the press room at the Metropolitan Opera House during the early 1980s in New York City. He died of AIDS in 1993.

the former kingdom of Bavaria during the short-lived Bavarian Soviet Republic, which lasted all of one month in 1919. The other was National Socialism, a hybrid that combined elements of Italian Fascism—such as putting private industry at the service of the state, rather than nationalizing it—with Adolf Hitler's own Aryan race theories and Wagnerian dreams of national grandeur. Hitler took over what had been the tiny German Workers Party (the *Deutsche Arbeiterpartei*, or DAP) and turned it into the National Socialist German Workers Party: to give it its German name, *Nationalsozialistische Deutsche Arbeiterpartei* (NSDAP); "Nazi" for short.

Socialism has long appealed to the Germans. In *Germania*, the historian Tacitus noted the Germans' relative (compared to the Romans, at least) lack of a hierarchy and their sense of community; practically from the beginning, it seems, the Germans have been fond of societies, brotherhoods, *Gesellschaften*. Another characteristic, as we might call it today, is their environmentalism: Germans are the original tree-huggers. And as for the German "blood" that has gotten them into so much trouble, Tacitus observes:

> For myself, I accept the view that the peoples of Germany have never contaminated themselves by intermarriage with foreigners but remain of pure blood, distinct and unlike any other nation. One result of this is that their physical characteristics, in so far as one can generalize about such a large population, are always the same: fierce-looking blue eyes, reddish hair, and big frames—which, however, can exert their strength only by means of violent effort.

Hitler's hijacking of the Bavarian-based DAP and its transformation within 13 months into the NSDAP was in part based on a leftist appeal to a working class that might otherwise have been susceptible to Communism, combined with a siren song of xenophobia and anti-Semitism that had been surging in the aftermath of Wilhelmine Germany's degrading defeat in World War I and the economic chaos that followed. It was a potent, and popular, combination.

In some senses, then, the Reds and the Brownshirts were two sides of the same coin, reactive and opportunistic; one militant, the other revanchist, and each opposed to the status quo of the *Junkers* and remnants of the Bismarckian ruling class. They battled it out not only in the streets, but also at the ballot box—in the Reichstag (parliamentary) election of November 1932, they roughly split the popular vote, with 11,737,000 votes for the National Socialists, 7,248,000 for the Social Democrats, and 5,980,000 for the Communists. That election made the National Socialists the largest party in the Reichstag, and thus Hitler was named chancellor on January 30, 1933.

Still, the Molotov-Ribbentrop "Treaty of Non-Aggression between Germany and the Union of Soviet Socialist Republics," which took effect on August 23, 1939, should not have come as a total surprise. True, Nazi ideology proclaimed the inferiority of both the Slavs and the Jews, and the Slavic Soviet Union, with its large Jewish[6] population, made an ideal target for its collective animus.

But the two states also had mutual interests: Nazi Germany and Communist Russia had been eyeing each other warily for six years across the territory of independent Poland as Hitler built up the German war machine; he had already gobbled up Austria, his birthplace, and—in the wake of the Munich Agreement with Britain, France, and Italy—Czechoslovakia, without firing a shot.

Under the Molotov-Ribbentrop Pact's protocols, some of them secret, Stalin and Hitler, via their foreign ministers, agreed to spheres of influence regarding Poland, the Baltics, and Finland. Little more than a week later, on September 1, 1939, Germany invaded Poland. The Soviets followed suit on the seventeenth. Poland vanished, bifurcated, and the Russians swallowed up the neighboring Baltics and invaded Finland.[7]

---

6. In addition, many of the early Bolsheviks were Jewish, among them Trotsky (born Lev Bronstein), Sverdlov, and Zinoviev. Lenin had a Jewish great-grandfather on his mother's side. Marx came from a long line of rabbis, but his father had converted to Lutheranism to minimize the effects of burgeoning anti-Semitism in Prussia. The Nazis considered Marxism-Leninism to be a Jewish economic and political philosophy. The Soviets, however, quickly purged their upper ranks of Jews and became a frankly anti-Semitic nation right up to the end.

7. For a time, the Soviets even considered joining Germany, Italy, and their erstwhile enemy, Japan, as a member of the Axis.

World War II was underway, with Germany and Russia on the same side.

The dishonor among thieves lasted just short of two years, ending when Hitler unleashed Operation Barbarossa on June 22, 1941, a three-pronged surprise attack on the Soviet Union. Army Group North headed for Leningrad (St. Petersburg); Army Group Center made for Moscow; and Army Group South barreled toward the industrial city on the Volga River called Stalingrad, formerly Tsaritsyn and today Volgograd. The Russians were taken completely unawares. Stalin had refused to believe intelligence reports that his ally was about to double-cross him, in part because he believed that Germany had learned a lesson from World War I—not to engage in a two-front war—and the two countries had become major trading partners. Even in the face of increasing German provocation, such as overflying Soviet airspace, Stalin continued to send raw materials to Germany while busying himself not with defense but with his political purges of the Red Army. But after the lightning-quick fall of France and the British escape at Dunkirk in May–June 1940, it was only a matter of time.

To the world in 1941, the importance of taking Leningrad and Moscow was obvious—those two cities were the seats of culture and the Soviet political system; it was still axiomatic then that when capitals fell, so did countries. Why this was thought universally true is something of a mystery—the Greeks abandoned Athens, their leading city, after the last stand at Thermopylae, and although the Persians vandalized it, the city was reclaimed fairly quickly and went on, restored, to even greater glory. Destroying the Soviet Union's principal cities would be the source of great personal satisfaction, and Hitler assumed that the same *Blitzkrieg* tactics he had just used on France (then considered far more formidable militarily than Russia) would work just as effectively.

Hitler, however, wanted not just territorial acquisition in western Russia—*Lebensraum* for the expanding German population with Slavs for slaves—but also a stinging personal humiliation of Stalin, and that is where Stalingrad came in. Sandwiched between the Don and the Volga Rivers, the city was a strategic target, a railhead and a major port, and the center of manufacturing (along with Kharkov, whose facilities had been evacuated to the east) for the fearsome and plentiful T-34 and other tanks. It also commanded the approach to the oil fields of the Caucasus around Baku—a vital objective for a country like Germany, with no natural resources of its own. Best of all, it bore Stalin's name. Stalingrad, however, lay farthest to the south and east of Leningrad and Moscow, so it took longer to get there. As a result, Hitler's plan to crush the Russians in all three cities simultaneously before the winter of 1941–42 set in proved overly optimistic.

Army Group South and the Red Army first collided in the southern Ukraine. The undertrained Russians were poorly led by a depleted officer corps and pushed back. A counterattack failed, and several Soviet divisions were surrounded and annihilated. The Germans rolled through the Ukraine and captured the Crimea. But resistance was still stubborn, and costly—all along the Russian front—and so the Germans failed in their objective to knock the Soviet Union out of the war in a single lightning campaign. True, Leningrad was under siege, but the thrust at Moscow had been stopped just outside the city as the Soviets rallied with an assist from General Winter. And Stalingrad was still out of reach.

So during the summer offensive for 1942—dubbed by the Germans *Fall Blau* (Operation Blue)—the principal objective became Stalingrad and the Caucasus. The Wehrmacht split Army Group South in half, sending Army Group A south to Baku and Army Group B[8] to Stalingrad, spearheaded by the Sixth Army under the leadership of Friedrich Paulus. This time, Stalin knew the Germans were coming and appointed one of his best if most brutal generals, Vasily Chuikov, the hard-drinking commander of the Soviet Sixty-Second Army, to defend the city—to the last man.

What-ifs are always fun, since there is no penalty for error. But a glance at the strategic situation in the latter half of 1942 shows how important it was for the Soviets to hold Stalingrad—and not just hold it, but to destroy the German Sixth Army in the process. The momentum

---

8. This army, under the overall command of Field Marshal Fedor von Bock, also included Italian, Romanian, and Hungarian units.

from the Soviet victory effectively reversed the entire thrust of the German attack, rendering the remainder of the war on the Eastern Front a long mopping-up action that finally ended in Berlin in 1945. Further, what had been a numerical superiority in manpower on the German side eventually turned decisively against the Wehrmacht as the war dragged on; the Russians (like the ancient Romans), it seemed, could magically summon whole new divisions at will, many of them composed not of Slavs but ethnic minorities from all over the Soviet Union, while the attrition in men and materiel eventually spelled German doom.

But, what if? For example, what if Hitler hadn't redirected units of Luftflotte 4 from Stalingrad to North Africa to counter the Allies' landings there, thus giving the Soviets air superiority for the first time in the battle? Had the Germans rolled through Stalingrad and annihilated the Red Army forces remaining in place as Stalin had ordered, the way would have been clear not only to seize the oil fields but to swing Army Group B northward again, this time to capture Moscow from a demoralized and possibly leaderless Kremlin—who knows what might have happened to Stalin?—and then to break the stalemate at Leningrad. Some of the Red Army might have escaped to the east, to wage a guerilla war, but the Germans had no intention of conquering the entire Soviet Eurasian land mass. They wanted semi-civilized European Russia, the Ukraine, and the Baltics, with some readymade infrastructure and a captive population of serfs. Further, with vast new natural resources opened up to them, their war machine would again rev up.

The German assault on Stalingrad from the west pushed the defending Soviets back to the Volga and across it, to Krasnaya Sloboda, where they set up their field hospitals and brought troops in from the Russian Far East by rail. For a time, the Russians only managed to hang on to small pockets of the city proper on the west side of the river, but those were of critical importance: their forces, ferrying across from the east bank, needed a place to land, especially since they were under constant shelling and strafing by the Luftwaffe. To make sure his officers stayed loyal, Stalin also dispatched a political commissar, Nikita

Khrushchev,[9] to oversee the defense of Stalingrad and ensure the commanders' loyalty.

The military situation at Stalingrad was vividly illustrated in the 2001 motion picture *Enemy at the Gates*, which depicts fresh-off-the-farm Soviets like sharpshooter Vasily Zaitsev[10] being ferried across the Volga in the teeth of ferocious air attacks, and then handed a rifle, one for every two conscripts; when the first man was killed, the second man, trailing behind him, was to pick up the rifle and carry on. The Soviet air force had been quickly knocked out, leaving the Stuka dive-bombers free to attack the infantry and Russian tanks at will. In the initial stages, Germans quickly occupied almost all of the city.

The Russian task, therefore, was not just to repel the Germans but also to retake the town, or whatever was left of it. This was an enormous undertaking. Normally the defender has certain advantages of terrain, especially on home turf, but in this case the Soviets were attempting a counterattack—dubbed Operation Uranus—along a broad front, hoping to punch through at a couple of strategic points and thus envelop Paulus's overextended main force. In order to do so, the Russians would have to absorb a terrific beating. As the battle commenced, the Germans had the upper hand in weapons, manpower, and training, but the Russians had one major advantage: this was not going to be a set-piece battle, or even a conventional siege, but—literally—a street fight. And in a street fight, the side that wants it more, and is willing to do and endure anything, generally wins.

"Hitler put the best he had against Stalingrad," Chuikov told a United Press correspondent in the immediate aftermath of the battle. "He did not spare quantity or quality. It was a battle for life or death. We were continuously attacked by great masses of infantry, tanks, artillery and planes. Our forces were not equal. The enemy had superiority at all points all the time. The German Command used its favorite method. It intended to smash us with a stunning blow. They thought we hadn't enough guts. . . . This was not the kind of fight we study at

---

9. Khrushchev would succeed Stalin as Soviet leader in 1953. He was toppled by a party coup in 1964, and was succeeded by Leonid Brezhnev.

10. Portrayed by Jude Law; Bob Hoskins played Khrushchev.

the military academies where enemies meet, engage in battle and then separate."

In preparation for the battle, Stalin had issued Order No. 227, which established the fighting principle of "Not One Step Back." Further, the Soviet dictator refused to allow any of the 400,000 or so civilians to leave, on the theory that his soldiers would fight harder defending their countrymen instead of empty buildings. Under this directive, penal battalions composed of soldiers who had been court-martialed were sent immediately to the front lines, and units were created in the rear with orders to shoot all deserters and cowards.

The Soviets had held Moscow, and, so far, Leningrad was surviving one of the bitterest sieges in history,[11] but Stalin understood—as Hitler came to—that Stalingrad would be the most important of the three German objectives. It would be, of necessity, the Soviets' last stand. Their armies had already been pushed back hundreds and hundreds of miles along a two-thousand-mile front from the Baltic to the Black Sea. Once past these three main population and industrial centers, there was basically no place for the Soviets to go, except Siberia. So Stalingrad it was to be, then.

What has come to be known as the Battle of Pavlov's House did not seem at first, in the gigantic scheme of the battle, of great importance. True, the block of flats commanded the 9th of January square, which lay close to the Red Army's fragile staging area on the west bank of the Volga, but by the time Pavlov and his men seized it from the Germans and occupied it, the principal fighting had turned north and west, to the Dzerzhinsky Tractor Works and other industrial sites. Paulus was intent on rolling up the Soviets all along the river, and with the area around the 9th of January Square under German control, he had moved his troops away, leaving elements of Alexander von Hartmann's 71st Infantry Division in the area.

Further, it didn't seem to have much chance of success. The officers of Pavlov's platoon had been killed or incapacitated, leaving Pavlov as the senior man. Their weaponry, of necessity, was modest: submachine

11. For a definitive and riveting account of its horrors and privations, see Harrison Salisbury's *The 900 Days: The Siege of Leningrad.*

guns, a light machine gun, rifles, small arms, but plenty of fragmentation grenades and ammunition. Most of the men, however, were killed in the fighting, leaving (according to the official Soviet version) only four men to garrison the building at first. About ten civilians were huddled in the basement; one of the women even gave birth during the siege. It would have surprised nobody if, had the Germans really set their minds to it, Pavlov's troops had been overrun in an hour or two.

The story goes on to relate that, after a few days, reinforcements from the 42nd Guards Rifle Regiment arrived, and this force, which included machine guns, automatic weapons, mortars, and four antitank rifles, was able to hold off various German counterattacks.[12] The Panzer IV tanks weren't able to elevate their turrets high enough to take out the Soviet riflemen on the roof, but their light top armor could be penetrated by the PTRS-41 antitank rifle's 14-millimeter shells. Meanwhile, infantry charges across the open square—the building had a clear view to the east, north, and south—were savagely rebuffed. Indeed, the bodies piled so high that the Russians were forced to leave the relative safety of the building to push them over so their lines of sight could be cleared.

In his order 179, General Chuikov made clear what his tactics would be: "Every trench and every dug out should be reinforced and each building shall become a towering fortress. To fulfill this task, new engineering works and obstacles must be built, buildings and houses turned into firing points for heavy machine guns, communications trenches dug, and minefields and barbed wire emplacements set out. Our strongpoints must also be equipped with anti-tank guns and mortars." He added: "All these measures are aimed at making our defense unbreakable—for all the furious attacks of the Fascist troops will shatter upon these obstacles as sea waves are broken by granite rock."

And that is exactly what happened at Pavlov's House.

It wasn't all fighting, all the time, of course. The basement offered some measure of protection against hostile fire, and down there was to be found a gramophone player, with only one record to help them pass the time, musically. But most of their waking hours—and they got very

12. Estimates are that the garrison eventually numbered as many as one hundred Soviet soldiers.

little sleep, owing to the constant German attacks—were involved with defensive preparation and fighting.[13] The men dug a trench over to the Soviet beachhead, through which they could bring in ammunition and food and through which reinforcements could arrive. Even so, the defenders could not have held out without calling in artillery strikes close to their own position as the Germans advanced on the building. They also forayed out to conduct operations in other nearby buildings around the square. Like the Texians at the Alamo and the French Foreign Legion, they fought like devils. Some of the men scrawled graffiti on the walls, identifying the structure as "Pavlov's House."

And thus did Pavlov and his men become the propaganda poster boys for the Soviet resistance at Stalingrad. The Russians needed heroes: two of their snipers—Zaitsev, credited with at least 242 kills, and the baby-faced teenager Anatoly Chekhov (who saw duty at Pavlov's House and elsewhere in Stalingrad), credited with 256—became icons of the Great Patriotic War. So did Pavlov: a common soldier elevated to greatness through his own deeds and the power of Soviet propaganda.

Finally, after 58 days, Pavlov and his men were relieved during a Soviet counterattack. As it happened, Pavlov's unit was ordered on November 24 to clear a building across the square, called the Milk House, of German occupiers. By then, they were commanded by a couple of lieutenants, including Ivan F. Afanasiev,[14] but the operation was a failure, and most of the men were killed in the Wehrmacht counterattack. Pavlov himself was wounded and sent away from the front. His propaganda value was now over, but the fight for the house lasted another two months, with the building changing hands several times before Paulus surrendered the Sixth Army on February 2, 1943. What had begun as the Soviet Union's last stand ended as the beginning of Germany's *Untergang*.

---

13. The Russian position was in some respects similar to that of Anielewicz's fighters in subterranean Warsaw, although vastly better armed.

14. Recent scholarship credits Afanasiev, who led the first wave of reinforcements into Pavlov's House, with organizing and commanding the defense of the building. Like Pavlov, he was wounded in the attempt to take the Milk House. But Pavlov's made a better story.

Indeed, the propaganda value of Stalingrad was one of the foremost considerations during the conduct of the battle itself, on both sides. Two stubborn socialist dictators dug in their heels: Stalin could not lose his namesake city to Hitler, and thus refused to allow the Red Army to conduct even a tactical retreat. For his part, Hitler denied repeated requests from a surrounded and starving Paulus that he be allowed to capitulate, even going so far as to promote him to the rank of field marshal late in the battle on the theory that the general would not wish to go down in history as the first German *Feldmarschall* ever to surrender his command. But he had no choice.

The Germans, of course, tried to spin the disaster to their best advantage. Having announced imminent victory for months, propaganda minister Joseph Goebbels issued a defensive and admonishing statement at the end of January, when the end was clear and inevitable: "The heroic struggle of our soldiers on the Volga should be a warning for everybody to do the utmost for the struggle for Germany's freedom and the future of our people, and thus in a wider sense for the maintenance of our entire continent."

Perhaps it was at this point that Hitler realized that a war he had envisioned as the highest form of *die heilige deutsche Kunst* that his musical idol, Richard Wagner, had celebrated in his opera *Die Meistersinger von Nürnberg*—leading to the establishment of the Third Reich, the successor to Charlemagne's Holy Roman Empire and the Wilhelmine Empire of Otto von Bismarck—was turning inexorably instead into the final installment of the "Ring" cycle, *Götterdämmerung*: the Twilight of the Gods. His spectacular foolishness, a malignant bravado born of ignorance and malice, would lead to the needless deaths of millions of soldiers, civilians, and innocents, the obscenity of the concentration and death camps, and the moral destruction of the most civilized country in Europe (whose sophistication had always just barely concealed the barbarism beneath[15]). The Roman general Varus, falling upon his own sword in the Teutoburg Forest, would have understood, just before

15. The more reversals the Germans suffered near the end of the war, the faster the Jews, Catholics, homosexuals, Russian prisoners of war, and gypsies were murdered in the camps.

the Germans decapitated his corpse and nailed his head to a tree. For his part, Paulus might have appreciated the strategic predicament at Cannae, his army pincered and scissored to death. As it was, his surrender prevented the complete slaughter of his troops, but just barely: 91,000 Germans were taken prisoner, and only 5,000 were repatriated after the war.

Chuikov was in Berlin during the final surrender on May 1, 1945. The chief of the German General Staff, Hans Krebs, crossed the lines to greet his Soviet counterpart with typical German arrogance but socialist solidarity: "Today is the first of May, a great holiday for our two nations," he said. At the end of the war, Krebs was still boasting of the ideological ties that bound the National Socialist German Workers Party with Soviet Communism: the rights of the working class. Inadvertently, he was also evoking the other meaning of May Day: a German pagan ritual celebrating the coming of spring and the driving out of evil spirits, as well as the Christian month of Marian feast days.

Chuikov responded: "We have a great holiday today. How things are with you over there it is less easy to say."

The Battle of Pavlov's House may have been, in the end, a sidelight of a much larger existential struggle, but it encapsulated, in the form of a reality-based myth, the Russian experience at Stalingrad. It became a metaphor for the entire Great Patriotic war—not a war for atheism or even Communism, but for the *Rodina*, the Third Rome against the pagan Third Reich.[16] The Germans, too, believed in the rightness of their destiny: after all, they had once sacked Rome and put a barbarian on the throne of Caesar. But this time, the better, more powerful God won.

In their darkest hour, the Russian people needed to believe that no matter how great the odds, they would somehow win through in the end, that men of humble origin, a lowly sergeant such as Pavlov, could rise to the occasion and fight for the motherland as heroically as any general. The Soviet canonization of Pavlov concluded his story when and where it did because that was what best served the narrative.

---

16. After the war, the roles of some of the "undesirable nationalities" were considerably downplayed. One of the men returned to his native village in Soviet Tajikistan without the slightest inkling that he was part of something famous.

That the Battle of Stalingrad was, in essence, a battle of two evils often goes unremarked. The Molotov-Ribbentrop Pact is practically forgotten today, since it served America's own propaganda interests during the war to present Stalin as kindly "Uncle Joe," the man who couldn't make an omelet without breaking a few eggs rather than the monster he really was. Communist sympathizers around the world, including Americans and Europeans who had joined the International Brigades during the Spanish Civil War to fight against Franco, were called "premature anti-Fascists" at a time when the Western democracies were still on cordial terms with Mussolini and Hitler—and have crowed about it ever since—but they were also an embarrassment to the Soviets during the Molotov-Ribbentrop Pact. War, like politics, makes strange bedfellows. Whereas the American enthusiasm for the various Bunds in the run-up to the war[17] disappeared with Pearl Harbor and Germany's irrational declaration of war on the United States, the residual sympathies for the Russian Communists remain a potent force in American politics.

What did emerge from Stalingrad and the postwar world were some truths and insights about the Russian character that might better inform attitudes toward Russia today were they heeded. For all the expansionism of the tsarist empire, Russia has never been a colonizing force: from Siberia to the Mongolian and Chinese borders far to the east was a largely uninhabited and uncontested area. Russia's principal geopolitical concerns have always lain in the west, from which Napoleon, Kaiser Wilhelm, and Hitler had mounted serious invasions. But its focus historically has been its battles with fellow Slavs, primarily the Ukraine, Georgia, and Poland—a struggle that during the height of the conflict between the two powers in the seventeenth century was as much about religion (Catholicism vs. Orthodox Christianity) as it was about territorial ambition. Aside from the ill-advised Russo-Japanese War of 1904–5, Russia has not sought military aggrandizement in the

17. Regrettable and much demonized today but in the context of the times not particularly surprising, since Germans comprised the largest single ethnic group in the United States. Few could predict, or endorse, what was to come.

Far East, and even the Warsaw Pact of captive nations after World War II was primarily a defensive perimeter.

Russia, however, would not have felt the need for such an Iron Curtain were it not for its fear of the Germans. The love-hate relationship between the two peoples went back centuries. There were for hundreds of years substantial German communities in Moscow itself, as well as the so-called Volga Germans who had settled in the heart of European Russia by invitation of the tsars in the eighteenth century. The West had the technological know-how the Russians needed and admired (Peter the Great spent some time, incognito, learning the shipbuilding trade in Holland), and the Germans brought not only their aptitude and their industry but also their abilities as traders and merchants. Gradually, however, the Germans came to treat the Slavs as their inferiors, and by the time of Hitler that contempt had evolved into murderous hatred. Stalingrad proved the hatred to be mutual.

Even evil can have its heroic side, when the men fighting in the mud, blood, snow, and ice are unaware of it. For the common soldier on both sides of the lines at Stalingrad, under orders from his supreme leader to stand his ground, come what may, death was a small price to pay for honor. Whether it was worth it is another matter, and perhaps not for us to say.

EPILOGUE

"IRON MIKE"

THE CHOSIN RESERVOIR, 1950

IT HAS BEEN THE THESIS OF THIS BOOK THAT WHILE TECHNOLOGY MAY change, human nature is immutable. The soldiers who went into action with Leonidas, Hannibal, Anielewicz, Roland, Harold, Röist, Zrínyi, Davy Crockett and Jean Danjou, Grant, Sitting Bull, Gonville, Gordon, and Pavlov differed in their arms and often in their tactics, but not a whit in their elemental masculinity. Even when all was lost, they turned a potential rout into a last stand by adhering to discipline, trusting in their drill and training—not to spare them from a fate that was almost certainly theirs, but from shame, disgrace, and dishonor.

Cynics may, and do, scoff that these are outmoded virtues (if indeed they were ever really virtues at all) from a bygone era, relics of barbarism, sexism, and "the patriarchy." In an age when nuclear annihilation is just a hot button away, what does it matter if men are willing to fight to the end? That some are willing to do just that never seems to occur to them. Only a nihilist or a fatalist could believe otherwise. Rome fell because its political class was exhausted and there were not enough real Romans left to fight, and so it was up to the naturalized barbarians to do the jobs Romans just wouldn't do: have babies and join the legions. The result was 476 A.D.

While armies are deployed in the defense of hearth and kin, in the field those are not the things men actually fight for. At Stalingrad, soldiers on both sides were fighting in macro for *honor*—the honor of their respective countries (not political systems or even their leaders; few were fighting for Hitler or Stalin personally, but rather for what they represented). They were not even fighting directly for their wives and children. In micro, they were fighting not even for themselves but for the men in their units, the men closest to them. In the Roman maniples, the thrust of your gladius often went to the right, into the man directly across from your buddy. One of the principal foundations of combat is the idea of "support." In a well-regulated platoon, company, battalion, regiment, brigade, division, or corps, it is the job of each man to make sure the next man can do his job. The lowly cook is in charge of feeding the men; the commanding general is in charge of winning the war. But as brilliant as he might be, he cannot do it without the cook.

The heart of any army is its infantry, the grunts, the body of the mighty spear that is to harpoon and pinion the enemy, and then to destroy him. All the other elements of combat, such as cavalry (whether equine or air), artillery, armored units, and naval forces, support the infantry. An army can survive and even win without air superiority, as the Russians did at Stalingrad, but no army can with only air power—as the Germans discovered during the Battle of Britain. And while the Allies bombed the German cities around the clock in the last phases of the European theater, Hitler only surrendered via suicide as the Russians came rolling down the Unter den Linden, heading for the Reichstag and the Brandenburg Gate. Even should the next war be fought with missiles, or from space, there will still be a need for the infantry, either on offense or defense in the aftermath of any nuclear exchange.

Until the infantry arrives, the war is not really over. Germany was bombed into rubble by the British and the Americans, but it was not until the Allies crossed the Rhine and the Russians crossed the Oder and finally met in Berlin that the conflict ceased. And while the Japanese capitulated after the firebombing of Tokyo and atomic bombings of Hiroshima and Nagasaki, it was the Marine Corps' island-hopping across the Pacific, fighting an archipelagic land war, that demonstrated the Americans' will and ability to win. At the Battle of Midway in June 1942, the U.S. Navy had torn the heart out of Admiral Yamamoto's carrier fleet, helping clear the way for the Marines' continuous amphibious assaults, drawing ever nearer to the Japanese homeland. However bloody it was going to be, the end was inevitable.

What lessons can we, in the twenty-first century, learn from these historical examples? Not much that comports with the received wisdom and disappointing results of the past 70 years of world conflict. Primarily, since Korea and Vietnam (in both its French and American incarnations), and continuing throughout the "endless wars" in the Middle East and the Hindu Kush that have followed in the wake of 9/11, there has been the abandonment of the concept of total victory and unconditional surrender—the notion that wars are meant to decide something, rather than be "expeditions" involving "proportionate responses" to often murderous provocations and exercises in "nation-building." As Sherman would tell us, these are all fool's errands that only serve to encourage the enemy and get more of our troops killed. No doubt Caesar would say the same thing.

We've also learned that tolerance of a great moral evil is no virtue, as Anielewicz at Warsaw and Grant at Shiloh realized; that "diversity" as a cardinal organizing principle is the death of unified societies, as the Roman Empire discovered too late; and that hate, properly channeled, can be a powerful protective emotion, as the Indians at the Little Bighorn and the Russians at Stalingrad proved. These are not lessons, however, particularly palatable to or compatible with modernity, which prizes talk over action, instinctively sympathizes with declared foes, and shies away from actual victory on the grounds that it would somehow be rude or unfair.

We've discovered that war heroes can be enlisted men or junior officers (Pavlov, Chard, and Bromhead); that high rank is no definitive measure of either capability or success (Varus, Roland); that sometimes the smaller force outwits the larger (Cannae, Rorke's Drift); and that sometimes there is nothing left to do but to die (Leonidas, Gordon).

And most of all, that war may be hell but it is often necessary. This may be regrettable, but unless one is a member of a suicide cult, it does neither an individual nor a nation any good to deny. In our iconoclastic era, in which a sizable segment of the American population thinks it somehow cathartic to tear down statues of great men of the past because they lacked the foresight to see how their actions and attitudes might play out hundreds or even thousands of years in the future, there can be no disagreement with transitory orthodoxy. The animated warriors of the "social justice" movement are quite brave when confronting inanimate objects; one wonders how far this bravado would extend to an existential threat. Let's hope we never have to find out, although one suspects they would suddenly discover the joys of conscientious objection, or a "higher loyalty" to nonviolence over their preferred goal of international, borderless brotherhood. Who knows, they might even pick up a gun, if only in inexpert self-defense.

History offers us a constant reminder of Kant's dictum, that the natural state of man is war. Our most fundamental myths and legends concern war, not peace. The destruction that results may be absolute but it is rarely useless. From the ruins of Rome sprang the diverse cultures of Europe and the Mediterranean. And, in any case, nothing will stop war, especially good intentions. The Kellogg-Briand Pact, signed in Paris in 1928, bound its signers to renounce war. The original signatories included Australia, Belgium, Canada, Czechoslovakia, France, Germany, India, Ireland, Italy, Japan, New Zealand, Poland, South Africa, the United Kingdom, and the United States. Other nations followed, including Afghanistan, Cuba, Finland, Nicaragua, the Soviet Union, Turkey, and the Kingdom of the Serbs, Croats, and Slovenes. Eleven years later, World War II broke out, rendering the treaty nugatory and resulting in the disappearance of several of the signatories.

Contemporary pacifists and feminists will argue that war is the result of "toxic masculinity," and that in a female-dominated world disputes will be amicably settled by tribal councils of conciliation and jawboning. Why, then, are contemporary feminists so adamant about women in the military? Why do they insist, against all historical and empirical evidence, that women are the equals of men in every respect, including physical strength and the nature of their emotions? Their ideal, the now-obsolete United Nations, is a monument on the East River to the naïveté of Kellogg-Briand. What has the U.N. brought us? Wars that drag on forever with "peacekeepers" in blue helmets there to referee, a bloated bureaucracy occupying valuable Manhattan real estate, and outbreaks of rape and exploitation in various hot zones around the world. Winston Churchill never said anything stupider than "jaw-jaw is better than war-war"—rich, coming from a man who also said (of his experience on the North-West Frontier between Pakistan and

Afghanistan), "Nothing in life is so exhilarating as to be shot at without result."

Talk rarely if ever settles anything. What it does do, though, is push the simmering resentments down into the emotions until they suddenly burst out, like a smoored fire that smolders and then catches flame once more. And then it will be up to the males to put out the flames, often literally fighting fire with fire, until the rage burns itself out in the ruins of Dresden or the ashes of Tokyo. Santayana's oft-quoted aphorism, "Those who forget the past are condemned to repeat it," is in a way supererogatory: the past will recur whether we remember it or not. Remembering it and learning from it, however, at least gives us a fighting chance.

And so, in the end, we come to the heart of the matter, which is also where we began: with the fighting man himself. Throughout this book, we have heard from primary and secondary sources from Herodotus forward about the nature of war and the men who have fought it. With the World War II generation pretty much gone, we still however have access to some of the combatants of the Korean War, and it is to one of them now we turn for a firsthand account of what it was like to survive and escape a last stand, the Battle of the Chosin Reservoir.

I present some biographical details here not simply as familial history but as an insight into the upbringing and formation of a typical American warrior. Unlike in England, where the Gonville Bromheads have long had a hereditary call on the officer corps, the American military has always been far more democratic. With the exception of blacks, who were finally integrated into the armed forces by President Truman in 1948,[1] boys from all ethnic groups and all walks of life could rise to command. Korea was, in fact, the first war in American history in which blacks and whites fought alongside each other as equals. And that included Indians.

When the 12,000 men of the First Marine Division, along with some

---

1. Via Executive Order 9981, which circumvented a threatened filibuster by Southern Democrats: "There shall be equality of treatment and opportunity for all persons in the armed forces without regard to race, color, religion, or national origin."

units of the U.S. Army, marched toward the Yalu River on the Chinese–North Korean border at Thanksgiving, 1950, they were very much on the attack. On June 25, the North Korean People's Army (NKPA) had invaded the Republic of Korea and routed its armed forces, capturing the South Korean capital of Seoul and pushing the ROK forces into what became known as the Pusan Perimeter in the extreme southeast of the country, threatening to drive them into the Sea of Japan. The peninsula had been divided since the end of World War II, while the Soviets, having entered the war against Japan very late in the conflict, sliced off pieces of the crumbling empire, including the Kuril Islands and Sakhalin Island. At the conclusion of hostilities, the Russians were occupying Korea north of the 38th parallel, while the Americans had possession of the south. The two Koreas, acting as proxies for the U.S.S.R. and the United States, had been battling ever since. Meanwhile, a newly Communist China under Mao Tse-tung was watching warily from the sidelines.

The new United Nations condemned the attack and sent ground forces under the overall command of Gen. Douglas MacArthur, whose long career had spanned both world wars, including a stint as supreme commander for the Allied Powers in Japan from 1945 to 1948—effectively the absolute ruler of Nippon, with the Emperor Hirohito allowed to continue as a figurehead. From his base in Japan, MacArthur became commander in chief of the United Nations Command for Korea, with the U.S. Eighth Army as its centerpiece and the First Marine Division under Maj. Gen. Oliver P. Smith as the tip of its spear.

The problem was, there wasn't much of the Marine Corps left. Despite—or perhaps because of—the Marines' pivotal role in the Pacific, there was an assiduous push by Army and civilian brass to downsize or even eliminate it, folding it into the two principal services, the Army and the Navy (the Marines are part of the Navy department). It wasn't until the National Security Act of 1947 that the Marines' existence was guaranteed. Calling in Marines from duty stations at home and in the Pacific, and using mostly rust-bucket American landing craft repurchased from the Japanese, MacArthur landed troops in Pusan, where they were able to stabilize the front and plan a counterattack against the North Koreans. In September, the Marines were withdrawn from Pusan, put aboard troop ships, and transported to the western port city of Inchon, where in a daring amphibious landing they secured the area and marched all the way to the occupied South Korean capital of Seoul, which was liberated on September 29.[2]

Emboldened by the rapid disintegration of the NKPA, Truman ordered MacArthur to destroy the North Korean People's Army and unify the peninsula. In short order, U.N. and South Korean forces crossed the North Korean border and were moving toward the Yalu River, the border with China. Despite warning from the People's Republic of China, acting at the behest of the Soviet Union, that it might enter the fray should the U.N. forces threaten its national security, MacArthur considered the threat empty, and so advised the president at their Wake Island conference on October 15, 1950.

That blunder set the stage for one of the greatest battles in Marine Corps history.

Among those Marines fighting from Pusan to Inchon to Seoul and then into North Korean territory was my father, 1st Lt. John J. Walsh. He was born in Malden, Massachusetts, on June 1, 1926—the same day as Marilyn Monroe, as it happens. His father, Joseph, was the son of two Irish immigrants from County Clare; his mother Mildred's parents were both Nova Scotians who had legally immigrated to America. Her father, Emanuel Dingle, had served in the Navy as an Ordinary Seaman during the Spanish-American War; her mother, Mary Adele "Addie" La Fave (LeFevre), was an Acadian-French-speaking Mic Mac Indian, always referred to by her husband—affectionately, one hopes—as "Squaw."

John was a standout athlete at Malden Catholic High School, outstanding at ice hockey, baseball, and, especially, football. Indeed, the Boston sportswriters dubbed him "Iron Mike" Walsh, a popular slang term in the first half of the twentieth century for men who were tough and brave, and because he took the hardest hits (in the days of leather helmets) and somehow managed to stay in the game. (In typical Irish fashion, I am named after him.[3])

---

2. The city eventually changed hands four times.

3. Thanks to the frequent use of certain Christian names—Michael, Patrick,

It was a moniker well earned. A star player on the Malden Catholic high school football team, he took a particular wicked shot in the face: "Two front teeth sticking down here, nose has never been correct, no medical care whatsoever. Coach said, sit down," he recalls. "Game is now in the last 30 seconds: go ahead back in there. So I go back in and I throw a touchdown and a friend of mine, he kicks the extra point and we tie the score. Nobody gave a damn about my injury. And that's the way I grew up. So I guess when I had a choice to go into the Marine Corps and fight people, it was the natural thing to do."

To this day, he marvels that he was ever accepted into the Corps. The beating he took as a high school athlete, including major knee injuries, has impacted him throughout his life. At about five feet, eight inches tall and, at his heaviest, no more than 180 pounds, he was never a big man by today's standards. But he was extremely strong, very tough, impervious to pain, and packed a wicked left hook. A natural left-hander, he writes and shoots with his right hand, a legacy of a time in Catholic-school education in which the nuns beat left-handedness out of the children in their keep.

Every soldier's story is the same, but every soldier's story is different. We don't have the first-person accounts of Lucius Vorenus and Tito Pullo, two of the men of Legion XI (the Legio XI Claudia) who fought with Caesar and whom he mentions by name in the *Commentaries*,[4] but we do have the testimony—as I have quoted throughout this book as much as possible—of soldiers throughout history who spoke or jotted down or in interviews gave their recollections, whether contemporaneously or decades later (like Grant, in his *Personal Memoirs*).

As a child, growing up, I heard none of these stories. This is in part due to my father's natural reticence, the fact that we are only twenty-three years apart in life, and that I graduated so quickly from schoolboy

---

John, Joseph, Mary, Margaret, etc.—the Irish often distinguish among relatives with the same names by adding a modifier or using a nickname whose meaning is often only clear within the family itself.

4. Book V, Chapter 44. They are also the principal characters in the HBO/BBC miniseries *Rome* (2005–7), in which they were portrayed by Kevin McKidd and Ray Stevenson.

and college student to professional that I hardly had a chance to know him when I was young—and am just doing so now, when we are both old men. Only later in his long life did he tell these tales, not to his children but to his grandchildren and even his great-grandchildren. When you first return from a war zone, no one wants to hear your stories, if you even want to relate them at all. It is enough that you are home. So you save them, nurturing them in your breast and in your heart, until near the end they come out, in a rush, the testimony of the eyewitness, the truth at last—or at least as you remember it.

So here is the story of an ordinary, but extraordinary, soldier, one who can bring to life the major themes of this book. Why do men fight? What do they fight for? What are their personal characteristics? When the shooting begins, when the perimeters of the battlefield close in, what are the virtues and circumstances that separate the living from the dead? Courage? Training? Discipline? Chance? What separates the quick and the dead? And what, after the battle, do the survivors experience, think, and tell themselves?

> I'm a loner because I was brought up that way. When I was three or four years old, my mother would ship me out across the street someplace while she and my father went to work, and my sister [Mary Lou, two years younger] would go someplace else. We were getting up and out of the house at five o'clock in the morning, and my sister was being carried, wrapped in her bundle, and we each had a paper bag, with a sandwich in it for lunch. Did we eat breakfast? I don't know. I don't remember. Being a loner, I had to make up my mind what my life was going to be like. My father would come home, completely exhausted just from going to work; he didn't seem to drink during the work week, but he drank like hell on Friday night. And so at age six or seven my mother would say to me, "go down to Peroni's beer house and get your father's pay check."

That, clearly, was not the life he wanted. For a man like my father, the idea of punching a time clock at the Boston Rubber Shoe factory, making Converse sneakers as his father did, was not for him. His Irish grandmother, who had learned English in America,[5] had come from nothing: a stone hut on a rocky slope west of Lisdoonvarna in County Clare, with a spectacular view of the Cliffs of Moher, the Atlantic Ocean, and the Aran Islands, but not much else. She settled in Lowell, Massachusetts, and labored in a textile factory until, bused down to a social in Boston, she met a Clare man who had come in through Philadelphia. They married in Lowell in 1892 and moved to the small city of Malden, just north of Boston, where they bought or built a double-decker home on Malden Street facing Devir Park, living on one floor and renting out the other. His Indian grandmother, who spoke Acadian French as her native language, had come from even less, born in 1873 in Belleville, Nova Scotia, near Yarmouth. She married Emanuel Dingle, also from Yarmouth, in Massachusetts in 1900 (it was her second marriage) and they settled in Wakefield.

Working-class Malden in those days was largely an Irish and Italian town, very Catholic, a town of churches, bars, and bakeries, where weddings between the two groups were considered "mixed marriages," with all of the racial overtones the phrase implies. It was also the Depression: poverty and straitened circumstances were the norm. Higher education—and in those days, that meant high school; college was a luxury beyond the reach of most—was not necessarily a given, especially for girls. His father never graduated from high school, and his mother never graduated into high school. Instead, she worked in a laundry for six years, earning $9.90 a week. For them, marriage was the way up and out.

"So she and my father got married when she was about 20 and my dad was 22, I believe, and they soon found out it was the worst time in the world because of the Depression. They couldn't buy a house, they couldn't pay rent, they couldn't do anything." The solution was to move

5. Mary O'Brien Walsh spoke Irish—*Gaeilge*—as her native tongue; I have the Irish-English dictionaries she possessed, along with various books of English-language poetry, among them a volume called *Scotia's Bards*—"Scotia" being the original name of Ireland. *Gaeilge* is part of the Goidelic language family of the Celts. Transplanted to Scotland, it turned into Scots Gaelic (Gallic). Mary LaFave Dingle spoke Acadian, a seventeenth-century dialect of French, older than Quebecois, generally found only in the Canadian Maritimes.

in with Joe Walsh's parents in the duplex on Malden Street, which is where John became acquainted with his Irish grandfather. "I can remember the grandfather, Patrick, sitting at the head of the stairs, going upstairs through the back door with his two cats, who hated me and I hated them. That would be about 1927. And the old man would be sitting up there, black mustache, the only thing I remember—he looked like any Irishman of the time—he didn't like me at all. So that contributed to my being almost a recluse." Meanwhile, Mary O'Brien Walsh, her long hair tied up in a bun, would be out in the backyard where she raised chickens. At dinnertime, "she would grab one by the neck and she'd twirl it a few times, kill it, and drop it in this boiling 55-gallon drum and somehow put a torch underneath it, and then when it was ready, she would go out there, pull all the feathers off and then gut it."

For a time, he was farmed out to his other set of grandparents, where he spent a couple of years being raised by his First Nations[6] grandmother in nearby Wakefield, where he walked every day to school through the woods. She taught him much about nature, packing him off to pick berries and other edibles to bring home. He was a restive, combative boy:

> I remember I was always getting in trouble. I was also fighting with the kids in the first and second grades. It became such that it was an armed combat with penknives, and it had to be that there was more of them than there was of me. At that age I took a defensive posture, a counterattack as we would say today. If they were harassing me to the point that I was fearful at that age, I would manage to trot, then run, and if that didn't get me safely to the front porch of my grandmother's house, I would open up the jackknife and I would sit there in a defensive mode until they chickened out and went home. I remember that very clearly.

Then it was back to Malden Street where Dan—my father's uncle—was living in the attic, a virtual hermit.[7] Across the street was Devir

---

6. It is noteworthy that three ethnic groups overrepresented in the Marines are the Irish, the American Indians, and the Southwestern Hispanics.

7. "Dan was my model as a recluse. Dan was what anybody told me Dan was. I

Park, where the neighborhood kids played and where the circus would pitch its tent when the big top came to town. But the focus of the Irish was not on recreation, but on the church: "From Lent to Easter I knew at age 12, maybe, that I was expected to be in the upstairs, kneeling down, saying my prayer, reciting all of the mysteries of the Rosary, and anything else that my Irish grandmother had brought over with her. They had statuettes of Mary, Joseph, Jesus—the only time I ever remember them displayed in the house, I think was maybe once. My grandmother knew I would be in the park someplace, running around, and she would holler out the window, 'John, time to go home. Time to go to prayer.' And I never disobeyed my grandmother. She had an Irish accent, and she had a complete Irish demeanor: I'm in charge and everybody knows I'm in charge."

Perhaps the formative experience of his young life came during a near-death experience while still a schoolboy. He and some other kids had climbed a rocky bluff behind his parish church, Immaculate Conception, on Salem Street. The brothers who taught at the primary school had warned everybody not to climb up the cliff, but of course, boys being boys, a few of them did. It was around the beginning of Lent: "So me and a guy I will never forget come out of church, all authority is out of sight, we and three other guys ended up going around behind the brothers' house and climbing to this higher level, which was flat. Cold, windy, slippery, and for some reason we were right over at the edge of it."

Something happened. The next thing John Walsh knew, he was lying on the street below with a fractured skull, a broken left wrist, and multiple cracked ribs. With the help of some of his buddies he somehow managed to stagger, nearly unconscious, to a nearby gas station, where the attendant shouted at him to get off the property because he was bleeding so profusely. "The next I know was that I wake up in the hospital, and I'm dying. Leaning over me is a priest, and he's giving me extreme unction." His Irish grandmother was also by his side, intoning

---

don't ever remember seeing him until I was about ten or eleven years old." When we were boys, my brother Stephen (who went on to a distinguished career in the Navy, retiring as a commander) and I used to imagine that Dan was busy writing the Great American Novel. Alas, it was not to be. He was just a bum.

a prayer to St. Bridget, widely venerated in Ireland as the patron saint of healing. It worked. To this day, he believes he was pushed by one of the boys. "He says I slipped. I didn't confront him but I had conversations with him later."

As he healed he realized he was in the pediatric burn ward, surrounded by other kids who hadn't been so lucky. "Every other kid was purple. Burned. Scalded. These kids had been victims of their mother or their father or themselves. When I left there, I know they were still there and some of them must have died there. I don't have a scar to speak of. But that started me on my adventure through life."

Now all the elements of the warrior were in play: the loner, the outsider, the wounded child who had already received the last rites of the Church, the man of faith with something to prove to society and to himself. The Romans would have recognized him immediately as the kind of man they needed as a centurion in the Legions. The kind of man who, already bloodied, could be counted on in combat. Who, having cheated death once, would no longer have any irrational fear of it. And so, after attending the College of the Holy Cross in Worcester under the accelerated V-12 Navy College Training Program, he was commissioned as a second lieutenant in the Marine Corps in 1947.

His early fortitude served him well: at Inchon on September 15, 1950, a concussion grenade (also called a percussion grenade, or a "flash-bang") exploded very near him as he scrambled up and over the wooden ladder of his LST and onto the concrete seawall. The grenade knocked him down and almost out cold; behind him, eleven of his men were wounded so badly they had to be evacuated to the aid station at sea. "The Gunnery Sergeant asked if I was okay and I answered yes. He said I was strong as steel. I was now one of the team." Iron Mike had come to Korea.

Something else happened on that beach at Inchon after it was secured, something not entirely uncommon in war, even in a hot zone, and yet always remarkable: "Sporadic enemy activity was ongoing. In the semi-darkness, a much distressed Korean 18-year-old mother, plus or minus, with baby and two-year-old child, appeared looking very confused. Instinctively, I picked up the two-year-old and by hand signals directed the mother to an area out of the path of other USMC coming ashore. Communist propaganda portrayed Marines as criminal bad guys, so she was probably scared to death when I grabbed the child; she likely thought we would kill and eat the baby. At dawn the next day my platoon was on the move toward Seoul. To my surprise about 20 Korean civilians, including the girl, were in the area smiling and waving to us. I guess my good deed with the babies proved that the communist propaganda was false."

Still, he was plagued by physical problems, the legacy of his early injuries. "The walk from Inchon to Kimpo resulted in my bad knee swelling and becoming very painful. I could not walk as the 'replacement' platoon leader—with three whole days of combat. I was embarrassed. What to do? I told my problems to my senior NCO [noncommissioned officer; in other words, a high-ranking sergeant] so that he could tell the platoon. I rode in my Jeep for the next two days. I called for help from above [i.e., from God] and as we were nearing Kimpo, the help came. The knee, believe it or not, was pain free and remained that way for my next nine months in Korea.[8] An officer who cannot do what the troops are doing is not much respected or followed." On September 18, on the road to Seoul, at Kimpo, a city near Inchon, he captured Maj. Ju Yeong-bok, one of the North Korean dictator Kim Il-sung's staff officers and translators, along with two NKPA enlisted men; Major Ju, a valuable security asset, remained as a prisoner of war in South Korea until 1953.

The first battle of Seoul was as brutal as they come. Dad was a mortar man, fighting with the 2/5—the most decorated unit in Marine Corps history, whose famous motto, "Retreat, Hell!" dates back to World War I. To this day, he does not vouchsafe much information about it. Door to door and house to house, it was urban fighting at its worse. Captured Americans could look forward to brutal interrogation and then a bullet in the back of the head. Korean civilians, including old

---

8. The Catholic faith has always played an important part in my father's life, with a special devotion to the Blessed Virgin Mary. With his wife, Nancy (d. January 19, 2017, just hours short of her ninety-first birthday), and his five children, he attended Mass every Sunday. At Inchon, he made a vow to Mary that if he survived the conflict and returned to his family (I was the only child at this time), he would always honor her. And so he has: even today her statue has a special place in his Florida garden.

women, would yank AK-47s from underneath their skirts and shoot the Marines in the back. Almost no one could be trusted. The fog of war combined with the darkness of the Korean night made it almost impossible to distinguish friend from foe. "In the black of night the security problems became intense," he recalled. "It was difficult to fight with POWs everywhere. Many times the thought of killing POWs was considered but never implemented."

After Inchon and Seoul, the Marines were put back on ships and transported around to the east side of the peninsula, to the port city of Wonsan, which was in U.N. hands. They had to wait a while for mines to be cleared. At this point, it was obvious that the Chinese had crossed the border and were now actively supporting the retreating North Korean troops. Whether they would attack Americans directly, and in what force, remained to be seen.

The Marines made their way north to Hungnam and then set out for the Yalu River, on the Chinese border. MacArthur wished to deliver a killing blow to the North Korean People's Army, and so, along with elements of the U.S. Army's X Corps, the 12,000 men of First Marine Division under the command of Maj. Gen. Oliver P. Smith began marching into the interior, heading for Haguru-ri, located at the base of the Chosin Reservoir.[9] At Hagaru, the Army split off, pushing north along the east side of the man-made reservoir, while the Marines took the west side, heading for Koto-ri and, ultimately, Yudam-ni. As in World War I, "Home for Christmas" was the watchword.

The enemy, however, also gets a vote. On the night of November 27, 1950, despite MacArthur's assurances to Truman that they would not enter the war, the Chinese arrived en masse—wave after wave. As at Stalingrad, the first wave was armed; the second wave would pick up the weapons from the dead and dying; the third wave consisted of commissars with burp guns ready to shoot any strays, sluggards, or cowards. At some points along the front, the Marines found themselves outnumbered ten to one. MacArthur's was a blunder born of overconfidence

---

9. "Chosin" is a variant of the Japanese name for the large body of water; in Korean, it is Changjin.

and hubris on the scale of Sherman's refusal to credit the scouting reports at Shiloh, or Custer's surprise at the Big Village:

> Simultaneous Chinese attacks occurred at Yudam—Hagaru—Koto-ri on 27 November. My battalion (2/5) was to fight at these towns from 27 Nov.–8 Dec. 1950. This time frame to me was "The Reservoir." After that it was over the bridge[10] to Hungnam and the ships.
>
> Yudam-ni lies in a valley about four miles long and one and a half to two miles wide. In this valley, surrounded by eight or nine hill masses four to five thousand feet high was the town. The 2/5 was positioned three miles west of Yudam-ni. For two days (27–28 Nov.) thirty thousand Chinese[11] and ten thousand USMC fought and left about ten thousand casualties in minus-30 temperatures on 29–30 November. USMC headed south and the Chinese followed. Subsequent major battles occurred along the MSR[12] over fifty miles during the next ten days.
>
> At Yudam-ni my 81mm platoon was positioned within the Fifth Marines perimeter and expended over one thousand mortar rounds in an area fronting the rifle companies. As the Chinese probed for weak spots in our perimeter, rifle companies were moved to strengthen these areas. During the mid-night of 27–28 November, I moved all 81mm mortars about one to two miles east toward the Yudam Valley. The Chinese had penetrated our northwest perimeter and we were under direct fire which results in one killed in action at our mortar site and also some short 105mm rounds from our Marine artillery which

---

10. This was the bridge at the Funchilin Pass, which had been destroyed by the Chinese. Had they not been able to cross the gorge, the Marines would have been trapped with no way out. American war planners had anticipated that the Chinese would blow the bridges along the Marines' route to the sea, so four sections of metal-and-wood Treadway bridge, just barely wide enough for both tanks and Jeeps, were airdropped, and the bridge reopened on December 9.

11. Across the entire Chosin front, the Chinese forces consisted of elements of 12 divisions, about 100,000 troops.

12. Main supply route. All in all, it was 78 miles from the Reservoir to the sea.

> was attempting to kill the Chinese who had penetrated our defense.
>
> We stayed in this position until 28-29 November when the 5th and 7th Marine Regiments were preparing to "bust-out" of Yudam-ni. I could see at this time that hundreds (perhaps thousands) of Chinese had overrun the 7th Marine perimeter in the valley and if not contained, they would cross the valley, seize the MSR and destroy our artillery, supply, our casualties and my 81mm platoon. Fortunately, this did not happen.

His terse matter-of-fact description, of course, cannot do justice to the experience. As a child, I never heard him discuss the war. I knew he had been in Korea, but I had no conception of what that meant, or what it had entailed. So in April 2019, I asked him about it, asked the questions with which we have been concerned throughout this book. At last, here was someone who had actually been at a last stand to respond to them: Were you scared? Did you fear death? What was going through your mind? His answers probably will come as no surprise:

> I don't ever remember being too excited. I remember that at the time that the Chinese did attack—I don't remember the details but we must have gotten a phone call from the battalion headquarters, which was about a mile and a half away from where I had the guns [mortars], and they were talking about, it looks like we're going to be overrun, and so—as far as I remember, being not too excited,[13] I gathered my two staff sergeants together and I said, "I've just been told that we'd better prepare." We're a quasi-infantry unit, meaning that we don't have barbed wire and we don't have mines, we don't have claymore mines, things that are designed to meet a charging enemy and kill him fifty yards or a hundred yards away. All we had was our own side arms and I said to the sergeants: you're infantry and I'm infantry but we're not

13. He means frightened, anxious.

> equipped to take a thousand Chinese on, but what we're gonna do is, we're gonna line up like Civil War types, because we had no depth to go into, and as I remember it was just a cool exchange between two sergeants who had been with this unit for two years at Camp Pendleton [between San Diego and Los Angeles] and me brand-new, since we went to Inchon. And so we came to the conclusion about three in the morning. So we went to work.

The Chinese held off that night. The Marines, however, were still under constant fire. But note the term "work." Soldiers from time immemorial have regarded combat as work—grim and grisly work, to be sure, but work nonetheless. There is nothing glamorous in it, just old-fashioned resolution. The randomness of injury and death in combat is something no soldier can prepare for—sometimes the bullet bounces off your sword, as Grant discovered, and sometimes it goes through your brain. The safest and best thing is to do your job. If you do, you might get killed, but if you don't, you *will* get killed.

The surprising truth is, most men are not killed in battle. In any enumeration of casualties, the number of wounded and missing outnumber deaths on the field. One's chances of surviving any given battle are actually relatively good; disease, or a wound that might otherwise have been attended to and thus rendered nonfatal, is usually the Grim Reaper. At Shiloh, Albert Sidney Johnston might have lived had something as simple as a tourniquet been applied to his leg after he was shot. Instant death on the battlefield came from the thrust of a *gladius*, an encounter with a halberd, the cleave of the Dane axe, a bouncing cannonball, the fatal lacerations from canister shot, an arrow through the eye, or a bullet to the head. Instantaneous, and thus not feared because you never saw it coming. One minute you were doing your job, and the next moment you were gone, eyes still open, staring blindly at the sky. Before the battle, you might prepare—write a testament or a letter to your girl or your parents, and then ask your buddy, should he survive and make it back home, to deliver it. Like William Penn Symons, you died facing the enemy.

The history of military warfare tells us this, over and over again. You do your duty. You obey the dictates of your discipline. You do what you have been trained to do. This is exactly what we should expect. When everything is falling apart, the one fixed point in a rapidly changing environment a soldier has to cling to is his training. You do the job—which is to say, you kill the man in front of you. And then you do it again until the fighting stops, one way or the other.

’Twas ever thus. The Greeks knew it was coming, the hail of arrows that would blot out the sun and allow them to fight and die in the shade. So did Vercingetorix at Alesia, invested twice over, against an implacable foe in Caesar who would, after the Roman fashion, show no mercy to a man who was defying him. Ditto Roland, fighting until his temple burst. Harold, felled by an arrow to the eye, sagging, leaning, falling. Custer, unable to form an effective perimeter and, like Gordon at Khartoum, waiting for help that never came. And yet, even in the midst of the action, there is hope of survival. It’s hard to hit a human target, even one that is relatively stationary; the reserved seats on the Paris Metro to this day are for the *mutilés de guerre*, the wounded war veterans from as far back as the First World War, and perhaps even those still hobbled by the Franco-Prussian War 30 years before the Metro opened, should those ghosts need a ride.

Few civilians understand how *loud* war is. The shell-shocked veterans of the Somme were not reacting to the carnage so much as to the ear-splitting noise produced by the big guns and personal firearms. It is literally deafening, which is why shooters on a gun range are forced to wear ear protection during target practice. There is a memorable moment early in Steven Spielberg’s masterpiece *Saving Private Ryan* where it takes Captain Miller (Tom Hanks) a few moments to shake off the effects of gunfire as he lands on Omaha Beach during Operation Overlord in 1944. Of such moments are the fog of war made. To live or die is not a matter of courage but of luck, born of discipline and preparation. “Tell everyone I died facing the enemy” is about all any warrior can ask.

And so, on the night of November 27, 1950, the Chinese attacked in full force, shooting off rockets and sounding gongs and noisemakers as they charged down the hills to attack. Mao’s goal was simple: to annihilate the First Marine Division and thus effectively destroy the entire Marine Corps. In temperatures that were as cold as 30 degrees below zero, he came very close to succeeding.

Let Lieutenant Walsh describe it in his own plain words, for this is as close as a modern reader will ever get to a living eyewitness account of Thermopylae, the Swiss Guard at the Vatican, or Rorke's Drift:

> I don't ever remember getting "what if" about it, except to say up and down the line: if you see a bunch a people, we're going to assume they're not friendly. We only had ammunition enough for—I would guess we had six or eight cartridge bandoliers, probably seventy rounds of ammunition apiece. I had since made up my mind that I was going to do an M-1 rifle in addition to my .45. I had shot expert in both of them and I had confidence in them, but with a .45 your best bet is within 25 yards, with your M-1 your best bet is within 300 yards. I liked that. The other thing about the 300 [the M-1]—we call it "battle sight"—the rise and fall of the bullet is almost flat, so you don't have to screw around, you just set your weapon at battle-300 yards, and you know that somebody coming up at five and a half, six feet tall, you're going to hit somebody.
>
> So what came across is a couple of Chinese regiments—this was 20–30 degrees below zero—dressed in their quilted uniforms. Other Chinese, who were coming down from the hills across the valley two miles away, had frozen to death. Otherwise they would have come in between our artillery which was in our southern perimeter, and our infantry people and all of their fighting might, but absent of air support, absent of artillery, no tanks. Just bazookas and M-1 rifles. The main thing for artillery in the perimeter is what they can do for perimeter defense, so when you can know the enemy is coming, you just throw everything you got at them.
>
> I can't remember being, oh Jesus we're all going to die, or what's going to happen. The thought might have crossed my mind that I don't want to be taken prisoner. I don't want to be a prisoner of war. I'm sure that happened.
>
> We knew we were in deep trouble because the Chinese had the high ground this time. And once you lose the high ground, and you gotta move trucks and troops and all that stuff, otherwise

> forget it. You'll have survivors and stragglers but you won't have a militarily operational unit coming back.

In the freezing conditions, the Marines stacked the dead bodies of the Chinese to use them as both breastworks and windbreaks. Many of the Chinese had essentially frozen alive, the only sign of life being their moving eyeballs. The Marines shot them. They relieved the dead of any usable clothing and unspent ammunition.

> Normally you go into a war with a three-day supply of whatever you think you need—350 rounds per mortar was a good estimate. I had six guns. That's almost two thousand rounds. You take with the guns a day's unit of fire, as they call it. And you have a day's worth backing that up a couple of miles away. Illumination, WP [white phosphorus], high explosives. At Hagaru we probably had about ten days of supply. Smith, the general, was thumbing his nose at the Army, who were telling him to hurry up, hurry up and get up to the Yalu River and don't worry about your resupply and all that. On the contrary, Smith was quadrupling the ammunition, quadrupling everything, so we had I would guess ten days of supply, and we damn near expended the whole thing in two days.
>
> All mortars had an adjustable fuse, to explode upon impact or to explode ten or fifteen feet above the ground. I'm now a mortar man, first time I've been one in my life, and there were thousands of Chinese, trying to get to where I was through the infantry I was supporting. I had an observer for each pair of guns that I had. So I had an observer with A company, B company, C company, Second Battalion, Fifth Marines, and they were spread out in an arc over three miles, I would say.
>
> The observer during the first day getting ready for the Chinese to come to us was marking out targets by grid coordinates, six-digit kind of thing, and coordinating back to his pair of guns, to his sergeant. And his sergeant and the other two sergeants doing the same thing were communicating with the two gunnery sergeants that I had back in my little command post, which was a

tent, which was nice because I had it close in to the infantry so we could turn it into an aid station for the wounded about halfway through this two days of constant work, whatever your job was.

The only moment of trepidation came when friendly fire from the Marine artillery rained down on his head:

During the night, when the fighting was at its heaviest, my guns were off a road between the 5th Marines and 7th Marines and as we were firing I could hear this whistle from something that I knew was a 105 mm howitzer shell from our guns which were five miles over in the valley away from us. And they had the wrong coordinates and all of a sudden: boom boom boom boom. And I yelled out: everybody get off the guns and get back on the cover of the hills. Looking back on it, it was kind of silly, because artillery comes in this way [from above] and they don't recognize hills too much. So after about four or five minutes after this barrage, I discovered that's what it was: one battery of four guns had misinformed a gun of the correct coordinates to shoot over there instead of over here. Scared the shit outta me.[14] They were about fifty yards away, and the range killing zone on a 105 is about thirty to forty yards. Awful close. That scared the hell out of everybody. But I listened, and then I said we'd better get back on the guns, because there wasn't any follow-on. And then we resumed killing the Chinese, for the support of the Fifth Marines.

During the first night our positons were mutually supporting within the battalion, but then the Chinese decided sometime during that first night that they were coming from the west, the north, and the east. For some reason—I think they coulda whipped us right there—they moved their western attacks and backed up their north to south and east to west attackers, because they were taking a beating and they needed some unplanned-for reinforcements rather than having reinforcements back five

14. One of the few times I have every heard my father curse. In general, and despite what you see in the movies, Marine officers don't use four-letter words.

miles to call in. So when they moved some time that night or early morning, when the Chinese pull back normally, because they don't like [to fight in] daylight, I decided to move my whole contingent—all the vehicles, the tent, everything—about 1,500 yards east. That's probably what screwed up the artillery, I didn't tell anybody, lesson learned, don't do that. Let everybody know where you are, because they've got bigger guns than you have. That turned out to be a very good move because it shortened my resupply line, guns and so forth. I was able to converse with the forward observer that I had up with the colonel who commanded the battalion.

The next night the Chinese really came in full force. I'm sure that the guns that I had for the area were so effective that the company commanders, when the battle was over, they were all happy. I didn't know any of them and they didn't know me, and I'm a recluse, so I didn't go out and say I'm so and so, and I did this, so I never got to meet ninety percent of the officers who were in the weapons company. I didn't give a shit what they were doing and I assumed they didn't care what I was doing. But I was doing my job, and so in the middle of the second night, when we were really harassed, I changed my firing attitude and, after talking to the FO [forward observer], I said, I'm gonna put an illumination shell up, and I'm going to fire what we call search and traverse missions. That means that each of the two guns in support of that company's sector on order would fire at nine points in a 100-yard square.

By this time the Chinese are pretty compressed,[15] trying to get into our weak spots. Now, what are they going to do? They're going to stand still, not gonna move. They got white coats on, snow is on the ground, hard to see 'em. I said I'm going to fire one round, which was different than firing the nine rounds before, and then they're going to stop someplace. And as soon as I got word of that, I would fire 20 seconds later the other eight

15. Like the Romans at Cannae. The bulk of the Chinese forces could not function effectively in the face of the terrain and the Marines' superior firepower. They had nowhere to run and nowhere to hide.

> shots, and then repeat that by moving at fifty yards time and time again. And I swear that, according to those guys, we must have killed a couple of thousand Chinese. Their political guys were killing them if they didn't attack; once they said you're gonna attack here, that made it easy for us to say OK: target number so and so. That to me was one of the significant moves that made it easy for us. If the Chinese hadn't tried to fortify what was the weakest part of our defense, if they hadn't done that, if they had reinforced just enough to get through our weak spots [on the west side] it would have been a different game. They would have had what we call double envelopment.

And so we come full circle, back to Thermopylae and Cannae and to the most elemental aspects of military tactics and strategy. Surround your enemy, cut him off from his supplies and reinforcements, and then crush him. What the Marines did in their "advance to the rear" was to elide their own last stand, escape under constant and heavy fire, and return home. It wasn't easy. As the 2/5 abandoned Hagaru, my father found himself in the rear guard:

> As the 2/5 attempted to break contact, the commanding officer, Lt. Col Roise,[16] ordered me to stay in the 81mm mortar firing position until further ordered. At that moment, about three or four hundred Chinese soldiers came off the high ground north of Hagaru about four hundred yards from my position. They stopped in Hagaru to forage. The Lt. Col ordered me south to rejoin the 2/5. As far as I know, I was the last Marine out of Hagaru.

There were some harrowing moments along the main supply route. As the frozen and wounded Marines made their way back to the Allied lines on foot or by Jeep, some of the men were too exhausted even to sit upright. "I was walking along the convoy when I saw a body fall from a vehicle and roll off the road toward a dropoff. I ran toward the Marine

---

16. History rhymes: Röist was the commander of the Swiss Guard in 1527.

(semi-conscious), a Second Lieutenant. As my Jeep came by I loaded him in the front seat and moved up and down the convoy to check on the 81mm vehicles. About five or ten minutes later, he fell out a second time and was in danger of falling down a slope and over a steep cliff. I managed to get him the second time, put him in my Jeep, tied him in and told him there would be no third fall and that I would kick his butt if it happened again." The man survived.

On December 12, the 2/5 boarded ship at Hungnam and headed for Pusan to rest and regain combat capability. At this point, my father weighed about 140 pounds, and had severe bronchitis. There was still more fighting to come, but the Battle of the Chosin Reservoir was over. He stayed in Pusan for about a month until, along with the rest of the battalion, he was deemed fit for combat again. On May 9, he received orders to leave Korea, traveled by ship via Japan to San Francisco, where he landed on May 25, and was assigned to Marine Barracks, Eighth and I Streets, in Washington, D.C., the oldest Marine post in the country, the location of the commandant's official residence, and its principal ceremonial grounds.

> From September to December 1950, my 81mm platoon had one killed in action, eleven wounded in action, and zero frostbite. Personally during that time, I was knocked down by a fragmentation grenade and struck by bullets which hit my cartridge belt and my backpack. No body wounds, no Purple Heart.
>
> Among infantry lieutenants the casualty rate was over sixty percent. Considering these numbers I was "lucky" with lots of help. Long time believers in the protective power of the Blessed Virgin Mary, Nancy and I had a grotto for the BVM visible from our homes' kitchen windows for most of our sixty-eight years married. Nancy gave me a pocket-sized Blessed Virgin Mary which I carried always in Korea. I came out of Korea in one piece thanks to two blessed ladies . . . the Blessed Virgin Mary and Ann Patricia Walsh.

This is about as good an explanation of why he fought as we're ever likely to get from him or any other soldier. In retrospect, the elements of his personal biography certainly seem to have pointed the way toward a military career, a framework from within which he could shed his sense as an outsider[17] and indulge his natural aggression. Had he been just a year or so older, he might have fought in the Pacific during the last year of World War II; as it was, he was just the right age to see action in both Korea and Vietnam.

Among his personal and unit awards were the Bronze Star[18] for heroism, the Navy Commendation, a "Combat V," six Korean War battle stars, and four presidential unit citations. He returned home from Korea to father four more children, see service in Southeast Asia (including a stint as a military representative to SEATO), retire from the Corps in 1967, and continue working in the Navy Department in Washington, D.C., until 1982, finally retiring for good to Florida, where he lives today.

He's had a long time to think this over. A voracious reader, even with only one good eye (he lost the other to botched cataract surgery some years ago), he devours books on military history, trying to fit his own first-blood infantryman's-eye-view of war with the view from 30,000 feet afforded by the best military historians. In his opinion, war always has and always will boil down to its most elemental factor: "As long as there's two guys and they're fighting each other, one's going to win over the other one. I don't think that the way to fight has ever changed from a man-to-man basis." He muses that perhaps the best way to settle disputes is the ancient ritual of single combat: "Two champions, one on this side and one on that side. Why don't we go back to that?"

Unrealistic, to be sure. But perhaps here endeth the lesson, where we began, with war at its most elemental, man to man. With Kant's dictum and Hobbes's evocation of Genesis. With the Greeks at Thermopylae, combing out their long hair and sharpening their weapons against the final assault they knew they would not survive. With the Swiss Guard, desperately fighting its way from the steps of the Vatican, across the Tiber. With Zrínyi and his men mounting one last desperate charge into

---

17. Interestingly, he seems to have experienced no prejudice as a part-Indian. But then, many New Englanders of his era had similar family trees, into which the Native American elements simply dissolved without comment.

18. See Extract 13.

the Turkish ranks. With Gordon in his study at Khartoum, defiantly illuminated as he watched the sands of time run out.

Try as man might, he has not yet found a way to elide the fates of Cain and Abel: not through the various peaces of Westphalia et al.; neither via the League of Nations, the Kellogg-Briand Pact, nor the United Nations. Not through negotiations, or even "peace through strength." The Pax Romana failed; so will the Pax Americana, and whatever follows it. In the end, it seems, there will be blood.

And then it is up to the warrior. The warrior is as the warrior does. In the field, the warrior does not negotiate, beg, or bargain, for it is no use. The warrior fights because it is his job. The warrior kills, or is killed, because that is part of the job too. History in retrospect may regard him as hero, villain, or simply anonymous cannon fodder. His bones may be honored or ground to powder. His sacrifice may be honored or mocked.

Whether he lives or dies, however, the warrior stays true—to his country, his tribe, his family, his comrades, and most of all to himself. No matter how distasteful we may find it, this is his code, and we abandon it at our civilizational peril, otherwise, there can never be peace.

Si vis pacem, para bellum, indeed.

ACKNOWLEDGMENTS

WITH THE POSSIBLE EXCEPTION OF HERODOTUS, NO HISTORIAN WORKS in a vacuum. Works of history, and interpretations of history, build upon the past with the sensibilities of the present, and generally with an eye to the future. And so, in undertaking a work of this kind, I would be remiss in not first thanking the "father of history" himself, as well as Livy, Tacitus, Polybius, Suetonius; the authors of the various books of the Bible in both the Old and New Testaments; Josephus; Gibbon, Creasy, du Picq, and many others. I would also like to thank the classical and military historians of our own time such as Victor Davis Hanson, Caleb Carr, Mackubin Owens, and Nick Lloyd, who read the manuscript in early draft and offered valuable suggestions of interpretation.

I must also thank the writing generals, including Caesar, Marcus Aurelius, Grant, and Custer, who left us crucial firsthand accounts of their roles in making history that repay reading even today, long after their political and personal purposes have expired. We honor the poets and artists as well, including Virgil, Miklós Zrínyi, the unknown author of *La Chanson de Roland*, the anonymous hands behind the Bayeux Tapestry, and, yes, even the makers of cinematic epics such as *The Fall of the Roman Empire, The Alamo, Zulu,* and *Khartoum.* However many historical liberties they took, their work brought these stories and countless others to millions of people around the world—among them, no doubt, future historians.

This book would not exist without its editor, Adam Bellow, and the exemplary team at St. Martin's Press, including Pronoy Sarkar, Ryan

Masteller, and Jennifer Fernandez; and my agent, Cristina Concepcion, at Don Congdon Associates, whose wise counsel is always invaluable. Most important of all, as has been true throughout my literary career, this book would not have become a reality but for my wife, Kate.

EXTRACTS

1) Genesis 22:6–13 (King James Version):

6. And Abraham took the wood of the burnt offering, and laid it upon Isaac his son; and he took the fire in his hand, and a knife; and they went both of them together.

7. And Isaac spake unto Abraham his father, and said, My father: and he said, Here am I, my son. And he said, Behold the fire and the wood: but where is the lamb for a burnt offering?

8. And Abraham said, My son, God will provide himself a lamb for a burnt offering: so they went both of them together.

9. And they came to the place which God had told him of; and Abraham built an altar there, and laid the wood in order, and bound Isaac his son, and laid him on the altar upon the wood.

10. And Abraham stretched forth his hand, and took the knife to slay his son.

11. And the angel of the Lord called unto him out of heaven, and said, Abraham, Abraham: and he said, Here am I.

12. And he said, Lay not thine hand upon the lad, neither do thou any thing unto him: for now I know that thou fearest God, seeing thou hast not withheld thy son, thine only son from me.

13. And Abraham lifted up his eyes, and looked, and behold behind him a ram caught in a thicket by his horns: and Abraham went and took the ram, and offered him up for a burnt offering in the stead of his son.

2) Livy, *The History of Rome*, Book 21:

They next came to a much narrower passageway on the rock face, where the cliff fell away so steeply that a soldier free of baggage could barely make it down by feeling his way and clinging with his hands to shrubs and roots projecting round about him. The spot had been naturally steep before, but it had now also been sheared off by a recent landslide, which had created a drop of fully one thousand feet. The cavalry halted at this point, thinking they had reached the end of the road and, as Hannibal wondered what was holding up the column, word that the cliff was impassable was brought back to him. He then went off to examine the location for himself.

The slippery path afforded no foothold, and on the incline it made the feet slide all the more quickly. If they used hands or knees to help themselves up, these supports themselves would slither away from under them, and they would fall again. And there were no stumps or roots around to provide leverage for either foot or hand—only glare ice and slushy snow on which they simply slithered about. The pack animals treading the snow would occasionally cut even into the bottom layer. They would then slip forward and, with their hoofs flailing more wildly in their efforts to get up, would break right through. As a result, a number became wedged in the ice, which was hardened and frozen to a great depth, as though they were caught in a snare.

Finally, with pack animals and men exhausted to no purpose, they pitched camp on the crest—and they had a very hard time clearing ground even for this, so much snow had to be dug up and removed. The men were then taken off to make a road down the cliff, which was the only possible way to go on. Solid rock had to be cut. They felled some massive trees in the area, stripped the branches from them, and made a huge pile of logs. This they set on fire when a strong breeze arose suitable for whipping up a blaze, and as the rocks became hot they made them disintegrate by pouring vinegar on them. After scorching the cliff-face with fires in this way, they opened it up with picks and softened the gradient with short zigzag paths so that even the elephants, not just the pack animals, could be brought down. Four days were spent at the cliff, during which the pack animals almost starved to death.

3) Gibbon, *The Decline and Fall of the Roman Empire*, Chapter One:

That public virtue which among the ancients was denominated patriotism, is derived from a strong sense of our own interest in the preservation and prosperity of the free government of which we are members. Such a sentiment, which had rendered the legions of the republic almost invincible, could make but a very feeble impression on the mercenary servants of a despotic prince; and it became necessary to supply that defect by other motives, of a different, but not less forcible nature; honour and religion. The peasant, or mechanic, imbibed the useful prejudice that he was advanced to the more dignified profession of arms, in which his rank and reputation would depend on his own valour; and that, although the prowess of a private soldier must often escape the notice of fame, his own behaviour might sometimes confer glory or disgrace on the company, the legion, or even the army, to whose honours he was associated. On his first entrance into the service, an oath was administered to him, with every circumstance of solemnity. He promised never to desert his standard, to submit his own will to the commands of his leader, and to sacrifice his life for the safety of the emperor and the empire. The attachment of the Roman troops to their standards was inspired by the united influence of religion and of honour. The golden eagle, which glittered in the front of the legion, was the object of their fondest devotion; nor was it esteemed less impious than it was ignominious, to abandon that sacred ensign in the hour of danger. These motives, which derived their strength from the imagination, were enforced by fears and hopes of a more substantial kind. Regular pay, occasional donatives, and a stated recompense, after the appointed time of service, alleviated the hardships of the military life, whilst, on the other hand, it was impossible for cowardice or disobedience to escape the severest punishment. The centurions were authorised to chastise with blows, the generals had a right to punish with death; and it was an inflexible maxim of Roman discipline, that a good soldier should dread his officers far more than the enemy. . . .

And yet so sensible were the Romans of the imperfection of valour without skill and practice, that, in their language, the name of an army was borrowed from the word which signified exercise. Military exercises were the important and unremitted object of their discipline. The recruits and young soldiers were constantly trained both in the morning and in the evening, nor was age or knowledge allowed to excuse the veterans from the daily repetition of what they had completely learnt. Large sheds were erected in the winter-quarters of the troops, that their useful labours might not receive any interruption from the most tempestuous weather; and it was carefully observed, that the arms destined to this imitation of war, should be of double the weight which was required in real action. It is not the purpose of this work to enter into any minute description of the Roman exercises. . . . The soldiers were diligently instructed to march, to run, to leap, to swim, to carry heavy burdens, to handle every species of arms that was used either for offence or for defence, either in distant engagement or in a closer onset; to form a variety of evolutions; and to move to the sound of flutes, in the Pyrrhic or martial dance. In the midst of peace, the Roman troops familiarised themselves with the practice of war; and it is prettily remarked by an ancient historian who had fought against them, that the effusion of blood was the only circumstance which distinguished a field of battle from a field of exercise.

4) Polybius, *The Histories*, Vol. 6:

The youngest soldiers or *velites* are ordered to carry a sword, javelins, and a target (*parma*). The target is strongly made and sufficiently large to afford protection, being circular and measuring three feet in diameter. They also wear a plain helmet, and sometimes cover it with a wolf's skin or something similar both to protect and to act as a distinguishing mark by which their officers can recognize them and judge if they fight pluckily or not. The wooden shaft of the javelin measures about two cubits in length and is about a finger's breadth in thickness; its head is a span long hammered out to such a fine edge that it is necessarily bent by the first impact, and the enemy is unable to return it. If this were not so, the missile would be available for both sides.

The next in seniority called *hastati* are ordered to wear a complete panoply. The Roman panoply consists firstly of a shield (*scutum*), the convex surface of which measures two and a half feet in width and four feet in length, the thickness at the rim being a palm's breadth. It is made of two planks glued together, the outer surface being then covered first with canvas and then with calf-skin. Its upper and lower rims are strengthened by an iron edging which protects it from descending blows and from injury when rested on the ground. It also has an iron boss (*umbo*) fixed to it which turns aside the most formidable blows of stones, pikes, and heavy missiles in general. Besides the shield they also carry a sword, hanging on the right thigh and called a Spanish sword. This is excellent for thrusting, and both of its edges cut effectually, as the blade is very strong and firm. In addition they have two *pila*, a brass helmet, and greaves. The *pila* are of two sorts—stout and fine. Of the stout ones some are round and a palm's length in diameter and others are a palm square. Fine pila, which they carry in addition to the stout ones, are like moderate-sized hunting-spears, the length of the haft in all cases being about three cubits. Each is fitted with a barbed iron head of the same length as the haft. This they attach so securely to the haft, carrying the attachment halfway up the latter and fixing it with numerous rivets, that in action the iron will break sooner than become detached, although its thickness at the bottom where it comes in contact with the wood is a finger's breadth and a half; such great care do they take about attaching it firmly.

Finally they wear as an ornament a circle of feathers with three upright purple or black feathers about a cubit in height, the addition of which on the head surmounting their other arms is to make every man look twice his real height, and to give him a fine appearance, such as will strike terror into the enemy. The common soldiers wear in addition a breastplate of brass a span square, which they place in front of the heart and call the heart-protector (*pectorale*), this completing their accoutrements; but those who are rated above ten thousand drachmas wear instead of this a coat of chain-mail (*lorica*). The *principes* and *triarii* are armed in the same manner except that instead of the *pila* the *triarii* [the most seasoned troops] carry long spears (*hastae*).

5) Tacitus, *The Annals of Imperial Rome*, Book Three:

Germanicus conceived a desire to pay his last respects to these men and their general. Every soldier with him was overcome with pity when he thought of his relations and friends and reflected on the hazards of war and of human life. Caecina was sent ahead to reconnoitre the dark woods and build bridges and causeways on the treacherous surface of the sodden marshland. Then the army made its way over the tragic sites. The scene lived up to its horrible associations. Varus's extensive first camp with its broad extent and headquarters marked out, testified to the whole army's labours. Then a half-ruined breastwork and shallow ditch showed where the last pathetic remnant had gathered. On the open ground were whitening bones, scattered where men had fled, heaped up where they had stood and fought back. Fragments of spears and of horses' limbs lay there—also human heads, fastened to tree-trunks. In groves nearby were the outlandish altars at which the Germans had massacred the Roman colonels and senior company commanders.

Survivors of the catastrophe, who had escaped from the battle or from captivity, pointed out where the generals had fallen, and where the eagles were captured. They showed where Varus received his first wound, and where he died by his own unhappy hand. And they told of the platform from which Arminius had spoken, and of his arrogant insults to the eagles and standards—and of all the gibbets and pits for the prisoners.

So, six years after the slaughter, a living Roman army had come to bury the dead men's bones of three whole divisions. No one knew if the remains he was burying belonged to a stranger or a comrade. But in their bitter distress, and rising fury against the enemy, they look on them all as friends and blood-brothers. Germanicus shared in the general grief, and laid the first turf of the funeral mound as a heartfelt tribute to the dead. Thereby he earned Tiberius's[1] disapproval. Perhaps this was because the emperor interpreted every action of Germanicus unfavourably. Or he may have felt that the sight of the unburied dead would make the army too respectful of its enemies, and reluctant to fight. . . .

1. Tiberius, the second of the five Julio-Claudian emperors, had succeeded Augustus upon the latter's death in 14 A.D.

6) Gibbon, *Decline and Fall*, Chapter One:

The principal conquests of the Romans were achieved under the republic; and the emperors, for the most part, were satisfied with preserving those dominions which had been acquired by the policy of the senate, the active emulations of the consuls, and the martial enthusiasm of the people. The seven first centuries were filled with a rapid succession of triumphs; but it was reserved for Augustus to relinquish the ambitious design of subduing the whole earth, and to introduce a spirit of moderation into the public councils. Inclined to peace by his temper and situation, it was easy for him to discover that Rome, in her present exalted situation, had much less to hope than to fear from the chance of arms; and that, in the prosecution of remote wars, the undertaking became every day more difficult, the event more doubtful, and the possession more precarious, and less beneficial. The experience of Augustus added weight to these salutary reflections, and effectually convinced him that, by the prudent vigor of his counsels, it would be easy to secure every concession which the safety or the dignity of Rome might require from the most formidable barbarians. Instead of exposing his person and his legions to the arrows of the Parthians, he obtained, by an honorable treaty, the restitution of the standards and prisoners which had been taken in the defeat of Crassus.

. . . [T]he northern countries of Europe scarcely deserved the expense and labor of conquest. The forests and morasses of Germany were filled with a hardy race of barbarians, who despised life when it was separated from freedom; and though, on the first attack, they seemed to yield to the weight of the Roman power, they soon, by a signal act of despair, regained their independence, and reminded Augustus of the vicissitude of fortune. On the death of that emperor, his testament was publicly read in the senate. He bequeathed, as a valuable legacy to his successors, the advice of confining the empire within those limits which nature seemed to have placed as its permanent bulwarks and boundaries: on the west, the Atlantic Ocean; the Rhine and Danube on the north; the Euphrates on the east; and towards the south, the sandy deserts of Arabia and Africa.

7) Josephus, *The Jewish War*:

In the end every one of them proved up to the enormity of what they had resolved, and all accounted for each member of their closest family, one after the other—poor wretched men, forced by necessity to decide that killing their own wives and children with their own hand was the lesser of two evils! Unable to bear any longer their anguish at what they had done, and feeling that it would wrong the dead if they outlived them for more than a brief moment, they quickly piled all their possessions into one heap and set fire to it. Then, after choosing by lot ten of their number to be the executioners of the rest, each man flung himself down by his wife and children where they lay dead, took them in his arms, and offered his throat to those charged with this painful duty.

They unflinchingly slaughtered them all, then set themselves the same lottery rule. Whoever drew the lot was to kill the other nine and himself last of all—such was their shared confidence that there was no difference in the way that any of them would either act or submit. So finally the nine presented their throats, and the one last survivor first checked that in the whole spread of bodies in this massive carnage there was no one still needing his hand to finish them: satisfied that all were dead, he set the palace ablaze, and then with all the force of his hand drove his sword right through his body, and fell dead alongside his family.

8) Urban II at Clermont:

Oh, race of Franks, race from across the mountains, race chosen and beloved by God as shines forth in very many of your works set apart from all nations by the situation of your country, as well as by your Catholic faith and the honor of the holy church! To you our discourse is addressed and for you our exhortation is intended. We wish you to know what a grievous cause has led us to your country, what peril threatening you and all the faithful has brought us.

From the confines of Jerusalem and the city of Constantinople a horrible tale has gone forth and very frequently has been brought to our ears, namely, that a race from the kingdom of the Persians, an accursed race, a race utterly alienated from God, a generation forsooth which has not directed its heart and has not entrusted its spirit to God, has invaded the lands of those Christians and has depopulated them by the sword, pillage and fire; it has led away a part of the captives into its own country, and a part it has destroyed by cruel tortures; it has either entirely destroyed the churches of God or appropriated them for the rites of its own religion. They destroy the altars, after having defiled them with their uncleanness. They circumcise the Christians, and the blood of the circumcision they either spread upon the altars or pour into the vases of the baptismal font. When they wish to torture people by a base death, they perforate their navels, and dragging forth the extremity of the intestines, bind it to a stake; then with flogging they lead the victim around until the viscera having gushed forth the victim falls prostrate upon the ground. Others they bind to a post and pierce with arrows. Others they compel to extend their necks and then, attacking them with naked swords, attempt to cut through the neck with a single blow. What shall I say of the abominable rape of the women? To speak of it is worse than to be silent. The kingdom of the Greeks is now dismembered by them and deprived of territory so vast in extent that it cannot be traversed in a march of two months. On whom therefore is the labor of avenging these wrongs and of recovering this territory incumbent, if not upon you? You, upon whom above other nations God has conferred remarkable glory in arms, great courage, bodily activity, and strength to humble the hairy scalp of those who resist you.

Let the deeds of your ancestors move you and incite your minds to manly achievements; the glory and greatness of king Charles the Great, and of his son Louis, and of your other kings, who have destroyed the kingdoms of the pagans, and have extended in these lands the territory of the holy church. Let the holy sepulcher of the Lord our Savior, which is possessed by unclean nations, especially incite you, and the holy places which are now treated with ignominy and irreverently polluted with their filthiness. Oh, most valiant soldiers and descendants of invincible ancestors, be not degenerate, but recall the valor of your progenitors.

But if you are hindered by love of children, parents and wives, remember what the Lord says in the Gospel, “He that loveth father or mother more than me, is not worthy of me.” “Every one that hath forsaken houses, or brethren, or sisters, or father, or mother, or wife, or children, or lands for my name's sake shall receive an hundredfold and shall inherit everlasting life." Let none of your possessions detain you, no solicitude for your family affairs, since this land which you inhabit, shut in on all sides by the seas and surrounded by the mountain peaks, is too narrow for your large population; nor does it abound in wealth; and it furnishes scarcely food enough for its cultivators. Hence it is that you murder one another, that you wage war, and that frequently you perish by mutual wounds. Let therefore hatred depart from among you, let your quarrels end, let wars cease, and let all dissensions and controversies slumber. Enter upon the road to the Holy Sepulcher; wrest that land from the wicked race, and subject it to yourselves. That land which as the Scripture says "floweth with milk and honey," was given by God into the possession of the children of Israel. Jerusalem is the navel of the world; the land is fruitful above others, like another paradise of delights. This the Redeemer of the human race has made illustrious by His advent, has beautified by residence, has consecrated by suffering, has redeemed by death, has glorified by burial. This royal city, therefore, situated at the centre of the world, is now held captive by His enemies, and is in subjection to those who do not know God, to the worship of the heathens. She seeks therefore and desires to be liberated, and does not cease to implore you to come to her aid. From you especially she asks succor, because, as we have already said, God has conferred upon you above all nations great glory in arms. Accordingly undertake this journey for the remission of your sins, with the assurance of the imperishable glory of the kingdom of heaven.

[Urban followed up the speech the next month with a "Letter of Instruction to the Crusaders," which reads:]

Urban, bishop, servant of the servants of God, to all the faithful, both princes and subjects, waiting in Flanders; greeting, apostolic grace, and blessing.

Your brotherhood, we believe, has long since learned from many accounts that a barbaric fury has deplorably afflicted and laid waste the churches of God in the regions of the Orient. More than this, blasphemous to say, it has even grasped in intolerable servitude its churches and the Holy City of Christ, glorified by His passion and resurrection. Grieving with pious concern at this calamity, we visited the regions of Gaul and devoted ourselves largely to urging the princes of the land and their subjects to free the churches of the East. We solemnly enjoined upon them at the council of Auvergne (the accomplishment of) such an undertaking, as a preparation for the remission of all their sins. And we have constituted our most beloved son, Adhemar, Bishop of Puy, leader of this expedition and undertaking in our stead, so that those who, perchance, may wish to undertake this journey should comply with his commands, as if they were our own, and submit fully to his loosings or bindings, as far as shall seem to belong to such an office. If, moreover, there are any of your people whom God has inspired to this vow, let them know that he [Adhemar] will set out with the aid of God on the day of the Assumption of the Blessed Mary, and that they can then attach themselves to his following.

9) Livy, *The History of Rome*, Book 5:

The consular tribunes had secured no position for their camp, had constructed no entrenchments behind which to retire, and had shown as much disregard of the gods as of the enemy, for they formed their order of battle without having obtained favourable auspices. They extended their line on either wing to prevent their being outflanked, but even so they could not make their front equal to the enemy's, whilst by thus thinning their line they weakened the centre so that it could hardly keep in touch. On their right was a small eminence which they decided to hold with reserves, and this disposition, though it was the beginning of the panic and flight, proved to be the only means of safety to the fugitives. For Bennus, the Gaulish chieftain, fearing some ruse in the scanty numbers of the enemy, and thinking that the rising ground was occupied in order that the reserves might attack the flank and rear of the Gauls while their front was engaged with the legions, directed his attack upon the reserves, feeling quite certain that if he drove them from their position, his overwhelming numbers would give him an easy victory on the level ground. So not only Fortune but tactics also were on the side of the barbarians.

In the other army there was nothing to remind one of Romans either amongst the generals or the private soldiers. They were terrified, and all they thought about was flight, and so utterly had they lost their heads that a far greater number fled to Veii, a hostile city, though the Tiber lay in their way, than by the direct road to Rome, to their wives and children. For a short time the reserves were protected by their position. In the rest of the army, no sooner was the battle-shout heard on their flank by those nearest to the reserves, and then by those at the other end of the line heard in their rear, than they fled, whole and unhurt, almost before they had seen their untried foe, without any attempt to fight or even to give back the battle-shout. None were slain while actually fighting; they were cut down from behind whilst hindering one another's flight in a confused, struggling mass. Along the bank of the Tiber, whither the whole of the left wing had fled, after throwing away their arms, there was great slaughter. Many who were unable to swim or were hampered by the weight of their cuirasses and other armour were sucked down by the current. The greater number, however, reached Veii in safety, yet not only were no troops sent from there to defend the City, but not even was a messenger despatched to report the defeat to Rome. All the men on the right wing, which had been stationed some distance from the river, and nearer to the foot of the hill, made for Rome and took refuge in the Citadel without even closing the City gates.

The Gauls for their part were almost dumb with astonishment at so sudden and extraordinary a victory. At first they did not dare to move from the spot, as though puzzled by what had happened, then they began to fear a surprise, at last they began to despoil the dead, and, as their custom is, to pile up the arms in heaps. Finally, as no hostile movement was anywhere visible, they commenced their march and reached Rome shortly before sunset. The cavalry, who had ridden on in front, reported that the gates were not shut, there were no pickets on guard in front of them, no troops on the walls. This second surprise, as extraordinary as the previous one, held them back, and fearing a nocturnal conflict in the streets of an unknown City, they halted and bivouacked between Rome and the Anio. Reconnoitering parties were sent out to examine the circuit of the walls and the other gates, and to ascertain what plans their enemies were forming in their desperate plight.

As for the Romans, since the greater number had fled from the field in the direction of Veii instead of Rome, it was universally believed that the only survivors were those who had found refuge in Rome, and the mourning for all who were lost, whether living or dead, filled the whole City with the cries of lamentation. But the sounds of private grief were stifled by the general terror when it was announced that the enemy were at hand. Presently the yells and wild war-whoops of the squadrons were heard as they rode round the walls. All the time until the next day's dawn the citizens were in such a state of suspense that they expected from moment to moment an attack on the City. They expected it first when the enemy approached the walls, for they would have remained at the Alia had not this been their object; then just before sunset they thought the enemy would attack because there was not much daylight left; and then when night was fallen they imagined that the attack was delayed till then to create all the greater terror. Finally, the approach of the next day deprived them of their senses; the entrance of the enemy's standards within the gates was the dreadful climax to fears that had known no respite.

10) Grant, *Personal Memoirs*, Chapter 55:

I have always regretted that the last assault at Cold Harbor was ever made. . . . At Cold Harbor no advantage whatever was gained to compensate for the heavy loss we sustained. Indeed, the advantages other than those of relative losses, were on the Confederate side. Before that, the Army of Northern Virginia seemed to have acquired a wholesome regard for the courage, endurance, and soldierly qualities generally of the Army of the Potomac. They no longer wanted to fight them "one Confederate to five Yanks." Indeed, they seemed to have given up any idea of gaining any advantage of their antagonist in the open field. They had come to much prefer breastworks in their front to the Army of the Potomac. This charge seemed to revive their hopes temporarily; but it was of short duration. The effect upon the Army of the Potomac was the reverse.

11) Grant, *Personal Memoirs,* Chapter 24:

About one P.M., not hearing from Wallace and being much in need of reinforcements, I sent two more of my staff, Colonel McPherson and Captain Rowley, to bring him up with his division. They reported finding him marching towards Purdy, Bethel, or some point west from the river, and farther from Pittsburg by several miles than when he started. The road from his first position to Pittsburg landing was direct and near the river. Between the two points a bridge had been built across Snake Creek by our troops, at which Wallace's command had assisted, expressly to enable the troops at the two places to support each other in case of need. Wallace did not arrive in time to take part in the first day's fight. General Wallace has since claimed that the order delivered to him by Captain Baxter was simply to join the right of the army, and that the road over which he marched would have taken him to the road from Pittsburg to Purdy where it crosses Owl Creek on the right of Sherman; but this is not where I had ordered him nor where I wanted him to go.

I never could see and do not now see why any order was necessary further than to direct him to come to Pittsburg landing, without specifying by what route. His was one of three veteran divisions that had been in battle, and its absence was severely felt. Later in the war General Wallace would not have made the mistake that he committed on the 6th of April, 1862. I presume his idea was that by taking the route he did he would be able to come around on the flank or rear of the enemy, and thus perform an act of heroism that would redound to the credit of his command, as well as to the benefit of his country.

Footnote: Since writing this chapter I have received from Mrs. W. H. L. Wallace, widow of the gallant general who was killed in the first day's fight on the field of Shiloh, a letter from General Lew. Wallace to him dated the morning of the 5th. . . . This modifies very materially what I have said, and what has been said by others, of the conduct of General Lew. Wallace at the battle of Shiloh. It shows that he naturally, with no more experience than he had at the time in the profession of arms, would take the particular road that he did start upon in the absence of orders to move by a different road.

The mistake he made, and which probably caused his apparent

dilatoriness, was that of advancing some distance after he found that the firing, which would be at first directly to his front and then off to the left, had fallen back until it had got very much in rear of the position of his advance. This falling back had taken place before I sent General Wallace orders to move up to Pittsburg landing and, naturally, my order was to follow the road nearest the river. But my order was verbal, and to a staff officer who was to deliver it to General Wallace, so that I am not competent to say just what order the General actually received.

12) Custer, *My Life on the Plains*, Chapter One:

It is but a few years ago that every schoolboy, supposed to possess the rudiments of a knowledge of the geography of the United States, could give the boundaries and a general description of the "Great American Desert." As to the boundary the knowledge seemed to be quite explicit: on the north bounded by the Upper Missouri, on the east by the Lower Missouri and Mississippi, on the south by Texas, and on the west by the Rocky Mountains. The boundaries on the northwest and south remained undisturbed, while on the east civilization, propelled and directed by Yankee enterprise, adopted the motto, "Westward the star of empire takes its way." Countless throngs of emigrants crossed the Mississippi and Missouri rivers, selecting homes in the rich and fertile territories lying beyond. Each year this tide of emigration, strengthened and increased by the flow from foreign shores, advanced toward the setting sun, slowly but surely narrowing the preconceived limits of the "Great American Desert," and correspondingly enlarging the limits of civilization. At last the geographical myth was dispelled. It was gradually discerned that the Great American Desert did not exist, that it had no abiding place, but that within its supposed limits, and instead of what had been regarded as a sterile and unfruitful tract of land, incapable of sustaining either man or beast, there existed the fairest and richest portion of the national domain, blessed with a climate pure, bracing, and healthful, while its undeveloped soil rivalled if it did not surpass the most productive portions of the Eastern, Middle, or Southern States. Discarding the name "Great American Desert," this immense tract of country, with its eastern boundary moved back by civilization to a distance of nearly three hundred miles west of the Missouri river, is now known as "The Plains," and by this more appropriate title it shall be called when reference to it is necessary.

13) Bronze Star Citation:

The President of the United States takes pleasure in presenting the
BRONZE STAR MEDAL to
FIRST LIEUTENANT JOHN J. WALSH
UNITED STATES MARINE CORPS
For service as set forth in the following
CITATION:

For heroic achievement as Assistant Platoon Commander, 81mm Mortar Platoon, weapons company, Second Battalion, Fifth Marines, First Marine Division (reinforced), during operations against enemy aggressor forces in Korea on 4 December 1950. Providing support for hard-pressed riflemen in a determined attempt to dislodge a well-concealed and heavily armed enemy force blocking the route of approach to Hagaru-ri, First Lieutenant Walsh led his men across 150 yards of open position from which to support the rifle company. Directing effective mortar fire from his new position, he contributed materially to the infliction of heavy casualties upon the enemy and to the eventual destruction of the hostile force. His outstanding leadership, courage and inspiring actions throughout were in keeping with the highest traditions of the United States Naval Service.
First Lieutenant Walsh is authorized to wear the Combat "V"

For the President,
Charles S. Thomas
Secretary of the Navy

INDEX